How did my problem spread?

Social Responsibility Therapy: Understanding Harmful Behavior Workbook 3

James M. Yokley, Ph.D.

I0103928

This workbook focuses on developing an understanding of "The Harmful Behavior Anatomy" that set the occasion for unhealthy harmful behavior to grow and spread to other areas. Case study examples for the intervention summaries in Exhibits 1- 3 in this workbook are described in Chapter 2 of the Social Responsibility Therapy treatment manual and in The Clinician's Guide to Social Responsibility Therapy listed in the references section.

The Social Responsibility Therapy focus on Understanding Harmful Behavior through "The Problem Development Triad" includes a three workbook series designed to help individuals with unhealthy, harmful behavior understand how they got that problem, what kept it going and how it spread to other areas.

Workbook 1- **"How did I get this problem?"** focuses on understanding how unhealthy, harmful behavior was acquired through The Risk Factor Chain (Yokley, 2010a)

Workbook 2- **"Why do I keep doing this?"** focuses on understanding how unhealthy, harmful behavior problems were maintained by The Stress-Relapse Cycle (Yokley, 2011a)

Workbook 3- **"How did my problem spread?"** focuses on understanding how unhealthy, harmful behavior problems were generalized to other areas using The Harmful Behavior Anatomy (present workbook)

A Social Solutions Healthy Behavior Lifestyle Development Project

> **Social Responsibility Therapy Mission Statement:**
> **"Reclaiming Dignity through Honesty, Trust,**
> **Loyalty, Concern and Responsibility"**

Information on Social Responsibility Therapy is available at www.srtonline.org.
The Social Responsibility Therapy treatment manual for adolescents and young adults,
Social Responsibility Therapy workbooks and The Clinician's Guide are available at
www.socialsolutionspress.com

Published by
Social Solutions Press
Post Office Box 444
North Myrtle Beach, South Carolina 29597
Second Printing

Who can benefit from this workbook?

Individuals with unhealthy, harmful behavior- in more than one area who are uncertain of how their harmful behavior grew and spread can benefit from the "Structured Discovery" approach of this workbook with therapy assistance. This workbook is a good support resource for Therapeutic Community program healthy lifestyle change efforts. In addition, those who are aware of some contributing factors but do not have a full understanding of "How did my problem spread?" are also likely to benefit. See back cover. Harmful behavior is unhealthy, excessive, compulsive or abusive and damaging to self or others. Social Responsibility Therapy (SRT) has a strong focus on developing honesty, trust, loyalty, concern and responsibility as competing responses to harmful behavior. These multicultural prosocial values are the healthy relationship success skills that employers, parents, partners and probation/parole officers are looking for in their workers, children, relationships and parolees. SRT is highly consistent with the family values of faith-based treatment organizations as well as the "Right Living" treatment approach of Therapeutic Communities and Twelve-Step Programs. The SRT healthy relationship and behavior success skills focus meets the rehabilitation goals of correctional institutions and social service group homes making it easy to integrate into those settings. This workbook is best suited for individuals over age 13 with good reading ability and basic arithmetic skills. Although developed for use with therapist input to help those in treatment become more active participants, it can also provide self-awareness and motivation for those considering therapy.

Mental Health Professional use in treatment plans and programs- The ten components of the Harmful Behavior Anatomy covered in this workbook allow mental health professionals to narrow their focus and build very brief skills-based treatment plans that utilize specific components based on individual client treatment needs. Information on developing focused treatment plans for time limited treatments is provided in Appendix A. The increased workbook structure includes step-by-step self-discovery directions This "Structured Discovery" approach addresses the self-awareness problems exhibited by many individuals with unhealthy, harmful behavior. The Awareness Training Goal for those who complete this workbook is to understand ten components in "The Harmful Behavior Anatomy" that enabled unhealthy, harmful behavior to grew and spread. The Responsibility training goal is to learn the healthy behavior success skills needed to address each component that supports the growth and spread of unhealthy, harmful behavior. Since the focus of this workbook is on the primary contributing factors that maintain multiple forms of unhealthy, harmful behavior, it is ideal for those who have a co-occurring harmful behaviors in addition to the one that resulted in their treatment referral. The present workbook is helpful for those with strong autonomy needs who value their independence, like to work on their own, take charge of their lives and help themselves deal with their own situations. It is ideal in limited resource public service or institutional settings that require group treatment by clients who must contribute to their treatment plans and support each other's goals. The three SRT workbooks on understanding harmful behavior was acquired, maintained and generalized can be used consecutively or individually for treatment focused on: insight (workbook 1); relapse prevention (workbook2) and; co-occurring problems (workbook 3). Workbook support materials are listed in the reference section.

Social Responsibility Therapy (SRT) Acknowledgements

A special thanks to: Christine Laraway and Brigette Bulanda for their help in implementing SRT with adolescents in Forensic Foster Care; Jennifer LaCortiglia for her help in adapting SRT for preteens; Rose Chervenak for her help in providing SRT to adolescents referred for sexual behavior problems in the residential Therapeutic Community setting; Chris Hewitt for his help in presenting Social Responsibility Therapy (SRT) to residential substance abuse clients and; Angie Roth for her program coordination of SRT for obesity patients in hospital-based treatment. Their feedback on the use of this workbook with clients exhibiting multiple forms of harmful behavior provided highly valuable treatment information.

Understanding how Harmful Behavior was Generalized: Social Responsibility Therapy Workbook 3

Workbook Completion Notes:
The ten components of the Harmful Behavior Anatomy covered in this workbook allows your therapist to develop a skills-based treatment plan that covers specific components based on your individual treatment needs. Also, this workbook has a "basic form" which allows you to skip portions in 8 of the 10 components. Please consult with your therapist about which components of this workbook you need to complete and whether you should complete the "basic form" or complete form. Review the first section entitled, "Introduction to Social Responsibility Therapy & Understanding Harmful Behavior" and update your answers even if you have completed it in workbook 1 or 2.

Table of Contents   Page

Table of Contents   Page

Introduction to Social Responsibility Therapy and Understanding Harmful Behavior

"If you're not working on the solution, you're part of the problem" -- Eldridge Cleaver [1]

Note: Read the "Workbook Completion Notes" (top of page iii) before starting this workbook.

Social Responsibility Therapy Summary

Social Responsibility Therapy addresses multiple forms of unhealthy, excessive, compulsive or abusive behavior that is harmful to self and/or others (i.e., "harmful behavior"). Traditional treatments typically focus on helping yourself. Social Responsibility Therapy focuses on helping yourself and others. In Social Responsibility Therapy, learning to care for yourself and others involves developing enough social maturity (i.e., honesty, trust, loyalty, concern and responsibility) and emotional maturity (i.e., self-awareness, self-efficacy/confidence and self-control) to avoid behavior that is unhealthy to you or harmful to others. Social Responsibility Therapy teaches multicultural prosocial values and behaviors that help prevent unhealthy, harmful behavior. In Social Responsibility Therapy, "If you're not working on the solution, you're part of the problem". If part of the problem is that unhealthy, harmful behavior got in the way of your education, work on the solution by reading this workbook with a dictionary and educate yourself by looking up the words you don't know.

What's in it for me? Less unhealthy, harmful behavior results in less consequences and a more healthy, positive life. More unhealthy, harmful behavior leads to more consequences and a less healthy, negative life. Unless you are keenly aware of your thoughts, feelings and motivations, you will make decision mistakes or slips that lead to "relapse" and falling back into unhealthy, harmful behavior. One type of decision that leads to relapse involves a problem with awareness referred to as a "foresight deficit decision" or foresight slip. Foresight is the ability to look ahead and think about what could happen in different situations. A foresight deficit decision often results in thoughtless decisions to enter high risk situations for slipping into harmful behavior. If you were ever asked, "What were you thinking?" you probably had a foresight slip into trouble. This is a very serious matter. Since your decisions control the path that your life will take, you need to locate the type of harmful behavior you want to change or that resulted in your referral for treatment in Appendix B (p. 184) and study the examples of decisions that led to relapse by individuals who lacked foresight and self-awareness. Don't worry if the connection between the decisions and the relapse that occurred is not clear to you right now. The primary purpose of this workbook is to help you develop enough self-awareness to make those connections and avoid falling back into harmful behavior or developing a new one after you have successfully stopped this one. Although you can use this workbook as a self-help tool to develop your own awareness and understanding of yourself, it is typically used in individual/family therapy or in group treatment programs and you are likely to benefit from therapeutic discussion of each section with others. The unhealthy, harmful behavior targeted by Social Responsibility Therapy covers a broad spectrum of behavior on the Harmful Behavior Continuum (Table 1) ranging in Social Responsibility impact from primarily hurting self (e.g., excessive eating or skipping medication) to hurting self and others (e.g., substance abuse or gambling debt) to primarily hurting others (e.g., acts of physical or sexual aggression) and in severity from relatively mild to socially devastating. The multiple forms of abusive behavior that Social Responsibility Therapy targets includes: trust abuse (e.g., lying, cheating, confidence scams, running away); substance abuse (e.g., drugs/alcohol, cigarettes, unhealthy eating); property abuse (e.g., theft, vandalism, fire setting, excess spending/shopping, gambling debt); physical abuse (e.g., school bullying, assault, kidnapping, robbery) and; sexual abuse (e.g., rape, child molestation, harassment).

Table 1.   The Harmful Behavior Continuum: Selected Behavior Examples

Primary Area of Impact ⟶

Behavior Impact Severity	Harmful to Self	Harmful to Self and Others	Harmful to Others
	Unhealthy Eating (Overeat/binge/purge/starve) **Medication Non-compliance** **Self Injury/Cutting** **Nicotine Abusers**		
		Workaholics	
	(Single)	(with partners or family)	
		Codependents	
	(Self-destructive relationships)	(Abuse enablers)	
		Money Abusers	
	(Single shopaholics)	(Gamblers with partners/family)	(Embezzlers, Credit card fraud)
		Sexual Compulsives	
	(Deviant masturbation, porno)	(Unprotected sex, affairs, prostitution)	(sexual harassment)
		Substance Abusers	
	(Single alcohol and drug abusers)	(Alcohol and drug abusers with partners/family)	(Drunk drivers, Drug dealers)
		Responsibility Abusers	
		(Work Neglecters)	(Child Neglecters)
		Trust Abusers	
		(Partner cheating)	(Professional con artists)
			Verbal/Power Abusers (employee harassment) **Property Abusers** (theft, vandalism, arson) **Physical Abusers** (bullying, assault, child abuse) **Sexual Abusers** (rape, child molestation) **Contract Killers** **Lust Murderers, Serial Killers**
	Source: Adapted with permission from Table 1.1 in Yokley (2008)		

Note: "The more difficult the problem, the harder it is to change" may not always be the case. Less severe harmful behaviors which impact more people can be more difficult to change because of...

1. Impact Rationalization- It's low on the social impact continuum, e.g., "It doesn't hurt others, it only hurts me"
2. Availability and associated Normalization- It's normal to eat, smoke, spend and sometimes over do it, e.g., "Everyone does it" or "Lots of people do it". For example, smoking lapses "were more likely to occur when smoking was permitted, when cigarettes were easily available and in the presence of other smokers" (p. 64, Shiffman et. al., 1996).
3. Severity Minimization- It's the least on the severity continuum (above) and "It's not illegal". You can get arrested for drinking or drugging and driving but you can't get arrested for overeating and driving. We have a highway patrol and drug court but there is no buffet patrol and the only food court that exists is in the Mall.

In Social Responsibility Therapy, harmful behavior relates to a lack of social responsibility which is the result of a pathological level of social-emotional immaturity. Thus, a very basic summary of Social Responsibility Therapy is an intervention which develops honesty, trust, loyalty, concern and responsibility as competing factors against sexual abuse, physical abuse, property abuse, substance abuse and trust abuse. The main focus of Social Responsibility Therapy is on whether the action being considered is helpful or harmful to self or others. If it is helpful to self and others it is socially responsible and needs to be reinforced. If it is harmful to self and others it is socially irresponsible and needs to be re-directed. Three important treatment goals in Social Responsibility Therapy are to:

1. **Stop the harmful behavior-** Develop the healthy behavior success skills (p. 18) needed to keep from repeating unhealthy, harmful behavior;
2. **Understand the harmful behavior-** Develop awareness of how the unhealthy, harmful behavior was acquired, maintained and generalized to other problem areas and;
3. **Demonstrate helpful behavior-** Develop the healthy relationship success skills (p. 17) needed for positive social adjustment.

The focus of this workbook is on understanding unhealthy, harmful behavior and it is structured to help you discover how that behavior was acquired. The healthy behavior success skills you need to keep from repeating the problem (i.e., **A**void trouble; **C**alm down; **T**hink it through and; **S**olve the problem) are integrated into each workbook section. Developing healthy relationship success skills through honesty, trust, loyalty, concern and responsibility is also included.

Introspection 101: Becoming a Careful Self-Observer
Introspection means looking inside of yourself at your motivations for what you do which is the key to developing self-awareness. Becoming a careful observer of others and pointing out their problems is easy but you have to train yourself to look at your problem thoughts, feelings and motivations. Social Responsibility Therapy uses a Structured Discovery approach to help you look at yourself through *structured* exercises that help you *discover* important thoughts and feelings that are connected to unhealthy, harmful behavior. This process increases your self-awareness which develops your self-efficacy (confidence) and helps you maintain your self-control responsibility. Self-control is needed to achieve your personal goals and maintain successful relationships. The social responsibility of self-control tends to get overlooked in our school systems which teach effective control of baseballs, basketballs and footballs but leave it up to you to develop effective control of thoughts, feelings and behaviors.

Developing self-awareness through the structured discovery exercises in this workbook is like playing cards. Each section represents a hand of cards with different statements that may apply to you. Your job is to get honest with yourself by carefully looking at each statement for connections between that information and your behavior (like drawing a new card to see if it can be used in your hand). If the statement applies to you or adds to your understanding of yourself, mark it, if not let it go (discard) and move on to the next piece of information to consider (draw another card). Having the courage to accept the workbook statements that apply to you will allow you to put together a winning hand of connections between thoughts, feelings and motivations.

These connections will provide you with an understanding of how you got involved with your unhealthy, harmful behavior. If you are a mental health professional and are reviewing this workbook for use with your clients, information is provided for you in Appendix A (page 178).

There are two basic things that you can't change in life, the past and other people's behavior. As mentioned earlier, it has been said that "If you're not working on the solution, you're part of the problem". This is the case with many individuals with unhealthy, harmful behavior whose energy is too focused on the past and other people's behavior. Individuals who have problems with unhealthy, harmful behavior tend to spend far too much time ruminating on (i.e., going over and over) past injustices done to them by others, trying to cover up past mistakes of their own and trying to influence other people's opinions of them. This negative coping style maintains unhealthy pride, diverts energy away from solving your harmful behavior problem and makes you feel helpless since you can't change the past or other people's behavior.

In Social Responsibility Therapy, the focus is on the present and your behavior. While it is true that you can't change the past, you can change your honesty about it and understanding of it. Working on your honesty, trust, loyalty, concern and responsibility (which includes self-control) develops healthy pride and dignity. Understanding how you got this problem and learning the healthy behavior success skills to manage it are the first steps toward positive change. In order to successfully complete this workbook, you need to be willing to "set your pride aside" and use this workbook as a mirror to see yourself by carefully considering each statement. This begins with getting honest about past behavior that has been unhealthy to you or harmful to others.

History of Unhealthy, Harmful Behavior
"The more extensive a man's knowledge of what has been done,
the greater will be his power of knowing what to do" -- Benjamin Disraeli (1804-1881)

Record the Type, Duration, Frequency, Severity and Impact on Others
Why go back through the past? That was then, this is now. What's in it for me to go through this again, other than bringing up bad memories? The answer is simple, to learn enough about the past to prevent your past history from repeating itself. In order to prevent history from repeating itself, you have to study history to make yourself aware of the problems and traps to avoid.

Circle all of the forms of harmful behavior on the Harmful Behavior Continuum (Table 1, p. 2) that you have ever been involved with in your life. Then complete the basic information about yourself below and then begin yourself understanding work.

Name: _____   **Date:** _____

Date of Birth: _____   Sex: _____   Race: _____

Education: _____   Occupation: _____   Marital Status: _____

Referral problem (What harmful behavior resulted in your referral for treatment or caused you to

get this workbook?): _____

Name of your current treatment program or provider: _____

Your current treatment Setting: __ Outpatient; __ Intensive Outpatient; __ Residential/Inpatient; __ Secure Residential/Correctional Facility; __ Self-help, not in treatment

<u>Check all of the types of harmful behavior you have done</u>. Then underline the parts that apply to you.

____ Trust abuse- For example, lying, cheating, conning, coercion, fraud, running away, child neglect, walking out on a friend in need, shifting loyalties to others when it benefits you or when things aren't going well for current friends, using people for what they have, saying "I love (or really care about) you" just to get sex or justify having it. Making false allegations or filing false charges. Problem priorities- for example: Parents putting involvement in relationships before family/child care (see Planning Problems, p. 196); Putting negative associates before positive friends/family; Doing too much work and forgetting about relationships or getting too involved in relationships and forgetting about responsibilities; Putting other life tasks or relationships before treatment. Doing too much for others and not caring for yourself or getting too caught up in your problems and forgetting about others.

____ Responsibility neglect- Letting your responsibilities go and just doing what you want, what is easiest, what you feel like doing or what makes you feel good at the time. Putting off responsibilities until someone else does them, making excuses to avoid doing things you just don't want to do, Youth example- making excuses to miss or skip school/work, not completing activities that are required of you. Adult example- failure to pay bills or being an absent parent to your children (see Planning Problems, p. 196).

____ Responsibility abuse- Refusal to accept responsibilities. Examples include quitting school or job training, quitting a job without getting another job first, defaulting on loans, not paying people back, not paying child support, using "survival" as an excuse for drug dealing addiction to "easy money", using not being able to find a job that pays enough as an excuse to live off of others without working at all. Cover-up for others abuse, not saying anything.

____ Responsibility overdose- Over-involvement in work/workaholic and neglecting relationships or family. Falling into becoming responsible for everyone and everything all the time, resulting in others always calling on you to get things done or help them out and not taking time to care for yourself (see Need Problems, p. 196).

____ Food abuse (i.e., overeating/overweight, excessive eating/binging, purging or starving self)

____ Substance abuse- legal substances (e.g., alcohol, prescription medications, cigarettes/tobacco or other legal substances- List here _____).

____ Substance abuse- illegal substances (e.g., marijuana, cocaine, methamphetamine, heroin or other recreational/street drugs- List here _____).

____ Property abuse- legal activity including money abuse (e.g., credit card debt, excessive borrowing, gambling debt, compulsive gambling, overspending or shopaholic)

____ Property abuse- illegal activity (e.g., theft, vandalism, arson, forgery, black mail or extortion/getting money by threats, or other property abuse- List here _____).

____ Physical abuse- harm to self (e.g., cutting self, pulling hair out, excessive scratching, picking skin off, injury from banging head or punching walls, suicide attempt)

____ Physical abuse- harm to others (e.g., assault, domestic violence, robbery, kidnapping, school bullying, physical intimidation, child physical abuse/excessive physical punishment)

____ Sexual abuse- harm to self or others (e.g., rape, child sexual abuse/molestation, sexual harassment, exhibitionism/flashing, voyeurism/peeping, prostitution, pandering/pimping, excessive/compulsive sexual behavior including cruising for sex, promiscuity, affairs, pornography, deviant masturbation, dangerous sex, unprotected sex with people I just met)

____ Other problem behavior (list-_____)

Referral Behavior History- Use the space below to write a history of the harmful behaviors and events that resulted in your referral for treatment, got you thinking you need to change or resulted in someone close to you telling you that you need to change. Include: **who** (your behavior hurt, self, others, both, be specific, give names); **what** (your referral behavior was, the primary reason you were referred for or need treatment); **when** (you started it and how long it has gone on); **where** (you usually did it or where it occurs often) and; **why** (you think you did it, include anything you can think of that can start it).

Who: _____

_____

_____

What: _____

_____

_____

_____

When: _____

_____

_____

Where: _____

_____

_____

Why: _____

_____

_____

_____

Introduction to The Problem Development Triad
"The power of man has grown in every sphere, except over himself"-- Sir Winston Churchill (1874- 1965)

Some individuals with unhealthy, harmful behavior have never had a reasonable period of abstinence or time in their life where they were free of that behavior. They were unable to successfully control their behavior because they never understood: 1) **How they got the problem** to begin with; 2) **Why they kept it up** and; 3) **How it spread** to other types and areas.

The Problem Development Triad components covered in this three workbook series will be used to help you understand the:
1. **Risk Factor Chain** that led to acquiring your harmful behavior (Yokley, 2010a)- How you got the problem;
2. **Stress-Relapse Cycle** that maintained it (Yokley, 2011a)- Why you kept it up once you started and;
3. **Harmful Behavior Anatomy** of factors that generalized it (present workbook)- How it spread to other types.

When you have finished the material needed to complete the summary worksheet at the end of each workbook you will have a graphic representation of how you got your problem (workbook 1), kept it (workbook 2) and spread it to other problem areas (workbook3). A summary of "The Problem Development Triad" used in Social Responsibility Therapy is provided in Figure 1. In Social Responsibility Therapy, our number one responsibility as human beings is self-control. Learning to control unhealthy, harmful behavior is the first and most important step toward getting what you want in life. In the words of Dr. Albert Ellis "We are all fallible human beings" so having serious problems is not the issue. The issue is developing enough:
1. **social maturity** to hold yourself accountable about problems when mistakes are made and reclaim your dignity through honesty, trust, loyalty, concern and responsibility (see Healthy Relationship Success Skills, p.18) and;
2. **emotional maturity** to learn from life mistakes by becoming aware of the high risk situations that trigger those mistakes, developing a sense of mastery (self-efficacy) and self control to handle those high risk situations with Healthy Behavior Success skills (p. 18).

Fork in the road- Life always has important junctions and the path we choose determines the way our life will turn out. The harmful behavior development fork in the road is at the end of the Risk Factor Chain when you first started your harmful behavior. The Risk Factor Chain sets you up for harmful behavior and can lead to a number of types of interpersonal abuse (e.g., physical, verbal, sexual or trust abuse) or substance abuse (e.g., drugs, alcohol, cigarettes or food abuse). If an individual has enough risk factors in each link of the Risk Factor Chain to lead them into a harmful behavior, their use of positive or negative coping determines what happens next.

The Awareness Training goal at the end of this workbook is for you to understand how you got your problem behavior with enough confidence to be able to explain it clearly to others. In order to reach this level of understanding you will need to complete each of the five links in "The Risk Factor Chain" and be able to give at least one specific example of a healthy behavior success skill that you have used to address each personal risk factor. If you are able to understand

Figure 1. The Problem Development Triad
(Managing these risk, stress and generalization problems is summarized in Exhibits 1-3, p. 175)

Figure 1. The Problem Development Triad: How Harmful Behavior Was Acquired, Maintained & Generalized Referred to as "The Abuse Development Triad" in cases of sexually and/or physically abusive behavior. Source: Yokley, 2008.

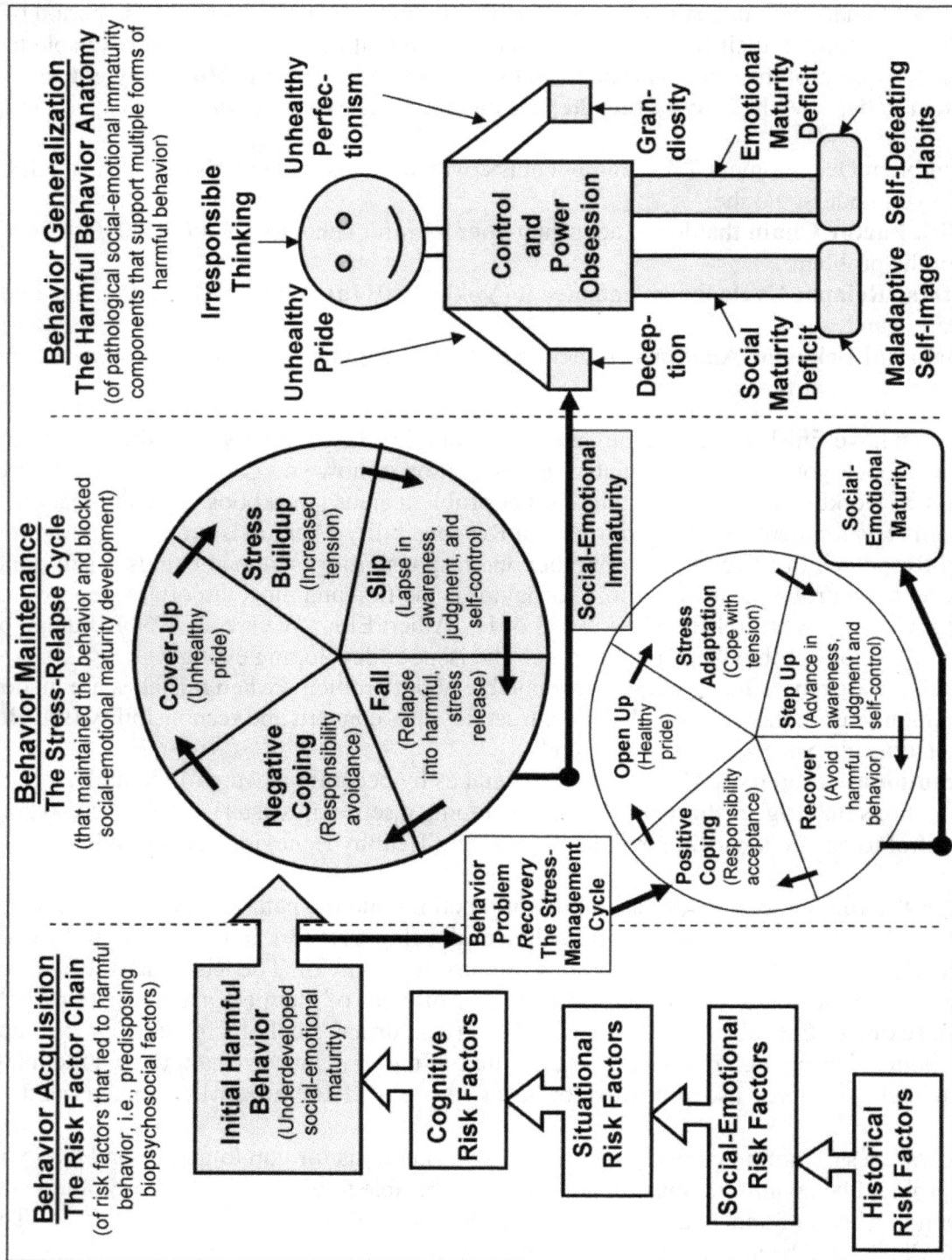

Behavior Generalization
The Harmful Behavior Anatomy
(of pathological social-emotional immaturity components that support multiple forms of harmful behavior)

- Unhealthy Perfectionism
- Irresponsible Thinking
- Unhealthy Pride
- Control and Power Obsession
- Grandiosity
- Deception
- Emotional Maturity Deficit
- Social Maturity Deficit
- Self-Defeating Habits
- Maladaptive Self-Image

Behavior Maintenance
The Stress-Relapse Cycle
(that maintained the behavior and blocked social-emotional maturity development)

- Stress Buildup (Increased tension)
- Slip (Lapse in awareness, judgment, and self-control)
- Fall (Relapse into harmful, stress release)
- Negative Coping (Responsibility avoidance)
- Cover-Up (Unhealthy pride)

Social-Emotional Immaturity

Behavior Problem Recovery
The Stress-Management Cycle

- Stress Adaptation (Cope with tension)
- Step Up (Advance in awareness, judgment and self-control)
- Recover (Avoid harmful behavior)
- Positive Coping (Responsibility acceptance)
- Open Up (Healthy pride)

Social-Emotional Maturity

Behavior Acquisition
The Risk Factor Chain
(of risk factors that led to harmful behavior, i.e., predisposing biopsychosocial factors)

- Initial Harmful Behavior (Underdeveloped social-emotional maturity)
- Cognitive Risk Factors
- Situational Risk Factors
- Social-Emotional Risk Factors
- Historical Risk Factors

and address these factors, you will have successfully decreased your risk for developing a new behavior problem in addition to developing your confidence in managing your present problem.

Using positive coping is the more difficult path to take after a period of harmful behavior because admitting the problem can result in unwanted consequences. However, positive coping has the added advantages of:

- Developing **honesty** and letting go of unhealthy pride that makes it worse by covering up;
- Repairing broken **trust** and developing the positive relationships needed to stay on track;
- Reducing stress-build up from anxiety about getting caught or guilt about what you did by doing the right thing and being **loyal** to family values (what is right for yourself and others);
- Showing **concern** for yourself and others by keeping your problem "up front" [2] and thinking ahead about the consequences of falling back into secret-keeping;
- Developing **responsibility** by holding yourself accountable and learning to solve problems by focusing on the present and your behavior, not the past and other people's behavior.

In summary, the drawbacks of positive coping are the consequences of honesty, i.e., "honesty has its price, but good news is you don't have to pay twice". A big advantage of positive coping is adapting to the stress of making mistakes and reclaiming your dignity through your social maturity (i.e., honesty, trust, loyalty, concern and responsibility). Positive coping leads to resilience (bouncing back) by learning from experience which develops social maturity and wisdom (see Figure 2). During the course of this workbook, you will develop your positive coping skills using the Situation Response Analysis Log in Appendix D (p. 202). Exhibits 1, 2 and 3 (p. 175- 177) provide positive coping summaries of for risk factor management, stress management and management of factors that support multiple forms of harmful behavior.

Figure 2.   The Prevention or Development of Harmful Behavior

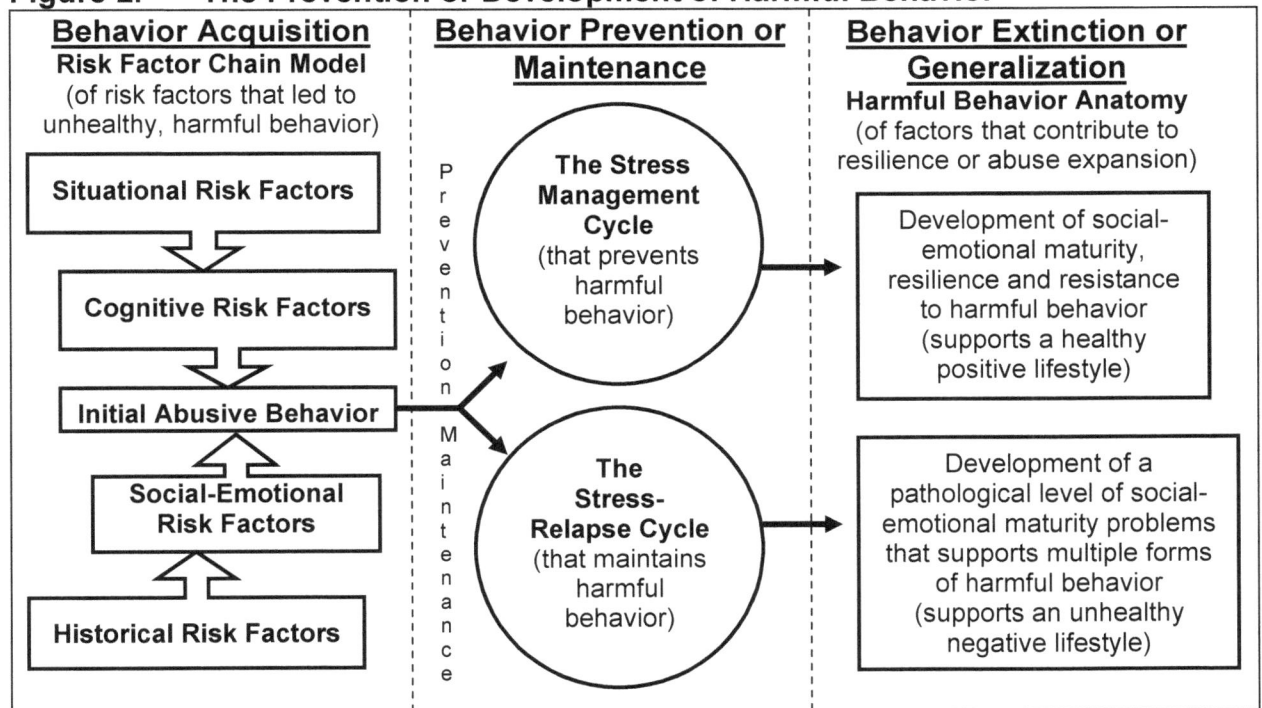

Using negative coping, denying the problem, and covering it up by acting like everything is alright, avoids dealing with the problem. Negative coping creates stress build-up. This eventually results in slipping up and taking a fall back into the Stress-Relapse Cycle (Yokley, 2011a) that maintains unhealthy, harmful behavior (Figure 1). Falling back into the cycle reinforces the social-emotional maturity problems that prevent learning from experience and supports multiple forms of harmful behavior that result in an unhealthy, unhappy, negative life. Over time, repeated relapse through the Stress-Relapse Cycle develops a level of social-emotional maturity problems that spreads one type of unhealthy, harmful behavior to other types or other areas of your life. Given this situation, the harmful behavior that brought you to treatment is often not your only harmful behavior. Also, the harmful behavior that resulted in your referral for treatment may not be the first harmful behavior that you developed. Examples include earlier alcohol abuse being in remission (now under control) but getting substituted with urges to take out feelings on others verbally and physically (i.e., the "dry drunk" syndrome). Earlier trust abuse (i.e., abusing the trust of others by lying, cheating, manipulating, conning, etc.) may go into remission (increasing boredom) but the excitement of trust abuse can get substituted by cocaine abuse. Perhaps excessive or risky sexual behavior is in remission but the untreated emotional maturity problem of self-control is now showing itself through excessive eating or risking money (gambling). Or maybe unhealthy overeating is in remission but is now being substituted with over-spending.

"Knowledge is power." The more we know about how we developed our present behavior patterns, what maintained that behavior and how it spread to other areas, the more confident we can be in understanding ourselves, understanding others, maintaining positive behavior change and achieving positive life goals. It takes a great deal of work to get a clear understanding of your unhealthy, harmful behavior. Not everyone will succeed. To achieve a positive lifestyle, developing self-understanding must include developing dignity through honesty, trust, loyalty, concern and responsibility. Not everyone will continue on the path to social responsibility. Those that do will develop the self-understanding that builds the self-confidence needed for self-control of unhealthy, harmful behavior and maintenance of a healthy, positive lifestyle.

Getting what we want in life

Getting what we want in life involves becoming who we want to be. "Who do we want to be?" can be a difficult question. Who we are is easy to answer and summarized in Table 2 below. According to the ancient Greek philosopher Aristotle (384 BC-322 BC), "We are what we repeatedly do".

Table 2. Who we are According to Aristotle

According to Aristotle...	On the other hand...
• If we repeatedly lie, we are a liar • If we repeatedly drink, we are a drunk • If we repeatedly steal, we are a thief • If we repeatedly beat people, we are a bully • If we repeatedly sexually abuse, we are a sex abuser • If we repeatedly commit crimes, we are a criminal	• If we are repeatedly honest, we are trustworthy • If we are repeatedly trustworthy, we are loyal. • If we are repeatedly loyal, we care • If we are repeatedly care, we are responsible

"Who do we want to be?" is a difficult question that gets people side tracked on <u>external characteristics</u> such as fortune, fame, beauty, brilliance and power. All of these external characteristics require one thing- other people acknowledging, admiring and appreciating them. An easy exercise to help us re-focus on important <u>internal characteristics</u> that we want to have is to simply to look at what we want from others.

What do we want from others? Table 3 below is a survey of over 100 groups of foster parents and youth who were asked… "If you were able to get online at www.godgiveme.com and select the ideal best friend, close family member and life partner (girlfriend, boyfriend, husband or wife), what characteristics would you want that person to have?"

Table 3. Summary of What We Want from Others
(i.e., What Youth, Parents, and Treatment Staff Want from Best friends, Close Family and Life Partners)

Honesty	Trust	Loyalty	Concern	Responsibility
Honest	Trustworthy	Loyal	Caring	Responsible
Assertive,	Obedient	Dependable	Loving	Financially stable
Expressive	Gives you	Sharing	Understanding	Good money
Truthful	space, not nosy	Faithful	Kindness	management
	Reliable	Not a	Nurturing	Respectful
	Not jealous	backstabber	Supportive	Neat, clean, and
	Not possessive	Not a gossip	Considerate	tidy
	Not	Not promiscuous	Nice	Sober, drug free
	overprotective	Not a prostitute	Pleasant	Helpful
		Doesn't cheat	Give and take	Socially mature
			Not selfish	Good morals
			Sensitive	Common sense
			Good listener	Role model
			Tolerant	Reliable
			Open-minded	Good hygiene
			Unconditional	Helps discipline
			love	Has life goals,
				College plans, a
				goal setter
				Self-control
				Work ethic,
				achiever,
				Employed, self-
				motivated
				Punctual, stays
				organized

Source: Reprinted with permission from Table 3.7 (Yokley, 2008).

The results were overwhelmingly consistent in revealing that both youth and adults alike want honesty, trust, loyalty, concern and responsibility in their best friends, close family members and life partners (girlfriend, boyfriend, husband or wife). This begs the question, "If honesty, trust, loyalty, concern and responsibility is what we want from other people in our life, what do we think they want from us?" The bottom line conclusion here is simple, since you can't get any of these things without giving them, if we want honesty, trust, loyalty, concern and responsibility from others, then this is what we should we be trying to develop in ourselves. That's very easy to say and very hard to do, because each of these things has consequences and takes both courage and good judgment to manage well. For example, while it is true that "the truth will set you free" (of guilt and worry about getting caught), the tremendous consequences that come with honesty is why we value it so much. Anyone who has been betrayed, played or back stabbed knows that trust and loyalty can be risky, takes courage and requires good judgment about who can be trusted and who to give your loyalty to. On the other side of the coin, if you are not trustworthy and are disloyal, you will eventually find yourself by yourself, without friends or the support from others needed to help maintain a positive healthy life. Concern and responsibility are also things that you have to learn to manage well. Caring too much about others who are not doing the right thing for themselves, eventually leaves you disappointed and depressed while not caring enough leaves you disconnected and deprived of healthy positive relationships. Likewise, being too responsible and doing too much for others, eventually leaves you resentful of having to carry their weight but not being responsible enough gets you resented by others who have to carry your weight, leaves you unemployed and unwanted by employers.

What do we need to change to get what we want in life?

Getting what we want in life involves changing the pathological social-emotional immaturity that supports multiple forms of unhealthy, harmful behavior in the Harmful Behavior Anatomy. Pathological social immaturity in SRT is defined as serious problems with honesty, trust, loyalty, concern and responsibility. For example, pathological social immaturity often results in deception to get what you want or avoid consequences instead of asking or apologizing or not understanding the difference between dishonesty by omission and diplomacy (p. 188). It typically involves not understanding that trust must be earned through a track record of responsibility and expecting it or giving it without that track record. It can be seen in too much loyalty to irresponsible people or not enough loyalty to responsible people. Social immaturity includes not enough concern for self (don't care attitude) or others (selfish) or too much concern for others and forgetting about self (e.g., compromising self to be accepted). Finally, social immaturity may involve taking on too much responsibility or avoiding it altogether. Developing social maturity requires practicing a healthy balance in honesty, trust, loyalty, concern and responsibility. This means learning to "act as if" [3] we are the positive person we want to be and practicing that behavior until it becomes automatic. Learning to "Act as if" we have social maturity is a very important practice skill because, "We are what we repeatedly do"-- Aristotle (384BC- 322BC). Social maturity is covered further in Component 5 of this workbook

In SRT, pathological emotional immaturity is defined as serious problems with self-awareness, self-efficacy (confidence) and self-control. This results in: 1) not understanding why you keep falling back into unhealthy, harmful behavior; 2) continuing to try the same methods to deal with your problems and; 3) not putting enough energy into stopping yourself from doing what you want to do and getting yourself to do what you need to do. Developing emotional maturity means gaining enough: self-awareness to know your high risk situations for relapse; self-efficacy (confidence) to step outside of your comfort zone by trying new solutions to old problems and;

self-control to take the first most important relapse prevention step by getting out of the high risk situation so that you can think before you act. Emotional maturity is covered further in Component 9 of this workbook.

"No one plans to spread their problem"

But it happens often. In fact it's hard to find a person with just one problem. After getting trapped in a cycle of unhealthy, harmful behavior, people usually feel anxious or depressed and try to make things better not worse. We don't typically tell ourselves, "This is getting boring, I need to spread out and try some new forms of unhealthy, harmful behavior". In reality there was an anatomy or structure of components working together to grow and spread your unhealthy, harmful behavior. This workbook will help you develop your:

- Awareness of the components that maintained your unhealthy, harmful behavior and allowed it to spread to other types or other areas in your life;
- Responsibility by learning how to handle the Harmful Behavior Anatomy components which decreases the chances of your unhealthy behavior growing or spreading and;
- Tolerance to change by increasing your social-emotional maturity.

Learning about your Harmful Behavior Anatomy is very important in recovery from unhealthy, harmful behavior because developing the social-emotional maturity that it takes to deal with the components in the Harmful Behavior Anatomy is also needed to get the positive life and healthy relationships we want.

Best Practice Treatment for Harmful Behavior

The best practice treatment for harmful behavior includes adopting the Therapeutic Community Pendulum Concept (Yokley, 2008) that "you have to go to the opposite extreme in order to meet the median."[4] In the Pendulum Concept values and associated behavior that were allowed to swing way over to the very negative, harmful side before treatment are required to swing way over to the very positive opposite extreme during treatment. This requirement focuses on developing an opposite extreme positive behavior track record during treatment so that after treatment when self-control naturally swings back some, our behavior will still be positive enough to meet the community behavior standard median and we can survive in that setting without relapse. This "over-correction" training approach of consistently "acting as if"[3] we are a positive person by practicing behavior that is the opposite extreme of our negative, harmful behavior is a therapeutic community training method.[4] This is similar to military boot camp where the physical stamina requirements exceed what may be needed during battle in order to insure that recruits can adjust to the battlefield and survive. In our goals to avoid death on the battlefield and avoid relapse in the community, "Hesitation kills". On the battlefield, hesitation to follow an order kills your ability to survive. In treatment, hesitation to do the opposite behavior, kills your ability to recover from your unhealthy, harmful behavior pattern. Since unhealthy thoughts lead to unhealthy behaviors, the Pendulum Concept needs to be applied to responsible self-statement substitution to help you correct unhealthy thinking by going to the opposite extreme with very healthy thinking (See description and examples in Appendix C., p. 188)

SRT Opposite Extreme Values and Behaviors

In SRT, honesty, trust, loyalty, concern and responsibility are reinforced to prevent harmful behavior because these multicultural prosocial values are the opposite extreme to the antisocial values used in harmful behavior and are not compatible with unhealthy, harmful behavior. For example, it is not possible to be a dishonest, irresponsible drug abuser while being honest and responsible or it is not possible to be a physically abusive cheating boyfriend while being concerned and loyal. In general, it is difficult to go through with harmful behavior while considering the impact of that behavior and "acting as if" by going to the opposite extreme helps break harmful behavior habits. In summary, SRT requires that we "go to the opposite extreme" of harmful behavior by modeling healthy, helpful behavior which is are not compatible with and thus competes against that harmful behavior. harmful behavior such as trust abuse, substance abuse, property abuse, physical abuse and sexual abuse require us to be dishonest, untrustworthy, disloyal, selfish and irresponsible, going to the opposite extreme and acting honest, trustworthy, loyal, concerned and responsible act as "blockers" to these harmful behaviors. Opposite extreme values are associated with opposite extreme behaviors used to help you break each phase of the stress-relapse cycle.[4] This is summarized in Table 4 below.

Table 4.
SRT Opposite Extreme Values and Behaviors

Negative Behavior Phases in the Stress-Relapse Cycle	Opposite Extreme Positive Behavior Phases in the Stress-Management Cycle
Negative coping- not accepting responsibility, dishonesty about problems (An honesty problem-denial to self)	**Positive coping**- accepting responsibility, honesty about problems, "To thine own self be true". Get honest with yourself
Cover up of problems to avoid consequences, unhealthy pride, untrustworthy (A trust problem-deception, lying to others, holding negative contracts)	**Open up** about problems, accept consequences, use healthy pride to hold self accountable "The truth will set you free" and hold others accountable, "Be your brother's keeper". Rebuild trust by getting honest with others.
Stress buildup- increased tension from not being loyal to what you know is right and who is right, cover up stress (A loyalty problem)	**Stress adaptation**- cope with tension by being loyal to what you know is right and who is right.
Slip- sliding back in awareness, judgment or self-control (A concern problem- about self not keeping problem "up front" and others not considering the impact of harmful behavior on others)	**Step Up** in awareness, judgment and self-control, show concern for self by keeping you problem "up front"[2] and for others by putting yourself in their shoes, thinking about the impact of your behavior.
Fall- relapse into harmful behavior, not protecting the welfare of self and others (A responsibility problem- "Our #1 responsibility is self-control")	**Recover**- Avoid or escape relapse. Be responsible by maintaining self-control in order to protect the welfare of self and pothers.

In order to help prevent harmful behavior relapse, SRT also sets opposite extreme positive rules [4] to prevent harmful behavior relapse based on the logic that setting the bar high opposite extreme moves a behavior slip (lapse) further away from a behavior fall (relapse). Put another way, "If you aim for the stars, you may hit the trees and if you aim for the trees you may hit the ground".[5] Examples of SRT opposite extreme positive treatment rules are provided in Table 5.

Table 5.
SRT Opposite Extreme Positive Rules

Harmful Behavior	Relapse Triggers
Sexual abuse	No pornography
Physical abuse	No threats or cursing others
Property abuse	No borrowing
Substance abuse	No cigarettes
Trust abuse	No excuses

SRT Opposite Extreme Healthy Behavior Success Skills

Opposite extreme healthy behavior success skills[6] are used to maintain opposite extreme positive rules and behaviors which are required to maintain our number one responsibility of self-control and avoid relapse. Opposite extreme healthy behavior success skills help counter the negative dysfunctional family law that, "What I want to do is right and the reason its right is because I want to do it" associated with harmful behavior. Understanding each SRT healthy behavior success skill involves a simple learning experience broken down into Awareness training, Responsibility training and Tolerance training. In life, what you do is more important that what you say. In growing up, many people have been told by adults that, "Your ACTS speak louder than your words". In SRT, your ACTS are your responsibility to: Avoid trouble; Calm down; Think it though and; Solve the problem. The ACTS healthy behavior success skills are outlined in Table 6.

Table 6. Opposite Extreme Healthy Behavior Success Skills

Harmful Behavior Stance	Opposite Extreme "ACTS"
Never back down, Stand your ground, Divide and conquer	**Avoid Trouble** (Relapse prevention)
Create chaos, Stir it up, Get worked up, Stay worked up, Work others up	**Calm Down** (Emotional regulation)
Go with your gut Act on impulse	**Think it through** (Decisional balance)
Forget fighting it, do what you want. Don't work it out, block it out. "That was then, this is now"	**Solve the problem** (Social problem solving)

Cycles, Cycles and More Cycles

Stress-relapse cycles are have been observed across a number of harmful behaviors. For example: the substance abuse relapse-recovery cycle (Scott, Dennis and Foss, 2005); the physical abuse cycle of violence (Dutton, 2007); the sexual abuse maintenance cycle (Kahn, 1996); the unhealthy eating binge-diet cycle (Schulherr, 1998; 2005); the gambling cycle (Nower and Blaszczynski, 2006) along with the cycle of change that illustrates the general (transtheoretical) behavior change stages including relapse (Passmore, 2012). With respect to harmful emotions an anger-relapse cycle (Clancy, 1996; 1997) and depression-rumination cycle (Law, 2005; Nolen-Hoeksema and Davis, 1999) have been described. The point is this, harmful behavior habits are repeating cycles that

Figure 3. The Stress-Relapse Cycle

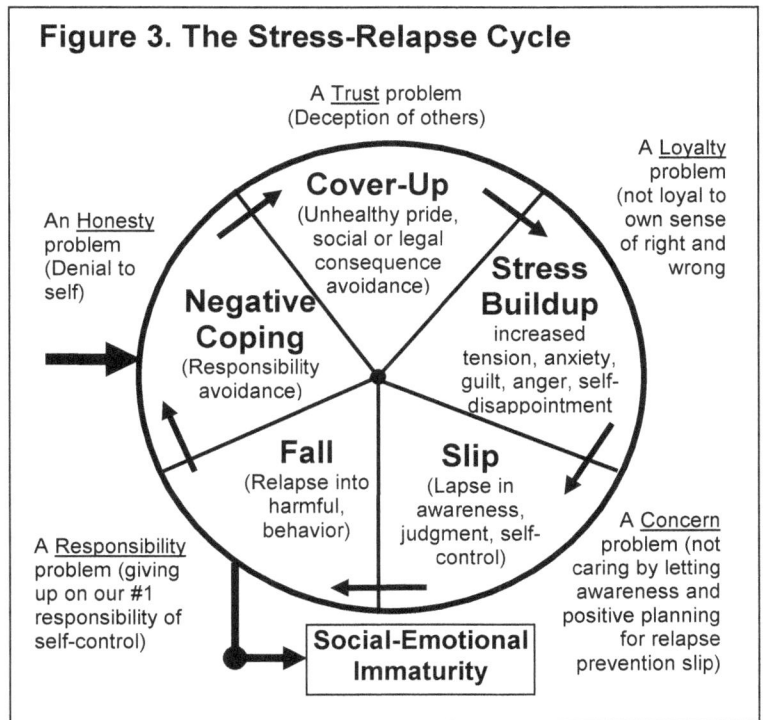

A Trust problem (Deception of others)

An Honesty problem (Denial to self)

A Loyalty problem (not loyal to own sense of right and wrong)

Cover-Up (Unhealthy pride, social or legal consequence avoidance)

Negative Coping (Responsibility avoidance)

Stress Buildup increased tension, anxiety, guilt, anger, self-disappointment

Fall (Relapse into harmful, behavior)

Slip (Lapse in awareness, judgment, self-control)

A Responsibility problem (giving up on our #1 responsibility of self-control)

A Concern problem (not caring by letting awareness and positive planning for relapse prevention slip)

Social-Emotional Immaturity

humans fall into and need to learn to break. The Stress-Relapse Cycle is used in SRT to help address multiple forms of unhealthy harmful behavior (See Figure 3).

The Fork in the Road after harmful behavior episode:
Positive vs Negative Coping, Recovery or Relapse?

After committing an abusive behavior, if you use positive coping, accept and work on the problem, don't make excuses and get honest, two things are likely. First, you are likely to get help to avoid doing it again and second there is likely to be consequences. In short, "Honesty has its price but the good news is you don't have to pay twice". If you use negative coping, you are likely to fall into the Stress Relapse Cycle that maintains harmful behavior.

The Stress-Relapse Cycle
"We are what we repeatedly do"- Aristotle (384 BC-322 BC)

The Stress-Relapse Cycle plays an important part in relapse prevention because it: 1) describes the cycle that maintains harmful behavior; 2) summarizes the basic factors in each phase of the cycle that increase relapse risk and; 3) provides the skills needed in each phase to break the Stress-Relapse Cycle. A Stress-Relapse Cycle summary is provided in Figure 1.

Breaking the Stress-Relapse Cycle

Breaking the Stress-Relapse Cycle involves being able to answer the following five basic relapse prevention questions in order to make a relapse prevention plan that works for you.

Making a Relapse Prevention Plan that Works for You:
Five Relapse Prevention Questions to Answer

1. After making a mistake and falling back into your harmful behavior, what did you tell yourself to deal with it?
2. What did you do to keep your harmful behavior from being detected?
3. What stressful thoughts, feelings and situations are you experiencing?
4. What slips have you noticed that can lead you to fall back into your harmful behavior?
5. What do you believe led you to fall back into your harmful behavior this last time?

Since these questions are easy to ask but hard to answer, the rest of this workbook is structured to help you discover the answers that fit your specific situation and how to use the ACTS healthy behavior success skills to develop a Stress-Management Cycle (Figure 1) that works for you.

Summary of Healthy Relationship and Behavior Success Skills

The awareness training focus of this workbook is on helping you understand how your unhealthy, harmful behavior spread through the Harmful Behavior Anatomy. During awareness training on how your problem spread, it is equally important to keep the problem under control. This requires a responsibility and tolerance training focus on: 1) the healthy behavior success skills needed to change that harmful behavior and; 2) the healthy relationship success skills needed to form a positive support network that will help maintain that positive change.

The healthy behavior success skills you need to keep from falling back into harmful, negative behavior are: **A**void trouble; **C**alm down; **T**hink it through and; **S**olve the problem.[6] The healthy relationship success skills you need for positive relationship development and to help you maintain behavior change are honesty, trust, loyalty, concern and responsibility. In relationships these are the things that we want from others in our life and that others want from us. Both healthy behavior and relationship success skills are needed for positive community adjustment and to get what you want in life. These skills are related to each other and support each other.

Healthy <u>Relationship</u> Success Skills (Description)

Honesty- Involves getting honest with yourself about your mistakes and with others about their mistakes. Tell yourself the truth about the feelings that others could have about your actions and how you feel about the actions of others. Getting honest involves learning to "Calm down" (see p. 22- 23) so that you don't justify lying based on fear of consequences and learning to "Think it through" (p. 24- 25) by weighing out the severity of the consequences to yourself and others on the reality scales. Confront deception (see p. 188) in yourself and others. List the benefits of honesty and how you can improve it. What could you do differently? Get others opinions.

_____

_____

_____

Trust- Involves: 1) <u>building trust</u> in others by taking responsibility to "Avoid trouble" (see p. 18), keeping your word and respecting others feelings along with; 2) <u>learning to trust</u> others by opening up about problems and picking the right people to trust. Avoid trust double standards (see p. 188). List the benefits of trust, how you can improve it, what you can do. Get others opinions.

_____

_____

_____

Loyalty- Involves <u>standing up for what you know is right</u> and who you know is right especially when there is social pressure to keep quiet, i.e., "If you don't stand for something, you'll fall for anything." This means learning to "Think it through" (see p. 24- 25) to avoid Irresponsible Loyalty (see p. 190) by going along with what is wrong just to get along, compromising yourself to be accepted or covering up for others. List the benefits of loyalty and how you can improve your loyalty below. What could you do differently? Get others opinions.

_____

_____

_____

Concern- Involves: 1) <u>helping self</u> by keeping problems "up front" [2] as a daily priority so that they don't get out of control again; 2) <u>helping others</u> by treating them the way they want to be treated; 3) blocking helplessness by taking responsibility to "Solve the Problem" (see p. 25- 27) instead of blaming others (i.e., "when you blame other people for your behavior, you give them control over your life") and 4) substituting the "Don't care attitude" (see p. 190) with the courage to care, share and try. In group and family therapy, use your PRAISE skills (p. 28) to show concern for others. List the benefits of concern, how to improve, what you can do. Get others opinions.

_____

_____

_____

Responsibility- <u>Our number one responsibility is self-control</u> which involves learning to: **A**void trouble; **C**alm down; **T**hink it through and; **S**olve the problem (see below). Other important responsibilities are making things right (emotional restitution), pulling our own weight and learning to accept feedback. Getting what we want in life requires awareness of responsibility issues (see p. 191). List responsibility benefits, how to improve, what you can do. Get others opinions.

_____

_____

_____

_____

Healthy <u>Behavior</u> Success Skills (Instructions)

Let's face it, most people who are completing a harmful behavior workbook at one point in their lives have been told to avoid trouble, calm down, think things through before acting or that they need to solve their problem. This was telling you what you already know, not what you really need to know. Everybody knows that what you do matters more than what you say. You have probably been told at some time in your life that your **ACTS** speak louder than your words. What you really need to know is "how to" **A**void trouble, **C**alm down, **T**hink it through and **S**olve the problem.[6]

How to **A**void trouble: Two Basic Skills
If you have had some treatment experience in the past, you may have heard the skills used to avoid trouble referred to as "relapse prevention". These skills basically involve becoming aware of your high risk situations for relapse into unhealthy, harmful behavior and then making relapse prevention plans to avoid or escape those situations. A high risk situation is a person, place or thing (often a thought or feeling) that sets the occasion for falling back into trouble (i.e., harmful behavior). In order to avoid trouble (relapse) you need to know how to deal with high risk situations. Dealing with high risk situations takes two basic types of skills. You need avoidance skills to help you identify high risk situations so you can get around them and you need escape skills to get out of high risk situations when you fall into them or when they find you. The focus in this workbook will be on learning to "Avoid Trouble" by learning high risk situation avoidance and escape skills.

High Risk Situation Avoidance

Use positive planning and fantasy fast forward to avoid trouble (p. 187). Since it's always easier to avoid trouble (high risk situations) than escape it once started, "If you fail to plan, you plan to fail". Use Positive Planning to avoid high risk situations. Know your high risk situations. Make a list with a positive plan for each high risk person, place or thing/emotion that could lead you back into harmful behavior trouble. "Keep your problem up front",[2] don't let your recovery planning guard down by and put a HALT on falling into high risk situations by not letting yourself get to Hungry, Angry, Lonely or Tired. Think about your last harmful behavior problem and list who you were with, where you were, what you were thinking and feeling at the time. Then list how these people, places and things set the occasion for trouble.

Referral problem- Harmful behavior that resulted in your treatment referral _____

High risk people- Who you were with and how they helped lead you into your referral problem?

_____

Positive plan (to avoid these people)- _____

_____

High risk places- Where were you and how that helped lead you into your referral problem?

_____

Positive plan (to avoid these places)- _____

_____

High risk things- What you were feeling and how did that lead to your referral problem?

_____

Positive plan (to deal with these feelings)- _____

_____

What you were thinking and how did that lead to your referral problem? _____

_____

Positive plan (to manage these thoughts)- _____

_____

> **Hint:** If you are not sure about your thinking, review the irresponsible thinking that can lead to trouble in Appendix C. This may help you become aware of your high risk thoughts that led to trouble.

Avoiding foresight slips into high risk situations

In reality, no matter how good our intentions are, if we don't use positive planning, Murphy's Law kicks in and "whatever can go wrong, will go wrong". If we don't stick to our recovery priorities and relapse prevention plan by avoiding high risk situations, using the reality scales (p. 24) to think our decisions through and weigh the possible consequences, we are likely to make a foresight deficit decision and fall back into harmful behavior trouble. Foresight deficit decisions are foresight slips that lead to falling back into harmful behavior from not being aware of high risk situations, not looking ahead and not thinking about what could happen. Foresight deficit decisions can result in relapse on many types of harmful behaviors. The key to avoiding foresight deficit decisions that lead to harmful behavior relapse is developing self-awareness of: 1) high risk situations for relapse and; 2) the irresponsible thinking (see Appendix C, p. 188) that allows you to enter those high risk situations. One simple way to help you avoid foresight deficit decisions is to use Fantasy Fast Forward (p. 187) where you pretend you are actually the main character in a movie and fast forward to the end in order to help you imagine what may go wrong if you stay in your present situation and don't change course. In short, fantasy fast forward involves learning to "Think ahead and plan ahead to get ahead". Then describe a foresight deficit decision that you have made on your referral problem behavior and how you could use fantasy fast forward to avoid the same harmful behavior trouble in the future. Sometimes it's easier if you break your foresight deficit decision down by starting at the end with the problem you fell into and working backwards to look at the situations or events you didn't think ahead about that led to that harmful behavior. Like anything else, fantasy fast forward takes practice. In order to get good at it, you have to look at what you could do different next time.

Foresight deficit decision: I fell into a problem with _____

when I didn't think ahead about what could go wrong from _____

_____

> **Hint:** A review of the foresight deficit decisions examples in Appendix B (p. 184) and the description of fantasy fast forward at the end (p. 187) should help you with this assignment.

Fantasy Fast Forward: If I think about being in a similar situation again and fast forward to the

end, I need to think ahead about _____

and avoid trouble by _____

High Risk Situation Escape

Use the Three-Step Social Responsibility Plan (i.e., "The 3 G's"- get out, get honest and get responsible) to escape trouble. Accept that when it comes to getting out of high risk situations, "hesitation kills recovery". Look at the high risk people, places and things that you listed in the previous section and describe how you could use your Three-step responsibility plan to escape.

1. **Get out** (Remove yourself) Involves getting out of the high risk situation by leaving without hesitation. No one thinks clearly in emotional situations. "You need to be laughing and leaving, not staying and stewing" because the longer you stay in the problem situation, the higher the risk of acting irresponsible. Be prepared to escape trouble by developing "concrete face saving mechanisms" (excuses to leave high risk situations that will work) to have ready if needed. Look at the high risk situations you listed above. What could you do or say to get

   away from these people and out of these places? _____

_____

_____

2. **Get honest** (Block irresponsible thinking by getting honest with yourself) about: 1) the likelihood of relapse if you return to those high risk situations and block the irresponsible thoughts that "I can handle it, no big deal, nothing will happen", etc. and 2) what will happen to your goals and feelings about yourself if you act on the unhealthy, harmful thoughts that get triggered by high risk people, places or feelings. Use "Fantasy fast forward" to play the tape in your head to the end consequences and tell yourself "I'm not falling into that". Tell yourself the truth that feelings can change over time but once you have done something, that can't be changed. If you can't deny the feeling, delay it by telling yourself "I can always come back here or do this tomorrow". What could happen next if you don't stay out of that

   situation and how will you will feel later? _____

   _____

   _____

   Using the reality scales described on page 24 can also help you get honest with yourself about the need to stay or escape your high risk situation. Rate the high risk situations you listed above on the scales below.

   Survival scale- "How necessary for my survival is it for me to stay in this situation?"

   0 = not necessary; 10 = necessary to save my life _____
   Success scale- "How important is it to my success in life for me to stay in this situation?"

   0= not important at all; 10= so important I will never succeed in life without it _____
   Severity scale- "How severe could the consequences be if I leave this situation?"

   0= not severe at all; 10= so severe I can't stand it and will need help to handle it _____

3. **Get responsible** (Use responsible self-statement substitution, p. 188). Replace the irresponsible thoughts about unhealthy, harmful behavior that (e.g., eating, drinking, drugging, smoking, spending, cheating, hitting, cursing, stealing, molesting, running away) that get triggered by high risk situations with responsible thoughts. Begin by asking yourself, "How will that help me? or Why should I hurt me just because other people or other things hurt me?" Then substitute responsible thoughts. For example, "I need to stay out of that situation", "It's not worth the risk", "I need to put my recovery first" and escape trouble.

   What I need to say to myself _____

   _____

   _____

   What I need to do _____

   _____

The ABC's of Calming Down: Emotional Regulation 101

The healthy behavior success skills needed to calm down involves emotional control. These skills are often referred to as "emotional regulation" in treatment manuals. Many unhealthy, harmful behaviors are justified by feelings while ignoring facts. Since you can't justify harmful actions based on unwanted feelings, without unwanted feelings. It is important to learn emotional regulation skills to deal with the discomfort of unwanted feelings. The core of acting feelings out is justifying actions based on feelings and the cure for acting feelings out is emotional regulation. If you were standing next to your best friend when a problem situation hit you, they would show you concern by talking you down, not working you up. Unfortunately, we are not usually standing next to our best friend when problems hit. In these situations we have to learn to talk to ourselves like our own best friend. We have to talk ourselves down, not work ourselves up.

The two basic skills emotional regulation skills we have to learn in order to talk ourselves down, deal with frustration, distress and stop acting feelings out are: 1) Emotional Dissipation- How to let go of unwanted feelings and; 2) Emotional Accommodation- How to hold on to unwanted feelings. In short, emotional regulation involves, knowing how and when to hold on to and let go of feelings. In this respect, dealing with feelings is like playing card hands in the game of life, "You gotta know when to hold 'em and know when to fold 'em"- Kenny Rogers

Emotional Dissipation (The ABC's of letting feelings go):

Emotional dissipation involves letting go of belief problems that are working you up. The ABC's of letting feelings go are as follows... **"A"** is the Action that occurred (the problem situation or event); **"B"** is the Belief problem, about the action that works you up and triggers problem feelings or urges (i.e., often contains the word "should" or "must"); **"C"** is Challenging the Belief problem about the action in order to stop following the feeling and let it go.[3] For example: Action that occurred- Supervisor in a hurry raises their voice to you on in front of others; Belief problem- Telling yourself "They should respect me" triggers feeling frustrated and angry. This can result in having the last word and getting consequences if you can't let the feelings go and keep talking; Challenging the Belief problem- "Where is the evidence that people in a hurry, should slow down and lower their voice, I don't" and "How is me doing the wrong thing going to get them to do the right thing?"

Think about the last time you got really upset and had a relapse urge. Apply the ABC's of letting feelings go to that situation and discuss it with your therapist or group if you are in treatment.

Action that occurred: _____

_____

Belief problem: _____

_____

Challenging the belief problem: _____

_____

Hint: You can use the who, what, when, where, how and why that you learned in school for writing a short story to challenge belief problems. "Who could prove that? or "I can't prove that" (Validity challenge) "What if the worst happens?" (Preparation challenge) "When/why should I have known better?" (Self-criticism challenge) "Where is the evidence that...?" (Objective challenge) "Why does it follow that...?" (Philosophical challenge), "How likely is it that the negative outcome will occur? (Probability challenge)

Note: The ABC's used here were condensed from Rational Emotive Behavior Therapy.[7]

Emotional Accommodation (The ABC's of holding on to feelings):

Physical accommodation is the hot tub example where you get used to the uncomfortable temperature by making yourself stay in the tub until your body gets used to it (i.e., accommodation). Typically your thoughts stop and all your focus is on the hot water sensation along with the cool air around you. Emotional accommodation is where you get used to the uncomfortable feeling by making yourself stay with it until you get used to it, you stop all your thoughts by focusing on your body sensations and the environment around you. This is similar to the cotton candy experience where it's big, it's blue and it's in your face right up until you take a bite out of it and realize there wasn't that much to it. The ABC's of holding on to feelings is structured to help you discover "the cotton candy effect" of facing unwanted feelings and letting yourself accommodate to them. Remember urges and cravings are feelings too!

"A" is Accept the distressing feeling (urge or craving). Accept that distress and discomfort are a real part of everyone's life that we need to accommodate. Accept the trigger situation. Receive the feeling. Don't avoid it. Don't deny that you're upset. Don't distract yourself with activity, slow down and let yourself feel. Be open to unwanted feelings and opinions. Don't change the subject or block others feedback out. All feelings and all opinions are valid because they are someone's view of the world and we are all allowed to have different views. List a feeling that puts you at risk for relapse and how to accept that feeling. What do you say to yourself and do?

_____

_____

_____

"B" is Begin getting used to the feeling (urge or craving). Give yourself permission to feel. Stay with the feeling. Hold on to it. Don't try to minimize it or rationalize it off. Think of a hot tub, don't get out, let yourself accommodate. Find a quiet place if you can. Accept the fact that feelings can't hurt you, but telling yourself "I can't stand it" triggers reactions that can hurt you. Tell yourself, "I dislike this feeling but I can deal with it and don't have to act it out" or "This feeling is disturbing and disappointing but not dangerous so there is no need to take action". Write how could you begin to get used to that feeling that puts you at risk for relapse.

_____

_____

_____

"C" is Channel the feeling (urge or craving) to the right place at the right time. Tell yourself, "I can always act on my feeling tomorrow" to give yourself time to settle. Use your responsible mind to focus all of your awareness on your sensations. Let your emotional mind coast to a stop and allow thoughtless peace right now. Stay in the moment. Continue to be aware of the body sensations associated with the feeling/urge, just notice them, don't attach any thoughts to them, don't fight or struggle with them, just be aware of your sensations and let them be. Sit with your sensations. Think of the Chinese finger trap, stop struggling and pulling against the feeling, just let it be so you can get free. Imagine you are surfing a big wave using your breath to steady the surfboard though the peak of the urge as it rises and you are staying with it as it slides all the way into the beach. When you have surfed the urge out and the feeling subsides, channel your energy into a positive future image of yourself as the person you want to be in the place you want to be. Stay with that positive image. If the unwanted feeling/urge was triggered by a problem, describe where you could take that problem.

_____

_____

_____

How to Think it through with the "Reality Scales": Decisional Balance 101

If you were ever asked "what were you thinking", chances are that you didn't think your decision through before you took action. Thinking it though by balancing the benefits against the drawbacks before making the decision is referred to as "decisional balance" in treatment manuals. Thinking it through is an important part of learning to talk to yourself like your own best friend. False friends who just want to be popular with everyone or people who want to stir up trouble, tell you what you want to hear. They help you minimize unhealthy, harmful behavior by using the words "just" and "only" (e.g., "It's a only little thing, no big deal" or "We'll just do it this one time"). Best friends are honest with you and tell you what you need to hear, not what you want to hear. If you were standing next to your best friend when you were hit with temptation to do something you shouldn't, they would give you a reality check. Your best friend would tell you that in reality, it's only a little thing if no harm can come to yourself or others and it's never just once. Since your best friend can't always be there to give you a reality check, you have to learn to do this yourself. "When in doubt, weigh it out". The *reality check* and *reality scales* described below will help you weigh things out during difficult decisions, think it through and guide yourself into responsible action.

Use the Social Responsibility Check (reality check) for on the spot "snap" decisions by asking yourself "Is what I'm thinking about doing helpful or harmful to myself or others?" All decisions that could be harmful to self or others need to be weighted out further on three reality scales, the Survival Scale, the Success Scale and the Severity Scale. The Survival Scale evaluates how necessary for my survival it is to do the behavior being considered on a scale of zero (not necessary at all) to ten (absolutely necessary to save my life). Ask yourself, "How necessary for my survival is it for me to do what I am considering?" "What will happen to my survival if I don't act?" The Success Scale evaluates how important for my success is doing the responsible thing or failing to do it on a scale of zero (not important at all) to ten (so important that it could change the entire course of my life). Ask yourself, "How important is it to my success in life for me to do what I am considering?" "Do I have to do this in order to succeed in life?" The Severity (or Awful) Scale ("Bad Scale" for young children) evaluates how severe the consequences of doing the responsible thing or failing to do it will be on a scale of zero (not severe, awful or bad at all) to ten (so severe that I can't stand it, must avoid it and need help to overcome it). On one side of this scale is the reality of what will likely happen if the harmful behavior is committed. For example, "In the worst case, how severe could the consequences be if I smoked, drank or ate this and do I need to avoid these consequences?", "In the worst case, how severe could the consequences be if I took or smashed this and do I need to avoid these consequences?" or "In the worst case, how severe could the consequences be if I hit or fondled this person and do I need to avoid these consequences?" On the other side of this scale is the reality of what will likely happen if the harmful behavior is not committed. "How severe would the consequences be if I do the right thing and decide not to do this? Could I handle these consequences?" In summary, the severity scale is used to show concern for yourself and others by weighing out the severity of the consequences to yourself and others before taking action. [3]

List a recent decision mistake that you made: _____

_____

_____

Apply the Social Responsibility Check to that decision. My decision was (check one)...
__Helpful to me but harmful to others   __Harmful to me but helpful to others

__Helpful to myself and others   __Harmful to myself and others

List an important life decision that you need to make: _____

_____

_____

Use the Reality Scales to weigh out your decision and discuss this with your therapist or group if you are in treatment.

Survival scale rating ___(0- 10); Success scale rating ___(0- 10); Severity scale rating ___(0- 10)

My decision: _____

_____

_____

How to Solve the problem: Social Problem Solving 101

Life always has problems that kick up feelings and require solutions. Behind every problem there is a goal. Problems are only problems when we are not meeting our goals to get what we want in life. The healthy behavior success skills used to solve the problems we face in life are referred to in treatment manuals as "social problem solving". Being able to "solve the problem" is needed to meet our goals to: get what we want; do as well as we want or; be treated the way we want in life. In order to get what you want in life, you need to get SET for solving problems in three steps: 1) Set your goal; 2) Evaluate your progress and options; 3) Take responsible action.

Set your goal. Setting your goal involves getting honest with yourself about your goal. Ask yourself, What is my goal? What do I really want? Get honest about the problem and your real goal. Look at actual problem-solving goals not feelings about the problem. There is a big difference between solving the problem and just venting your feelings. For example, imagine you are a young person in a treatment program and your real goal is independence. You feel held back by adults because you are certain you can make it on your own if they just let you go. They keep reminding you that you haven't finished high school and believe you need more treatment to avoid relapse. You keep getting caught up in arguments over whether or not you can make it on your own.

Evaluate your progress and options. Evaluate your progress by asking yourself, "How well is what I am doing working in getting me what I want?" and "How will things likely to turn out for me if I continue this way?" This requires getting honest with yourself about your progress. For example, admitting that "Arguing over whether I can make it on my own if they just get out of my life is getting caught up in venting feelings, has not changed their minds and is not getting me any closer to actually being out on my own." Evaluate your options- Ask yourself, "What are my options?", "What can I change?", "What really needs to get done?" Make as long of a list as you can, be creative ask others for ideas. List all possible options and choices that could get you to your goal, then write it out for yourself. For example, "To be independent, I need my own place which takes money. My options are stealing, dealing, working going into the military or moving in with someone. I can change getting side-tracked in arguments on whether or not I can make it on my own, start really looking at what independence takes, 'keep my eyes on the prize', and figure out a way to get what I want. If I continue to vent my feelings over feeling held back without making a convincing plan to succeed, nothing will change. If I don't show them I know how to avoid relapse, I won't get out of treatment."

Take responsible action involves taking responsibility to change your method by getting honest with yourself about what needs to change and correcting your course. This involves answering the questions, "What do I need to do differently to reach my goal?", "What is the best way to get what I want?" and "What should I try first?" For example, "I need to do two things differently to reach my goal. First, I need to accept that reaching my goal will take more than just getting other people off my back and moving in with someone who will take care of me is not really making it on my own. In all honesty, I need a good job with health benefits or I need to get into the military. Both of these require graduating from high school and not relapsing back into another treatment program. Second, I need to stop letting my feelings get in the way of my goal to be on my own, stop arguing, start studying and finish treatment. I just got so mad when they told me 'you need to stop breeding and start reading' that I let my feelings get in the way of my goal. The best way to get what I want is to make the best relapse prevention plan I can. What I should try first is increased treatment participation and regular study hours." [3]

List a current problem that you are having: _____

_____

Use the steps above to "solve the problem" and discuss this with your therapist or group if you are in treatment.

Set your goal: _____

_____

Evaluate your progress _____

_____

and options: _____

_____

_____

_____

Take responsible action: _____

_____

_____

You can remember the healthy behavior success skills: **A**void trouble; **C**alm down; **T**hink it through and; **S**olve the problem by remembering that "actions speak louder than words" and thinking about your **ACTS**. Make a healthy relationship and behavior success skills cue card out of Table 7 below and carry it with you as a reminder of the skills you need to practice.

Table 7.
Healthy Behavior Success and Relationship Skills Cue Cards

Keep your Skill Cards with you at all times
"There are two basic types of knowledge in life, Knowing it and knowing where to get it" [8]

Social Responsibility Therapy- Healthy <u>Behavior</u> Success Skills[a]
Getting what we want in life involves learning to...

Avoid trouble (relapse prevention)- Use the 3-step social responsibility plan: <u>Get out</u> (Remove yourself)- "You need to be laughing and leaving, not staying and stewing"; <u>Get honest</u> (Block the thought)- Tell yourself the truth, feelings change but actions can't be changed. If you can't deny the thought delay it. Tell yourself "I can always do this tomorrow". <u>Get Responsible</u>[b] (Substitute a more responsible thought)- Weigh out your decision on the "Reality Scales".

Calm down (emotional regulation)- The ABC's of letting feelings go: "A" is the <u>Action that occurred</u>; "B" is the <u>Belief problem</u>, i.e., the word "should" or "must" that is triggering the feeling; "C" is <u>Challenging the Belief problem</u> in order to stop working yourself up, prevent following feelings and let it go.[b] (See Ellis & Bernard, 2006; Ellis & Velten, 1992). Use the ABC's of holding on to feelings if needed (see p. 23).

Think it through (decisional balance)- Do a Responsibility Check, ask yourself- "Is what I'm considering helpful or harmful to myself and others?" If harmful or unhealthy[b] use the three <u>Reality Scales</u> (0 to 10 scales):
Survival scale- How important to my survival is it for me to... ? ("Am I safe right now?")
Success scale- How important for my success is it for me to...? ("Will this change my life forever?")
Severity scale (Bad or Awful scale)- How severe would the consequences be if I...?

Solve the problem (social problem solving)- Get <u>SET</u> for solving problems: 1) <u>S</u>et your goal;
2) <u>E</u>valuate your progress and options; 3) <u>T</u>ake responsible action[b]

Table 7. (continued)
Healthy Behavior Success and Relationship Skills Cue Cards

Social Responsibility Therapy- Healthy Relationship Success Skills[c]
What do we want from others in our life and what do they want from us?
Developing the relationships we want in life requires mutual...

Honesty- Involves getting honest <u>with yourself and others</u> by taking responsibility for mistakes along with getting honest about others mistakes to keep them from getting in worse trouble later.

Trust- Involves <u>building trust</u> in others by keeping your word and respecting their feelings along with <u>learning to trust</u> others by opening up about problems and picking the right people to trust.

Loyalty- Involves <u>standing up for what you know is right</u> and who you know is right when there is peer pressure to keep quiet, "If you don't stand for something, you'll fall for anything."

Concern- Involves <u>helping self</u> by keeping personal problems "up front" [2] so they don't get out of control again and <u>helping others</u> by treating others the way they want to be treated.

Responsibility- <u>Our number one responsibility is self-control.</u> Three others are emotional restitution (making things right), pulling our own weight and learning to accept feedback.

Social Responsibility Therapy PRAISE Group Process Skills[d]
Group Participation Motivation Skills

Helping yourself and others get the most out of the group learning experience requires...

Pulling people in- "Can I borrow that from you? That's a really good point we need to discuss" (Making them a part/Integration), (p. 38, Yokley, 2008)

Responsible reinforcement- "That [took a lot of courage, was impressive, etc] let's give him a hand for his... [honesty, trust, loyalty, concern, responsibility]" (p. 33, 105, Yokley, 2008) or "Thank you for your honesty"

Acknowledgement - "What they are teaching us is..." (p. 38, Yokley, 2008), "An important thing that I got from of what you said was..."

Instant identification- "Please raise your hand if you have also..." followed by head count "one, two, three... people here also..." for awareness development (rapid identification/validation of shared experience), p. 192, Yokley, 2008.

Social mathematics by finding the least common denominator (p. 192 Yokley, 2008) during successive group introductions and when two or more members disclose similar issues- "These two/three have a couple things in common, what are they?/did you notice?" or after introductions, "What does this group have in common?" (Cumulative Identification).

Enabling responsibility- "It's not pick on John time or Let's not put John in the hot seat or Help me take John off the spot, please raise your hand if like John, you have ever (been accused of/made the mistake of)..." Setting the occasion for accepting responsibility and the "no more secrets policy" (p. 176, Yokley, 2008) by getting honest.

Table 7. Footnotes

a. SRT early stage recovery skills to help stabilize and prevent relapse into unhealthy harmful behavior.
b. Do the responsible thing. "Act as if" you are the positive person you want to be (p. 12) and go to the opposite healthy, helpful extreme.
c. SRT late stage recovery skills to help maintain healthy, helpful behavior.
d. SRT group recovery skills to build unity and enhance motivation for participation.

"Maturity comes not with age but with the acceptance of responsibility.
You are only young once but immaturity can last a lifetime!" -- Edwin Louis Cole

Understanding How Harmful Behavior Generalized to other Areas: The Harmful Behavior Anatomy

This third workbook in the Social Responsibility Therapy series focuses on developing an understanding how unhealthy, harmful behavior was generalized or spread to other forms of harmful behavior through the Harmful Behavior Anatomy (i.e., Section 3 of Problem Development Triad). Developing this understanding will be accomplished by getting you familiar with the components common to many types of harmful behavior which set the occasion for harmful behavior in general. Understanding harmful behavior generalization is extremely important if you want to lead a life free of all types of harmful behavior, not just the type of harmful behavior that caused you to be referred for treatment.

Introduction to Harmful Behavior Generalization

No one plans to spread their problem. After getting trapped in a cycle of unhealthy, harmful behavior, people usually feel anxious or depressed and try to make things better not worse. We don't typically tell ourselves, "This is getting boring, I need to spread out and try some new forms of unhealthy, harmful behavior". What happens is that over time, repeated falling back into the Stress-Relapse develops a pathological level of social-emotional immaturity made up of 10 basic components that support multiple forms of unhealthy harmful behavior. Once you have an entire set of components that support multiple forms of unhealthy harmful behavior, it's easy for your unhealthy, harmful behavior to spread from one type to another or bounce back and forth between problems. In Social Responsibility Therapy, the components that work together to support and spread unhealthy, harmful behavior are referred to as "The Harmful Behavior Anatomy ".

Social-Emotional Maturity Problems

Many individuals with behavior that is harmful to self or others suffer from a serious deficit in social and emotional maturity referred to as "Pathological Social-Emotional Immaturity". Individuals with Pathological Social-Emotional Immaturity often have action oriented styles that inhibit vicarious learning (i.e., learning by watching what happens to others) and requires learning by experience. Others have problems getting so far into something that they get obsessed with it, can't get it out of their minds and feel compelled to do it, particularly when experiencing stress. Many are often involved in power struggles with others, putting others down to build themselves up. They frequently use anger to manipulate others or to get others to back down. Their role reversal deficit (i.e., problems imagining what others might think or how they might feel) and emotional turmoil keeps them caught up in their own world which interferes with their concern for others. Individuals with social-emotional maturity problems don't fight fair and take advantage of others using intimidation, manipulation, impression formation and people pleasing to get what they want. If this sounds childlike, it's because social-emotional maturity problems keep people from acting their age.

Pathological Social-Emotional Immaturity includes a preoccupation with injustices or things that don't seem fair which leads to:
1. Avoidance of social responsibility- procrastination on change either because of expecting that others should change or waiting for them to care take of or solve your problems when it's up to you (your responsibility);
2. Avoidance of personal responsibility- always looking outside self for responsibility/blame or solutions to problems;
3. Avoidance of financial responsibility- "the world owes me a living" mentality, feeling entitled to be supported by others, "they should make it up to me" for bad past experiences.

Social-Emotional Maturity Problems Support Multiple Forms of Harmful Behavior
A pathological level of social-emotional immaturity supports multiple forms of unhealthy, harmful behavior and allow generalization from one type to another (See Figure 4).

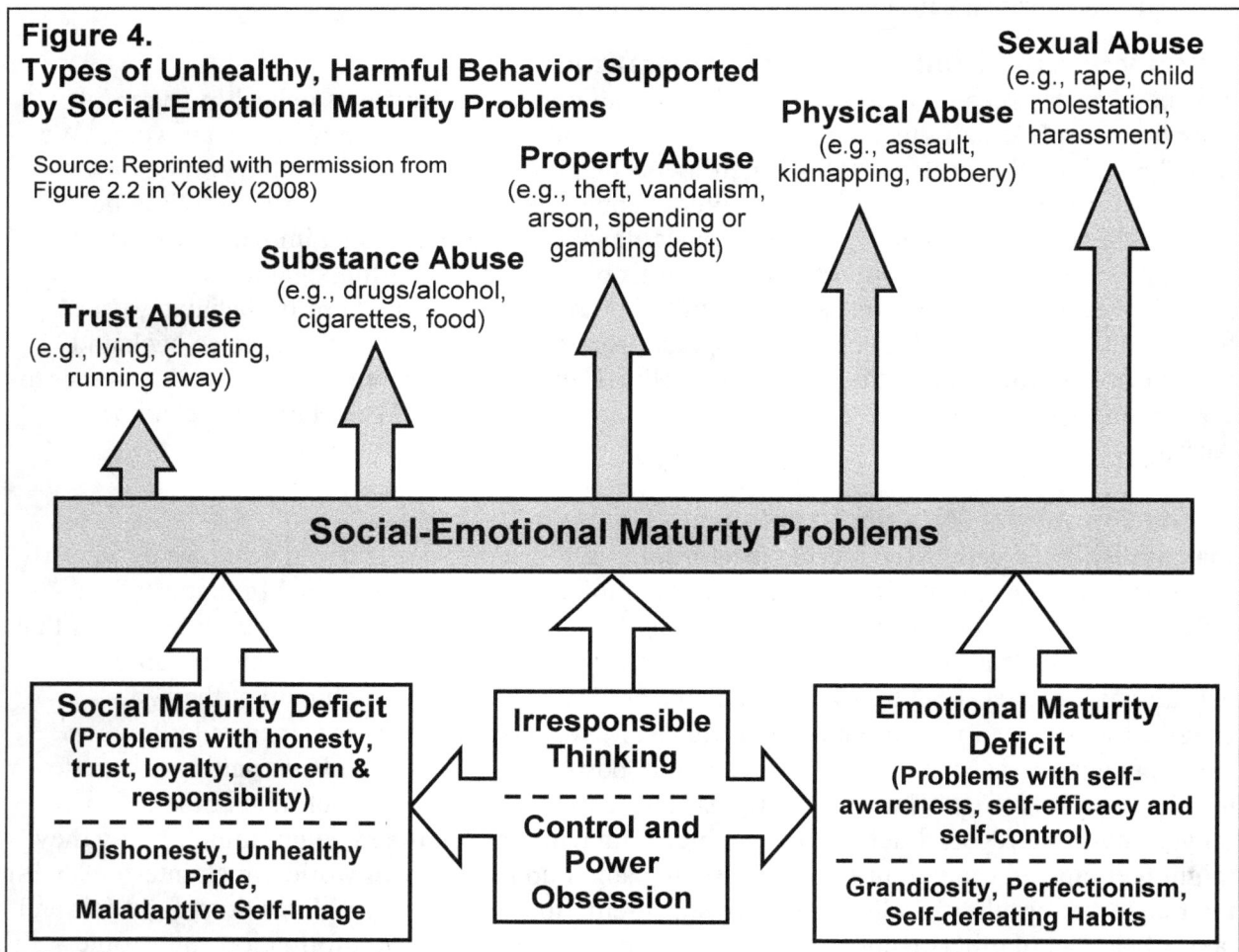

Figure 4.
Types of Unhealthy, Harmful Behavior Supported by Social-Emotional Maturity Problems

Source: Reprinted with permission from Figure 2.2 in Yokley (2008)

Sexual Abuse (e.g., rape, child molestation, harassment)

Physical Abuse (e.g., assault, kidnapping, robbery)

Property Abuse (e.g., theft, vandalism, arson, spending or gambling debt)

Substance Abuse (e.g., drugs/alcohol, cigarettes, food)

Trust Abuse (e.g., lying, cheating, running away)

Social-Emotional Maturity Problems

Social Maturity Deficit (Problems with honesty, trust, loyalty, concern & responsibility)
- - - - - - - - - - - -
Dishonesty, Unhealthy Pride, Maladaptive Self-Image

Irresponsible Thinking
- - - - - - - - - -
Control and Power Obsession

Emotional Maturity Deficit (Problems with self-awareness, self-efficacy and self-control)
- - - - - - - - - - - -
Grandiosity, Perfectionism, Self-defeating Habits

Harmful behavior involves problems with self-control and control of others

Self-control problems with harmful behavior involves not being able to hold back an urge to do something that could be harmful to self or others and trying to control moods by forcing a desired mood or blocking an undesired one. For example, in substance abuse this involves getting high to feel good or relieve negative feelings with drugs/alcohol (e.g., decreasing anger by smoking marijuana, anxiety by taking narcotics, depression or boredom by taking stimulants), cigarettes (calming self) or food (i.e., "comfort eating"). In addition, thrill seeking behaviors such as gambling, shoplifting or vandalism may control moods by breaking boredom and feeding an exaggerated need for excitement.

In social forms of harmful behavior, control of others or their property may serve the purpose of building self-up by putting others down through dominating them or getting over on them and making self feel smarter. Sexual or physical abuse involving winning by intimidation to control others or get what you want also feeds power needs through domination of others. Property abuse "thrill crimes" such as shoplifting can gratify powerful feelings of excitement during the behavior and result in superiority feelings after getting away with it.

Unhealthy, harmful behavior can sometimes serve a dual purpose, for example control of others through sexual abuse that involves forcing or tricking a person to feed power needs also gratifies excitement needs. Likewise, sexual abuse behavior such as rape may gratify an exaggerated need for excitement and vent anger at the same time. Property abuse behavior such as vandalism may also gratify an exaggerated need for excitement and vent anger at the same time. Substance abuse relapse behavior with alcohol, tobacco or overeating, such as accepting an invitation to go out for a drink or a buffet dinner at a smoking restaurant with a friend can gratify an exaggerated need for acceptance and control or decrease social anxiety at the same time.

Many substance abusers (e.g., drugs, alcohol, cigarettes, food) are social abusers (e.g., of people their property and their trust) and many social abusers are substance abusers. However, it is important not to confuse definitions used in substance abuse with social abuse. Substance abuse treatment divides the seriousness of the problem into two levels by using definitions of Abuse (meaning someone whose behavior is excessive but still under their willful control) and Dependence (or addiction, meaning someone whose behavior is excessive, has become compulsive and no longer entirely under their willful control).

While the substance abuse treatment concept of addiction is appropriate for those whose behavior is primarily harmful to self (e.g., overeaters, drinkers, smokers), it is not appropriate for treatment of individuals whose behavior is primarily harmful to others (e.g., physical and sexual abusers). It is too tempting for social abusers to use a label of addiction as an "I couldn't help it" as an excuse to avoid responsibility for their abuse of others. The only distinction that is important in Social Responsibility Therapy is whether the person in treatment has behavior problems that hurt themselves or others and whether they are willing to take responsibility for that behavior. This means keeping your problem, up front all of the time including group therapy introductions that begin with, "Hi my name is Diego and I am responsible for my unhealthy, harmful behavior".

Individuals may have the right to abuse themselves but they certainly have no right to abuse others. If you were referred for an abuse behavior that is primarily harmful to self by individuals who care about you deeply, you need to stay in touch with the fact that when you hurt yourself you are hurting them. Regardless of what other types of diseases, addictions or historical trauma you may have, if you have hurt others, it is important that you hold yourself accountable and take responsibility for your behavior by enrolling and completing treatment. If you have hurt others, you need to reclaim your dignity through your honesty about your behavior. If you don't hold yourself accountable to the social responsibility of reclaiming your dignity through your honesty you will never develop the social maturity required to have true meaningful relationships with others based on honesty, trust, loyalty, concern and responsibility. The reason we value honesty so much is the tremendous price attached and the tremendous courage it takes.

"Abuse is abuse"-- Gail Ryan (founder of National Adolescent Perpetration Network)
Unhealthy, harmful behavior is supported by a pathological level of social-emotional immaturity. Given this situation, although there is always a need to separate predators from their prey, there is no real need to have separate groups for different types of substance abusers or separate groups for different types of social abusers. In substance abuse treatment, there are alcoholics that express their disgust at having drug addicts in their groups. This is interesting because outside of group some actually hang out with people worse off to help them minimize their own problems. In social abuse treatment, there are rapists that express their disgust at having child molesters in their groups. This common thinking among substance and social abusers is an example of the Unhealthy Pride (i.e., not wanting to associate with "the serious cases") and Control and Power Obsession (i.e., putting others down to build self up) in their Pathological Social-Emotional Immaturity. The same thing occurs across the spectrum of abuse behavior severity. For example, in examining Table 1 on page 2, it would be common for food abusers to tell themselves that their problem is not as serious as the alcohol abusers who tell themselves that their problem is not as serious as the drug abusers who tell themselves that their problem is not as serious as the wife beaters who tell themselves that their problem is not as serious as rapists who tell themselves that their problem is not as serious as the murderers. This comparison and contrast minimization of harmful behavior is observable in just about every setting. Near the end of this workbook revision, a morbidly obese patient told me "I just binge, I don't stick my finger down my throat." Another patient asked me for a cigarette and said, "This hospital's making a bum out of me. They don't have cigarettes here and I have to bum them. A smoker's gotta do what a smoker's gotta do. It's not like I'm gambling or anything". However, abuse is abuse and harmful behavior to self or others often relates to a pathological level of social-emotional immaturity.

The Harmful Behavior Anatomy
Social Responsibility Therapy utilizes a Harmful Behavior Anatomy model to help individuals with unhealthy, harmful behavior understand ten components that contribute to the pathological level of social-emotional immaturity needed to support multiple forms of unhealthy, harmful behavior. This in turn allows the generalization or spread of one type of harmful behavior to another type along with symptom substitution (i.e., starting another type of harmful behavior after successfully stopping the referral form harmful behavior that was on your treatment plan).

Review Your History of Unhealthy, Harmful Behavior

When asked to give their history, some people say "I did this already at the beginning of this workbook (along with workbook 1 and 2 if you have completed them) so what's in it for me to go through this again?" The answer is simple, each time you look at something that you have examined before, if you look close enough your will see something new which will help you plan your recovery. Put another way, "The more extensive a man's knowledge of what has been done, the greater will be his power of knowing what to do" -- Benjamin Disraeli (1804-1881).

Using your Situation Response Analysis during the Risk Factor Chain in workbook 1 and Stress-Relapse Cycle in workbook 2 has probably made you aware of more types of unhealthy, harmful behaviors than when you first started your Social Responsibility Therapy. If you have completed workbook 1, review the Link #5 section of The Risk Factor Chain in workbook 1 and update it adding additional harmful behaviors that you have noticed. If this is your first SRT workbook, review Table 1, The Harmful Behavior Continuum and underline all of the types of harmful behavior that you have ever committed.

It's never too late to reclaim your dignity through your honesty. It is difficult for some people to view their problem behavior as unhealthy, harmful or abusive and take responsibility for letting it go too far. Some prefer to view their behavior as "traps" that they fell into which ensnared them to the point where it took over, put their life on hold, alienated them from others. They seem upset at external, uncontrollable things which they believe prevented them from forming positive, healthy relationships and achieving their life goals. Those who avoid taking responsibility, avoid the language of responsibility. They substitute "It happened" for "I did it" and describe criminal charges with "I caught a case" as if it were a cold that someone else sneezed on them. Take a minute and think back through the types of harmful behavior that you have reported in this workbook. Then take responsibility and list any other types of unhealthy, harmful behavior that you need to get honest about or any further details that you need to disclose in the space provided below. After that, complete the questions A, B and C.

_____

_____

_____

A. List your **referral behavior** (harmful behavior that resulted in your treatment referral).

_____

This behavior is primarily harmful to (check one) __self; __others; __both self and others.

B. List your top three **most severe** types of harmful behavior (In order of seriousness).

1) _____ Was it harmful to (check one) __self; __others; __both?

2) _____ Was it harmful to (check one) __self; __others; __both?

3) _____ Was it harmful to (check one) __self; __others; __both?

C. List your top three **most frequent** harmful behaviors (In order of how often you did them).

1) _____ Was it harmful to (check one) __self; __others; __both?

2) _____ Was it harmful to (check one) __self; __others; __both?

3) _____ Was it harmful to (check one) __self; __others; __both?

D. List the form of **harmful behavior causing you the most trouble now.**

_____

_____

This behavior is primarily harmful to (check one) __self; __others; __both self and others.

List your multiple forms of harmful behavior

Record your referral behavior, your #1 most serious harmful behavior, your #1 most frequent behavior and the behavior you are having the most trouble with now in the space provided on your Harmful Behavior Anatomy worksheet (page 161).

Almost all forms of harmful behavior involve varying symptoms and degrees of Pathological Social-Emotional Immaturity. Thus, if you don't get treatment for your social-emotional maturity problems, your harmful behavior is at risk for generalizing (spreading) to another type or form. This section covers ten social-emotional immaturity components that you need to address in order to prevent: 1) your harmful behavior from generalizing to other types and; 2) starting another type of harmful behavior after stopping the one that resulted in your referral to treatment.

Start Completing your Harmful Behavior Time Line (Appendix F)

If you are in treatment, now is the time to start a discussion with your therapist and/or treatment group about your harmful behavior history. After you have recorded the harmful behavior that you directed towards yourself and/or others, bring up (with your therapist and/or treatment group) the past harmful things that you have experienced, that were done to you by others. Be sure to take social responsibility by disclosing everything you did that was harmful before you start discussions about what others have done. Hold yourself accountable first by looking at your behavior/issues. After you have outlined the basics of both the harmful behavior you did as well as what you experienced, set these two topics aside. We will get back to them after completing your work on the ten Harmful Behavior Anatomy components that support harmful behavior.

Record your history of multiple forms of harmful behavior on the bottom half of the Harmful Behavior Time Line form in Appendix F of this workbook. Do your time line work in this order. Record: 1) your birth date under "birth" and your current age under "now"; 2) the types of unhealthy, harmful behavior that you did to yourself and others at the bottom of your time line and; 3) the types of unhealthy, harmful behavior and treatment you have experienced at the top of your time line.

The Ten Components in the Anatomy of Social-Emotional Maturity Problems that Support Multiple forms of Unhealthy, Harmful Behavior

Remember what's in it for you. Two important motives for understanding the anatomy of components that contribute to multiple forms of harmful behavior are to help: 1) develop a healthy, responsible lifestyle free of any form of unhealthy, harmful behavior and; 2) decrease the probability of "symptom substitution" to another form of harmful behavior after you have learned to successfully control your referral behavior. The categories selected for inclusion in the Harmful Behavior Anatomy of characteristics associated with pathological social-emotional immaturity and related multiple forms of harmful behavior are listed in Table 8 below.

Table 8.
The Harmful Behavior Anatomy of components
that support multiple forms of harmful behavior

Head: Irresponsible Thinking	**Heart/Torso:** Control & Power Obsession
Right Arm: Unhealthy Pride	**Left Arm:** Unhealthy Perfectionism
Right Hand: Deception	**Left Hand:** Grandiosity
Right Leg: Social Maturity Deficit	**Left Leg:** Emotional Maturity Deficit
Right Foot: Maladaptive Self-Image	**Left Foot:** Self-Defeating Habits

Most psychology models of behavior seek to establish independent key contributing factors. In contrast, the anatomy model seeks to establish how key components help each other support unhealthy harmful behavior, similar to the way key organs of the human body help each other support human life. For example, it is easy to see how the right hand of deception is the logical extension of the right arm of unhealthy pride and serves to protect that pride. A summary of The Harmful Behavior Anatomy of components that support multiple forms of unhealthy, harmful behavior is provided on Figure 5.

What's in it for me? Understanding what generalizes harmful behavior to other forms is extremely important if you want to avoid transferring to another type of unhealthy, harmful behavior after you have stopped the behavior that you were referred for during treatment.

When most people think of problems generalizing or spreading, they think in terms of going up the severity scale on Table 1 (page 2) but harmful behavior can spread even if you come into treatment for a harmful behavior that is at the top of the severity scale. Harry, a 17-year-old male in residential youth sex offender treatment gave the following brief summary of how his harmful behavior spread as a result of developing a Control and Power tolerance. "After a while sexual abuse wasn't enough for me, I went to picking on a couple of kids I singled out at school (physical abuse), moved on to getting high (substance abuse) and increased my lying (trust abuse) to cover everything up".

Figure 5.
How Harmful Behavior was Generalized

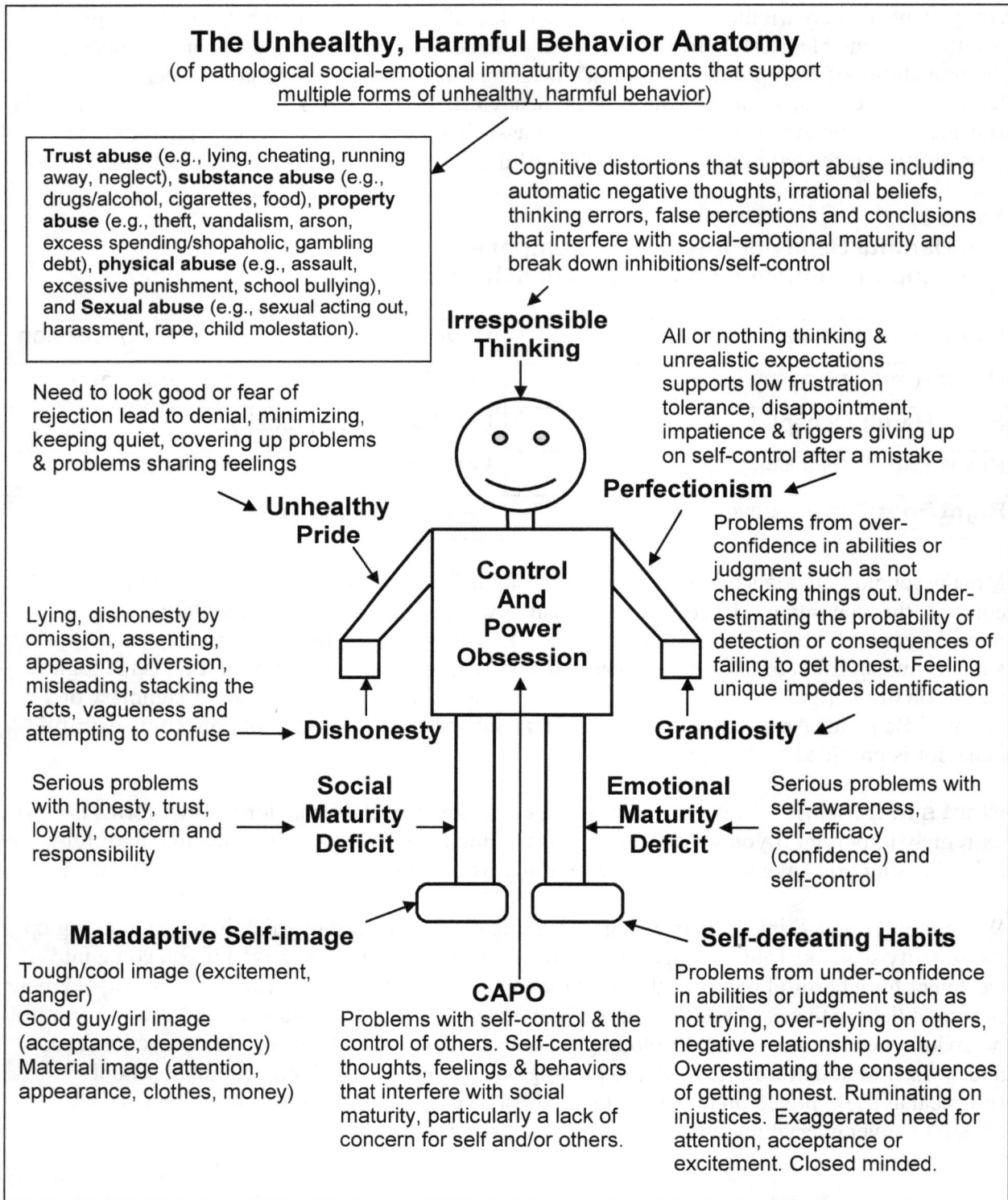

The Unhealthy, Harmful Behavior Anatomy
(of pathological social-emotional immaturity components that support
<u>multiple forms of unhealthy, harmful behavior</u>)

Trust abuse (e.g., lying, cheating, running away, neglect), **substance abuse** (e.g., drugs/alcohol, cigarettes, food), **property abuse** (e.g., theft, vandalism, arson, excess spending/shopaholic, gambling debt), **physical abuse** (e.g., assault, excessive punishment, school bullying), and **Sexual abuse** (e.g., sexual acting out, harassment, rape, child molestation).

Cognitive distortions that support abuse including automatic negative thoughts, irrational beliefs, thinking errors, false perceptions and conclusions that interfere with social-emotional maturity and break down inhibitions/self-control

Irresponsible Thinking

Need to look good or fear of rejection lead to denial, minimizing, keeping quiet, covering up problems & problems sharing feelings

All or nothing thinking & unrealistic expectations supports low frustration tolerance, disappointment, impatience & triggers giving up on self-control after a mistake

Unhealthy Pride

Perfectionism

Lying, dishonesty by omission, assenting, appeasing, diversion, misleading, stacking the facts, vagueness and attempting to confuse

Control And Power Obsession

Problems from over-confidence in abilities or judgment such as not checking things out. Under-estimating the probability of detection or consequences of failing to get honest. Feeling unique impedes identification

Dishonesty

Grandiosity

Serious problems with honesty, trust, loyalty, concern and responsibility

Social Maturity Deficit

Emotional Maturity Deficit

Serious problems with self-awareness, self-efficacy (confidence) and self-control

Maladaptive Self-image

Tough/cool image (excitement, danger)
Good guy/girl image (acceptance, dependency)
Material image (attention, appearance, clothes, money)

CAPO
Problems with self-control & the control of others. Self-centered thoughts, feelings & behaviors that interfere with social maturity, particularly a lack of concern for self and/or others.

Self-defeating Habits

Problems from under-confidence in abilities or judgment such as not trying, over-relying on others, negative relationship loyalty. Overestimating the consequences of getting honest. Ruminating on injustices. Exaggerated need for attention, acceptance or excitement. Closed minded.

The Harmful Behavior Anatomy Component 1: Irresponsible Thinking

"Change your thoughts and you change your world" -- Norman Vincent Peale (1898- 1993)

Name: _____   Date: _____

Definition: Irresponsible Thinking is the head of the Harmful Behavior Anatomy that controls the type, frequency, and severity of unhealthy, harmful behavior that has been learned and gets expressed. Irresponsible Thinking supports multiple forms of unhealthy, harmful behavior. Since the same irresponsible thinking can trigger multiple forms of unhealthy, harmful behavior, once you get in the habit of using that thinking, your harmful behavior can spread from one type to another. The basic types of unhealthy, harmful behavior that are supported by Irresponsible Thinking is illustrated in Figure 6. below.

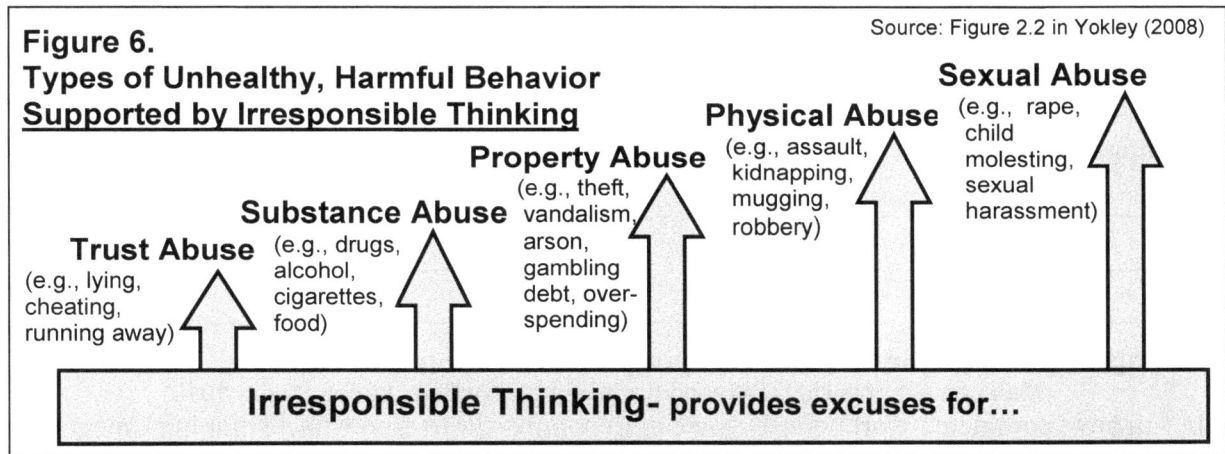

Figure 6.
Types of Unhealthy, Harmful Behavior
Supported by Irresponsible Thinking
Source: Figure 2.2 in Yokley (2008)

Trust Abuse (e.g., lying, cheating, running away)

Substance Abuse (e.g., drugs, alcohol, cigarettes, food)

Property Abuse (e.g., theft, vandalism, arson, gambling debt, over-spending)

Physical Abuse (e.g., assault, kidnapping, mugging, robbery)

Sexual Abuse (e.g., rape, child molesting, sexual harassment)

Irresponsible Thinking- provides excuses for...

Irresponsible Thinking involves cognitive distortions that support unhealthy, harmful behavior including automatic negative thoughts, thinking errors and misattributions (i.e., attributing an incorrect meaning to a behavior such as telling yourself something was done on purpose that was really an accident). These distortions interfere with social-emotional maturity, break down inhibitions and interfere with self-control. Irresponsible Thinking also involves irrational beliefs (i.e., telling yourself things that are not realistic), misperceptions (i.e., looking at things from a biased point of view) and false perceptions (not seeing things the way they really are) that stop you from adapting, growing or succeeding in life..

Behavior Anatomy Question #1: What type of things can people tell themselves that enable or justify unhealthy, harmful behavior?

Examples of Irresponsible Thinking that support multiple forms of unhealthy, harmful behavior and allows your problems to spread from one type to another are provided in Table 9. Circle any of the 15 Irresponsible Thinking statements in Table 9 above that you have used. Then write any other things you said to yourself that have allowed you to go ahead and do an unhealthy, harmful behavior in the space provided under Table 9. If you want, just change the Table 9 statements to fit you.

Table 9.
Examples of Irresponsible Thinking that Supports Multiple Harmful Behaviors

Harmful Behavior	Minimizing	Justifying Actions	Victim View	Extremism (all or nothing)
Trust Abuse	"It was just a white lie"	"They cheated on me so I deserved to do it"	"I had to lie to they would kill me"	"I always get blamed so I lie"
Substance Abuse	"It was only beer, not drugs"	"Anyone would get high after what happened"	"Relapse wasn't my fault, she left me"	"I always relapse & will never make it"
Property Abuse	"I just stole a few dollars"	"I had to take it because they might have said no if I asked"	"It's not my fault that I don't have money"	"I'll never get caught"
Physical Abuse	"I only slapped her once"	"They made me hit them by disrespecting me"	"I shouldn't be blamed, they started it"	"If you never hit, you will always get hit"
Sexual Abuse	"It was just fondling, not rape"	"It's OK to do it to others because it was done to me"	"I couldn't help it, she got me excited"	"They always say no when they really mean yes"

Source: Adapted with permission from Table 2.3 in Yokley 2008

Other things I have said to myself that allowed or excused unhealthy, harmful behavior are...

_____

_____

_____

A. Recognize and Replace your Irresponsible Thinking

"Man can alter his life by altering his thinking"-- William James (1842- 1910)

If you have completed workbook 1, you can Recognize 20 Irresponsible Thinking Categories that can trigger harmful behavior and Replace it. Review Appendix C (page 188) and underline all of the Irresponsible Thinking that you have used. Then review the Responsible Alternatives suggested under each type. Look at the material you have underlined on the 20 types of Irresponsible Thinking, circle the numbers of the top three that of you have used (i.e., those types with the most symptoms underlined) and record them in the space below.

Irresponsible Thinking Type #1 (from list of 20 in Appendix C, page 188)

Recognize the Irresponsible Thinking that I have (list the type and symptoms you underlined).

Type or Irresponsible Thinking- _____

Symptoms (Things I underlined)- _____

_____ -_____

Replace the Irresponsible Thinking- List what you need to say to yourself when you recognize it.

_____

_____

Irresponsible Thinking Type #2 (from list of 20 in Appendix C, page 188)

<u>Recognize</u> the Irresponsible Thinking that I have (list the type and symptoms you underlined).

Type or Irresponsible Thinking- _____

Symptoms (Things I underlined)- _____

_____ - _____

<u>Replace</u> the Irresponsible Thinking- List what you need to say to yourself when you recognize it.

_____

_____

Irresponsible Thinking Type #3 (from list of 20 in Appendix C, page 188)

<u>Recognize</u> the Irresponsible Thinking that I have (list the type and symptoms you underlined).

Type or Irresponsible Thinking- _____

Symptoms (Things I underlined)- _____

_____ - _____

<u>Replace</u> the Irresponsible Thinking- List what you need to say to yourself when you recognize it.

_____

_____

Keeping your Irresponsible Thinking "Up Front"

Keeping something "up front" means staying aware of it at all times. If you don't recognize it, you can't replace it. Life can move fast and sometimes we need a few memory tricks so that things don't slip by us. You can recognize several basic types of Irresponsible Thinking that support multiple forms of unhealthy, harmful behavior, create problems and can get in the way of your recovery with the acronym **"JOBS MAN"** easily remembered by the sentence "JOBS are a Must to Always have and Never lose".

"**J**ust" and "**O**nly" helps you become aware of when you are minimizing (p. 202) a behavior or issue, e.g., "It's OK, I'll just do it a little or only do it once"
"**B**ut" helps you recognize excuses involving responsibility issues (p. 194), blaming, "I can't belief" or justifying, e.g., "I know it was wrong, but it wasn't my fault because…"
"**S**hould" and "**M**ust" helps you recognize irrational beliefs, e.g., "These thugs should treat me with respect", "I must be the best at whatever I do"
"**A**lways" and "**N**ever" helps you become aware of over-generalizing (all or nothing extremism, p. 199) which is important because things don't <u>always</u> go wrong and we are <u>never</u> right all of the time.

In Social Responsibility Therapy, it is your social responsibility to hold yourself accountable on a daily basis through structured self-evaluation of responses to problem situations. This type of structured adaptive thinking was designed to combat irresponsible thinking and is referred to as

Situation Response Analysis. If you have completed workbook 1 and 2, you have already been holding yourself accountable by analyzing your responses to situations on your daily Situation Response Analysis Log (Appendix D) and addressing your irresponsible thinking.

Begin using your Situation Response Analysis Log

This is a very important part of increasing your self-awareness of the Irresponsible Thinking that you use on everyday problem situations. Make time to sit down every evening to review your day and record events in your log. The Situation Response Analysis Log and instructions are provided for you in Appendix D. Be sure to make at least one log entry every day as you will be using what you learned from this log in your treatment sessions and later in workbook 3. Use this log as a way to become more aware of your thoughts feelings and behavior in difficult situations. Don't forget to record using "the 3 G's", i.e., your three-step social responsibility plan (p. 20) when you use it as a Positive Coping response to a problem situation. Consult with your therapist or staff about whether to complete the Candy Bar Exercise on high risk situation access in Appendix D or whether to wait and discuss this exercise in the Self-Control portion of the Component 9- Emotional Maturity Deficit in workbook 3.

Monitor your irresponsible thinking closely on your Situation Response Analysis log. Putting consistent effort in to identifying and changing irresponsible thinking is one of the most important things you can do to keep from falling back into your Stress-Relapse cycle of harmful behavior. The more self-awareness of your thinking that you develop and the better you get at making the corrections listed in Appendix C, the more self-control you will develop. The more self-control you develop, the more you will avoid falling back in to your Stress-Relapse cycle. Your knowledge about how to manage your harmful behavior and avoid falling back into your cycle will increase your self-efficacy (confidence) and decrease the unwanted consequences that result from unhealthy, harmful behavior.

B. Complete and Score (or Update) Your Awareness and Honesty Examination

If you have not completed workbook 1 or 2, complete and score your Awareness and Honesty Exam in Appendix G (p. 207). If you have completed your Awareness and Honesty Exam in workbook 1 or 2, it is now time to see how much the Situation Response Analysis Log that you began using during your work on the Risk Factor Chain and/or Stress-Relapse Cycle has helped you improve your self-awareness of Irresponsible Thinking. Review your Awareness and Honesty Examination (in Link 4 of workbook 1 or Appendix F of workbook 2). Then complete the Awareness and Honesty Exam in Appendix G of this workbook to update your ratings and show the improvement in awareness that occurred as a result of your use of the daily Situation Response Analysis Log (Appendix D).

C. Compare your the types of Irresponsible Thinking that you have the most symptoms of with the types that you used most frequently

"Recognize and Replace" is the key to changing the irresponsible thinking that allows unhealthy, harmful behavior. Since "practice makes perfect", let's review recognizing and replacing your irresponsible thinking again but this time using all of the information you became aware of from the "Irresponsible Thinking Categories & Responsible Alternatives" you reviewed (Appendix C) and from your "Awareness and Honesty Exam" (Appendix G) .

Compare results of your Awareness and Honesty Exam in Appendix G (p. 207) showing the top five types of irresponsible thinking that you used most frequently with the irresponsible thinking that you listed in section A above. Then list those that overlap in the space provided below (i.e., Irresponsible Thinking that you underlined the most symptoms of and listed in section A above along with the irresponsible thinking that you rated as most frequent in Appendix G. If there is no overlap, list all eight (i.e., the three with the most symptoms underlined that you listed in section A above followed by the five most frequent from Appendix G)

Irresponsible Thinking that I had the most symptoms of and used most frequently:

1) _____

2) _____

3) _____

4) _____

5) _____

6) _____

7) _____

8) _____

Which of the above types of irresponsible thinking listed above do you believe had the strongest impact on you and led to your treatment referral? List your personal quotes (i.e., self-statements, what you would say to yourself that showed the type of thinking you listed above).

Personal Quote #1 _____

Personal Quote #2 _____

Personal Quote #3 _____

Next you have to <u>replace</u> the irresponsible thinking that you recognize with responsible thinking to develop healthy, helpful behavior. Review the responsible alternatives that need to be substituted for each of the 20 types of Irresponsible Thinking listed in Appendix C. Then use the space below to write a responsible self-statement to replace the Irresponsible Thinking that you listed in the "Recognize and Replace" section above.

1) _____

2) _____

3) _____

4) _____

5) _____

6) _____

7) _____

8) _____

D. Identify the top three types of Irresponsible Thinking that supported your harmful behavior.

Review your most frequent Irresponsible Thinking types (section 1 above), your thinking before, during and after harmful behavior (section 2 above) along with your thinking that created social-emotional maturity problems (section 3 above), circle any similarities that you see and write about any connections that you are able to make in the space provided below. Then review the top three forms of Irresponsible Thinking that you recorded on your Harmful Behavior Anatomy worksheet (page 161) and update it if needed.

_____

_____

_____

_____

The ART of Avoiding Trouble

An important part of the ART of Avoiding Trouble (Relapse Prevention), particularly in the area of escaping situations that are high risk for relapse is learning to manage the Irresponsible Thinking that maintains those situations. The **ART** of avoiding trouble involves: <u>A</u>wareness training on identifying high risk situations for unhealthy, harmful behavior; <u>R</u>esponsibility training on learning high risk situation avoidance and escape skills and; <u>T</u>olerance training on learning to tolerate and utilize behavior feedback on relapse triggers and barriers to success (Figure 7).

Whenever you become aware of a high risk situation you need to immediately use your "3 G's", i.e., Three Step Social Responsibility Plan (p. 20) to: <u>G</u>et out (remove yourself from the situation); <u>G</u>et honest (by telling yourself the truth about what could happen if you do the harmful behavior) and; <u>G</u>et responsible (substitute a responsible thought that will keep you out of the high risk situation and avoid

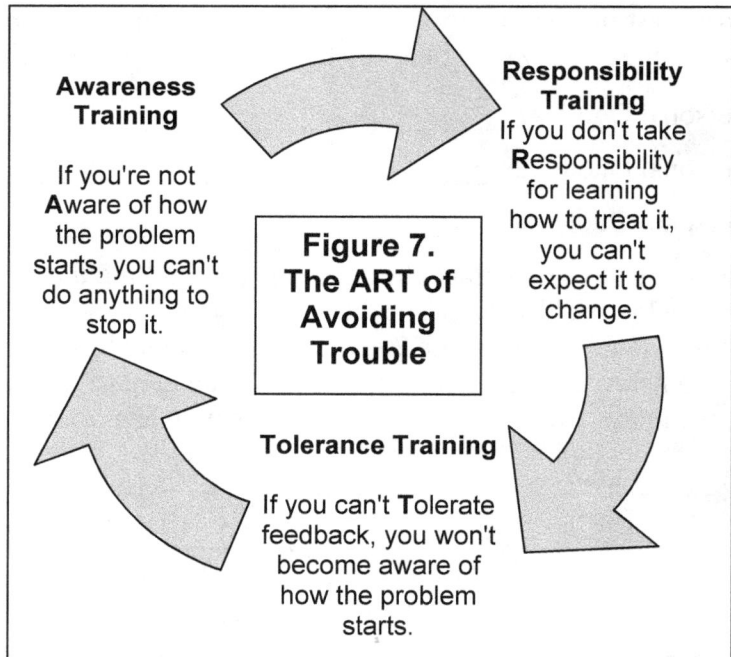

Awareness Training

If you're not **A**ware of how the problem starts, you can't do anything to stop it.

Responsibility Training
If you don't take **R**esponsibility for learning how to treat it, you can't expect it to change.

Figure 7. The ART of Avoiding Trouble

Tolerance Training

If you can't **T**olerate feedback, you won't become aware of how the problem starts.

relapse). "You are only limited by your creativity" when dealing with life problems. See Exhibit 3 (p. 177) for a description of another ACTS skill you can use to deal with irresponsible thinking.

Awareness training: In the ART of avoiding trouble, if you're not **A**ware of the Irresponsible Thinking that enables your contact with high risk people/places/things or results in high risk feelings that trigger your unhealthy, harmful behavior, you can't do anything to stop it. Awareness training focuses on identifying the irresponsible thinking that sets the occasion for to relapse. Review what you have learned in Section A through D of this component about high risk Irresponsible Thinking that can trigger your unhealthy, harmful behavior and answer the question "What kind of Irresponsible Thinking" can trigger relapse for me? List that thinking and give examples of how it can lead to unhealthy, harmful behavior relapse below

Irresponsible Thinking   Unhealthy, Harmful Behavior

_____

_____

_____

Hint: Look at your high risk situations on p. 20 and write what you tell yourself that allows you to enter them or stay in them.

Responsibility training: While Awareness training is a necessary first step, if you don't take **R**esponsibility for learning how to avoid trouble, you can't expect to change. It does you no good to develop your awareness to the point where you can recognize your high risk situations, if you stay in those situations until a relapse is triggered. Responsibility training involves learning positive self-statements to substitute for irresponsible thinking because "When we know better, we do better". Review "How to Avoid trouble: Two basic Skills" (p.20- 23) and describe how to avoid and escape the unhealthy, harmful behavior that can be triggered by the Irresponsible Thinking by substituting responsible thinking.

List Irresponsible Thinking that allows you to enter high risk situations
(Review Appendix C., p. 188 and see High Risk Situation Avoidance, p. 19)

_____

_____

How I can avoid trouble? Responsible self-statement substitution (see definition, p. 188)

_____

_____

Using the "3 G's", i.e., The Three Step Social Responsibility Plan (p. 20)
Imagine you just ran into a high risk person who took you to a high risk place where you used to do your unhealthy, harmful behavior.
List that person and place here- _____
Then complete the exercise below on using your three step social responsibility plan to escape that situation in order to prevent relapse.
1. **Get out** (Remove yourself). Use responsible thinking. Write what you need to say to yourself to get yourself out of this high risk situation.

_____

2. **Get honest** (Block irresponsible thinking by getting honest with yourself). Use responsible thinking. Write the real truth about what would likely happen if you stayed in that situation and the real truth about how you would feel afterwards.

_____

Hint: "Not to make a decision, is to make a decision." This insight was pointed out by Harvard Medical School professor and philosopher William James (1842- 1910). Often referred to as the father of American psychology, James stated, "When you have to make a choice and don't make it, that is in itself a choice". Thus, not to make a decision to "Get out" of a high risk situation for relapse, is to make a decision to set yourself up for relapse.

3. **Get responsible** (Substitute more responsible thoughts). Write what you need to say to yourself to stay out and not go back.

_____

Tolerance training: If you can't **T**olerate change, you won't be able to maintain decisions to change. Learning to tolerate change involves going to the opposite extreme with all of the things that can help with self-control of your unhealthy, harmful behavior (e.g., your irresponsible thinking triggers, your high risk feeling triggers, your high risk people triggers). Reasons this is needed include learning to keep a healthy distance between you and your relapse triggers along with getting yourself used to the extra effort that it takes to avoid relapse back into unhealthy, harmful behavior. Answer the question, "What would be the opposite extreme?" of the unhealthy, harmful, irresponsible thinking you listed in the Awareness training section above. Describe the opposite healthy, helpful, responsible thinking that you need to practice regularly. Do it like this. Look at your awareness training section above and make a sabotage plan listing plans to be around and stay around high risk people, places and things including the Irresponsible Thinking that will make it OK for you. Then go to the opposite extreme and write the healthy, responsible thoughts that will prevent a relapse. Use the workspace on page 227 if needed.

Irresponsible Relapse Thinking   Opposite Responsible Relapse Prevention Thinking

_____

_____

E. Make a Positive Plan and Commitment to Change
Review the three types of Irresponsible Thinking you listed on your Harmful Behavior Anatomy worksheet (page 161). What can you do about it now? How are you going to change, what are you going to do? (Consult with your therapist)

1) _____

2) _____

3) _____

Get honest about the Irresponsible Thinking that you have become aware of with your therapist or treatment group. Log the date you discussed this and your positive plan to change along with who you discussed it with in the space provided below.

Date: _____ Discussed with: _____

"The greatest power that a person possesses is the power to choose" -- J. Martin Kohe

Name: _____   **Date:** _____

Definition: Unhealthy, harmful behavior is often the expression of control and power issues. A control and power obsession can be considered at the heart of multiple forms of harmful behavior because most forms of unhealthy, harmful behavior involve problems with power, self-control, and the control of others. A Control and Power Obsession (CAPO) can be expressed through: controlling/manipulating people with lies and deceit (i.e., Trust abuse); controlling/decreasing depression, anxiety or anger with drugs, alcohol or food (i.e., Substance Abuse); controlling/elevating excitement with gambling, vandalism, shoplifting or arson (i.e., Property Abuse); controlling/venting anger with harassment, bullying and assault (i.e., physical abuse) and controlling people and elevating sexual excitement with molestation and rape (i.e., sexual abuse).

Many survivors of abuse, neglect or over-controlling relationships experience feelings of helplessness, powerlessness, and inadequacy. These feelings can create exaggerated needs for control and power. Thus, it is not unusual for CAPO behavior to involve an abuser who was abused themselves. Since the same Control and Power Obsession can be expressed through multiple forms of unhealthy, harmful behavior, once you develop exaggerated needs for control and power, your harmful behavior can spread from one type to another (Figure 8).

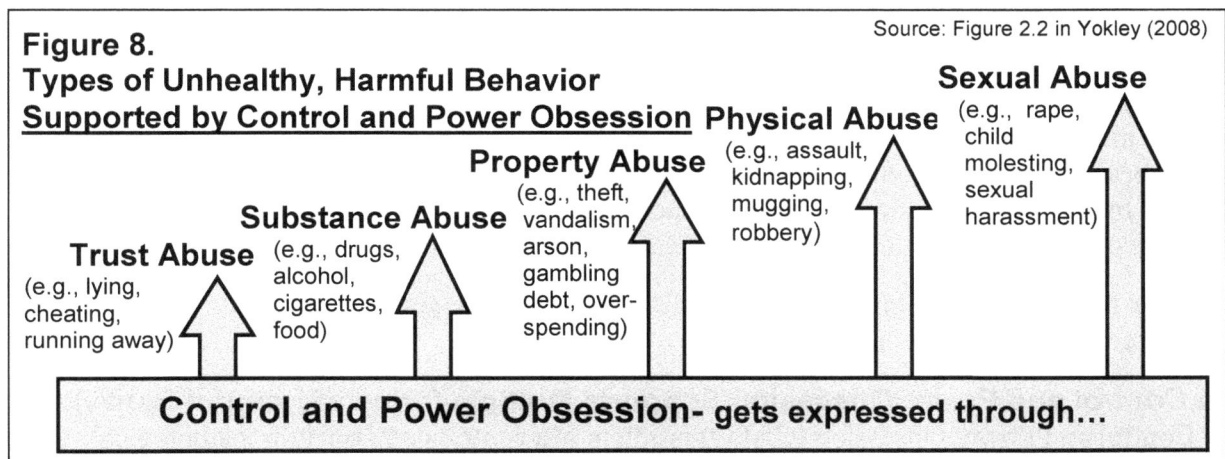

Figure 8.
Types of Unhealthy, Harmful Behavior Supported by Control and Power Obsession
Source: Figure 2.2 in Yokley (2008)

Trust Abuse (e.g., lying, cheating, running away)

Substance Abuse (e.g., drugs, alcohol, cigarettes, food)

Property Abuse (e.g., theft, vandalism, arson, gambling debt, over-spending)

Physical Abuse (e.g., assault, kidnapping, mugging, robbery)

Sexual Abuse (e.g., rape, child molesting, sexual harassment)

Control and Power Obsession- gets expressed through...

The word capo itself has two meanings that relate to both of the above points. In music, a capo (short for capo tasto or head fret in Italian) is a guitar clamp that acts on all six strings in the same manner that a Control and Power Obsession gets acted out through virtually all forms of unhealthy, harmful behavior. In World War II history, a Nazi death camp capo was a guard who was also a prisoner distinguished by a yellow armband bearing the black letters c-a-p-o and armed with a club or a whip enabling these victims to become abusive to their fellow condemned prisoners in much the same way that a Control and Power Obsession enables a past abuse victim to exhibit current abusive behavior towards others.

There are a wide variety of CAPO symptoms including: a preoccupation with past injustices; keeping score and getting even; enjoying matching wits with others in power struggles with an intense need to win (including winning by intimidation); resisting authority/rule refusal; severe selfishness with interpersonal manipulation (including splitting or playing people against each other); an exaggerated need to get "my way" right away (i.e., immediate gratification problem); acceptance problems (e.g., can't take "no" for an answer) and; serious resistance to change (e.g., refusal to back down or compromise). In addition to other problems, CAPO involves what Dr. Ruth Greenberg (1992) has referred to as "I or You Thinking". This thinking is based on the assumption that only one person in a discussion can have dignity, value, empowerment, merit, control, success or good intentions. This view prevents sharing, mutual respect, compromise or win-win interactions and sets the occasion for conflict and power struggles.

CAPO characteristics are common in individuals who abuse people, property and substances. In addition to the serious behavior exhibited during a behavior relapse episode, the CAPO involves less serious ongoing negative behavior patterns that have become functionally autonomous or independent of the persons conscious decision making by habit (i.e., automatic, over learned responses). While CAPO characteristics are common in individuals with unhealthy, harmful behavior, externalizers and internalizers may have different CAPO symptoms or express the same symptoms differently. Many externalizing CAPO characteristics are referred to as "King Baby" behavior in substance abusers who exhibit Low Frustration Tolerance fall into "feeding the PIG" (Problem of Immediate Gratification) by showing little patience when their needs are not immediately met. The "King Baby" style involves a cluster of CAPO characteristics such as hostility, grandiosity, dominance, and narcissism that can create a view of self as different in a unique and special way deserving of special treatment differently based on their unique situation. CAPO behavior can involve a severe selfishness which prevents adequate development of honesty, trust, loyalty, concern and responsibility. Internalizing CAPO characteristics can include becoming overly controlling and taking on too much responsibility in order to be accepted by meeting dependency needs of others or over-controlling mood with alcohol, cigarettes or food. You could even view Unhealthy Perfectionism as a CAPO with yourself.

Behavior Anatomy Question #2: What past experiences have you had that could result in a need to keep things under control?

The Control and Power Obsession Supports Multiple forms of Harmful Behavior
The Control and Power Obsession (CAPO) problem is a central component in pathological social-emotional immaturity and the generalization of harmful behavior. The CAPO is made up of self-centered thoughts, feelings and negative behavior patterns that demonstrate a lack of concern for self and/or others, support thrill seeking or other forms of irresponsible gratification and prevent the adequate development of honesty, trust, loyalty, concern and responsibility. These patterns have been reinforced by many repetitions of the Stress-Relapse Cycle to the point where they have become functionally autonomous habits that struggle for independence from the

persons values. Although most CAPO behavior is irresponsible, since it acts to artificially boost self-efficacy at the expense of others, that reinforcement continues its use. Once a method to boost self-efficacy has been found, no other coping strategies are tried. Think about driving to a new work location. Once you find a way to get there on time you don't keep looking for new and more efficient routes. You just go with what you have learned that works. Since all coping acts to reduce stress, this is why you use your old negative coping and reenter a Stress-Relapse Cycle as opposed to looking for new positive coping to avoid falling back onto the cycle. Feeling better, getting relief and increasing self-efficacy through behavior that is harmful to self or others are CAPO issues, which underlie multiple forms of harmful behavior.

Spreading unhealthy, harmful to a similar type of problem- It is easy to see how generalization could occur when the types of unhealthy, harmful behavior are similar to each other such as different types of substance abuse, verbal abuse or physical abuse. It's no problem to see how a substance abuser with self-control problems could generalize from smoking marijuana to drinking alcohol because the purpose of each behavior is to get high or feel better while increasing self-efficacy (i.e., feelings of control and confidence).

Spreading unhealthy, harmful behavior to a different type of problem- Since the central issue of control and power (i.e., controlling mood, getting power needs met or "my way") is easily shifted from self to others, the presence of a CAPO also sets the occasion for easy generalization from one type of abuse to another. Examples include generalizing from substance abuse (alcohol to control separation anxiety) to physical abuse (inducing fear to control others from leaving) or physical abuse (anger-based assault and battery) to sexual abuse (anger-based rape). Since Cover Up deception is often involved in many types of unhealthy, harmful behavior, it is common for trust abuse (lying) to accompany sexual abuse, physical abuse, property abuse and substance abuse.

Review all of the CAPO information up to this point, underline any part that has applied to you in the past and use the space below to give a specific example of what you consider your most serious or most frequent past CAPO characteristics.

_____

_____

_____

_____

Almost all individuals with unhealthy, harmful behavior have some CAPO characteristics but different individuals with unhealthy, harmful behavior may have different symptoms of that condition. Please complete the following steps below which were designed to help you clarify and become more aware of the CAPO characteristics that you have developed.

A. Review your Awareness and Honesty Exam (Appendix G), record your CAPO
   Problem ratings in the spaces provided below and add up all of your ratings to get a total

Since your self-awareness may have improved from your use of the Situation Response Analysis log, you may need to update your ratings. Enter your ratings total in the space provided below.

Control and Power Problems (26 items from Awareness and Honesty Exam, p. 207)

___ 2) Respect double standards	___108) Score keeping and getting even
___ 9) Commitment to always stay in control of the situation	___122) Closed minded
___ 18) No tolerance for disagreement	___123) Refusal to tolerate "no"
___ 29) Exaggerated "my way" needs	___133) Putting others down to build self up
___ 49) Played people to get what I want	___134) Offender stance
___ 54) Eavesdropping	___136) Played people to avoid consequences
___ 69) Winning by intimidation	___137) Communication double standards
___ 74) Relationship jealousy or possessiveness	___139) Blocking people out
___ 77) Justifying actions based on feelings	___140) Disagreement defensiveness
___ 88) Emotional blackmail	___142) Refusal to back down
___ 90) Arguing for control or fun	___148) Using anger to put accusers on the defensive
___ 94) Creating chaos	___152) Ignoring authorities
___ 96) Manipulated for sympathy	___156) Felt others must cooperate with me
	Total = _____

Consult with your therapist or treatment program staff to determine if you are completing the basic form of this component or are completing the entire section.

<u>End of basic form</u>- **Stop here and skip to part C, "Control and Power Obsession Structured Discovery Exercise" on page 52 if you are completing the basic form. Otherwise, continue on with the section B questions below.**

B. Rate the following CAPO characteristics.
Use the numbered ratings on the scales provided below to rate the frequency of your past thoughts or behaviors on the statements listed in this section.

0	1	2	3	4
Never	**Sometimes**	**Half of the time**	**Often**	**Almost Always**

___ 1) I have spent time being angry about past injustices that were done to me.

___ 2) I have spent time being angry about other people's behavior towards me.

___ 3) It was easy for me to get away with things that I know I probably shouldn't have been doing.

___ 4) Truthfully, I have enjoyed matching wits and out thinking others in order to get my way.

___ 5) I have been called selfish or self-centered.

___ 6) People have said I need to learn how to consider the feelings and rights of others.

___ 7) I have been crafty and easily fooled others.

0	1	2	3	4
Never	Sometimes	Half of the time	Often	Almost Always

____ 8) I have been able to get others to do what I want without trying too hard.

____ 9) I have resisted authority & have had authority conflicts.

____ 10) I have been quick to take issue with those I thought were telling me what to do or were trying to enforce rules on me.

____ 11) I have argued over rules just for the sake of arguing and not really because the rules didn't make sense.

____ 12) I have been a person who wants to be in control and to control other people.

____ 13) I have broken rules just because they were rules.

____ 14) I have enjoyed matching wits with authorities to see if I could get around the rules.

____ 15) I have been angry at or afraid of authorities.

____ 16) I have played people against each other in order to get my way.

____ 17) I have been able to make good first impressions and start up new relationships easily.

____ 18) I have had problems maintaining long term relationships.

____ 19) I have had difficulty accepting personal criticism, got defensive or angry when criticized.

____ 20) I went to extremes and didn't know when to quit.

____ 21) I have had a "sick need for excitement" and done dangerous things or things that were wrong just for the thrill.

____ 22) I have used power-seeking to feel better (e.g., acting out or becoming a negative leader to hold the attention of others).

____ 23) I have liked being at the center of attention and tried to be entertaining, glamorous or really nice when around others.

____ 24) I have had a problem hearing the word "no" and took it to heart.

____ 25) I have acted like I believed people wanted me to be or acted in a way that I believed others liked.

____ 26) I tried to win friends by being very friendly and charming.

____ 27) I have tried to be in on all the talk going around about myself and my associates.

____ 28) I let others know that when I did them a favor, they owed me one.

____ 29) I competed to be the center of attention when others were around.

____ 30) I entertained people with my wit, stories or words and enjoyed it a lot.

____ 31) I tried to get things "my way" and people have called me stubborn.

____ 32) I focused a lot on how others have mistreated me and felt better when I saw that others felt sorry for me.

0 Never	1 Sometimes	2 Half of the time	3 Often	4 Almost Always

___ 33) I would quit when others tried to boss me around or get me to do things their way.

___ 34) I have been called immature or told to "grow up".

___ 35) I have gotten my way by being loud with others.

___ 36) I have refused to give in because I can't stand the frustration of not getting what I want.

___ 37) I have been a take charge kind of person who would get an idea and act on it right away.

___ 38) I have done things in a hurry.

___ 39) My first reaction to being confronted was to look at who said it.

___ 40) I felt good when able to get one over on someone and take advantage of them.

___ 41) I have enjoyed getting in power struggles and scheming to win.

___ 42) I liked to go it on my own and found it hard to work with groups.

___ 43) I have spent a lot of energy trying to get power and control in order to feel good inside.

___ 44) I have used shouting, the silent treatment, tears or sulking to get my way.

___ 45) Others have tried to talk me into doing right but I couldn't stand acting like the kind of wimp or boring looser that they wanted me to be.

___ 46) Instead of stopping me, being watched or supervised just made trying to do what I wanted or trying to get away with something a challenge or exciting.

___ 47) I have worn people out who tried to get me to change and have proved that I can out last them or are better at the game than they are.

___ 48) I have put a lot of time and energy into figuring out how to get around the rules.

___ 49) I have had a short temper, little patience or low frustration tolerance and wanted everything right away.

___ 50) I have been a smooth talker, found it easy to charm others, win their confidence or make a good first impression.

___ 51) I have had strong needs for power or to be in control of things.

___ 52) I have had a strong need for excitement.

___ 53) I have had strong needs to be in the center of what's going on, in the middle of it all.

___ 54) I know what makes me feel good and have had strong needs to do it.

___ 55) I have had strong needs to know what to expect and have tried to find out information about everything going on around me.

___ 56) I gave others the impression that I was mature, could handle things and protect them if they stuck with me.

___ 57) I have expected attention from those that I allowed to be with me.

0	1	2	3	4
Never	Sometimes	Half of the time	Often	Almost Always

___ 58) I have formed new relationships very easily.

___ 59) I have been involved in relationships with others where I was possessive, invading their personal/emotional space, demanding, attacking and conquered the persons will to resist what I wanted.

___ 60) I have had strong control needs and have ended up making demands on partners.

___ 61) I would try to change things to fit me as opposed to trying things that were suggested.

___ 62) It's OK to plan to do something wrong as long as you don't do it because people judge you by your actions not your thoughts.

___ 63) I didn't worry about what would happen to me until after getting accused or caught.

___ 64) I have felt like I "must" win or succeed in power struggles and do whatever it takes to get my way.

___ 65) I have thought that everyone else does the same things I do but just doesn't get noticed or caught.

___ 66) I got caught up in thinking about problems with other people's behavior that annoyed me or that wasn't right.

___ 67) I can't stand being sick or sick people irritate me.

___ 68) I have told myself that you only have to go by the rules until you work your way up and are in charge.

___ 69) Thought people in lower job positions, grades or privilege levels should have to put up with whatever I tell them because that's the way it was for me when I was in their position.

___ 70) Thought rules and laws are for those who can't handle themselves without being told what to do, not for people like me.

___ 71) I have told myself that nobody follows all of the rules so why should I try.

___ 72) I have felt like I know which rules you can ignore and which ones are important.

___ 73) I have felt like I could handle my own life fine if people would just leave me alone and let me make my own decisions.

___ 74) I have thought that given the rotten things that the world has done to me, it's about time that they realize they owe me for it.

___ 75) I have believed that the best defense was to attack or found myself automatically attacking when confronted.

___ 76) I have found myself saying "yes but" and giving reasons why a suggestion will not work as opposed to trying it first.

___ 77) When upset, got the attitude of "Don't get mad, get even" and thought about how I was going to do it.

___ 78) I didn't think much about people or things that I was grateful for.

0	1	2	3	4
Never	**Sometimes**	**Half of the time**	**Often**	**Almost Always**

___ 79) I have thought I had to act the way I did because I believed that people are either victims or offenders, winners or losers and I was tired of being the loser.

___ 80) I have thought that once I'm done with treatment then I can go back to doing things my way.

___ 81) Thought that in a conflict only one person can come out on top and be seen as the one who succeeded, had good intentions or was in control.

___ 82) Got caught up in anger power fantasies about being in fights.

___ 83) Got caught up in sexual fantasies about getting what I want.

Use the space provided below to list and rate any other CAPO characteristics that have been a problem for you in the past which were not included on the statements provided above. Discuss this with your treatment group and/or therapist. Include their feedback.

_____

_____

_____

C. Control and Power Obsession Structured Discovery Exercise
On the following five numbered topics, if you are completing the basic form refer only to what you underlined and wrote about your most serious or most frequent CAPO problems on p. 47 along with your ratings in part A. For the complete form include your ratings in part B.

1. **Select your top ten CAPO characteristics.**
Review the statements that you rated in sections A and B. Pick out the top ten (10) statements that described your particular CAPO behavior the most (i.e., that you rated the highest in sections A and B) and circle the numbers of those statements. Examine the top ten CAPO characteristics that you circled and number them in rank order with the #1 statement being the statement that most described your CAPO style, #2 the second most and so on. Use the space provided below to list the top ten CAPO characteristics that you circled. Place your #1 ranked statement in the space provided next to #1 and so on.

Top Ten CAPO characteristics (complete first 5 for the basic form)

1) _____

2) _____

3) _____

4) _____

5) _____

6) _____

7) _____

8) _____

9) _____

10) _____

2. **Record at least your top three CAPO characteristics** in rank order (highest rated statement first) in the space provided on your Harmful Behavior Anatomy worksheet (page 161). If you have a tie, circle the one that most applies to you and underline the other one. Put your ties (other highly ranked phrases that you underlined) on the back of your Harmful Behavior Anatomy Worksheet in the space provided. Although descriptive phrases (short versions of the questions you have answered) have been provided for you in part A, you will need to make up your own descriptive phrases for part B that will fit on your Harmful Behavior Anatomy worksheet. Don't limit yourself to the top three points if there are important parts that fit in this area. Make sure that you do not leave out any important information about yourself on this topic.

3. **Compute and enter your CAPO score.**
   If you are completing the basic form of this exercise, use the Awareness and Honesty Exam questions that were summarized with descriptive phrases in part A of this section to compute your average rating score by dividing your rating total by the 26 questions you rated. After you have recorded your average rating score in the space provided below and on your Harmful Behavior Anatomy Worksheet at the end of this section, you can move on to the next section.

Total part A ratings on Awareness and Honesty Exam (_____) divided by 26 = _____.
If you are completing the entire exercise, add up all of your part B question ratings. An easy way to do that is to fill in the chart below.

How many questions did you rate as 4? _____	Multiply that by 4 and enter the answer here _____
How many questions did you rate as 3? _____	Multiply that by 3 and enter the answer here _____
How many questions did you rate as 2? _____	Multiply that by 2 and enter the answer here _____
How many questions did you rate as 1? _____	Multiply that by 1 and enter the answer here _____
How many questions did you rate as 0? _____	Add this column, Total part B = _____
(Total should be 83) Total = _____	

Compute your average rating score by adding up your part A and part B total scores, then dividing the total by all 109 questions that you rated. Record your average rating score in the space provided below and on your Harmful Behavior Anatomy worksheet (page 161).

Total part A (_____) + Total part B = _____ divided by 109 = _____.

4. Write what you have discovered about yourself through this structured exercise
Use the space provided below to explain how your CAPO characteristics affected your social-emotional maturity. Use the workspace on page 227 if needed.

Social maturity (honesty, trust, loyalty, concern and responsibility).

Honesty-_____

_____

Trust- _____

_____

Loyalty-_____

_____

Concern- _____

_____

Responsibility- _____

_____

Hint: If you're having trouble with this, just take the ten CAPO characteristics that you listed (p. 52) and ask yourself questions comparing each CAPO characteristic to each component of social maturity. Then take a step by step approach to look for a connection. For example, "How did *my refusal to back down* affect my (honesty, trust, loyalty, concern or responsibility)?", "How did my *need to always stay in control of the situation* affect my (honesty, trust, loyalty, concern or responsibility)?", "How did my *relationship jealousy* affect my (honesty, trust, loyalty, concern or responsibility)?", "How did my *justifying actions based on feelings* affect my (honesty, trust, loyalty, concern or responsibility)?", "How did my *ignoring authorities* affect my (honesty, trust, loyalty, concern or responsibility)?"

Emotional maturity (self-awareness, self-efficacy/confidence, self-control).

Self-awareness- _____

_____

Self-efficacy- _____

_____

Self-control- _____

_____

Hint: Use the same step by step process with each component of emotional maturity comparing each CAPO characteristic that you listed (p. 52). For example, "How did my *closed minded attitude* affect the development of my (self-awareness, self-efficacy, self-control)?", "How did my *lack of tolerance for disagreement* affect the development of my (self-awareness, self-efficacy, self-control)?", "How did my *score keeping and getting even* affect the development of my (self-awareness, self-efficacy, self-control)?" Some connections are easy to see, others require asking for help.

5. **List the best personal example you can recall** of how your CAPO characteristics caused a major problem or crisis in your life. Use the workspace on page 227 if needed. Note: An honesty accomplishment award is generally administered for the best example in treatment groups.

_____

_____

_____

_____

_____

_____

Awareness training: In addition to becoming aware of the CAPO characteristics in sections A though C above, it is important to develop an understanding that real power comes from self-control, not control of others (e.g., getting your way by manipulation or intimidation) or moods (e.g., self-medicating with drugs, alcohol, cigarettes, food, or pleasurable activity).

Developing awareness of basic control styles of (1) approach "knowledge is power" (i.e., controlling emotions by learning all there is to know about the problem), or (2) avoidance "What you don't know won't hurt you" (i.e., controlling emotions by limiting information input to prevent stimulus overload) is the first step toward developing a new coping approach. That being said, use the space below to list the unhealthy, harmful behavior you have been involved with and the Control and Power Obsession characteristics that you believe may have supported that behavior.

Unhealthy, Harmful Behavior   Control and Power Obsession

_____   _____

_____   _____

_____   _____

Responsibility training: While Awareness training is a necessary first step, if you don't take Responsibility for learning how to manage your CAPO characteristics, you can't expect to change. Review your ACTS Healthy Behavior Success Skills (p.20- 28). Pick the best skill to help you deal with the CAPO characteristics you described above. Then follow the instructions for skill you picked and describe how to use that skill to manage the CAPO characteristics that you listed in the space below.

_____

_____

_____

_____

_____

_____

_____

_____

_____

> **Hint**: "You are only limited by your creativity" when dealing with life problems. See Exhibit 3 (p. 177) for an idea that may help you with CAPO issues.

Tolerance training: Involves learning to let go of control and power struggles, beginning with accepting that walking away from a conflict is taking control of yourself. Learning to tolerate authority by accepting that the only proper response to authority is, "Thank you I'll take care of that" is important. Be aware that exaggerated autonomy needs can result in authority problems and find the right person-environment fit, perhaps running your own business but accept that before you can give orders you must learn to take them. Learning to tolerate minor injustices is key to success in the workplace. This involves "Earning the right to complain" by finishing an assignment given to you by mistake before complaining that it wasn't your responsibility. Think about it. If you don't finish it first, you haven't been inconvenienced and really have nothing to complain about. Letting go of the need to have the last word and accepting that "If your words are no better than silence, silence is far better than words" is a good step in controlling the CAPO need to build self up by putting others down.

Answer the question, "What would be the opposite extreme?" of the unhealthy, harmful, CAPO characteristics you listed in the Awareness training section above. Describe the opposite healthy, responsible behavior that you need to "Act as if" (p. 12) you already have and practice regularly.

CAPO behavior   Opposite Healthy, Helpful Behavior

_____

_____

_____

D. Make a Positive Plan and Commitment to Change

Review the three CAPO characteristics that you listed on your Harmful Behavior Anatomy worksheet (page 161). What can you do about it now? How are you going to change these, what are you going to do? (Consult with your therapist)

1) _____

2) _____

3) _____

Get honest about your CAPO characteristics with your therapist or treatment group. Log the date you discussed your CAPO characteristics and who you discussed them with below.

Date: _____ Discussed with: _____

"Pride goes before a fall" -- Late 14th Century English adaptation of Proverbs 16:18

Name: _____   **Date:** _____

Definition: Unhealthy pride can be considered a strong arm in the commission of multiple forms of unhealthy, harmful behavior because it provides motivation for the dishonesty needed to maintain the veil of secrecy that enables unhealthy, harmful behavior. Unhealthy Pride involves reluctance and even refusal to admit mistakes which reflects personal weakness (i.e., of fear of looking bad, rejection, ridicule). On the other hand, healthy pride reflects personal strength (i.e., the courage to get honest, admit mistakes and back down when wrong). Since Unhealthy Pride leads to the cover up of unhealthy, harmful behavior, unhealthy Pride supports multiple forms of unhealthy, harmful behavior. Once you get in the habit of covering up mistakes to maintain Unhealthy Pride, your harmful behavior can spread from one type to another (Figure 9).

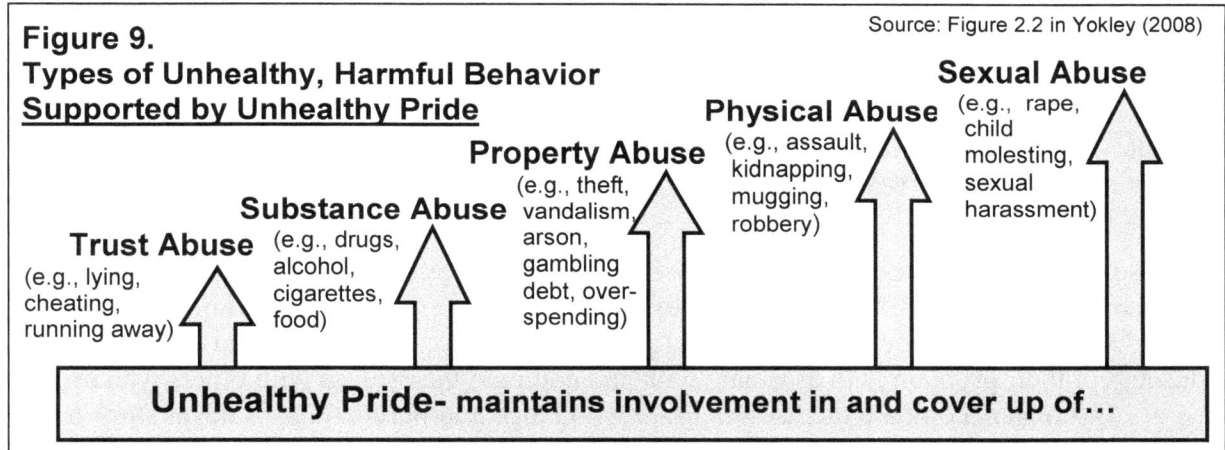

Figure 9.
Types of Unhealthy, Harmful Behavior Supported by Unhealthy Pride

Source: Figure 2.2 in Yokley (2008)

Trust Abuse (e.g., lying, cheating, running away)

Substance Abuse (e.g., drugs, alcohol, cigarettes, food)

Property Abuse (e.g., theft, vandalism, arson, gambling debt, over-spending)

Physical Abuse (e.g., assault, kidnapping, mugging, robbery)

Sexual Abuse (e.g., rape, child molesting, sexual harassment)

Unhealthy Pride- maintains involvement in and cover up of...

Unhealthy pride involves an exaggerated need to look good (acceptance) and/or fear of looking bad (rejection). Other unhealthy pride symptoms include denial, minimizing, keeping quiet, covering up problems, suppressing (stuffing) feelings and difficulty expressing (sharing) feelings along with difficulty admitting mistakes and apologizing. Individuals with unhealthy, harmful behavior tend to have some Unhealthy Pride characteristics but different individuals may have different symptoms of that condition. One type of unhealthy pride is criminal pride which involves acting tough, cool or in control ("I got it covered"), taking pride in criminal activity, getting over on the authorities and the criminal code of not "snitching" on others. Unhealthy pride goes before a fall because stuffing feelings leads to Stress Build-Up and falling back into acting feelings out through harmful behavior. Criminal pride goes before a fall because not snitching means having to take a fall for others when trouble comes down. Criminal pride supports the "Jailhouse Image of a Man", a socially callous self-image (see Table 11, p. 93), which ends up either killing the person or killing their chances at success.

Behavior Anatomy Question #3: What could happen if you were to admit a mistake or back down in a conflict?

Examples of Unhealthy Pride that support multiple forms of unhealthy, harmful behavior and allows your problems to spread from one type to another are provided in Table 10 below.

Table 10.
Examples of Unhealthy Pride that Support Multiple Harmful Behaviors

Harmful Behavior	Cover Up	Denial to self "I don't have a problem…	Fear of rejection (image pride)
Trust Abuse	Negative contracts- "I'll cover for you if you cover for me" Making up an alibi.	everybody lies"	"I have to lie, I don't want to be called a snitch"
Substance Abuse	Covering marijuana smell by smoking cigarettes or drinking with mouthwash. Using eye drops to get rid of red eyes.	everybody drinks"	"I have to get high, everyone in the group I hang with does" or "I can't get honest about drinking, others will look down at me"
Property Abuse	Getting a friend to cover your theft, "They were with me". Putting it on someone else.	everybody borrows things"	"I had to steal from the store, everyone else did and it seemed like it was my turn"
Physical Abuse	Wearing sunglasses or a long sleeve shirt to cover bruises. Skipping school/work after a fight	everybody gets in fights"	"I had to fight, I couldn't let it go, everyone was watching"
Sexual Abuse	Providing a cover story, "I didn't fondle them, we were just wrestling"	everybody experiments with sex"	"I can't let anyone find out, what would they think of me?"

Comparison and contrast strategy- Unhealthy Pride can interfere with getting help and making positive changes in your life by causing you to minimize your problem to the point where you feel you don't need to set your pride aside and get. One way people minimize and deny the seriousness of their problem is to associate with and compare themselves with others who are worse off. Overeaters compare themselves those who binge and purge, (e.g., "I never stuck my finger down my throat to make myself throw up"). Crack cocaine or methamphetamine smokers compare themselves to heroin addicts , (e.g., "I never stuck a needle in my arm"). Rapists compare themselves with child-molesters, (e.g., "At least I pick on people my own size"). Physical abusers compare themselves to murderers, (e.g., "I don't kill people, I just teach them respect").

Circle any of the 15 unhealthy pride statements in Table 10 above that you have used. Then write any other types of unhealthy pride that kept you covering up unhealthy, harmful behavior or building up your image in the space below. Don't forget the comparison and contrast strategy. If you want, just change the Table 10 statements to fit you.

_____

_____

_____

Please complete the following steps below which were designed to help you clarify and become more aware of Unhealthy Pride characteristics that you need to address.

A. Review your Awareness and Honesty Exam (Appendix G), record your Pride Problem ratings in the spaces provided below and add up all of your ratings to get a total.

Since your self-awareness may have improved from your use of the Situation Response Analysis log, you may need to update your ratings. Enter your ratings total in the space provided below.

Pride Problems (8 items from Awareness and Honesty Exam, p. 207)

___ 11) You can't show emotions or admit mistakes	___110) Avoiding or blocking out problems
___ 31) Worry about being put down	___120) Refusal to change
___ 37) Excuses to justify mistakes	___157) Others with my problem shouldn't act like they can help me
___ 40) Hard on self about mistakes	
___ 82) Not asked for help	Total = _____

Consult with your therapist or treatment program staff to determine if you are completing the basic form of this exercise or are completing the entire section.

<u>End of basic form</u>- **Stop here and skip to part C, "Pride Problem Structured Discovery Exercise" on page 61 if you are completing the basic form. Otherwise, continue on with the section B questions below.**

B. Rate the following Pride Problem characteristics.
Use the numbered ratings on the scales provided below to rate the frequency of your past thoughts or behaviors on the statements listed in this section.

0	1	2	3	4
Never	**Sometimes**	**Half of the time**	**Often**	**Almost Always**

___ 1) I have refused to admit that "my way" doesn't work or isn't best.

___ 2) I have not tried because of being afraid of failing.

___ 3) I held hurt feelings and emotional pain inside.

___ 4) I would laugh or joke to cover up feeling hurt.

___ 5) I have not admitted my feelings to others because of how they might view me.

___ 6) I have refused to be the first one to get back to the other person after an argument and try to work it out.

___ 7) When accused of a problem, I would make sure that others know why my actions were necessary or what caused the problem.

___ 8) When accused of a problem, I would make sure others know who actually started the situation.

___ 9) I have bragged about things that I did wrong.

___ 10) I have refused to apologize, even when I knew I was wrong

0	1	2	3	4
Never	Sometimes	Half of the time	Often	Almost Always

____ 11) I have kept my problems and feelings secret.

____ 12) I have admitted that I needed help with a problem not because I really believed it but more as a smart move or to just get people off my back.

____ 13) I have had to have the last word after being criticized.

____ 14) I have found it hard to admit mistakes to others.

____ 15) I have had problems asking for help.

____ 16) Feeling helpless or like there is nothing I can do to control the situation is difficult for me to handle but I won't let on.

____ 17) I have felt the need to maintain an image or appearance that I believe others want to see.

____ 18) I have acted confident like I can handle my problems but felt hopeless about ever turning things around.

____ 19) I have been looked up to by others and felt the need to keep up appearances for them.

____ 20) I have had a hard time admitting mistakes or backing out of things that I started to take in the wrong direction.

____ 21) I have refused to accept help from others because I believed that I must handle it myself.

____ 22) Success has gotten to me and I have had to remind myself that I'm not perfect.

____ 23) I have listened to other peoples problems but when it was my turn to talk, I talked about things that were not my problems.

____ 24) I took immediate action against someone who disrespected me in front of others.

____ 25) I felt I had to cuss someone out because of what they said or did that made me angry.

____ 26) I had to hit someone because of what they said or did that made me angry.

____ 27) I wouldn't admit childish behavior because that would be humiliating myself which no one should have to do.

____ 28) I got angry and said things I wish I didn't say but wouldn't take it back.

____ 29) If I didn't get what I thought was fair, I would feel that I must take immediate action to get what I believed was due me.

____ 30) When admitting a mistake, if the other person also was at fault, I have added "but" or "however" at the end and then pointed out their part.

____ 31) I have been head strong and wouldn't start to look at what others were saying until backed into a corner where I had to stop and listen.

____ 32) I have enjoyed winning against or getting over on those in authority.

____ 33) I have been more willing to give help than receive it.

____ 34) Had the attitude that if you admit feelings or mistakes, this will leave you open to criticism from others.

____ 35) Told myself "I can handle it myself, I don't need help".

0	1	2	3	4
Never	Sometimes	Half of the time	Often	Almost Always

___ 36) Thought I'm not like other people whose problem was more serious and really need help.

___ 37) Told myself I know right from wrong and am a responsible person which is all that is needed to handle my own problems.

___ 38) Thought that a person should be able to solve their own problems and it's a weakness to seek help.

___ 39) Told myself or others that no one knows me or understands me so they have no right to say that I have certain problems.

___ 40) Thought that once I'm done with treatment, I will know all I need to know to make it and I won't have to keep listening to suggestions.

___ 41) I had the attitude that you shouldn't talk about personal problems to others.

___ 42) It has been very difficult for me to admit a mistake and apologize.

___ 43) I have got caught up in fantasies about proving I was right all along.

___ 44) I have had negative contracts to cover up others problems so they would cover up mine.

___ 45) I have kept secrets about problem behavior because of how people might look at me.

___46) I would cover up unhealthy, harmful behavior to avoid being accused of a problem.

Use the space provided to list and rate any other unhealthy pride characteristics that have been a problem for you in the past which were not included on the statements provided above. Get feedback from your treatment group and/or therapist. Use the page 227 workspace if needed.

___

C. Pride Problem Structured Discovery Exercise
On the following five numbered topics, if you are completing the basic form refer only to what you circled in Table 10, wrote about your Unhealthy Pride problems on p. 58 and your ratings in part A (p. 59). For the complete form include your ratings in part B above.

1. **Select your top ten Pride Problem characteristics**.
   Review the statements that you rated in sections A and B. Pick out the top ten (10) statements that described your particular Pride Problem behavior the most (i.e., that you rated the highest in sections A and B) and circle the numbers of those statements. Examine the top ten Pride Problems that you circled and number them in rank order with the #1 statement being the statement that most described your Pride Problem style, #2 the second most and so on.

   Use the space below to list the top ten Pride Problems that you circled. Place your #1 ranked statement in the space provided next to #1 and so on.

Top Ten Pride Problem characteristics (complete first 5 for the basic form)

1) _____

2) _____

3) _____

4) _____

5) _____

6) _____

7) _____

8) _____

9) _____

10) _____

2. **Record at least your top three Pride Problem characteristics** in rank order (highest rated statement first) in the space provided on your Harmful Behavior Anatomy worksheet (page 161). If you have a tie, circle the one that most applies to you and underline the other one. Put your ties (other highly ranked phrases that you underlined) on the back of your Harmful Behavior Anatomy Worksheet in the space provided.

    Although descriptive phrases (short versions of the questions you have answered) have been provided for you in part A, you will need to make up your own descriptive phrases for part B that will fit on your Harmful Behavior Anatomy worksheet. Don't limit yourself to the top three points if there are important parts that fit in this area. Make sure that you do not leave out any important information about yourself on this topic.

3. **Compute and enter your Pride Problem score.**
    If you are completing the basic form of this exercise, use the Awareness and Honesty Exam questions that were summarized with descriptive phrases in part A of this section to compute your average rating score by dividing your rating total by the 8 questions you rated. After you have recorded your average rating score in the space provided below and on your Harmful Behavior Anatomy worksheet (page 161), you can move on to the next section.

Total part A ratings on Awareness and Honesty Exam (_____) divided by 8 = _____.

If you are completing the entire exercise, add up all of your part B question ratings. An easy way to do that is to fill in the chart below.

How many questions did you rate as 4? _____ Multiply that by 4 and enter the answer here _____

How many questions did you rate as 3? _____ Multiply that by 3 and enter the answer here _____

How many questions did you rate as 2? _____ Multiply that by 2 and enter the answer here _____

How many questions did you rate as 1? _____ Multiply that by 1 and enter the answer here _____

How many questions did you rate as 0? _____   Add this column, Total part B = _____

(Total should be 43) Total = _____

Compute your average rating score by adding up your part A and part B total scores, then dividing the total by all 51 questions that you rated. Record your average rating score in the space provided below and on your Harmful Behavior Anatomy worksheet (page 161).

Total part A (_____) + Total part B = _____ divided by 51 = _____.

4. **Write what you have discovered about yourself through this structured exercise**
    Use the space provided below to document how your Pride problems affected your social-emotional maturity. Use the workspace on page 227 if needed.

Social maturity (honesty, trust, loyalty, concern and responsibility).

_____

_____

_____

_____

_____

Emotional maturity (self-awareness, self-efficacy/confidence, self-control)

_____

_____

_____

> **Hint:** If you're having trouble with this, just take the top Pride Problem characteristics that you listed on page 61- 62 and ask yourself questions comparing each Pride Problem characteristic to each component of social maturity looking for a connection. For example, "How did my unhealthy pride affect my (honesty, trust, loyalty, concern, responsibility)?" Do the same with each component of emotional maturity. For example, "How did my unhealthy pride affect my (self-awareness, self-efficacy, self-control)?"

5. **List the best personal example you can recall** of how Pride Problem characteristics caused a major problem or crisis in your life on the space provided below.

_____

_____

_____

_____

_____

_____

The ART of Thinking it Through

The ART of Thinking it through (Decisional Balance), is important in managing the Unhealthy Pride that supports unhealthy, harmful behavior. Thinking it Through involves considering the benefits and drawbacks of getting honest and "blowing your image" by setting unhealthy pride aside to get help for unhealthy, harmful behavior. The **ART** of Thinking it through involves: Awareness training on the impact of your decisions to self and others; Responsibility training on learning decisional balance by weighing the benefits and drawbacks of your decisions and; Tolerance training on learning to tolerate change, frustration and barriers to success (Figure 10). Whenever you are considering the whether you should get honest about a problem or get help for one, you need to do a "Reality check" and weight your decision out on three Reality Scales that measure the impact of your decision in terms of survival, success and severity (p. 24). "You are only limited by your creativity" when dealing with life problems. See Exhibit 3 (p. 177) for a description of another ACTS skill you can use to deal with Unhealthy Pride.

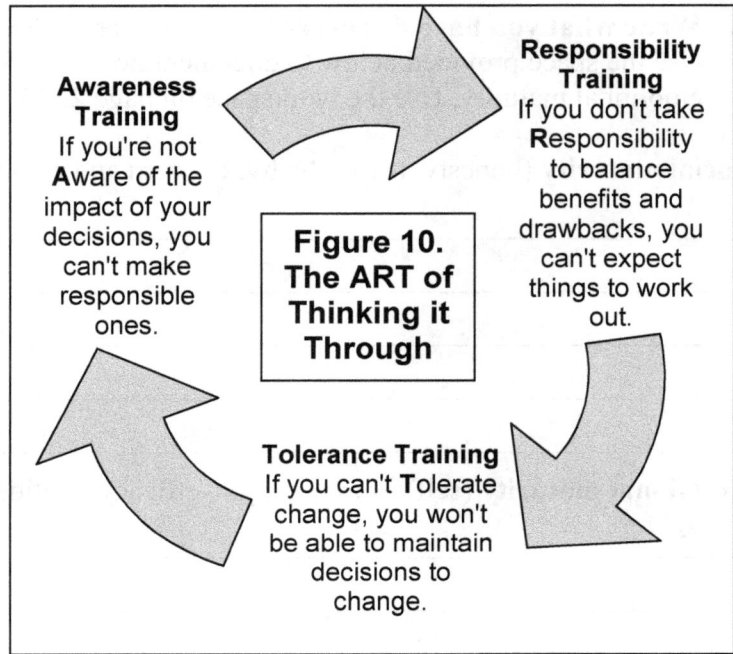

Awareness Training
If you're not **A**ware of the impact of your decisions, you can't make responsible ones.

Responsibility Training
If you don't take **R**esponsibility to balance benefits and drawbacks, you can't expect things to work out.

Figure 10. The ART of Thinking it Through

Tolerance Training
If you can't **T**olerate change, you won't be able to maintain decisions to change.

Awareness training: In the ART of thinking it through, if you're not **A**ware of the impact of your decisions, you can't make responsible ones. If you're not **A**ware of the Unhealthy Pride that focuses you on how you will look if you get honest or get help, then making responsible decisions based on the actual impact of your decisions will not possible. Unless you learn to set your pride aside and start making decisions based on impact, your unhealthy pride will continue to maintain your involvement in and cover up of unhealthy, harmful behavior. Review what you have learned in Section C of this component about the Unhealthy Pride that supports your unhealthy, harmful behavior and answer the question "What kind of Unhealthy Pride" supports my unhealthy, harmful behavior? Use the space below to list examples of how unhealthy pride led to cover up or continued involvement in unhealthy, harmful behavior (Hint: "Getting scared or getting dared". Worrying about how other will view you if you get honest about problems or don't "go along to get along").

Unhealthy Pride   Unhealthy, Harmful Behavior

_____

_____

_____

Responsibility training: While Awareness training is a necessary first step, if you don't take **R**esponsibility to balance benefits and drawbacks, you can't expect things to work out. Responsibility training involves learning to own responsibility for mistakes and use the reality scales to let go of unhealthy pride get honest, take personal responsibility, and drop negative contracts (i.e., mutual cover-up). It does you no good to develop your awareness to the point where you can recognize your unhealthy pride if you tell yourself, "It's better to look good than to do good" continue your unhealthy harmful behavior and keep covering it up. Review "How to Think it through" (p.25) and describe how to do a reality check (Social Responsibility Check) and use the reality scales to weigh out your decision to get honest about (or get help for) the harmful behavior that was supported by the unhealthy pride you described in the Awareness training section above. Don't forget to include your reality scale ratings in your description of "How to Think it through".

My "reality check" on unhealthy pride- _____

How I can use the reality scales to weigh out my decision to get honest- _____

_____

_____

Think of the last time you automatically said something that was not entirely honest and did not correct yourself. Then weigh out the need to preserve that Unhealthy Pride on the reality scales. What I said that was not entirely honest: _____

How important to my survival was it for me to not speak up and correct myself?

Survival scale rating (0 = not important; 10= could kill me if I didn't): _____

How important for my success was it for me to not speak up and correct myself?

Success scale rating (0 = not important; 10= would stop me from ever succeeding): _____

How severe would the consequences be if I spoke up and corrected myself?

Severity scale rating (0 = not severe at all; 10= extremely severe): _____

In reviewing your reality scale scores above, if you made the same mistake today, do you still think you need to keep quiet about it? ___Yes; ___No

Tolerance training: Tolerance training on Unhealthy Pride involves more than just "diversity training" on tolerating different people by accepting different cultural backgrounds as equally important and deserving of respect. Tolerance training also involves learning to tolerate feedback from others (i.e., different opinions) and tolerate doing things differently if we want to change. If you can't tolerate feedback, you will continue to block out what others have to say and won't become aware of the impact of your decisions. In order to tolerate feedback, you have to value feedback. In order to value feedback instead of just reacting to it and blocking it out (e.g., "You don't know me!"), you need to see a benefit from it. Using the "Mirror Concept" is the opposite extreme of the "You don't know me!" reaction that blocks out valuable feedback. Use the space on the following page to list the benefits of feedback from others.

The benefits of feedback from others- _____

_____

_____

> **Hint:** Read "Learning to value feedback" on page 139 and "Use the Mirror Concept" on page 200.

Feedback Tolerance- Just like humans can develop a tolerance for drugs/alcohol, overeating, gambling risk, sexual risk or thrill crime risk. Humans can develop a tolerance for cultural diversity. Leaning more about others builds our comfort level with them. If we want to feel comfortable in a diverse cultural neighborhood, we can't stay on our street, we need to get out there and interact with others in the neighborhood in order to learn more about them.

The same thing is true for personal growth feedback. To benefit, you have to push yourself out of your comfort zone. In order to let go of unhealthy pride and get honest, you have to learn to tolerate unwanted feedback (e.g., about the consequences of your actions) and unwanted feelings (e.g., ashamed, embarrassed, stupid). Tolerance training on unhealthy pride involves getting yourself ready to hear what you don't want to hear and stopping yourself from doing what you want to do about it. Anyone who has ever been to the dentist for a cavity knows that, "things always get worse before they get better". Coaches always tell us "no pain, no gain" which is a positive take on getting through difficult situations that helps us realize the need to push past our feelings and tolerate discomfort in order to improve ourselves. It's much easier for humans to change if we are aware of the thoughts, feelings and behaviors that maintain our problem. Learning more about ourselves, builds our confidence to change which is known as "self-efficacy". Put another way, "Self-awareness builds self-efficacy which develops self-control" or "The more we know, the more we can grow".

Developing a callous on your belly- When you see someone at a funeral really sobbing over the loss of a loved one, you can see their belly heaving in and out with emotion. Tolerating feedback means being able to encounter the thoughts, feelings and opinions of others without blocking them out. Since "the truth hurts", tolerating honest feedback can involve tolerating unwanted feelings. Just like practicing pull-ups on the high bar develops calloused hands that can tolerate heavy exercise, practicing pulling yourself up to the level of awareness that others have of you will "develop a callous on your belly" that allows you to tolerate honest feedback from others and use that feedback to change your behavior.

Reacting to feedback- In order to benefit from feedback you have to keep yourself from "reacting". Reacting means getting defensive and justifying what you say or do based on your emotional reaction, not the facts. Reacting can be: low level defensiveness that results and blocking out what is being said; moderate level reacting, striking back verbally and saying something negative or; high level reacting with verbal aggressiveness or physically threatening "up in your face" posture. Reacting is serious. Reacting can cost you a job in a supervisor conflict at work. It can cost you your entire bankroll in a high stakes poker game and it can cost you your life in a state where concealed weapons are legal in bars.

To prevent reacting, you have to get good at "finding facts, not following feelings". At first while the person giving you the feedback is speaking you may need to imagine that you are reading that information in a letter, e-mail or text message instead of hearing it. If you feel yourself reacting, delay the reaction using the survival scale (p. 24) to ask yourself, "how important is it to my survival to say something right now?" and remind yourself that "Sticks and stones can break my bones but words can never hurt me". Write the feedback you are receiving, and look at it later. Writing has the added advantage of allowing you to look down at the paper, avoid reacting to facial expression and stay focused on the words you are writing, not the tone of voice you are hearing. First master using just the words to help you see yourself. After you get a little "callous on your belly" and can tolerate feedback without reacting, move on to using tone of voice and facial expression to help you become aware of the reactions you trigger in others. Applying feedback is done by asking yourself, "What did I learn from this experience that was helpful to myself or others?" and "How can I use this information to change?" Avoiding reacting to feedback involves getting good at "The Window Concept" of holding on to feedback that can help you but not over-reacting or magnifying feedback that isn't helpful, i.e., "If it doesn't apply, let it fly". Give one example of helpful feedback you should apply and one you should "let fly".

_____

_____

| **Hint:** Read "Use the Window Concept" on page 200. |

In order to learn to tolerate feedback, you have to encounter feedback. If we accept that: 1) "If you want to grow more, you need to know more" and; 2) the only way to step outside of our own view and get more information about ourselves is to get feedback from others, then; 3) we need to set up situations that allow us to encounter the feedback of others. Developing feedback tolerance requires putting yourself in a position to encounter feedback and practice dealing with it. The "Envelope exercise" is one way to start practicing feedback tolerance.

Practicing feedback tolerance: The envelope exercise- Since you can't see facial expression or hear tone of voice when reading something, writing is a good place to start practicing tolerating feedback from others. In the "Envelope Exercise", you write the problem thoughts, feelings or behaviors that you are aware of (and listed in Awareness training section above) on a piece of paper and seal it in an envelope. Then you ask others for their feedback on your behavior and the thinking behind it. Say something like, "Based on what you hear me say and see me do, what types of Irresponsible Thinking do you believe I need to look at in order to avoid falling back into unhealthy, harmful, behavior?" If you are in individual therapy, you give the envelope to your therapist. If you are in group therapy, give the envelope to the person who you believe knows you the best. Then look down so you can't see facial expression while they write their feedback about what you say and do along with the thinking most likely behind it. When they are done, open the envelope and discuss the similarities and differences between what you are aware of on the inside and what other people see on the outside. If you are in group, ask for the feedback of others. Ask for help to identify: the irresponsible behavior you tend to fall into; the irresponsible thinking/attitude underneath that behavior and; what you need to say to yourself to change the irresponsible thinking/attitude to prevent further irresponsible behavior. Don't focus on differences between what you see and others see, look for similarities. If you can do this, it will be very good practice in tolerating feedback and using other people as a mirror to better see yourself. Write what you learned about yourself tolerating feedback (i.e., your feelings during the process) from the envelope exercise. Use the exercise workspace on page 230 if needed.

Envelope Exercise: What I learned- _____

_____

_____

Tolerating conflict- The most difficult feedback to deal with is a conflict. Think about a serious feedback conflict where the other person was angry and saying disrespectful or hurtful things that pushed your buttons and made you want to react. Imagine you start to slip and think about doing a harmful behavior to them to get even or doing an unhealthy behavior yourself to calm down and forget about the conflict. In the residential Therapeutic Community environment when unhealthy criminal pride starts to leak out, residents are immediately told to "deal with it" and "drop a slip" with the person's name that you have feelings for in the encounter group box. This makes sure you to take it to the right place (group) at the right time and avoid "reacting on the floor" (i.e., venting your feelings in the wrong place at the wrong time"). The Three Step Social Responsibility Plan is the outpatient version of dealing with conflicts. Use the space below to list a real conflict that ended up in you doing something harmful to others or unhealthy to yourself. Then describe how you can use "the 3 G's", i.e., your Three Step Social Responsibility Plan (p. 20) to avoid that type of trouble in the future. Use the workspace on page 227 if needed.

_____

_____

Tolerating change- Answer the question, "What would be the opposite extreme?" of the Unhealthy Pride you listed in the Awareness training section above. Describe the opposite healthy pride that you need to practice regularly in the space below.

_____

_____

D. Make a Positive Plan and Commitment to Change- Review the three Unhealthy Pride problems that you listed on your Harmful Behavior Anatomy worksheet (page 161). What can you do about it now? How are you going to change these things, what are you going to do? (Consult with your therapist or staff and write your plan below)

1) _____

2) _____

3) _____

Get honest about Unhealthy Pride with your therapist or treatment group. Log the date you discussed your Unhealthy Pride and who you discussed it with in the space provided below.

Date: _____ Discussed with: _____

"If you are speaking the truth you don't have to remember anything" -- Mark Twain

Name: _____   **Date:** _____

Definition: Deception can be considered the powerful right fist of unhealthy, harmful behavior because it provides the veil of secrecy needed required by Unhealthy Pride for covering up multiple forms of unhealthy, harmful behavior. Unhealthy, harmful behavior that is legal is still difficult to continue in front of people who care about you. Unhealthy, harmful behavior that is illegal is difficult to continue in front of witnesses. Thus, deception is needed to cover up multiple forms of unhealthy, harmful behavior. Once you get good enough at deception to the point where you feel you can cover up or talk your way out of anything, you are less likely to worry about consequences and more likely to do the wrong thing. This allows your unhealthy, harmful behavior to spread from one type to another (Figure 11).

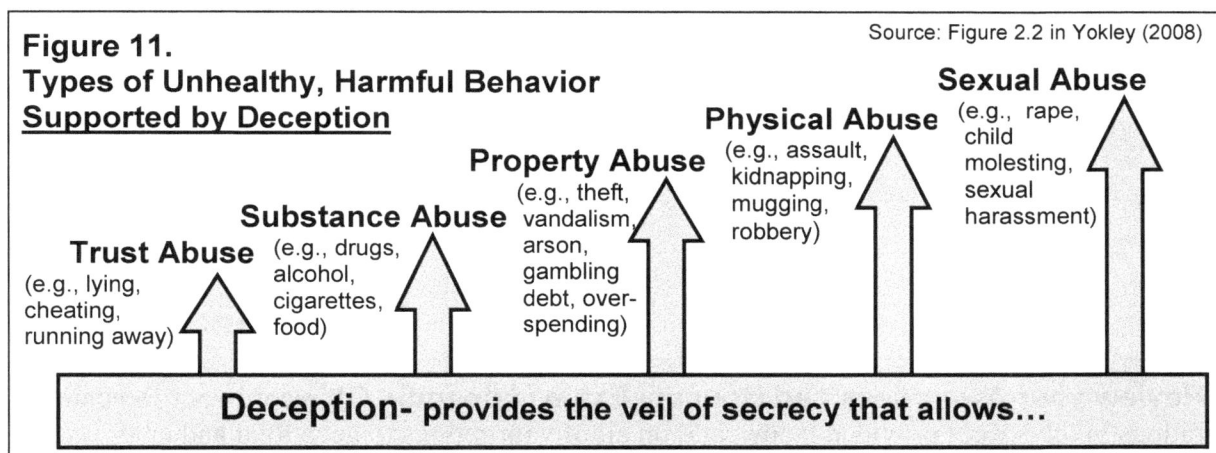

Figure 11.
Types of Unhealthy, Harmful Behavior Supported by Deception

Source: Figure 2.2 in Yokley (2008)

Trust Abuse (e.g., lying, cheating, running away)

Substance Abuse (e.g., drugs, alcohol, cigarettes, food)

Property Abuse (e.g., theft, vandalism, arson, gambling debt, over-spending)

Physical Abuse (e.g., assault, kidnapping, mugging, robbery)

Sexual Abuse (e.g., rape, child molesting, sexual harassment)

Deception- provides the veil of secrecy that allows...

There are many types of deception that involve not being entirely truthful to others. Basic deceptions include: *lying* to avoid consequences or cover up harmful behavior; telling people what they want to hear (*appeasing*); purposefully leaving out part of the truth (*dishonesty by omission*) and; agreeing with no intent to cooperate or comply (*assenting*). Deception also includes various forms of *diversion* such as changing the subject (diverting the conversation) to avoid getting honest about the subject at hand. The "diversion sandwich" is a more complex version that involves putting the deception in the middle of two honest/responsible statements. For example, "I'm going to the library (honest/responsible), to Jerry's (dishonest drug addict) and then to the church youth group (honest/responsible). This causes the person being deceived to "assume" that because they know the beginning and end of the sentence was honest and responsible, that the whole sentence was honest and responsible.

Other deceptions include *misleading* others with exaggerated/inaccurate information or by *stacking the facts* to minimize your part (usually by telling the other persons part first), using *vagueness* to avoid the truth and *attempting to confuse* the truth by bringing up a lot of things that don't have anything to do with the topic you want to avoid. Since deception is often used to cover up problems in order to avoid consequences, it can lead to a flawed definition of honesty. This involves not seeing honesty as valuable or needed for dignity, self-respect or respect by others. It also involves not understanding that the reason that we value honesty so much is the tremendous price attached and the courage it takes to get honest, putting personal comfort and avoidance of social or legal consequences over honesty. Not understanding that deception avoids immediate consequences while honesty builds trust which gets you the privileges in life that you want is a serious problem. This problem includes not understanding that honesty is a value that people try to achieve by maintaining a track record of keeping themselves aware of what they say and holding themselves accountable when they slip. It also includes double standards in viewing self as an honest person because they have had the courage to tell the truth on occasion while viewing others as dishonest or deceptive if they ever slipped and lied at any time during their entire life. Deception also includes not being truthful with self about having an unhealthy, harmful behavior problem or about the seriousness of the problem (i.e., "denial").

Behavior Anatomy Question #4: What types of things do people do to avoid detection, cover up or deceive others about their harmful behavior?

Deception to cover up unhealthy, harmful behavior comes in many shapes and forms. Review all of the deceptions above, underline any that have applied to you in the past. Then use the space below to give an example of your most serious or most frequent past deception.

_____

_____

_____

_____

A. **Review your Awareness and Honesty Exam (Appendix G),** record your Deception ratings in the spaces provided below, add up all of your ratings to get a total and enter it in the space provided below. Since your self-awareness may have improved from your use of the Situation Response Analysis log, you may need to update your ratings.

Deception (11 items from Awareness and Honesty Exam, p. 207)

____ 1) Appeasing- Telling others what you think they want to hear	____ 81) Purposeful vagueness
____ 21) Assenting- Agreeing without meaning it	____ 101) Silence to avoid honesty
	____ 117) Changing the subject
____ 41) Dishonesty by omission	____ 144) "Throwing out a bone"- Diversion by admitting less serious problems
____ 61) Lying	____ 154) Honesty double standards
____ 80) Engrossment- Blowing the facts out of proportion	____ 158) Confusing things so facts aren't clear
	Total = _____

End of basic form- **Consult with your therapist or treatment program staff** and stop here and skip to part C, "Deception Structured Discovery Exercise" on page 73 if you are completing the basic form. Otherwise, continue on with the section B questions below.

B. Rate the following Deception characteristics.

Use the numbered ratings on the scales provided below to rate the frequency of your past thoughts or behaviors on the statements listed in this section.

0 Never	1 Sometimes	2 Half of the time	3 Often	4 Almost Always

___ 1) Lied to avoid consequences to yourself (e.g., Said "I forgot" or "you forgot to tell me").

___ 2) Lied to cover for someone else.

___ 3) Used "assenting" or telling people what you think they want to hear just to get them off your back or to be accepted (e.g., Said "Yes" to the authorities but told yourself that you won't cooperate or cursed at them in your head).

___ 4) Been dishonest by omission to avoid consequences (i.e., Told the part of the problem that wasn't your fault and left out parts of the story that was your fault).

___ 5) Made excuses to be dishonest by omission, (e.g., Kept problems or trouble to yourself saying "why get everyone upset").

___ 6) Used the "diversion" method of "a hop over" or changing the subject to avoid having to get honest about yourself.

___ 7) Used the "diversion" method of pointing out what others who were involved did to avoid having to get honest about yourself.

___ 8) Engaged in "throwing out a bone" or "setting a brush fire" (e.g., opening up a discussion or treatment session by bringing up a minor mistake to draw attention away from a problem you want to avoid sort of like confessing to a misdemeanor to avoid discussion of a felony).

___ 9) Used vagueness or purposefully answering or explaining in broad, general terms to avoid getting honest.

___ 10) Attempted to confuse others in order to avoid answering a direct question honestly (i.e., introducing many other issues that are not relevant to the issue you want to avoid).

___ 11) In situations where I was caught off guard, I have lied out of habit or automatically without thinking.

___ 12) Have found yourself automatically lying to cover up earlier lies without thinking.

___ 13) Told people what they wanted to hear to avoid consequences of disappointing them.

___ 14) Told people what they wanted to hear just to shut them up or get them off my back.

___ 15) Told people what they wanted to hear so that they would give me what I wanted.

___ 16) I have acted like I agree even when I didn't agree.

___ 17) When asked about a problem or mistake, I have answered "no" if any part of what was being said was not correct even if some of it was true.

___ 18) When asked about a problem or mistake, I have told the truth but left out parts that I did or that would make me look bad.

___ 19) When asked about a problem or mistake, I have brought up things that did not relate to the questions being asked to change the subject or side track the conversation.

0	1	2	3	4
Never	Sometimes	Half of the time	Often	Almost Always

____ 20) When asked about a problem or mistake, I have been unclear, leaving out details and stating things in general terms.

____ 21) I have joked about things that I was really serious about.

____ 22) I am an honest person who only bends the truth or leaves things out when I have to, like to avoid getting in trouble.

____ 23) Honesty has not been valuable to me, it has not made me feel better to admit problems.

____ 24) I have planned what to say in terms of whether it could get me out of trouble or get me something I wanted without caring about what I said or even trying to get the facts strait.

____ 25) My first instinct has been to deny the things that other people confront me with just for the principle of the thing. Even if it was true or not that big of a deal, I have noticed myself automatically saying, "That's not true" or "I don't do that".

____ 26) When asked about a problem or mistake, I have answered questions by going around them and avoiding giving a strait answer. For example, I have said things like "what ever", "I'm not really sure" or "I can't recall exactly" as opposed to "yes" or "no".

____ 27) When asked about a problem or mistake, I have added a lot of unnecessary details to the story to confuse others and make my part in the problem less clear.

____ 28) When asked about a problem or mistake, I have said that I already told everything when in fact I told a different part to several different people and never told any one person the whole story.

____ 29) I have thought that when you do something wrong, you really have nothing to gain by telling the truth, honesty only brings you consequences.

____ 30) Had the attitude that "Since everyone lies, why should I even try to be honest".

____ 31) Thought that since everyone lies some so it doesn't hurt to do it once in a while as long as you don't let it get out of line.

____ 32) Told myself "You are either honest or dishonest and there isn't any in between".

____ 33) Thought that "If you have ever lied, that makes you a liar".

____ 34) My attitude has been that anyone who lies or has lied has no business talking to me about being more honest.

____ 35) Thought that being honest hasn't done anything for me except get me in more trouble.

____ 36) My attitude towards getting things from others has been, "when opportunity knocks, open the door".

____ 37) Thought the truth is just a point of view and honesty is just about your side of the story.

Use the space provided below to list and rate any other deception characteristics that have been a problem for you in the past which were not included on the statements provided above. Discuss your deception with your treatment group and/or therapist. Include their feedback.

_____

_____

C. Deception Structured Discovery Exercise

On the following five numbered topics, if you are completing the basic form refer only to what you underlined and wrote about your most serious or most frequent Deception problems on p. 70 and your ratings in part A. For the complete form include your ratings in part B.

1. **Select your top ten Deception characteristics**.

   Review the statements that you rated in sections A and B section. Pick out the top ten (10) statements that described your particular Deception behavior the most (i.e., that you rated the highest in sections A and B) and circle the numbers of those statements. Examine the top ten Deception characteristics that you circled and number them in rank order with the #1 statement being the statement that most described your Deception style, #2 the second most and so on. Use the space provided below to list the top ten Deception characteristics that you circled. Place your #1 ranked statement in the space provided next to #1 and so on.

   Top Ten Deception Characteristics (complete first 5 for the basic form)

   1) _____
   2) _____
   3) _____
   4) _____
   5) _____
   6) _____
   7) _____
   8) _____
   9) _____
   10) _____

2. **Record at least your top three Deception characteristics** in rank order (highest rated statement first) in the space provided on your Harmful Behavior Anatomy worksheet (page 161). If you have a tie, circle the one that most applies to you and underline the other one. Put your ties (other highly ranked phrases that you underlined) on the back of your Harmful Behavior Anatomy Worksheet in the space provided.

   Although descriptive phrases (short versions of the questions you have answered) have been provided for you in part A, you will need to make up your own descriptive phrases for part B that will fit on your Harmful Behavior Anatomy worksheet. Don't limit yourself to the top three points if there are important parts that fit in this area. Make sure that you do not leave out any important information about yourself on this topic.

3. **Compute and enter your Deception score.**

   If you are completing the basic form of this exercise, use the Awareness and Honesty Exam questions that were summarized with descriptive phrases in part A of this section to compute your average rating score by dividing your rating total by the 11 questions you rated. After you have recorded your average rating score in the space provided below and on your Harmful Behavior Anatomy Worksheet at the end of this section, you can move on to the next section.

Total part A ratings on Awareness and Honesty Exam (_____) divided by 11 = _____.

If you are completing the entire exercise, add up all of your part B question ratings. An easy way to do that is to fill in the chart below.

How many questions did you rate as 4? _____	Multiply that by 4 and enter the answer here _____
How many questions did you rate as 3? _____	Multiply that by 3 and enter the answer here _____
How many questions did you rate as 2? _____	Multiply that by 2 and enter the answer here _____
How many questions did you rate as 1? _____	Multiply that by 1 and enter the answer here _____
How many questions did you rate as 0? _____	Add this column, Total part B = _____
(Total should be 37) Total = _____	

Compute your average rating score by adding up your part A and part B total scores, then dividing the total by all 48 questions that you rated. Record your average rating score in the space provided below and on your Harmful Behavior Anatomy worksheet (page 163).

Total part A (_____) + Total part B = _____ divided by 48 = _____.

4. **Write what you have discovered about yourself through this structured exercise**
   Use the space provided below to document how your Deception affected any part of your social-emotional maturity. Use the workspace on page 227 if needed.

Social maturity (honesty, trust, loyalty, concern and responsibility).

_____

_____

_____

_____

Emotional maturity (self-awareness, self-efficacy/confidence, self-control)

_____

_____

_____

Hint: If you're having trouble with this, just take the top Deception characteristics that you listed on page 73 and ask yourself questions comparing each Deception characteristic to each component of social maturity looking for a connection. For example, "How did my deception affect my (honesty, trust, loyalty, concern, responsibility)?" Do the same with each component of emotional maturity. For example, "How did my deception affect my (self-awareness, self-efficacy, self-control)?"

5. **List the best personal example you can recall** of how your Deception caused a major problem or crisis in your life. Use the workspace on page 227 if needed. Note: An honesty accomplishment award is generally administered for the best example in treatment groups.

The three steps of working through the truth (about yourself or others) are as follows:
I.   Get honest with yourself- "To thine own self be true" (Shakespere)
II. Accept the truth- The truth hurts and "The truth will set you free, but first it will piss you off" (Mal Pancoast)
III. Get honest with others- "The truth shall set you free" (John 8:32), but only if you get it out

_____

_____

_____

Awareness training: In addition to becoming aware of the Deception characteristics in sections A though C above, it is important to be aware of deceiving yourself (i.e., "To thine own self be true") by paying attention to your irresponsible thinking such as "I can't belief", grandiosity, the victim view, justifying, extremism, minimizing and maximizing (see Appendix C). A second important recovery point about deception has to do with being aware that a history of unhealthy, harmful behavior builds a pattern of secret keeping about unhealthy, harmful thoughts, feelings, and behavior that need to come out in the open. Put another way, "The truth will set you free" does not apply to things you say in confidence, confession or individual therapy sessions which should be viewed as practice for getting honest in group therapy along with significant/involved others when appropriate. List the unhealthy, harmful behavior you have been involved with and the Deception you used to support that behavior in the space below.
Unhealthy, Harmful Behavior   Deception that supported it

_____

_____

_____

Responsibility training: While Awareness training is a necessary first step, if you don't take **R**esponsibility for letting go of your Deception habits, you can't expect to change. Review "How to think it through" with the Reality Scales (p. 24) to help you arrive at a responsible decision to get honest by weighing out how much you actually need deception to survive, succeed, or avoid consequences. Pick the last mistake you made and covered up with deception, then weigh out the need to do that next time on the reality scales below.

My mistake that I covered up with deception: _____

How important to my survival was it for me to cover that mistake up with deception?

Survival scale rating (0 = not important; 10= could kill me if I didn't): _____

How important for my success was it for me to cover that mistake up with deception?

Success scale rating (0 = not important; 10= would stop me from ever succeeding): _____

How severe would the consequences be if I got honest about what I did?

Severity scale rating (0 = not severe at all; 10= extremely severe): _____

In reviewing your reality scale scores above, if you made the same
mistake today, do you still think you need to cover it up with deception? ___Yes; ___No
"You are only limited by your creativity" when dealing with life problems. See Exhibit 3 (p. 177)
for an idea that may help you with deception issues and note your thoughts below.

_____

Tolerance training: Letting go of deception involves learning to tolerate the consequences of
getting honest. In letting go of deception, it helps to realize that the reason we respect honesty so
much is the tremendous courage that it takes to face the consequences of getting honest. It also
helps to realize that "honesty has its price but the good news is you don't have to pay twice" (i.e.,
once you get honest, you do not have to face the consequences of doing it again). Probably the
best treatment model out there for letting go of deception and developing honesty is the
Therapeutic Community model that has a saying, "When you're looking bad, you're looking
good" (DeLeon, 2000, p. 83). That is, when you think you are making yourself look bad by
admitting a mistake, you are actually looking good by getting honest which is respected by all.
Another way to help you tolerate the consequences of getting honest is to admit to yourself that
"dishonesty is disrespect". Put another way, if your want to show someone respect, you have to
get honest with them.

Answer the question, "What would be the opposite extreme of the top three deception
characteristics that you listed in section C?" Describe the opposite healthy, responsible behavior
that you need to "Act as if" (p. 12) you already have and practice regularly in the space below.

  Deception   Opposite Healthy, Helpful Behavior

1)_____

2)_____

3)_____

D. Make a Positive Plan and Commitment to Change
   Review the three Honesty problems that you listed on your Harmful Behavior Anatomy
   worksheet (page 161). What can you do about it now? How are you going to change these
   problems, what are you going to do? (Consult with your therapist or staff and write your plan
   below)

1) _____

2) _____

3) _____

Discuss your Deception with your therapist or treatment group. Log the date you discussed your
deception and who you discussed it with in the space provided below.

Date: _____   Discussed with: _____

"Character, not circumstances, makes the man" -- Booker T. Washington (1856-1915)

Name: _____   Date: _____

Definition: In the anatomy of unhealthy, harmful behavior, a social maturity deficit provides a strong support leg for multiple forms of unhealthy, harmful behavior. In Social Responsibility Therapy, a Social Maturity Deficit is defined as serious problems with honesty, trust, loyalty, concern and responsibility. These problems were predisposing factors that set up or enabled your unhealthy, harmful behavior. This deficit frequently occurs as a result of the historical (e.g., past trauma), social-emotional (e.g., impaired social skills and unwanted feelings), situational (e.g., people, places and things that trigger trouble) and cognitive (e.g., thoughts, views and attitudes) risk factors that you experienced in the Risk Factor Chain that led to your harmful behavior. Going through the Stress-Relapse Cycle makes things worse, advancing underdeveloped social maturity to a pathological level where serious problems with honesty, trust, loyalty, concern and responsibility are created. Social maturity problems interfere with all forms of relationships including those with partners (romantic), peers (social), teachers (school) and supervisors (work). Individuals involved in unhealthy harmful behavior are frequently described as having problems with honesty, trust, loyalty, concern and/or responsibility. These social maturity problems support multiple forms of unhealthy, harmful behavior which enables it to spread from one type to another (Figure 12).

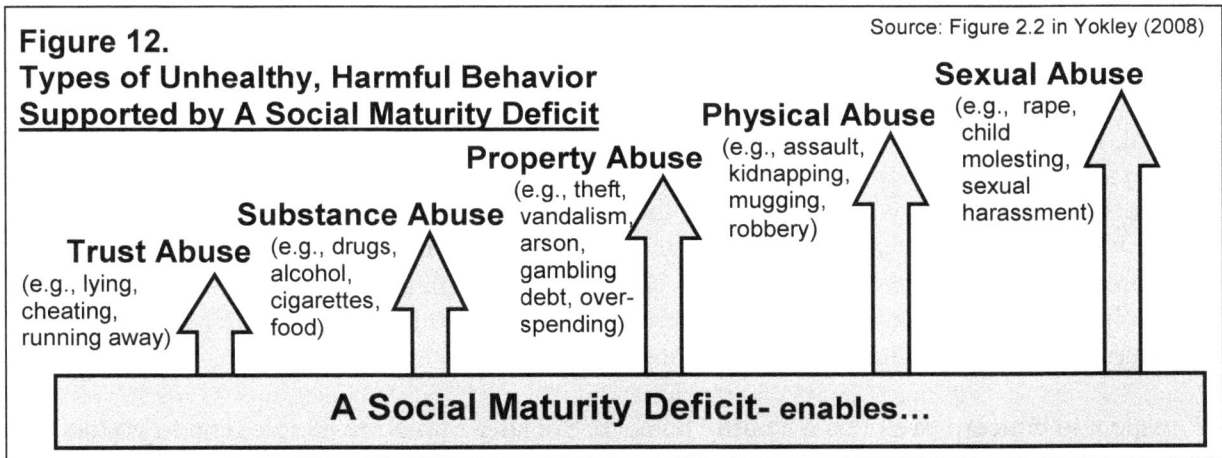

Figure 12.
Types of Unhealthy, Harmful Behavior Supported by A Social Maturity Deficit

Source: Figure 2.2 in Yokley (2008)

Sexual Abuse (e.g., rape, child molesting, sexual harassment)

Physical Abuse (e.g., assault, kidnapping, mugging, robbery)

Property Abuse (e.g., theft, vandalism, arson, gambling debt, over-spending)

Substance Abuse (e.g., drugs, alcohol, cigarettes, food)

Trust Abuse (e.g., lying, cheating, running away)

A Social Maturity Deficit- enables...

In Social Responsibility Therapy, the definition of social maturity is a healthy development of honesty, trust, loyalty, concern and responsibility. Let's break this down and clear up "what's in it for me" to be honest, trustworthy, loyal, concerned and responsible. When it comes to honesty, the first thing that comes to most people's minds is that honesty brings consequences. If we are standing in front of the judge when they ask "How do you plead?" and answer, "Guilty your honor", we know that our honesty will bring consequences. So here's the drill, we need to accept that the reason people value honesty so much is the tremendous consequences attached to it. If it were easy and carried no consequences, everybody would be honest all of the time. We have to get real with ourselves, admit that we look up to people who are honest, not only because we can trust what they say but because. "Honesty has its price, the good news is you don't have to pay twice". On the flip side of honesty, "dishonesty is disrespect". The people who lie to you are disrespecting you by treating you like a know nothing chump who will never figure it out or a nobody who just doesn't deserve the truth. If you keep disrespecting people by being dishonest, you lose every friend who values honesty and end up surrounded by liars who disrespect you through their dishonesty.

Let's move on to trust. A socially immature belief about trust is that getting respect has more to do with being tough than being trustworthy. Let's think that one through. In life it's win some, lose some, you can't win all the card games, arguments or fist fights. Since socially immature people don't know the difference between disrespect, disagreement, respect and fear. They mistake disagreement for disrespect and mistake fear for respect. As a result, they turn a disagreement with you into a fistfight if they can't change your mind. Because they mistake fear for respect, they view using fear to get agreement as getting respect. Be honest, after someone beats you down, when they are walking away running their mouth about you, what are you really thinking? Do you really tell yourself, "I really respect that person and want to be more like them?" or are you really thinking, "What an immature a##hole" when they pull that baby crap. So here's a question you have to get honest with yourself about... Can people demand your respect by bullying you or do they have to earn your respect by being trustworthy? The really good news here is that you don't have to trust people to be trustworthy; all you have to do is what you say you will do. In short, respect is earned by being trustworthy and responsibility builds trust.

In the area of loyalty, without going into great detail, relationship disloyalty is just too dangerous to put up with in today's HIV world. Picking looks over loyalty has always resulted in emotional heartbreak but now the penalty for that decision can include a premature death. In the area of family loyalty picking negative peers over positive family may help you hear what you want from others but it prevents you from hearing the truth from positive people who have your best interests in mind. Getting relationship and decision opinions from positive people who have your bests interests in mind is very important. Not being loyal enough to positive people can put you behind in life as a result of poor decisions and being too loyal to negative people can put you behind bars, in rehab or in the emergency room.

With respect to concern, we need a healthy balance. Socially immature people tend to go too far in both directions with concern. Some spend too much time following their need for acceptance, doing for others and putting more into relationships than they get out. Picking companionship over concern and compromising themselves to be accepted in unhealthy or abusive relationships does eliminate loneliness and guarantees companionship but results in resentment for putting in too much or regret for bringing on unwanted emotional drama and physical trauma. On the flip side, others spend too much time following their needs for attention or excitement, doing what they want, when they want for the reason they want and taking much more from relationships than they put in. These "take-aholics" don't consider the impact of their selfish behavior on others, focusing only on, "You got to look out for number one". The socially mature balancing act here involves being able to accept that, "You're number one but there are other numbers" and take good care of yourself so you can take good care of those you care about most.

Responsibility does not mean having a great job, owning your own company or having an important title like attorney, doctor or president. Responsibility means that you can be counted on to finish what you start and to give 100% of your ability to your obligations, whether that involves building houses or taking care of your household. Responsible people are people who can be counted on, they are the "go to" people you call when you need something done well.

The bottom line here is simple, when you call someone "immature" you are almost always referring to their problems with social maturity (i.e., honesty, trust, loyalty, concern or responsibility) and anytime we are told to "just grow up", it means to let go of our social immaturity and start acting honest, trustworthy, loyal, concerned and responsible. Who really wants to be around socially immature people? Social maturity problems interfere with developing a "right living" [3] positive lifestyle (i.e., based on the multicultural prosocial values of honesty, trust, loyalty, concern and responsibility) and prevents us from having a healthy, positive life with healthy, positive relationships. Even if you tell yourself that developing a "right living" positive lifestyle by being honest, trustworthy, loyal, concerned and responsible is boring, you have to admit that you don't like people who are not that way with you which means, if you want acceptance instead of rejection from others you need to act this way. Think about it. How long would you continue to do business with someone who has problems with honesty, trust, loyalty, concern and responsibility? The bottom line here is simple. Dishonesty is disrespect. If you respect someone, you're honest with them. If you respect someone, you can be trusted by them and you trust them. If you respect someone, you're loyal to them. If you respect someone, you're concerned about them. and if you respect someone, you're responsible with them.

Honesty, trust, loyalty, concern and responsibility is what …
• We want from others
• We need to survive in the community by avoiding trouble and protecting our freedom
• We need to get and keep real friends
• We need to succeed (i.e., get and keep privileges, jobs, promotions, raises
• We need to get along with different people in different parts of the country and world
• Others (partners, peers and parents) want from us

Think about it, if right now you were looking for a best friend in the whole world, a girlfriend or life partner (husband/wife) and started to make a list of what you are looking for in others, it doesn't take long to realize that these things would definitely be on the list. If you really think about it, these are also the things you want from your parents, teachers and boss. No one looking for a best friend or life partner purposefully picks someone who lacks honesty, trust, loyalty, concern and responsibility. So if this is what you want in other people, what do you know they want from you?

Socially mature people have honesty, trust, loyalty, concern and responsibility. Immature people have problems with honesty, trust, loyalty, concern and responsibility. If you are picking a life partner or best friend, no matter how much fun they are, if they are immature and don't have honesty, trust, loyalty, concern and responsibility, the relationship won't last. Here's why...

Honesty- We don't stick with people who lie to us because, "dishonesty is disrespect".
Trust- We don't stick with people we can't trust.
Loyalty- We don't stick with people who are not loyal, talk behind our back (or cheat). You can get a relationship with looks but you can't keep it without loyalty.
Concern- We don't stick with people who don't care as much about us as we do about them.
Responsibility- Our #1 responsibility is self-control and we don't stick with people who can't control themselves and are always creating problems. We also don't stick with people who are not responsible and always rely on us to pay their way.

In summary, since we want honesty, trust, loyalty, concern and responsibility from those who are a part of our lives and they want the same thing from us, it is obvious that if we want to be desirable and successful in our personal, family and business relationships, we need to develop our honesty, trust, loyalty, concern and responsibility.

Behavior Anatomy Question #5: How could your past experiences have affected your honesty, trust, loyalty, concern & responsibility?

Social Maturity 101: Multicultural Prosocial Values
In addition to being key components of social maturity, honesty, trust, loyalty, concern and responsibility are also multicultural prosocial values. No one around the world from Chile to China wants a dishonest neighbor. Everyone worldwide wants to be around others who we can trust, are loyal, concerned and responsible. These multicultural prosocial values are needed as a shared framework in our diverse society and have a long history. Since these multicultural prosocial values were needed for humans to survive, they probably date back to the beginning of mankind. Here are some examples written between 100 and 2500 years ago by individuals that you may have heard of in your lifetime that are still betting circulated today.

- "Honesty is the best policy" was coined by Miguel de Cervantes,1547-1616 (author of Don Quixote).
- "Every kind of peaceful cooperation among men is primarily based on mutual trust" was pointed out by Albert Einstein (1879-1955)
- "Consider loyalty and faithfulness to be fundamental" is a Confucius saying (c. 551- 479 BC)
- "Do unto others as you would have others do unto you" is "The Golden rule" of concern for others that dates back to Confucius 500BC, Aristotle 325BC & Jesus.
- Finally, "None of us can hope to get anywhere without character, moral courage and the spiritual strength to accept responsibility" was written by Thomas Watson (1874-1956).

The Multicultural Values Respect Goal- Involves the transmission of respect from one generation to another. If you respect someone: you're honest with them; you can be trusted by them; you're loyal to them; you're concerned about them and; you're responsible with them. Socially immature people mistake fear for respect and have not realized that dishonesty is disrespect.

Review all of the Social Maturity Deficit deception information above, underline any part that has applied to you in the past and use the space below to give a specific example of what you consider your most serious or most frequent past social maturity problems.

_____

_____

_____

_____

_____

A. Review your Awareness and Honesty Exam (Appendix G)

Record your Social Maturity Deficit ratings (i.e., problems with honesty, trust, loyalty, concern and responsibility) in the spaces provided below and add up all of your ratings in each category to get a total. Since your self-awareness may have improved from your use of the Situation Response Analysis log (Appendix D), you may need to update your ratings. Enter your ratings totals in the spaces provided below.

Honesty Problems (11 items from Awareness and Honesty Exam, p. 207)

___ 1) Appeasing- Telling others what you think they want to hear	___ 81) Purposeful vagueness
___ 21) Assenting- Agreeing without meaning it	___ 101) Silence to avoid honesty
___ 41) Dishonesty by omission	___ 117) Changing the subject
___ 61) Lying	___ 144) "Throwing out a bone"- Diversion by admitting less serious problems
___ 80) Engrossment- Blowing the facts out of proportion	___ 154) Honesty double standards
	___ 158) Confusing things so facts aren't clear
	Total = _____

Trust Problems (7 items from Awareness and Honesty Exam, p. 207)

___ 42) Felt entitled to trust	___ 141) Angry when others don't trust you
___ 103) Trust double standards	___ 149) Assuming others will use what you say against you.
___ 118) Accused those who didn't trust you of not caring	___ 153) Problems trusting others
___ 135) Premature trust of others	Total = _____

Loyalty Problems (10 items from Awareness and Honesty Exam, p. 207)

___ 3) Loyalty to one-sided relationships	___ 84) Depending on undependable people
___ 23) Loyalty priority problems- putting negative peers first	___ 112) Relationship approach-avoidance
___ 43) Defending negative relationships	___ 127) Enabling- Covering for others
___ 52) Putting others down behind their back	___ 143) Shifting loyalties
___ 63) Negative contracting- Mutual cover-up	___ 145) Loyalty double standards
	Total = _____

Concern Problems (18 items from Awareness and Honesty Exam, p. 207)

___ 4) Looking out for #1, every man for himself	___ 85) Putting others down behind their back
___ 17) Justifying actions based on feelings	___ 99) Not caring about self
___ 24) Not considering impact of behavior	___105) Rationalizing harmful behavior towards self
___ 34) Let teasing go too far	___107) Role reversal deficit
___ 44) Minimizing behavior impact on self	___116) Normalizing harmful behavior
___ 55) Minimizing behavior impact on others	___119) Putting others down for what they said
___ 57) Justifying wrong doing	___128) Concern double standards
___ 64) Called selfish	___129) Blame others for negative impact
___ 67) Not worrying about anyone else	
___ 75) Rationalizing harmful behavior towards others	Total = _____

Responsibility Problems (28 items from Awareness and Honesty Exam, p. 207)

Personal/Social Responsibility

___ 14) Forgetting to return borrowed items	___ 53) Not thinking about consequences
___ 15) Excusing problem responsibility	___ 76) Blaming responsibility on others, "They caused it"
___ 16) Responsibility denial, "It's not my fault", "I always get blamed"	___150) Shifting responsibility to others
___ 35) Minimizing problem responsibility	___151) No concept of behavior change track record
___ 36) Shifting responsibility to others who encouraged you	___160) Placing responsibility on the victim

Work/School/Home Responsibility

___ 6) "I forgot" responsibility avoidance	___ 97) Not doing your part
___ 13) Disorganized	___106) Avoiding boring responsibilities
___ 26) Doing things half way	___111) Late and/or missed appointments
___ 46) Lack of responsibility effort	___121) Putting fun before responsibilities
___ 65) Excuses to avoid things you don't want to do	___130) Physical excuses for inability to do responsibilities
___ 66) Refusal to accept responsibility	___138) All or nothing work attitude
___ 73) Failure to plan for future	___146) Expressing annoyance when reminded
___ 83) Responsibility double standards	___155) Problems finishing things
___ 87) Dragging your feet, "It can wait"	___159) Not earning the right to complain Total = _____

B. Social Maturity Deficit Structured Discovery Exercise

On the following five numbered topics, refer to what you underlined/wrote about your most serious or most frequent Social Maturity problems on p. 81 along with your ratings in part A.

1. **Select your top three Social Maturity Deficit characteristics in each category.**
Review the statements that you rated in the previous section. Pick out the top three (3) statements that described your particular Social Maturity Deficit behavior the most (i.e., that you rated the highest) in each category and circle the numbers of those statements. Use the space provided below to list the top three Social Maturity Deficit characteristics that you circled in each category. Record your #1 ranked summary phrases from the category boxes above in the space provided next to #1 and so on.

Top Three Social Maturity Deficit characteristics in each category

Honesty Problems	Trust Problems
1) _____	1) _____
2) _____	2) _____
3) _____	3) _____

Loyalty Problems	Concern Problems
1) _____	1) _____
2) _____	2) _____
3) _____	3) _____

Personal & Social Responsibility Problems	Work/School/Home Responsibility Problems
1) _____	1) _____
2) _____	2) _____
3) _____	3) _____

2. **Record your #1 Social Maturity Deficit in each category**.
   Record your #1 descriptive phrase from each Social Maturity category (#1 Honesty Problem, #1 Trust Problem, #1Loyalty Problem, #1 Concern Problem and #1 Personal/Social Responsibility Problem) in the space provided on your Harmful Behavior Anatomy worksheet (page 161). If you have a tie, circle the one that most applies to you and underline the other one. Put your #1 Work/School/Home Responsibility along with your ties (other highly ranked phrases that you underlined) on the back of your Harmful Behavior Anatomy Worksheet in the space provided.

3. **Compute and enter your Social Maturity Deficit scores.**
   Add all five problem category rating totals together to get your Social Maturity Deficit Total. Divide by the total number of items in each category to get the average score (round off to one decimal place) and record your average Social Maturity Deficit rating score in the space provided on the following page and on your Harmful Behavior Anatomy Worksheet at the end of this section.

		Strength & Weakness
Honesty Problem	Total = ____ divided by 11 items = _____ (Average score)	+ or -
Trust Problem	Total = ____ divided by 7 items = _____ (Average score)	+ or -
Loyalty Problem	Total = ____ divided by 10 items = _____ (Average score)	+ or -
Concern Problem	Total = ____ divided by 18 items = _____ (Average score)	+ or -
Responsibility Problem Total = ____ divided by 28 items = _____ (Average score)		+ or -
Social Maturity Deficit Total = _____ divided by 74 items = _____ (Average score)		

Social Maturity strengths (+) and weaknesses (-). Now compute your category scores for honesty, trust, loyalty, concern and responsibility problems. Circle the plus sign (+) next to your Social Maturity strength (lowest score) and circle the minus sign (-) next to your Social Maturity weakness (highest score). Then mark on your Social Maturity strength and weakness with a plus and minus sign on the Harmful Behavior Anatomy Worksheet at the end of this section.

4. Irresponsible Thinking Impact on Social Maturity
Use the space provided below to give examples of how your Irresponsible Thinking supported problems with Social-Emotional Maturity. Use workspace on page 227 if needed.

Social Maturity Problems	Irresponsible Thinking
Honesty Problems (list below)	Thoughts that stop you from being honest
Trust Problems (list below)	Thoughts that stop you from trusting
Loyalty Problems (list below)	Thoughts that stop you from being loyal
Concern Problems (list below)	Thoughts that stop you from caring
Responsibility Problems (list below)	Thoughts that stop you from being responsible

Hint: Look at your Irresponsible Thinking and personal quotes (p. 41). Some common thinking and self-statements that support Social Maturity Problems include, "It was no big deal", "They'll kill me if I tell", "Anything you say will be used against you", "What they don't know won't hurt them", "You have to look out for number one", "They got me upset and made me do it", "It's not my problem", "I'll do it later"

5. The Risk Factor Chain Impact on Social Maturity

As was mentioned at the beginning of this Harmful Behavior Anatomy Component, problems with honesty, trust, loyalty, concern and responsibility typically result from various parts of the Risk Factor Chain which involves historical (e.g., past trauma), social-emotional (e.g., impaired social skills and unwanted feelings), situational (e.g., people, places and emotions that trigger trouble) and cognitive (e.g., thoughts, views and attitudes) risk factors that you experienced in the Risk Factor Chain that led to your harmful behavior. The Risk Factor Chain is capable of delaying Social Maturity to the point where serious problems with all forms of relationships occur.

For Example, in Link 1, past personal problems consisting of historical life stressors such as toxic parenting can create **dishonesty** to avoid inappropriate criticism. Abusive parent discipline can trigger dishonesty to avoid irrational consequences. Parent neglect can result in a **distrust** of authorities and model a **lack of concern** for others. Family substance abuse can model **irresponsible behavior**. All of these family problems can result in moving away from family towards **negative peer loyalty**. These are just a few examples of how Link 1 can affect honesty, trust, loyalty, concern and responsibility, there are many others and each Link has its own connection to problems with honesty, trust, loyalty, concern and responsibility. It's now your job to come up with the connections that occurred in your life. Review the Risk Factor Chain (Figure 13, p. 87) and your Risk Factor Chain Worksheet in Workbook 1 if you completed it. Then make connections to your Risk Factor Chain in sections a- e below.

a. Review the top three **Honesty Problems** that you listed above and ask yourself, "Where was that coming from?" (What was your motivation) or "What did that relate to?" (What triggered it). Review each link on your Risk Factor Chain (Figure 13) in order to make a connection. Then list your answer in the spaces provided below.

1) _____

Motivation & trigger→_____

2) _____

Motivation & trigger→_____

3) _____

Motivation & trigger→_____

> **Hint:** If your #1 honesty problem was lying and that came from trying to avoid the physically abusive beatings that you recorded on your Link 1 historical factors, you would write "Lying- to avoid beatings" in space #1 below. If your #2 honesty problem was dishonesty by omission and that related to severe criticism for making mistakes that you recorded on your Link 1 historical factors, you would write "Dishonesty by omission- to avoid being put down" in space #2 below. If your #3 honesty problem was appeasing and that came from wanting to be liked and accepted by friends that you recorded on your Link 2 historical factors, you would write "Appeasing- to be liked and accepted by friends" in space #3 below.

b. Review the top three **Trust Problems** that you listed above and ask yourself, "Where was that coming from?" (What was your motivation) or "What did that relate to?" (What triggered it) Look back and review each link on your Risk Factor Chain in order to make a connection. Then list your answer in the spaces provided on the following page.

1) _____

    Motivation & trigger→ _____

2) _____

    Motivation & trigger→ _____

3) _____

    Motivation & trigger→ _____

c. Review the top three **Loyalty Problems** that you listed above and ask yourself, "Where was that coming from?" (What was your motivation) or "What did that relate to?" (What triggered it) Look back and review each link on your Risk Factor Chain (p. 87) in order to make a connection. Then list your answer in the spaces provided below.

1) _____

    Motivation & trigger→ _____

2) _____

    Motivation & trigger→ _____

3) _____

    Motivation & trigger→ _____

d. Review the top three **Concern Problems** that you listed above and ask yourself, "Where was that coming from?" (What was your motivation) or "What did that relate to?" (What triggered it) Look back and review each link on your Risk Factor Chain (p. 87) in order to make a connection. Then list your answer in the spaces provided below.

1) _____

    Motivation & trigger→ _____

2) _____

    Motivation & trigger→ _____

3) _____

    Motivation & trigger→ _____

e. Review the top three **Responsibility Problems** that you listed above and ask yourself, "Where was that coming from?" (What was your motivation) or "What did that relate to?" (What triggered it) Look back and review each link on your Risk Factor Chain (p. 87) in order to make a connection. Then list your answer in the spaces provided.

1) _____

    Motivation & trigger→ _____

2) _____

    Motivation & trigger→ _____

3) _____

    Motivation & trigger→ _____

Figure 13. The Risk Factor Chain: How Harmful Behavior was Acquired

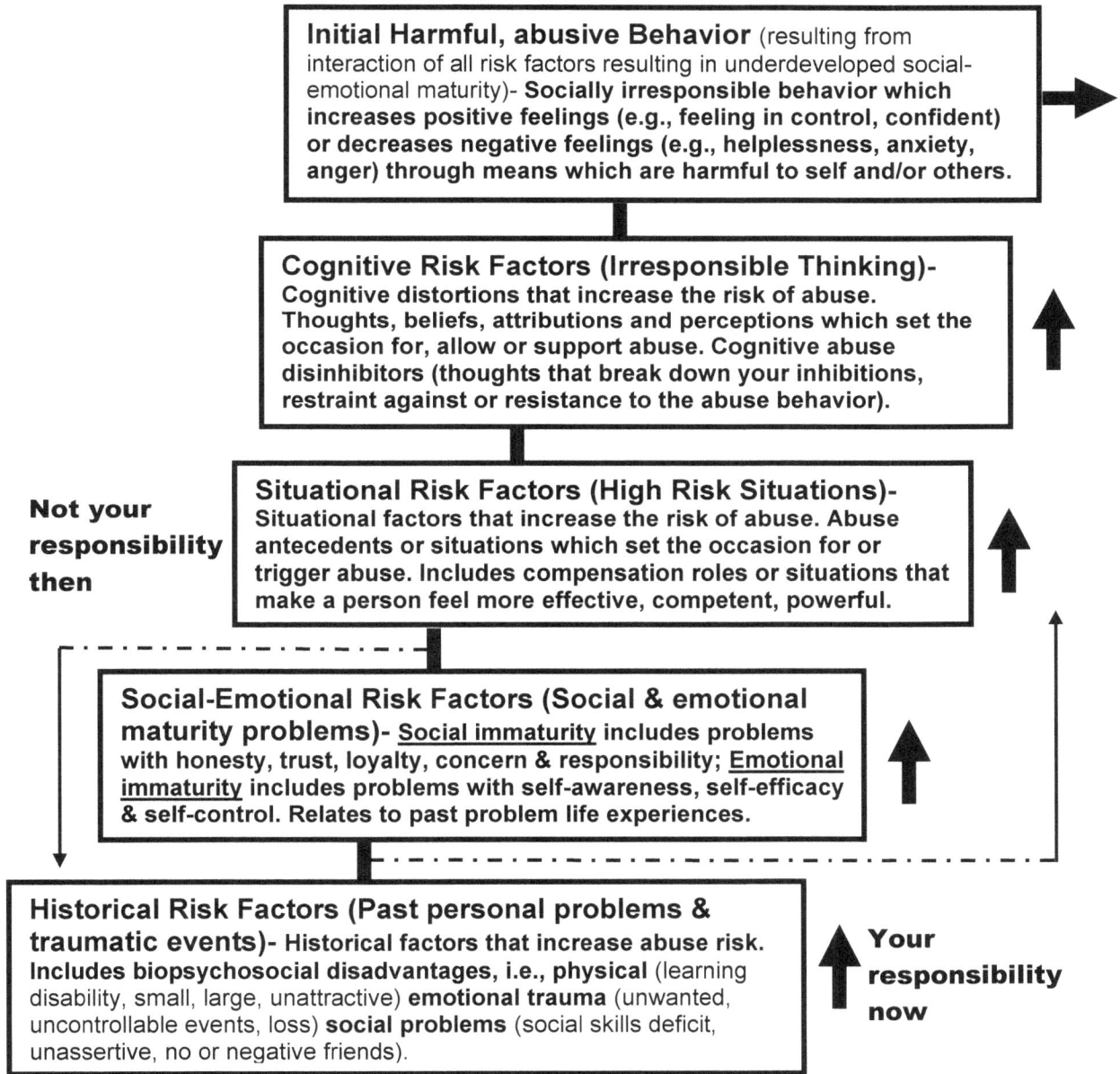

Initial Harmful, abusive Behavior (resulting from interaction of all risk factors resulting in underdeveloped social-emotional maturity)- **Socially irresponsible behavior which increases positive feelings (e.g., feeling in control, confident) or decreases negative feelings (e.g., helplessness, anxiety, anger) through means which are harmful to self and/or others.**

Cognitive Risk Factors (Irresponsible Thinking)- **Cognitive distortions that increase the risk of abuse. Thoughts, beliefs, attributions and perceptions which set the occasion for, allow or support abuse. Cognitive abuse disinhibitors (thoughts that break down your inhibitions, restraint against or resistance to the abuse behavior).**

Not your responsibility then

Situational Risk Factors (High Risk Situations)- **Situational factors that increase the risk of abuse. Abuse antecedents or situations which set the occasion for or trigger abuse. Includes compensation roles or situations that make a person feel more effective, competent, powerful.**

Social-Emotional Risk Factors (Social & emotional maturity problems)- <u>Social immaturity</u> includes problems with honesty, trust, loyalty, concern & responsibility; <u>Emotional immaturity</u> includes problems with self-awareness, self-efficacy & self-control. Relates to past problem life experiences.

Historical Risk Factors (Past personal problems & traumatic events)- Historical factors that increase abuse risk. **Includes biopsychosocial disadvantages, i.e., physical** (learning disability, small, large, unattractive) **emotional trauma** (unwanted, uncontrollable events, loss) **social problems** (social skills deficit, unassertive, no or negative friends).

Your responsibility now

Note: Management of these risk factors is summarized in Exhibit 1 (p. 175)

6. Write what you have learned about yourself through this structured discovery exercise
Use the space provided below to summarize the ways that your Risk Factor Chain affected your
Social Maturity (honesty, trust, loyalty, concern and responsibility). Use the workspace on page
227 if needed.

_____

_____

_____

_____

Use the space provided below to summarize how your problems with honesty, trust, loyalty,
concern and responsibility affected your Emotional Maturity (self-awareness, self-
efficacy/confidence, self-control). Use the workspace on page 227 if needed.

_____

_____

_____

_____

Hint: Just take a step by step approach to look for a connection, e.g., "How did my problems with
(honesty, trust, loyalty, concern or responsibility) affect my (self-awareness, self-efficacy/confidence, self-
control)?" Some connections are easy to see like: how automatic dishonesty about feelings (e.g., "I'm not
afraid") blocks self-awareness; how not being responsible and finishing things results in failure
experiences that lower self-efficacy/confidence or; how loyalty to negative peers involves letting go of
self-control and doing things with them you know you shouldn't. Others require looking closer.

7. List the best personal example you can recall of how your problems with honesty, trust,
loyalty, concern and responsibility caused real trouble in your life. Use the workspace on
page 227 if needed.

_____

_____

_____

Awareness training: In order to develop social maturity, we have to admit that: 1) we all want
honesty, trust, loyalty, concern, and responsibility from others (i.e., parents, peers, partners, and
employers); 2) these are the characteristics that others want from us and; 3) we cannot get these
things from others without giving them. List the unhealthy, harmful behavior you have been
involved with and the Social Maturity Deficit you used to support that behavior in the space
provided on the following page..

Unhealthy, Harmful Behavior   Social Maturity Deficit that supported it

_____

_____

_____

_____

Responsibility training: While becoming aware that honesty, trust, loyalty, concern and responsibility are what we all want from each other is an important first step, we need to make a commitment to improve in these five areas if we want to stop our unhealthy, harmful behavior. Review all of the social maturity deficit information in this section, check off the area that you believe needs the most improvement and write out what you need to change and why.

I need to improve most on my: __honesty, __trust, __loyalty, __concern, __responsibility

My self-improvement plan is: _____

_____

_____

_____

_____

"You are only limited by your creativity" when dealing with life problems. See Exhibit 3 (p. 177) for an idea that may help you with Social Maturity issues.

Tolerance training: Old habits die hard and letting go of social immaturity means learning to tolerate doing more work. Specially: being honest means no more excuses; being trustworthy means doing just as well when others aren't watching; being loyal means doing the right thing, not the fun thing; being concerned means looking out for others and not just yourself and being responsible means finishing what you start and putting in 100% effort. Honesty, trust, loyalty, concern and responsibility are competing factors against trust, substance, property, physical and sexual abuse. For example...

- It is very hard to be a dishonest, irresponsible drug abuser while being honest and responsible parent or;
- It is very hard to be a cheating, physically abusive boyfriend while being loyal and concerned partner.

Since it is hard to do both, if you practice one, it will compete against and help block the other. Given this situation, it is important for you to go to the opposite extreme in improving your social maturity in order to stop unhealthy, harmful behavior.

Answer the question, "What would be the opposite extreme of the social maturity problem that you listed in responsibility training as needing the most improvement?" Use the space on the next page to describe the opposite healthy, responsible behavior that you need to "Act as if" (p. 12) you already have and practice regularly.

<u>Social Maturity Deficit</u>   <u>Opposite Healthy, Helpful Behavior</u>

_____

_____

_____

Use the workspace below to explain why **what you do isn't who you are** and why social maturity is more important than social status. Then give a talk to your therapist or group that will convince them that your title on a school sports team (e.g., first string, second string) or in the workforce (e.g., director, assistant director) is not who you are, your social maturity (i.e., level of honesty, trust loyalty, concern and responsibility) is who you are. Log the date you discussed this issue and who you discussed it with in the space provided below.

_____

_____

_____

Hint: What eventually happens to people whose title is bigger than their social maturity?

C. Make a Positive Plan and Commitment to Change
Review the three Social Maturity problems that you listed on your Harmful Behavior Anatomy worksheet (page 161). What can you do about it now? How are you going to change these problems? (Consult with your therapist or staff and write your plan below)

1) _____

What I can do about it→ _____

What I am going to do about it→ _____

2) _____

What I can do about it→ _____

What I am going to do about it→ _____

3) _____

What I can do about it→ _____

What I am going to do about it→ _____

Hint: Try playing your values against your harmful behavior. For example, if honesty is a strength and hanging out with negative peers after work/school is a relapse trigger, make a commitment to meet a positive peer after work/school. If honesty is a strength, you will keep your word and avoid trouble.

Get honest about your Social Maturity Problems with your therapist or treatment group.
Log the date you discussed this issue and who you discussed it with in the space provided below.

Date: _____ Discussed with: _____

The Harmful Behavior Anatomy Component 6: Maladaptive Self-Image

"Great beauty, great strength and great riches are really and truly of no use.
The right heart exceeds all" -- Benjamin Franklin (1706-1790)

Name: _____   Date: _____

Definition: Humans can have adaptive or maladaptive self-images. A maladaptive self-image provides firm footing for unhealthy, harmful behavior. Your self-image is your view of who you are including who you want to be which is influenced by your past experience and expressed by what you repeatedly do. Maladaptive is a word that means doesn't help you adapt, grow or succeed in life. Maladaptive images are often based on maladaptive "schemas" which are repeating thought and feeling patterns that stem from childhood experiences.[14] There are many types of maladaptive self-images. The motivation behind each varies and includes but is not limited to a need to present self in a manner to command respect, gain status, take control or get needs met. These maladaptive self-image problems support multiple forms of unhealthy, harmful behavior and allow it to spread from one type to another (Figure 14).

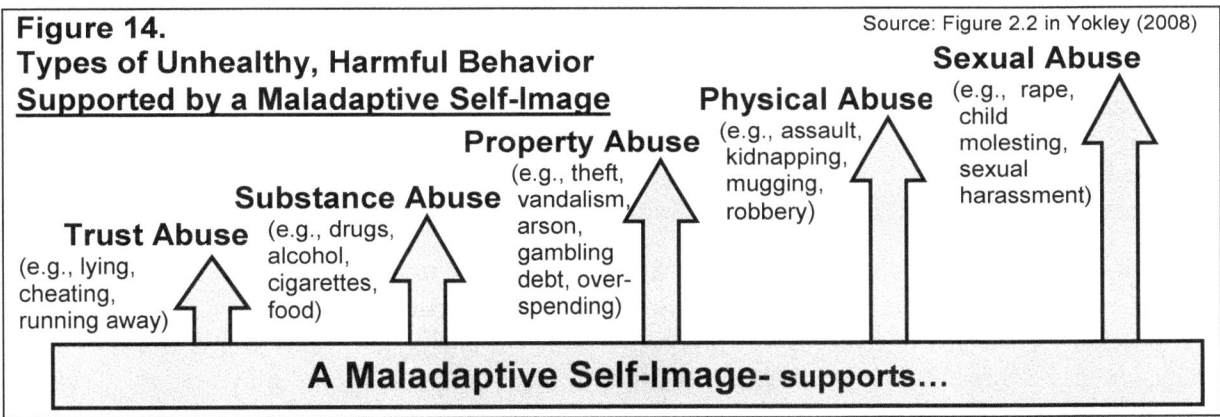

Figure 14.
Types of Unhealthy, Harmful Behavior Supported by a Maladaptive Self-Image

Source: Figure 2.2 in Yokley (2008)

Trust Abuse (e.g., lying, cheating, running away)

Substance Abuse (e.g., drugs, alcohol, cigarettes, food)

Property Abuse (e.g., theft, vandalism, arson, gambling debt, over-spending)

Physical Abuse (e.g., assault, kidnapping, mugging, robbery)

Sexual Abuse (e.g., rape, child molesting, sexual harassment)

A Maladaptive Self-Image- supports...

Some individuals with unhealthy, harmful behavior and unhealthy pride project a maladaptive good guy/girl image that involves deception to cover mistakes. These individuals often have relationship dependency and exaggerated needs for acceptance. They feel insecure and project a strong (but deceptive) good guy/girl image gets others to lean on them so they will feel either needed, strong or both. Others project a tough guy image with criminal pride that involves dishonesty to cover the unhealthy, harmful behavior of themselves and others. These individuals often have relationship control issues and exaggerated needs for excitement. In one case, the individual is afraid of tarnishing their image by looking less than perfect (i.e., unhealthy pride); in the other case, the individual is afraid of tarnishing their image by looking less than tough (i.e., criminal pride). Since they are afraid to self-disclose or disclose on others due to unhealthy pride or criminal pride they frequently misperceive confrontation with concern directed towards themselves or others as either character assignation or "snitching". Another maladaptive self-image involves a material focus on external attributes such as appearance, clothes, money as opposed to internal characteristics such as honesty, concern and responsibility, This is can be motivated by an exaggerated need for attention or acceptance.

A socially callous maladaptive self-image includes overcompensation for feeling inadequate through a preoccupation with getting respect. Many individuals with this maladaptive self-image confuse respect with fear as opposed to admiration and appreciation of positive attributes such as maturity or wisdom. They often seek external, artificial, short cut methods to get respect quickly (e.g., appearance, status, drugs, violence) without earning it through a relationship track record of honesty, trust, loyalty, concern and responsibility. Attempting to get respect through power and control fosters insecurity as it relies on other people's reactions which can't always be controlled. In addition to inducing feelings of insecurity, using power and control to get respect alienates themselves from others and further compounds their problems with genuine emotional attachment to others. The extreme end of self-images based on insecurity, power and short-cut methods to get respect quickly that build self up by putting others down can be race-based or gang affiliated. Using power tactics and successfully "winning through intimidation" reinforces that Control and Power Obsession. Using control tactics and successfully "winning through manipulation" reinforces Grandiosity. The socially callous like to fight, don't like to fail and have the insecure, over-controlling attitude that "I must win or I'm worthless". In order to win, they don't argue fairly. Fair arguments stay in the present. Unfair arguments drag out past issues which is a tactic to avoid losing the present argument by using the distraction of past issues to avoid defeat. Unfair arguments and harboring grudges are signs of social-emotional immaturity. These insecure, over-controlling characteristics make it difficult to develop real feelings of self-efficacy, genuine confidence and enduring relationships that come from self-awareness, self-discipline and steadfast loyalty to prosocial values (i.e., honesty, trust, loyalty, concern and responsibility). In summary, many individuals with a socially callous maladaptive self-image never learn that you get real respect by learning to control yourself, not others.

Insecurity can cause individuals with a maladaptive self-image to devalue the accomplishments of others and have distain, jealousy or envy, not admiration for those who have made significant achievements. "I shouldn't be afraid" and feeling shame for crying are often found. Being inconsistent and inconsiderate are considered rights. Honesty is considered unnecessary. Trust is replaced with the belief that if you don't use people to your advantage, they will use you or you might as well use a naive person because if you don't someone else will anyway. Since it's "every man for himself", loyalty doesn't apply. Shifting loyalties to whoever meets your needs best relates to a combination of: 1) the survival need to always keep back up relationships open and; 2) taking the path of least resistance and paying attention to only what suits you. These selfish manipulator characteristics overrule the need for consideration and concern for others.

Behavior Anatomy Question #6: How could your past experiences have affected your self-image and how you want others to view you?

Your self-image can be connected to your skills (i.e., how well you do what you do) or your social status (i.e., how popular or well-accepted you are in your social group). Your self-image can also be connected to your social-emotional maturity (i.e., how consistent you are in maintaining your honesty, trust, loyalty, concern, responsibility, self-awareness, self-efficacy and self-control). Among other things, self-image is comprised of various proportions of skills, social status, and social-emotional maturity. The three self-image categories focused on in Social Responsibility Therapy are summarized in Table 11.

Table 11.
Basic Self-Image Categories: Adaptive and Maladaptive Types

Skills-based Self-Image	

Adaptive Type
Professional skills-based image
Pride in a valued skill is first. Money earned is second.
    Pride in professional skills as a...
basketball player, business owner, carpenter, guitarist, plastic surgeon, psychotherapist, research scientist, student, teacher, etc.
(Professional pride)
	Maladaptive Type
	Material skills-based image
	Pride in a money earning skill is first. Type if skill developed is second. Developing a skill that gets money fast or easy is valued.
	    Pride in money earning skills as a...
	drug dealer, bank robber, burglar, car thief, shoplifter, card shark, con artist, pimp, prostitute, computer hacker, etc." (Criminal pride)

Social Status–based Self-Image	

Adaptive Type
Positive social-status based image
Pride in social status achievement by...
clergy members, entertainers, comedians, talk show hosts, philanthropists, industry leaders, law makers, heads of state who also use their positions to help others.
    Social status, popularity, looks, charm and charisma are used for positive purposes, e.g., English Royalty or American political figures use their head of state and leadership positions to promote a charity auction for abused children.
	Maladaptive Type
	Negative social-status based image
	Social status development is used for negative purposes. A deceptive good guy/girl image is used to cover harmful behavior. This self-image can be believed by the person with harmful behavior, e.g., wife beater views self as a good person because of his love of dogs and regular animal shelter volunteer work or teacher who is sexually active with students views herself as a good person because of the many students she has helped graduate.
	    Social status, popularity, looks, charm and charisma are used for negative purposes, e.g., a respected teacher or boy scout troop leader uses their youth leadership position to molest children.

Social Responsibility–based Self-Image	
Adaptive Type **Socially Mature Self-Image** Pride in social-emotional maturity by parents, foster parents, daughters/sons, aunts/uncles, family members, neighbors and human beings who strive to: develop dignity through honesty; earn trust through responsibility; be loyal to what is right and who is right; show concern for self and others; take responsibility to change mistakes; be aware of high risk situations for trouble; build self-efficacy by trying new solutions to old problems and; focus on controlling self not others.	**Maladaptive Type** **Socially Callous Self-Image** Tough guy image is reflection of pathological social-emotional immaturity by those who: view honesty as optional; see trust as a liability; are more loyal to negative peers than positive family; show concern only for self by taking without giving (womanizer or player); deny responsibility for mistakes; remain in high risk situations for trouble; use "winning by intimidation" to get what they want and; focus on controlling others not self. Thug mentality or "Jailhouse Image of a Man" [10]

Self images are not like "one size fits all" clothes so you may have to tailor them to fit you better. Circle any of the types of self images in Table 11 above that seems to fit you. Then use the space below to add any further information about your self-image (your view of who you are) to make that description fit better. If none fit, then underline all of the self-image information in this section, put your own self-image together out of those pieces and write it in the space below.

_____

_____

_____

_____

A. Review your Awareness and Honesty Exam (Appendix G), record your Maladaptive Self-Image ratings in the spaces provided below and add up all of your ratings to get a total.

Since your self-awareness may have improved from your use of the Situation Response Analysis log, you may need to update your ratings. Enter your ratings total in the space provided below.

Maladaptive Self-Image (10 items from Awareness and Honesty Exam, p. 207)

___ 3) Put more in a relationship than I got out	___ 92) Being afraid shows weakness
___ 7) Putting success before anything else	___102) Not "snitching" about a problem
___ 27) Put getting ahead over family/friends	___109) Inferior image, others are better
___ 47) Will do anything to succeed	___124) "No fear" image
___ 51) Looking good is most important	
___ 71) Being tough is necessary to get respect	Total = _____

Consult with your therapist or treatment program staff to determine if you are completing the basic form of this exercise or are completing the entire section.

End of basic form- Stop here and skip to part C, "Maladaptive Self-Image Structured Discovery Exercise" on page 97 at end of this section if you are completing the basic form. Otherwise, continue on with the section B questions below.

B. Rate the following Maladaptive Self-Image characteristics.
Use the numbered ratings on the scales provided below to rate the frequency of your past thoughts or behaviors on the statements listed in this section.

0	1	2	3	4
Never	Sometimes	Half of the time	Often	Almost Always

___ 1) Being rejected hits me very hard and I try hard to avoid it by seeking approval of others.

___ 2) Been afraid that others will discover that I am not what they expect of me and won't want me around anymore.

___ 3) Felt bad about myself, am not happy with myself or not satisfied with who I am.

___ 4) Imagined myself doing something that makes me a hero or famous.

___ 5) Done things to be accepted that I know were wrong just to fit in or win approval.

___ 6) Changed stories or said things to get accepted by the group of people that I was around.

___ 7) Needed to be involved in a relationship with someone.

0	1	2	3	4
Never	Sometimes	Half of the time	Often	Almost Always

____ 8) Felt socially anxious, insecure and lacked confidence around others.

____ 9) Didn't feel like I was worth much.

____ 10) Tried to be nice to people.

____ 11) Acted the way I think people want me to be or that seems to be popular.

____ 12) Tried not to cry and have stopped myself when I felt like it.

____ 13) Exaggerated stories to entertain others, get a laugh or hold the attention of the group.

____ 14) It was important to me to have a boy/girl friend to care about.

____ 15) It was more important to have money, nice things and nice clothes than anything else because people judge you by how you look or what you have.

____ 16) I have felt like I didn't fit in with others or any specific group.

____ 17) Tried hard to be accepted.

____ 18) It was important to me to have family to care for me.

____ 19) Being viewed as cool or tough was more important than trying to be honest, trustworthy, loyal, concerned or responsible.

____ 20) Judged myself based on others opinions of me as opposed to how well I am able to handle myself (i.e., deal with stress, criticism).

____ 21) Tried hard to please people, not make waves or stir up trouble.

____ 22) Having material things such as nice clothes was more important than personality or interests.

____ 23) Had strong needs for everyone to like me.

____ 24) It was very important to me to have a boy/girl friend to care for me.

____ 25) Told myself, "If you don't impress others they won't have anything to do with you".

____ 26) Thought that I won't ever be liked, cared about or amount to anything unless I do something that makes me important or a hero.

____ 27) Thought that there was no harm in hanging out with negative others, in fact it is more fun than being with regular people who are boring at times.

____ 28) Felt that what made me attractive/popular was my lack of respect for those who like me.

____ 29) Felt that what made me attractive or popular was my lack of respect for authority.

____ 30) Felt that I am going to be abandoned, rejected or left by others.

____ 31) Told myself that people view kindness as weakness so it's important to look tough.

____ 32) Felt that people view being humble or not acting big as a sign of being a loser or nerd.

0	1	2	3	4
Never	Sometimes	Half of the time	Often	Almost Always

____ 33) Had the attitude that that since I learn best from people that I like, there is no sense in listening to people I don't really like.

____ 34) Had the attitude that people who I like and seem to like me must always agree with me.

____ 35) Felt that people who talk about their problems are weak and looking for sympathy.

____ 36) Thought that bad feelings should be dealt with yourself, not shared with others.

____ 37) Thought that a success is someone who makes lots of money, has a nice car and lives in a nice place.

____ 38) Thought that a failure is someone who doesn't make much money or have nice things.

____ 39) Thought you can tell who has it together by looking at their clothes and what they have.

____ 40) Had the attitude that how others look at you is the most important thing, even more important than what kind of person you really are.

____ 41) Told myself that who you are is who people think you are and you're only worth as much as people think of you.

____ 42) In terms of the future, just think about general things like wanting to be rich, famous or happy and don't get into anything specific like steps I need to take.

____ 43) I have thought that appearance is the most important quality that you need to be liked and accepted.

____ 44) I have thought that a man should never cry.

____ 45) I have thought that since to most people, you are what you appear to be, it is much better to look good than to feel good.

____ 46) It has seemed to me that most people judge you by your appearance more than what you really can do or how you act.

____ 47) I have thought that a man should be able to handle every situation without asking others for help.

____ 48) I have thought that a man is tall, tough and takes no crap from anyone.

____ 49) I have thought that being "somebody" means being popular or liked by others.

____ 50) I have thought that being "somebody" means being successful or having money.

____ 51) I have thought that being "somebody" means being feared by others.

____ 52) I have thought that being "somebody" means being looked up to or respected by others.

____ 53) I have thought that people will only respect you if they fear you.

____ 54) I have thought that people who act like they care are just doing it to get something for themselves.

____ 55) I have thought that people who act kind or talk nice to you just do it because they are weak and afraid to stand up to you.

____ 56) Got caught up in fantasies about being respected as really cool, popular or tough.

Use the space below to list and rate any other Maladaptive Self-Image characteristics that have been a problem for you in the past which were not included on the statements provided above.

_____

_____

C. Maladaptive Self-Image Structured Discovery Exercise

Maladaptive Image of a Man/Woman

Think about who taught you about what was important in being a man or a woman. For example, if you are male did your father give you the impression that a man must always fight or that a man never cries? If so, then you were set up to be disappointed in yourself if you ever avoided a fight or cried. If you are female, did your mother give you the impression that you must always have someone around that you can count on? If so then you were set up to believe that you couldn't stand being alone or couldn't make it on your own.

Think about who brought you up. Were they consistent and considerate or were they unpredictable and inconsiderate. Would they discipline you one minute and want to play the next? Would they come home and take out their bad day on you? Did they seem to be angry, easily frustrated, selfish and inconsistent?

What parts of the description above apply to you? What maladaptive image of a man/woman have you learned or adopted? What irresponsible thinking is involved in the above maladaptive image? Where did you get your image beliefs about a man/woman?

_____

_____

_____

Hint: Review what you circled on Table 11 and wrote on p. 93

What is a man/woman? "There can be no courage without fear"[11]

A Social Responsibility-Based Self-Image is developed by facing fears as illustrated by Dr. Alro, a psychologist when he addressed a young man near the end of his unhealthy, harmful behavior treatment who was too afraid to attend his first day at a local community college. Dr. Alro asked the young man a question in the form of a story. It went like this… "If I get up in the morning scared to death when I look myself in the mirror but I shave and shower and go out there and do what I gotta do. And get up the next day scared to death when I look myself in the mirror but shave and shower and go out there and do what I gotta do. And so on each day... Am I a man?" The young man answered, "Yes you are". When Dr. Alro asked "Why?" he was told "because you're facing your fears". The young man accepted that "There can be no courage without fear", attended his classes each day, facing his fears which decreased over time and resulted ultimately in a Socially Mature image of a man and a college degree.

What is your definition of a real man or woman? What do you think a man/woman is (or should be) and what priorities should a real man or woman have, that is what should really be important to them in their life?

Definition- A real man/woman is...	Priorities for a real man/woman
_____	_____
_____	_____
_____	_____
_____	_____
_____	_____
_____	_____
_____	_____
_____	_____
_____	_____
_____	_____

On the following five numbered topics, if you are completing the basic form refer only to your ratings in part A, for the complete form refer to your question ratings in both part A and part B.

1. **Select your top ten Maladaptive Self-Image characteristics**.
   Review the statements that you rated in sections A and B and recorded above. Pick out the top ten (10) statements that described your particular Maladaptive Self-Image behavior the most (i.e., that you rated the highest in sections A and B) and circle the numbers of those statements. Examine the top ten Maladaptive Self-Image characteristics that you circled and number them in rank order with the #1 statement being the statement that most described your Maladaptive Self-Image style, #2 the second most and so on. Use the space provided below to list the top ten Maladaptive Self-Image characteristics that you circled. Place your #1 ranked statement in the space provided next to #1 and so on.

Top Ten Maladaptive Self-Image characteristics (complete first 5 for the basic form)

1) _____
2) _____
3) _____
4) _____
5) _____
6) _____
7) _____

8) _____

9) _____

10) _____

2. **Record at least your top three Maladaptive Self-Image characteristics** in rank order (highest rated statement first) in the space provided on your Harmful Behavior Anatomy worksheet (page 161). If you have a tie, circle the one that most applies to you and underline the other one. Put your ties (other highly ranked phrases that you underlined) on the back of your Harmful Behavior Anatomy Worksheet in the space provided. Although descriptive phrases (short versions of the questions you have answered) have been provided for you in part A, you will need to make up your own descriptive phrases for part B that will fit on your Harmful Behavior Anatomy worksheet. Don't limit yourself to the top three points if there are important parts that fit in this area. Make sure that you do not leave out any important information on this topic.

3. **Compute and enter your Maladaptive Self-Image score.**
   If you are completing the basic form of this exercise, use the Awareness and Honesty Exam questions that were summarized with descriptive phrases in part A of this section to compute your average rating score by dividing your rating total by the 10 questions you rated. After you have recorded your average rating score in the space provided below and on your Harmful Behavior Anatomy Worksheet at the end of this section, you can move on to the next section.

Total part A ratings on Awareness and Honesty Exam (_____) divided by 10 = _____.

If you are completing the entire exercise, add up all of your part B question ratings. An easy way to do that is to fill in the chart below.

How many questions did you rate as 4? _____	Multiply that by 4 and enter the answer here _____
How many questions did you rate as 3? _____	Multiply that by 3 and enter the answer here _____
How many questions did you rate as 2? _____	Multiply that by 2 and enter the answer here _____
How many questions did you rate as 1? _____	Multiply that by 1 and enter the answer here _____
How many questions did you rate as 0? _____	Add this column, Total part B = _____
(Total should be 56) Total = _____	

Compute your average rating score by adding up your part A and part B total scores, then dividing the total by all 66 questions that you rated. Record your average rating score in the space provided below and on your Harmful Behavior Anatomy worksheet (page 161).

Total part A (_____) + Total part B = _____ divided by 66 = _____.

4. **Write what you have discovered about yourself through this structured exercise**
    Use the space provided below to document how your Maladaptive Self-Image characteristics affected your social-emotional maturity. Use the workspace on page 227 if needed.

Social maturity (honesty, trust, loyalty, concern and responsibility)

_____

_____

_____

_____

Emotional maturity (self-awareness, self-efficacy/confidence, self-control)

_____

_____

_____

_____

> **Hint:** If you're having trouble with this, just take the top Maladaptive Self-Image characteristics that you listed on page 98 and ask yourself questions comparing each Maladaptive Self-Image characteristic to each component of social maturity looking for a connection. For example, "How did my Maladaptive Self-Image affect my (honesty, trust, loyalty, concern, responsibility)?" Do the same with each component of emotional maturity. For example, "How did my Maladaptive Self-Image affect my (self-awareness, self-efficacy, self-control)?"

5. Use the space below to **list the best personal example you can recall** of how your Maladaptive Self-Image characteristics caused a major problem or crisis in your life. Note: An honesty accomplishment award is generally administered for the best example in treatment groups. Continue on page 227 workspace if needed.

_____

_____

_____

Awareness training: In order to develop a positive self-image, you first need to become aware of the maladaptive self-image that you were projecting around others and some of your reasons (e.g., to be desired, admired, respected, trusted, accepted, etc.). Some people get caught up in all or nothing thinking with their self image, and think "You're either a hero or a zero", "You're a champ or chump". Since very few people are number one in any area of interest, when they fall short, they fall into a maladaptive self-image, e.g., "If I can't be the best of the best, I'll be the best of the worst". Review all of the Maladaptive Self-Image deception information in this section, underline any part that has applied to you in the past and use the space below to give a specific example of what you consider to be the maladaptive self image that you projected to others. Then see if you can draw a connection between your self-image, why you used it and your unhealthy, harmful behavior.

_____

_____

_____

_____

Responsibility training: While becoming aware of your maladaptive self-image an important first step, "image isn't everything" and we need to start to re-evaluate how we want to be viewed by others beginning with our choices in friends. Check off the image choices you have made in the past from the list below.

__Honesty	OR	__Money/Job (gets you financial security)
__Trustworthy	OR	__Popular (gets you attention)
__Loyalty	OR	__Looks (or cool image)
__Concern	OR	__Companionship (anybody who accepts me to avoid being alone)
__Responsibility	OR	__Excitement (someone who is fun)

Use the space below to write how your image choices have created problems for you in the past.

_____

_____

_____

Hint: "You are only limited by your creativity" when dealing with life problems. See Exhibit 3 (p. 177) for an idea that may help you with Maladaptive Self-image issues.

Tolerance training: We don't live on a desert island and regardless of what people say humans are herding animals like cows. How else can you explain all of the money spent on fashion if we don't want to fit in. this is a particular problem in the area of unhealthy, harmful behavior because the people doing it want to get us involved and we want to fit in. Put another way, our herding instinct puts us at risk for compromising ourselves to be accepted. In the area of social pressure it is important to weigh your decision on whether to go along to get along on the reality scales (p.25). Pick the last time you went along with something that you shouldn't have, then weigh out the need to do that next time on the reality scales below.

I went along with _____ even though I shouldn't have.

How important to my survival was it for me to go along and do what I did?

Survival scale rating (0 = not important; 10= could kill me if I didn't): _____

How important for my success was it for me to go along and do what I did?

Success scale rating (0 = not important; 10= would stop me from ever succeeding): _____

How severe would the consequences be if I didn't go along and do what I did?

Severity scale rating (0 = not severe at all; 10= extremely severe): _____

In reviewing your reality scale scores above, if you had to make the same
decision today, do you still think you need to go along and do it again? ___Yes; ___No

Answer the question, "What would be the opposite extreme of the maladaptive self-image
problem that you listed in awareness training above as needing the most improvement?" Use the
space below to describe the opposite healthy, responsible self-image that you need to project,
"Act as if" (p. 12) you already have and practice regularly.

Maladaptive Self-Image	Opposite Healthy, Helpful Behavior

D. Make a Positive Plan and Commitment to Change

Review the three Maladaptive Self-Image problems that you listed on your Harmful Behavior
Anatomy worksheet (page 161). What can you do about it now? How are you going to
change these, what are you going to do? (Consult with your therapist or staff and write your
plan below)

1) _____

2) _____

3) _____

Explain why **the image you project isn't who you are** and why social maturity is more
important than your image. Continue on page 227 workspace if needed. Then give a talk to your
therapist or group that will convince them that your image (e.g., popular, cool, good guy/girl
image or tough guy) is not who you are and your social maturity (i.e., level of honesty, trust
loyalty, concern and responsibility) is what people value in you. Log your talk date → _____

_____

_____

_____

Hint: What eventually happens to people whose self-image (and image they try to present to others) is
better than their social maturity?

Get honest about your Maladaptive Self-Image with your therapist or treatment group.
Log the date you discussed this issue and who you discussed it with in the space provided below.

Date: _____ Discussed with: _____

"When you aim for perfection, you discover it's a moving target" -- Geoffrey F. Fisher (1887-1972)

Name: _____   **Date:** _____

Definition: Perfectionism can act as another strong arm that support multiple forms of unhealthy, harmful behavior. Perfectionism can be categorized as healthy/positive or unhealthy/negative. Individuals with unhealthy perfectionism typically have unrealistic expectations for self and others based on irrational beliefs and all or nothing thinking about recovery (i.e., recovery perfectionism) that sets the occasion for relapse. These Unhealthy Perfectionism problems set the occasion for multiple forms of unhealthy, harmful behavior and can allow it to spread from one type to another (Figure 15).

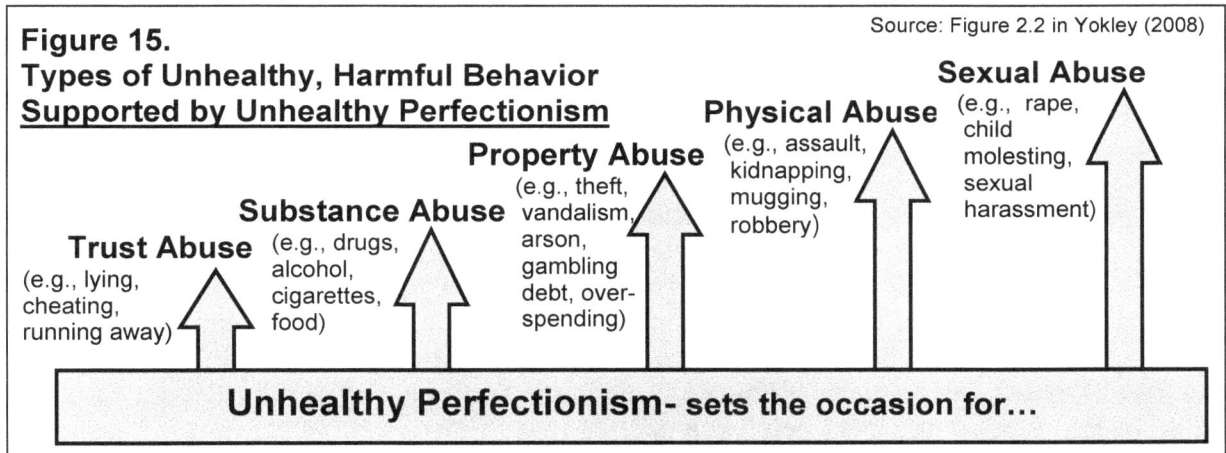

Figure 15.
Types of Unhealthy, Harmful Behavior Supported by Unhealthy Perfectionism

Source: Figure 2.2 in Yokley (2008)

Sexual Abuse (e.g., rape, child molesting, sexual harassment)

Physical Abuse (e.g., assault, kidnapping, mugging, robbery)

Property Abuse (e.g., theft, vandalism, arson, gambling debt, over-spending)

Substance Abuse (e.g., drugs, alcohol, cigarettes, food)

Trust Abuse (e.g., lying, cheating, running away)

Unhealthy Perfectionism- sets the occasion for...

Types of Unhealthy Perfectionism

In addition to the positive, healthy perfectionism that we want in our surgeons and air traffic controllers, perfectionism has several unhealthy, negative types that can contribute to unhealthy, harmful behavior. For example, self-oriented perfectionism can result in trying to compensate for feelings of inadequacy through career overachievement to the extent of family and child neglect. Other-oriented perfectionism has been associated with arrogant, dominant, and vindictive (i.e., control and power obsession) characteristics for both men and women that sets the occasion for interpersonal conflict and domestic violence. Socially prescribed perfectionism involving the belief that one must live up to exaggerated expectations that are assumed to be held by significant others can result in "excel at any cost" blind ambition including violating the rights of others to get ahead along with a "conceal at any cost" motive to protect the perfect public image.

Whether applied to self, others or socially, Unhealthy Perfectionism often involves all or nothing thinking along with overly high standards and unrealistic expectations for self and others, e.g., "You're either a hero or a zero". Since standards are set too high, individuals often don't measure up which creates disappointment along with feelings of inadequacy (not being good enough). Unrealistic expectations support impatience along with low frustration tolerance and acts to set the occasion for building self up by putting others down. Unhealthy Perfectionism can involve unhealthy criticism of self and others (name calling) along with and unhealthy competition by comparing self to others and focusing on faults. There is nothing wrong with trying your best and coming in second but with unhealthy perfectionists "second place is the first loser". Things must be done "perfectly" (which often means "my way") or they may get upset and quit.

Recovery Perfectionism

Recovery perfectionism is a serious threat to recovery from unhealthy, harmful behavior. Recovery perfectionism results in falling back into the Stress-Relapse Cycle after a single behavior slip (see Yokley, 2011a). When Recovery Perfectionism results in drug/alcohol relapse, it has been referred to as "the abstinence violation effect". With some unhealthy, harmful behaviors, abstinence must be replaced by goals (e.g., weight loss programs where you can't be abstinent from food). Thus when Recovery Perfectionism results in diet relapse, it has been referred to as "the goal violation effect". When Recovery Perfectionism results in breaking home, probation, parole or treatment rules, it is referred to as "the rule violation effect". The key concept underlying all of these behavior violation effects is "The Slip, Give Up Trigger"

"The Slip Give Up Trigger"

"The Slip Give Up Trigger" is the Recovery Perfectionism chain of events that results in giving up on your abstinence, goals or rules. In "the Slip Give Up Trigger", Recovery Perfectionism thinking (i.e., "all or nothing" extremism, perfectionist thinking) sets you up to give up on self-control after a slip (i.e., a single or minor mistake). This basically involves telling yourself that since you already slipped, your perfect track record is blown so you might as well just continue or do what you want. In this chain of events, the slip or mistake creates self-disappointment and/or conflict with others. Self-disappointment is followed by a self-defeating "I can't" belief which results in justifying actions of doing (or continuing) unhealthy, harmful behavior based on feelings of self-disappointment or helplessness.

In summary, taking a recovery Fall (i.e., relapse) through "the Slip Give Up Trigger" involves the following basic steps. "Since I slipped and broke my [promise, sobriety, rule, goal or parole], I completely blew it and can't turn things around so I might as well just give up [on self-control] and do what I want [or keep going]. Besides, if I stop now, there will still be consequences." [having to tell my AA sponsor/group, apologize, start my goal over, get grounded at home, start treatment over, have a probation/parole violation hearing]. In short, "I blew it so screw it, I give up" (i.e., on self-control and recovery from unhealthy, harmful behavior). Table 12 provides examples of how recovery perfectionism results in relapse through "the Slip Give Up Trigger" across multiple forms of harmful behavior.

One type of Unhealthy, Harmful Behavior can Trigger Another

The same "all or nothing" Recovery Perfectionism thinking that results in the "Slip Give Up Trigger" within each unhealthy, harmful behavior treatment plan when trying to maintain abstinence, goals or rules, i.e., "Since I already slipped and blew my [sexual, physical, property, substance or trust abuse] treatment plan, I might as well just give up and keep going" (Table 12) can occur between unhealthy, harmful behaviors.

104

For example...

- "Since I've already overcharged my credit card (trust abuse), I might as well go out drinking on it (triggers substance abuse). Besides, if I stop now I'm still not going to be able to pay and will get a late charge anyway."
- "Since I already got high and flirted with a friend (substance abuse), I might as well cheat on my partner. Besides, if I stop now it will look like I did anyway (triggers trust abuse)."
- "Since I already stole from them (property abuse), I might as well use the money to get high (triggers harmful behavior)."
- "Since I already fondled them (sexual abuse), I might as well threaten beat and them (triggers physical abuse) to see if I can keep them from telling."

Table 12.
Recovery Perfectionism "Slip Give Up Trigger" Examples

Example	Since I already slipped and...	I blew it so I might as well just...	Besides, if I stop now, I will...
Trust Abuse	gave them my number	cheat [**give up** on couples therapy]	not be able to get it off my mind
Substance Abuse (including cigarettes, food)	had one: sip, hit, snort, shot, line, smoke, drag, bite, etc.	keep going [**give up** on AA, NA, CA, OA, smoke-enders, etc.]	still have to start my recovery program over
Property Abuse	put it in my pocket	leave the store with it [**give up** on probation]	get caught putting it back
Physical Abuse	threatened them	beat their ass [**give up** on anger management]	have to take their crap
Sexual Abuse	was seen alone with a child	get sex [**give up** on SO treatment]	still get a parole violation

Behavior Anatomy Question #7: How has high standards, high expectations and needing things to be perfect caused problems in your life?

Review all of the Unhealthy Perfectionism information above, underline any part that has applied to you in the past and use the space below to give a specific example of what you consider your most serious or most frequent problem with unhealthy perfectionism.

_____

_____

_____

_____

_____

_____

_____

_____

Most individuals with unhealthy, harmful behaviors have some Unhealthy Perfectionism characteristics but different individuals may have different symptoms of that condition. Please complete the following steps below which were designed to help you become more aware of your Unhealthy Perfectionism characteristics.

A. Review your Awareness and Honesty Exam (Appendix G), record your Unhealthy Perfectionism ratings in the spaces provided below & add up all of your ratings to get a total.

Since your self-awareness may have improved from your use of the Situation Response Analysis log, you may need to update your ratings. Enter your ratings total in the space provided below.

Unhealthy Perfectionism (6 items from Awareness and Honesty Exam, p. 207)

___ 38) Performance perfectionism ___ 58) If it can't be done just right, why do it ___ 59) Recovery perfectionism ___ 78) I must be the best	___ 93) Putting things off until the last minute ___119) Impatient with others Total = _____

Consult with your therapist or treatment program staff to determine if you are completing the basic form of this exercise or are completing the entire section.

<u>End of basic form</u>- **Stop here and skip to part C, "Unhealthy Perfectionism Structured Discovery Exercise" on page 109 if you are completing the basic form. Otherwise, continue on with the section B questions below.**

B. Rate the following Unhealthy Perfectionism characteristics.
Use the numbered ratings on the scales provided below to rate the frequency of your past thoughts or behaviors on the statements listed in this section.

0 Never	1 Sometimes	2 Half of the time	3 Often	4 Almost Always

___ 1) Have put things off because it wasn't the right time and more planning was needed.

___ 2) Called people names in my head or under my breath when they acted stupid or frustrated me.

___ 3) Called people names in front of others when they acted stupidly or frustrated me.

___ 4) Would find fault with or "punch holes" in people's plans or suggestions.

___ 5) Have been a competitive person and tried hard to win against others.

___ 6) Have put others down to build myself up.

___ 7) Have had problems listening to criticism without interrupting and saying something back.

___ 8) Found myself pushing myself too hard to get something right.

0	1	2	3	4
Never	Sometimes	Half of the time	Often	Almost Always

___ 9) It was so important how others looked at me that I got tense when around others.

___ 10) Have been dissatisfied that things didn't work out better in my life.

___ 11) Unless I had the chance to make it big right away, I was not likely to try at all.

___ 12) Been easily critical of others and would find myself pointing out their problems.

___ 13) Got upset, frustrated and angry with myself when things didn't go the way they should.

___ 14) Waited to do things, telling myself that I must get something accomplished first before doing something else that was more important.

___ 15) Made other things a priority over getting help or doing treatment related things.

___ 16) Could easily see where a plan would fall apart or why a suggestion wouldn't work or seemed to need assurance of success before trying something new.

___ 17) Have had very strong needs to achieve important things or get ahead in life.

___ 18) Have found other people frustrating to work with because they don't try hard enough and don't do things right the first time.

___ 19) Would go over mistakes a lot in my mind and call myself names or feel like a failure.

___ 20) Have set very high goals, had a "Go for the Gold" attitude and would get disappointed when things don't work out, telling myself I should have been able to make it.

___ 21) Taking risks by trying new things has gotten me tense and nervous.

___ 22) Have tried to be perfect so I wouldn't have to worry about others criticizing me.

___ 23) Have not felt very good about myself and tried to look good to others or appear perfect to feel better.

___ 24) Got upset, frustrated and angry with others when things weren't done right.

___ 25) Didn't try things because I was afraid of how others would look at me if I failed or didn't do well.

___ 26) Tried to do things perfectly and liked it when people commented on how good I was able to do certain things.

___ 27) Have thought that other people should try harder and then I wouldn't have to point out their stupidity.

___ 28) Believed that I must be the best or I'm not worthwhile.

___ 29) Felt like "If you want something done right you have to do it yourself" and wasted time doing things that others could have done.

___ 30) Felt like "there is no room for making mistakes in life".

___ 31) Have worried about "What if I make a mistake?"

___ 32) Felt like, "I must be approved of by everyone".

___ 33) Felt like, "You're either a hero or a zero" & when I don't do perfect, I feel like a failure.

0	1	2	3	4
Never	**Sometimes**	**Half of the time**	**Often**	**Almost Always**

____ 34) I have thought that others should be on time to things and feel like I must be on time.

____ 35) Put things off that I needed to do by telling myself, "I won't have enough time to finish it if I start now", "I can do it later" or that I need to do something else which was more important first.

____ 36) Felt everyone should give 110% at anything they do and get annoyed at those who do just enough to get by.

____ 37) Felt that poor performance or so called "mistakes" by others is more likely on purpose.

____ 38) Had "All or nothing thinking" about success and felt a lot of pressure to succeed so I don't feel like a loser.

____ 39) Compared myself to others and felt that I'm not good enough.

____ 40) Thought that since I try to do my best to please others, they should try to do some things for me in return without being asked.

____ 41) Thinking, "I must do perfectly or why try at all" has caused me to put off trying things.

____ 42) Told myself that I must do things just right as well as have others do them just right.

____ 43) Felt that the only thing that matters is winning and "I tried my best" isn't good enough.

____ 44) Felt like I should always be able to do my best.

____ 45) Felt like I must be perfect to be accepted by others.

____ 46) Judged myself harshly and found myself saying things like "you idiot" to myself when I made a mistake.

____ 47) Felt like there is no room for mistakes in life.

____ 48) Thought people are either all good or all bad, nice or nasty, decent or crooked.

____ 49) Been disappointed at others performance who have been on my team or workforce.

____ 50) Told myself, "I can't get too involved in this relationship, what if I find someone better?" (Relationship perfectionism got in the way of commitment).

____ 51) Got caught up in fantasies about recognition for effort, competition or being #1.

Use the space provided below to list and rate any other perfectionism characteristics that have been a problem for you in the past which were not included on the statements provided above. Discuss your perfectionism issues with your treatment group and/or therapist. Include their feedback.

_____

_____

_____

_____

C. Unhealthy Perfectionism Structured Discovery Exercise

On the following five numbered topics, if you are completing the basic form refer only to what you underlined and wrote about your most serious or most frequent Unhealthy Perfectionism problems on p. 105 along with your ratings in part A. For the complete form, include your question ratings in part B above.

1. **Select your top ten Unhealthy Perfectionism characteristics**.
   Review the statements that you rated in sections A and B. Pick out the top ten (10) statements that described your particular Unhealthy Perfectionism behavior the most (i.e., that you rated the highest in sections A and B) and circle the numbers of those statements. Examine the top ten Unhealthy Perfectionisms that you circled and number them in rank order with the #1 statement being the statement that most described your Unhealthy Perfectionism style, #2 the second most and so on.

   Use the space provided below to list the top ten Perfectionism Problems that you circled. Place your #1 ranked statement in the space provided next to #1 and so on.

Top Ten Unhealthy Perfectionism characteristics (complete first 5 for the basic form)

1) _____

2) _____

3) _____

4) _____

5) _____

6) _____

7) _____

8) _____

9) _____

10) _____

2. **Record at least your top three Unhealthy Perfectionism characteristics** in rank order (highest rated statement first) in the space provided on your Harmful Behavior Anatomy worksheet (page 161). If you have a tie, circle the one that most applies to you and underline the other one. Put your ties (other highly ranked phrases that you underlined) on the back of your Harmful Behavior Anatomy Worksheet in the space provided. Although descriptive phrases (short versions of the questions you have answered) have been provided for you in part A, you will need to make up your own descriptive phrases for part B that will fit on your Harmful Behavior Anatomy worksheet. Don't limit yourself to the top three points if there are important parts that fit in this area. Make sure that you do not leave out any important information on this topic.

3. **Compute and enter your Unhealthy Perfectionism score.**
   If you are completing the basic form of this exercise, use the Awareness and Honesty Exam questions that were summarized with descriptive phrases in part A of this section to compute your average rating score by dividing your rating total by the 6 questions you rated.

   After you have recorded your average rating score in the space provided below and on your Harmful Behavior Anatomy Worksheet at the end of this section, you can move on to the next section.

Total part A ratings on Awareness and Honesty Exam (_____) divided by 6 = _____.

If you are completing the entire exercise, add up all of your part B question ratings. An easy way to do that is to fill in the chart below.

How many questions did you rate as 4? _____ Multiply that by 4 and enter the answer here _____

How many questions did you rate as 3? _____ Multiply that by 3 and enter the answer here _____

How many questions did you rate as 2? _____ Multiply that by 2 and enter the answer here _____

How many questions did you rate as 1? _____ Multiply that by 1 and enter the answer here _____

How many questions did you rate as 0? _____   Add this column, Total part B = _____

(Total should be 51) Total = _____

Compute your average rating score by adding up your part A and part B total scores, then dividing the total by all 57 questions that you rated. Record your average rating score in the space provided below and on your Harmful Behavior Anatomy worksheet (page 161).

Total part A (_____) + Total part B = _____ divided by 57 = _____.

4. **Write what you have discovered about yourself through this structured exercise**
   Use the space provided below to document how your Unhealthy Perfectionism affected your social-emotional maturity. Use the workspace on page 227 if needed.

Social maturity (honesty, trust, loyalty, concern and responsibility)

_____

_____

_____

_____

_____

_____

Emotional maturity (self-awareness, self-efficacy/confidence, self-control)

_____

_____

_____

> **Hint:** If you're having trouble with this, just take the top Unhealthy Perfectionism characteristics that you listed on page 109 and ask yourself questions comparing each Unhealthy Perfectionism characteristic to each component of social maturity looking for a connection. For example, "How did my Unhealthy Perfectionism affect my (honesty, trust, loyalty, concern, responsibility)?" Do the same with each component of emotional maturity. For example, "How did my Unhealthy Perfectionism affect my (self-awareness, self-efficacy, self-control)?"

5. **List the best personal example you can recall** of how your Unhealthy Perfectionism caused a major problem in your life. Use the workspace on page 227 if needed. Note: An honesty accomplishment award is generally administered for the best example in treatment groups.

_____

_____

_____

_____

_____

_____

Awareness training: In addition to becoming aware of the types of unhealthy perfectionism, it is important to become aware of the unhealthy perfectionism self-statements that can set the occasion for unhealthy, harmful behavior. Review the types of unhealthy perfectionism described earlier (p. 103), then complete the sentences below to become aware of how using "should" or "must" can move unhealthy perfectionism into unhealthy, harmful behavior.

Self-oriented perfectionism: Telling yourself, "I must... _____ "

Can result in... _____

Other-oriented perfectionism: Telling yourself, "They shouldn't have... _____

_____

Can result in... _____

Socially prescribed perfectionism: Telling yourself, "I have to (live up to/be like)... _____

_____ "

Can result in... _____

<u>Recovery perfectionism</u>: Telling yourself, "Since l already blew my perfect track record today and have to start over tomorrow." Can result in... _____

_____

Responsibility training: While becoming aware of the perfectionist self-statements that set the occasion for unhealthy, harmful behavior is important, in order to prevent relapse, you have to take responsibility to challenge those self-statements and interrupt the Slip-Give Up Trigger. Review Table 12 above. Then write your own example of how you fell into the Slip Give Up Trigger in the space provided below.

My Slip Give Up Trigger Example

Example List the type of relapse that you have had below	**Since I already slipped and…**	**I blew it so I might as well just…**	**Besides, if I stop now, I will…**
My relapse was on...	Write what you did...	Write what you said to yourself...	Write what you said to yourself...
Use the numbered statements below to help you pick the number of the best thing you could say to yourself to interrupt each stage ➡	I could use number...	I could use number...	I could use number...

Ten things I can say to myself that will help me interrupt my slip give up trigger and avoid relapse are...
1. Where is the evidence that I blew it and might as well give up? Giving up is really the only way that I will blow it.
2. The only thing worse than slipping is using it as an excuse to give up on self-control so you can just do what you want.
3. The worst thing that will happen if I stop now is that things won't get any worse.
4. A slip only becomes a fall if you refuse to correct it. I need to turn this around right now.
5. You don't have to be perfect to succeed, you just have to be honest with yourself and others.

6. Time to get real. If I stop now I don't get do what I want, I also don't get the consequences for doing what I want.
7. I need to go to the opposite extreme and do something completely opposite of my slip to prevent taking a fall.
8. Recovery is two steps up, one back, two up, one back until you get there. Since I just slipped back a step, I need to take two steps up.
9. I need to get honest with myself. what stopping now really means is stopping my baby excuses about quitting and starting to do something about it.
10. Would I rather have an imperfect day that I cleaned up after blowing my perfect track record or would I rather have a completely shot day where I kept on doing the wrong thing?

"You are only limited by your creativity" when dealing with life problems. See Exhibit 3 (p. 177) for ideas that may help you with Unhealthy Perfectionism issues and write anything else you can think of to block the slip give up trigger in the space provided below.

_____

_____

_____

_____

Tolerance training: Unhealthy perfectionism involves the self-defeating habit of rumination (i.e. going over and over something in your mind) on shortcomings and mistakes. Learning to tolerate not being perfect involves learning to let go of rumination about self and others not being perfect. A good first step is to weigh out the consequences of just letting it go with the Reality Scales (p. 24). Write the last unhealthy, harmful behavior slip you made below. Remember, slip is a lapse in self-control when you get started or move towards trouble, while a fall is a relapse back into trouble. With behavior that isn't harmful to others, a slip would be entering a high risk situation for unhealthy, harmful behavior while a fall would be continuing after you started.

I slipped by _____

_____

How important is it for me to go over and over this slip in order to survive?

Survival scale rating (0 = not important; 10= could kill me if I didn't): _____

How important is it for me to go over and over this slip in order to succeed in life?

Success scale rating (0 = not important; 10= would stop me from ever succeeding): _____

How severe will the consequences be if I continue to keep this slip a secret going over and over it and getting more and more upset?

Severity scale rating for ruminating (0 = not severe at all; 10= extremely severe): _____

How severe will the consequences be if I decide to stop ruminating about it, hold myself accountable for my slip, get honest about it and change it before it becomes a fall?

Severity scale rating for not ruminating (0 = not severe at all; 10= extremely severe): _____

In reviewing your reality scale scores above, if you had to make the same
decision today, do you still think you need to go along and do it again? ____Yes; ____No

Answer the question, "What would be the opposite extreme of the most serious or most frequent
problem with unhealthy perfectionism that you listed in this section. Use the space below to
describe the opposite healthy, responsible behavior that you need to "Act as if" (p. 12) you
already have and practice regularly.

Unhealthy Perfectionism   Opposite Healthy, Helpful Behavior

_____   _____

_____   _____

_____   _____

D. Make a Positive Plan and Commitment to Change

Review the three Perfectionism problems that you listed on your Harmful Behavior Anatomy
worksheet (page 161). What can you do about it now? How are you going to change these
problems, what are you going to do? (Consult with your therapist or staff and write your plan
below)

1) _____

2) _____

3) _____

Use the space below to explain why **your performance isn't who you are** and why social
maturity is more important than your task performance. Then give a talk to your therapist or
group that will convince them that your task performance (e.g., highest grades in school, #1 sales
record at work) is not who you are but your social maturity (i.e., level of honesty, trust loyalty,
concern and responsibility) is who you are. Log the date of your talk here → _____

_____

_____

_____

_____

Hint: What eventually happens to people whose task performance is better than their social maturity?

Get honest about your Unhealthy Perfectionism with your therapist or treatment group.
Log the date you discussed this issue and who you discussed it with in the space provided below.

Date: _____   Discussed with: _____

The Harmful Behavior Anatomy Component 8: Grandiosity

The worst disease which can afflict executives in their work is not, as popularly supposed, alcoholism; it's egotism-- Robert Frost (1874- 1963)

Name: _____   Date: _____

Definition: Grandiosity lends another hand in the commission of unhealthy, harmful behavior. Grandiosity comes in both adaptive and maladaptive forms. Adaptive grandiosity provides artists with the enormous belief in their own capacity and ability to stick to it that is needed to master their area and create great works. It is what is needed by battlefield soldiers or children from dysfunctional families to succeed against all odds. Adaptive grandiosity may be reflected in hero fantasies to fight off feelings of helplessness along with a "can do" or "I'll show you" attitude needed to overcome doubt or feelings of inadequacy and go on to succeed despite real disadvantages. Since maladaptive grandiosity is most common, it is just labeled "grandiosity". Grandiosity has been referred to as egotism (i.e., inflated self-esteem), meglomania (i.e., over-estimation of their power), super-optimism and is a central component of two of the three types of narcissism (i.e., the malignant type where grandiosity includes a thirst for power and the reactive type where grandiosity is a defense against feelings of inadequacy or inferiority). Like adaptive grandiosity, the third type of narcissism is seen in high functioning individuals characterized as self-important, articulate, energetic, and outgoing. The point here is that we need to use adaptive grandiosity to help us take on and stick to difficult tasks or get through tough situations without giving up while keeping a watchful eye on regular grandiosity so that it doesn't get us in trouble.

Common threads in conditions that share grandiosity symptoms are over-confidence and unrealistic optimism. Grandiose over-confidence allows entering or staying in high risk situations through an "I can handle it" attitude. Grandiose optimism results in telling self that the behavior won't hurt you despite known problems with others, that you won't get caught or that if the behavior is noticed there won't be consequences. These grandiosity symptoms set the occasion for relapse in multiple forms of unhealthy, harmful behavior (Figure 16).

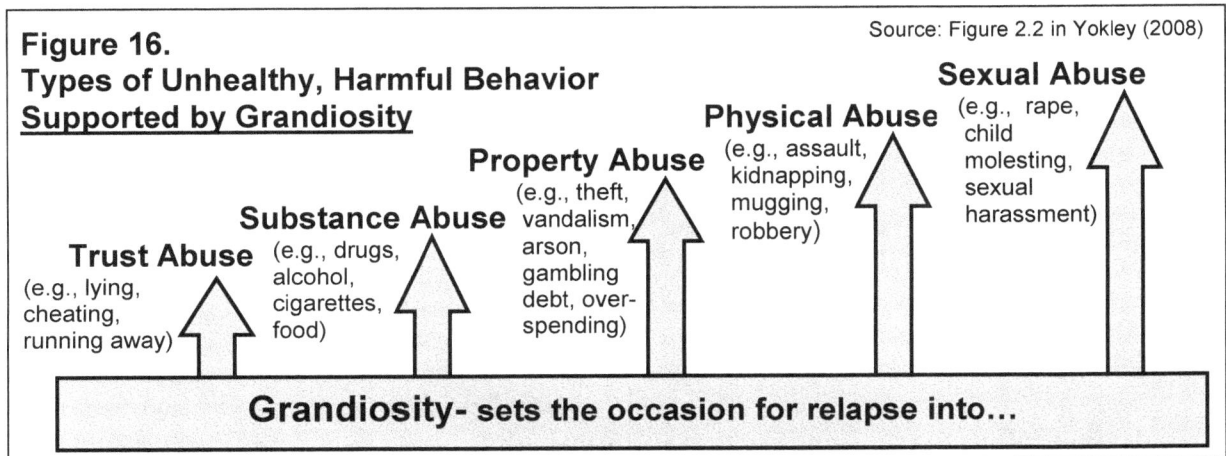

Figure 16.
Types of Unhealthy, Harmful Behavior Supported by Grandiosity

Source: Figure 2.2 in Yokley (2008)

Sexual Abuse (e.g., rape, child molesting, sexual harassment)

Physical Abuse (e.g., assault, kidnapping, mugging, robbery)

Property Abuse (e.g., theft, vandalism, arson, gambling debt, over-spending)

Substance Abuse (e.g., drugs, alcohol, cigarettes, food)

Trust Abuse (e.g., lying, cheating, running away)

Grandiosity- sets the occasion for relapse into...

"If you fail to plan, you plan to fail"- Grandiose over-confidence can result in a lapse of judgment from not checking situations out and making plans to deal with them as a result of "No problem, I got this" assumptions. This over-confidence can also interfere with relapse prevention, e.g., "I don't have to avoid trouble because I can always talk my way out of it". Grandiose optimism involves under-estimating the probability of detection or the consequences of failing to get honest (often in combination with the self-defeating habit of over-estimating the consequences of getting honest). Grandiose feelings about ability can lead to feeling unique and different from others. Uniqueness prevents identification with others which blocks developing a recovery support system. Uniqueness also allows discounting of treatment advice "which is for others that are not like me".

Behavior Anatomy Question #8: How has your strong confidence and "I can handle it" attitude gotten you in trouble or put you at risk for relapse?

Different individuals with different unhealthy, harmful behaviors may have different Grandiosity symptoms. Review all of the Grandiosity information above, underline any part that has applied to you in the past and use the space below to give a specific example of what you consider your most serious or most frequent problem with Grandiosity.

_____

_____

_____

_____

Please complete the following steps below which were designed to help you clarify and become more aware of the Grandiosity characteristics that you have developed over the years.

A. Review your Awareness and Honesty Exam (Appendix G), record your Grandiosity Problem ratings in the spaces provided below and add up all of your ratings to get a total.

Since your self-awareness may have improved from your use of the Situation Response Analysis log, you may need to update your ratings. Enter your ratings total in the space provided below.

Grandiosity Problems (16 items from Awareness and Honesty Exam, p. 207)

___ 10) Felt I could do anything if not held back	___ 113) Angry at criticism & criticized back
___ 19) Jumped to conclusions based on the situation	___ 114) No since trying for something that will take too long
___ 30) Annoyed by directions from inferiors	___ 115) Felt more attention and concern was due
___ 39) So confident that didn't need to verify	___ 125) Felt more cooperation was due
___ 50) People have been jealous of me	___ 126) Viewed self as mature for age
___ 70) Able to talk self out of problems	___ 132) Viewed disagreements as dishonesty
___ 89) Selective listening to what you want to hear	___ 138) All or nothing employment attitude
___ 91) 100% confident in handling problems	___ 147) Treatment resistance by uniqueness
	Total = _____

Consult with your therapist or treatment program staff to determine if you are completing the basic form of this exercise or are completing the entire section.

End of basic form- Stop here and skip to part C, "Grandiosity Problem Structured Discovery Exercise" on page 120 if you are completing the basic form. Otherwise, continue on with the section B questions below.

B. Rate the following Grandiosity Problem characteristics.

Use the numbered ratings on the scales provided below to rate the frequency of your past thoughts or behaviors on the statements listed in this section.

0 Never	1 Sometimes	2 Half of the time	3 Often	4 Almost Always

___ 1) Been confident that I look good to others.

___ 2) Been told that I think the world revolves around me or I am the center of the universe.

___ 3) Resented people who get in my business by telling me they want to help.

___ 4) Others have called me selfish.

___ 5) Been better at doing most things than others.

___ 6) Had problems following the directions or done better organizing others.

___ 7) I am an excellent judge of people and situations, my assumptions are very accurate.

___ 8) I've just blown people off who aren't on my level.

___ 9) Had low frustration tolerance and would get impatient easily.

___ 10) Would become determined and stubborn about changing my mind when I got an idea to do something.

___ 11) Said what was on my mind without considering others feelings.

___ 12) Negative things people have said about me didn't really affect me much.

___ 13) I don't waste energy doing things that others can do especially simple tasks that anyone can do.

___ 14) Have taken everything that I can get from others.

___ 15) Felt like everyone should agree with me more.

___ 16) It has been easy for me to fool others.

___ 17) Have listened patiently to ignorant authorities who didn't know what they were talking about and agreed just so they would stop talking.

___ 18) Angry about not getting what I was entitled to or deserved.

___ 19) Others may have believed that I was not grateful for their help when in reality I just didn't need it.

0	1	2	3	4
Never	**Sometimes**	**Half of the time**	**Often**	**Almost Always**

____ 20) I have been an achiever and think about the future success that I expect.

____ 21) People I have been close to have tried to get me jealous.

____ 22) Felt pressure or a need to act and do what I think when I get an idea.

____ 23) Admitted things to get others off my back, not because I really believe I'm in the wrong.

____ 24) Felt like I have the ability to succeed at anything I decide to do if I put my mind to it.

____ 25) Built myself up to others and exaggerated some things about myself.

____ 26) Been frustrated at others who should accept what I say and go along with me.

____ 27) Felt like I deserve to have more of my needs met after all that I have been through.

____ 28) Viewed myself as a person with certain talents or abilities that made me more likely to make it on my own than others who have had problems like me.

____ 29) Felt like since so many bad things have happened to me, I deserve some positive attention or support to help make up for it.

____ 30) Felt like other people should appreciate me more but they don't.

____ 31) Felt like since so many bad things have happened to me, I deserve some understanding for the mistakes I made.

____ 32) Have had big plans for myself in the future.

____ 33) Been very sure about how others are viewing me or feeling about me because I know how I would think or feel if I were them.

____ 34) Felt like life was frustrating, unrewarding and not what I deserved.

____ 35) Been completely confident that I can control my problems.

____ 36) Been or have the ability to be an excellent leader or supervisor.

____ 37) Haven't needed to plan things out a lot and have been able to get things done or get what I want by thinking on my feet and taking action on the spur of the moment.

____ 38) Felt like, if given the chance, I will prove that I'm somebody.

____ 39) Have had strong opinions about things and pushed hard to get what I wanted.

____ 40) I have been upset about getting treated just like everyone else when I know I'm different or have special abilities.

____ 41) Felt like others talk about me and I have been on their minds a lot.

____ 42) I have been a powerful person whose mind was not easily changed by others.

____ 43) When it comes to people, I have known what's going on a lot more that others do.

____ 44) Felt like everyone should like me more.

0	1	2	3	4
Never	Sometimes	Half of the time	Often	Almost Always

____ 45) I've been a leader, not one of the pack.

____ 46) Anything I did I would go all the way with because I have been very sure of myself.

____ 47) Felt like I should be the one in charge because most of the time I know what's going on and others don't.

____ 48) I have been a person who gets things done and have not held myself back by waiting to take action.

____ 49) Had fairly strong opinions about things, felt certain about my views and have not doubted myself.

____ 50) Felt like I'm worth a lot more than people give me credit for.

____ 51) Told myself or others that nobody understands me.

____ 52) Believed in myself as someone with special abilities who is capable of becoming an important person and achieving great things in life.

____ 53) Considered myself somebody that can't be ignored and felt that others will realize this in the future.

____ 54) Thought that in order to get things done right, people need to listen and do it like I tell them.

____ 55) Been looking out for opportunities that could benefit me because I believe "When opportunity knocks, open the door".

____ 56) Thought that you have to fight hard for yourself and not give in because people are either winners or losers, right or wrong, strong or weak.

____ 57) I have thought that friends should agree with you and support you no matter what.

____ 58) I have had unique and special qualities which made me different from others.

____ 59) I have thought that rules are made basically for those who don't know what to do without getting directions, not for individuals like me who can handle themselves.

____ 60) It seemed to me that the people who would tell me I had a problem were just plain unhappy and looking for someone to blame it on.

____ 61) I have thought that there are a lot of people who have more problems than me.

____ 62) I have thought that I shouldn't have to go along with things that I don't believe are fair.

____ 63) Felt that I deserved a lot more than I got in life.

____ 64) It seemed to me that others would often get the breaks and rewards that I should get because I was better, they were just lucky.

____ 65) Others have been jealous of me because of my abilities or looks.

____ 66) I have thought that people who won't listen to me or go off on their own will end up crawling back on their knees.

____ 67) I have thought that people that don't listen to me or go off on their own will have to find out the hard way that they're wrong.

0 Never	1 Sometimes	2 Half of the time	3 Often	4 Almost Always

___ 68) Felt that I know how to handle myself and only got in trouble out of bad luck.

___ 69) Felt that I haven't gotten the recognition I deserved or was entitled to.

___ 70) I have thought that being supervised sends a message that others think I'm someone who you better look out for and is worth watching.

___ 71) Felt that I could handle my problems if others would just stay out of my business.

___ 72) Thought that too many people were busy telling me what to do when I already knew I could make it without their help.

___ 73) Felt that if things hadn't gone wrong for me and if other people hadn't gotten in the way, I would have done OK on my own.

___ 74) It seemed to me that taking the advice of others is for people who can't handle themselves and need to be told what to do.

___ 75) I had the ability to be a great success but needed a break that will allow me to make it.

___ 76) Felt that since I am the only one who understands me, everyone else is wrong and should keep their opinions to themselves because "You don't know me!"

___ 77) Got caught up in fantasies about great wealth, success or becoming famous.

Use the space provided below to list and rate any other grandiosity characteristics that have been a problem for you in the past which were not included on the statements provided above. Discuss your grandiosity issues with your treatment group and/or therapist. Include their feedback.

_____

_____

_____

_____

C. Grandiosity Problem Structured Discovery Exercise
On the following five numbered topics, if you are completing the basic form refer only to what you underlined and wrote about your most serious or most frequent Grandiosity problems on p. 116 along with your ratings in part A. For the complete form, include your question ratings in part B above.

1. **Select your top ten Grandiosity Problem characteristics**.
Review the statements that you rated in sections A and B. Pick out the top ten (10) statements that described your particular Grandiosity Problem behavior the most (i.e., that you rated the highest in sections A and B) and circle the numbers of those statements. Examine the top ten Grandiosity Problems that you circled and number them in rank order with the #1 statement being the statement that most described your Grandiosity Problem style, #2 the second most and so on.

Use the space provided to list the top ten Grandiosity Problems that you circled. Place your #1 ranked statement in the space provided next to #1 and so on.

Top Ten Grandiosity problems (complete first 5 for the basic form)

1) _____

2) _____

3) _____

4) _____

5) _____

6) _____

7) _____

8) _____

9) _____

10) _____

2. **Record at least your top three Grandiosity Problems** in rank order (highest rated statement first) in the space provided on your Harmful Behavior Anatomy worksheet (page 161). If you have a tie, circle the one that most applies to you and underline the other one. Put your ties (other highly ranked phrases that you underlined) on the back of your Harmful Behavior Anatomy Worksheet in the space provided.

Although descriptive phrases (short versions of the questions you have answered) have been provided for you in part A, you will need to make up your own descriptive phrases for part B that will fit on your Harmful Behavior Anatomy worksheet. Don't limit yourself to the top three points if there are important parts that fit in this area. Make sure that you do not leave out any important information about yourself on this topic.

3. **Compute and enter your Grandiosity Problem score.**

If you are completing the basic form of this exercise, use the Awareness and Honesty Exam questions that were summarized with descriptive phrases in part A of this section to compute your average rating score by dividing your rating total by the 16 questions you rated. After you have recorded your average rating score in the space provided below and on your Harmful Behavior Anatomy Worksheet at the end of this section, you can move on to the next section.

Total part A ratings on Awareness and Honesty Exam (_____) divided by 16 = _____.

If you are completing the entire exercise, add up all of your part B question ratings. An easy way to do that is to fill in the chart on the following page.

How many questions did you rate as 4? _____ Multiply that by 4 and enter the answer here _____

How many questions did you rate as 3? _____ Multiply that by 3 and enter the answer here _____

How many questions did you rate as 2? _____ Multiply that by 2 and enter the answer here _____

How many questions did you rate as 1? _____ Multiply that by 1 and enter the answer here _____

How many questions did you rate as 0? _____

Add this column, Total part B = _____

(Total should be 77) Total = _____

Compute your average rating score by adding up your part A and part B total scores, then dividing the total by all 93 questions that you rated. Record your average rating score in the space provided below and on your Harmful Behavior Anatomy worksheet (page 161).

Total part A (_____) + Total part B = _____ divided by 93 = _____.

4. **Write what you have discovered about yourself through this structured exercise**
   Use the space provided below to document how your Grandiosity Problems affected your social-emotional maturity. Use the workspace on page 227 if needed.

Social maturity (honesty, trust, loyalty, concern and responsibility)

_____

_____

_____

_____

_____

_____

_____

Emotional maturity (self-awareness, self-efficacy/confidence, self-control)

_____

_____

_____

_____

Hint: If you're having trouble with this, just take the top Grandiosity problems that you listed on page 121 and ask yourself questions comparing each Grandiosity problem to each component of social maturity looking for a connection. For example, "How did my Grandiosity affect my (honesty, trust, loyalty, concern, responsibility)?" Do the same with each component of emotional maturity. For example, "How did my Grandiosity affect my (self-awareness, self-efficacy, self-control)?"

5. **List the best personal example you can recall** of how your Grandiosity Problems caused a major problem or crisis in your life. Use the workspace on page 227 if needed. Note: An honesty accomplishment award is generally administered for the best example in treatment groups.

_____

_____

_____

_____

_____

_____

_____

_____

_____

Awareness training

Two aspects of grandiosity that can be great barriers to successful treatment and recovery are uniqueness and over-confidence. It is very important to recognize how feeling special and unique can prevent us from accepting treatment for a particular unhealthy, harmful behavior. This is because uniqueness makes us feel we aren't like the others that the treatment was designed to help. This is particularly an issue in group therapy where in the early days of AA, alcoholics viewed themselves as unique and not like the heroin addicts despite the fact that both had lost their job, their car, their wife and their life. In sex offender therapy, we have seen rapists view themselves as unique and different from the child molesters in the group "because at least I pick on people my own size", despite both being registered sex offenders in supervised housing. The same goes for obese overeaters who view themselves as unique and different from the binge-purge eaters, "because I never stuck my finger down my throat to make myself throw up" after overeating despite both having lost complete control over their eating. Focusing on developing what we have in common (i.e., the multicultural, prosocial values of honesty, trust, loyalty, concern and responsibility) as opposed to our differences is very important in preventing uniqueness from interfering with getting help and developing relationships with others who can support our recovery.

> "The common ground is greater and more enduring than the differences that divide"
> -- Nelson Mandela (1999)

Uniqueness Exercise-

Write down the type of unhealthy, harmful behavior that resulted in you completing this workbook in the space provided below. Then look at Figure 16 (p. 115) in this section and pick a type of unhealthy, harmful behavior that seems much different than yours and write it down in the space provided on the following page.

My Unhealthy, Harmful Behavior	The Unhealthy, Harmful Behavior Most Different than mine
_____	_____
_____	_____
_____	_____

Now imagine you are in group therapy with someone who has that unhealthy, harmful behavior that seems much different than yours this person. Imagine that both of you want a positive life free from your unhealthy, harmful behavior. List all of the things you can think of that you may have in common in the space below.

_____

_____

_____

_____

> **Hint:** Think about your goals, values, needs, expectations, what you want in relationships with others, what you want in life, etc.

Another important aspect of grandiosity to become aware of is how grandiose over-confidence in abilities can result in unhealthy, harmful behavior. Over-confidence in ability to keep unhealthy, harmful behaviors that involve others undetected supports self-defeating risk taking and is unrealistic because, "Three can keep a secret if two of them are dead"- Benjamin Franklin. Over-confidence in ability to tolerate high risk situations (people, places or things/feelings) that can trigger relapse results in entering those risky situations. Over-confidence in being able to talk your way out of trouble prevents you from leaving risky situations. Over-confidence in judgment allows jumping to conclusions and irresponsible assuming.

Over-confidence Exercise-

In addition to becoming aware of the symptoms of how grandiose over-confidence can result in relapse, it is important to become aware of the self-statements that are behind grandiosity. Imagine that:
1. you haven't done your unhealthy, harmful behavior for a month;
2. you just ran into someone that used to do it too and;
3. they suggest doing it again, "just this one last time".

Write out self-statements that would make you over-confident, keep you in that high risk situation and could lead to relapse. Use the space on the following page to write in self-statements that would support the type of over-confidence listed in the left column.

Type of Over-Confidence	Self-statement that would support that type of over-confidence
Over-confidence in ability to keep things quiet	1)
Over-confidence in ability to tolerate high risk situations	2)
Over-confidence in being able to talk your way out of trouble	3)
Over-confidence in judgment (jumping to conclusions)	4)

Responsibility training

While becoming aware of the self-statements that set the occasion for unhealthy, harmful behavior through over-confidence is important, in order to prevent relapse, you have to take responsibility to challenge those self-statements. Review your ACTS Healthy Behavior Success Skills (p.20- 28). Pick the best skill to help you deal with the grandiose over-confidence you described in the exercise above. Then follow the instructions for the ACTS skill you picked and describe how to use that skill to manage the Grandiosity characteristics that you listed in the space below. Start by writing what you need to say to yourself to keep from becoming over-confident and falling back into your unhealthy, harmful behavior.

_____

_____

_____

_____

_____

_____

_____

> **Hint:** "You are only limited by your creativity" when dealing with life problems. See Exhibit 3 (p. 177) for a suggestion of an ACTS skill you can use to deal with Grandiosity.

Tolerance training

Learning to tolerate grandiose over-confidence involves letting go of reactive grandiosity (p. 115) and practicing going to the opposite extreme with responsible thinking. Imagine you have a form of reactive grandiosity from feeling inferior that makes you to think, "The only way I'll ever matter is by doing something grand/big/heroic to make me famous/infamous" which is causing you to bend the rules to get what you want. Review "Emotional Dissipation" (p.22) and use the space on the following page to list how to use the ABC's of letting feelings of inferiority go in order to begin dealing with this problem.

Action that occured:_____

_____

Belief problem:_____

_____

Challenging the belief problem:_____

_____

The opposite extreme from grandiose over-confidence is responsible thinking. Review the four self-statements that support over-confidence you wrote in the Awareness Training over-confidence exercise above and use the space below to write an opposite extreme responsible thinking self-statement to block each of the grandiose over-confidence statements you wrote.

Self-Statements that show Responsible thinking (Opposite of grandiose thinking)

1) _____

2) _____

3) _____

4) _____

D. Make a Positive Plan and Commitment to Change

Review the three Grandiosity problems that you listed on your Harmful Behavior Anatomy worksheet (page 161). What can you do about it now? How are you going to change these problems, what are you going to do? (Consult with your therapist or staff and write your plan below)

1) _____

What I can do about it➔_____

What I am going to do about it➔_____

2) _____

What I can do about it➔_____

What I am going to do about it➔_____

3) _____

What I can do about it➔_____

What I am going to do about it➔_____

Get honest about your Grandiosity Problems with your therapist or treatment group.
Log the date you discussed this issue and who you discussed it with in the space provided below.

Date: _____ Discussed with: _____

"To be angry is to revenge the faults of others on ourselves" -- Alexander Pope (1688-1744)

Name: _____   Date: _____

Definition: In the anatomy model, an Emotional Maturity Deficit provides another strong support leg for multiple forms of unhealthy, harmful behavior. In Social Responsibility Therapy, an Emotional Maturity Deficit is defined as serious problems with self-awareness, self-efficacy and self-control, particularly of emotions. Self-awareness is being aware of the thoughts, feelings and sensations that motivate you to act. Increasing self-awareness about the self-defeating harmful behavior motivation as well as the harmful impact on self and others makes it hard to continue that behavior. Thus, in general processes that reduce self-awareness (i.e., like blocking out warnings from others) are needed to continue unhealthy, harmful behavior while treatment interventions which target increasing self-awareness are needed to help prevent it. Self-efficacy is the belief that you can be effective in mastering skills, handling situations and getting things done. It's the opposite of helplessness, sort of like confidence. Low self-efficacy includes feeling ineffective, helpless, incompetent and experiencing a control and power loss. Low self-efficacy is the opposite of grandiose over-confidence and involves problems with under-confidence in abilities or judgment. This results in not trying, over-relying on others and negative relationship loyalty. High or low self-efficacy determines whether we think in positive or negative ways. This can determine whether we quit or continue in the face of difficulties which determines whether or not we learn to deal with stress, overcome barriers and achieve our goals. Self-control is stopping yourself from doing what you do want to do (i.e., the wrong thing) and getting yourself to do what you don't want to do (i.e., the right thing). This is a big problem in emotional immaturity, where actions are justified by feelings before finding out the facts. Individuals involved in unhealthy harmful behavior are frequently described as having problems with self-awareness, self-efficacy and self-control. Emotional maturity problems support multiple forms of unhealthy, harmful behavior which enables it to spread from one type to another (Figure 17).

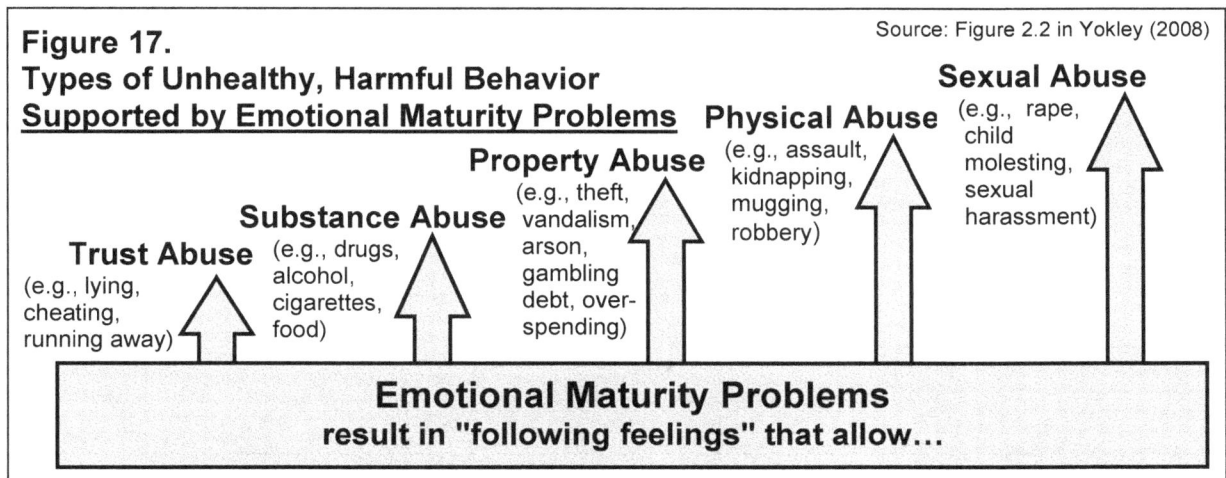

Figure 17.
Types of Unhealthy, Harmful Behavior
Supported by Emotional Maturity Problems

Source: Figure 2.2 in Yokley (2008)

Sexual Abuse (e.g., rape, child molesting, sexual harassment)

Physical Abuse (e.g., assault, kidnapping, mugging, robbery)

Property Abuse (e.g., theft, vandalism, arson, gambling debt, over-spending)

Substance Abuse (e.g., drugs, alcohol, cigarettes, food)

Trust Abuse (e.g., lying, cheating, running away)

Emotional Maturity Problems
result in "following feelings" that allow...

It's easy to see how an Emotional Maturity Deficit supports multiple forms of unhealthy, harmful behavior because you can follow many different types of feelings into many different types to trouble. Justifying actions based on feelings is a primary contributing factor to multiple forms of unhealthy, harmful behavior. You can get depressed, embarrassed or jealous (just to name a few) and then justify doing an unhealthy, harmful behavior based on your unwanted feelings. Selected examples of justifying actions based on feelings along with other types of Irresponsible Thinking related to Emotional Maturity Problems are provided in Table 13.

Table 13.
Irresponsible Thinking related to Emotional Maturity Problems: Selected Examples

Harmful Behavior	Justifying Actions based on feelings	Magnifying (blowing things out of proportion)	Assuming (jumping to conclusions)
Trust Abuse	"They made me jealous by flirting with others so I cheated on them"	"Looking bad is too awful to take so I just lie about mistakes"	"I assumed that they would blame me so I lied and said I was with somewhere else"
Substance Abuse	"I got really depressed after we broke up so I got high". "My social anxiety hit me hard at a party so I drank to relax"	"Since I took a sip during a party toast to my boss, I totally failed and decided I might as well just get drunk"	"I just know that my friends won't have anything to do with me if I don't high with them"
Property Abuse	"I got really embarrassed about my old shoes and not being able to buy new ones, so I stole them"	"I can't stand having to take the bus, it's awful so I borrowed their car while they were out of town"	"I know they were laughing about my car so I slashed their tires."
Physical Abuse	"I got really angry over what they said and punched them out"	"Because they disagreed with me, they totally disrespected me so slapped their mouth"	"Because they kept staring at me, I knew they wanted to fight, so I gave them what they were asking for"
Sexual Abuse	"They got me really excited talking to them, so I got them alone and did what I wanted"	"I can't stand these urges, they're too much to take so I have to act on them"	"Because she flirted with me, she must want me to take it the rest of the way"

Behavior Anatomy Question #9: How could your past experiences have affected your self-awareness, self-efficacy & self-control?

Circle any of the 15 the Irresponsible Thinking statements related to Emotional Maturity Problems in Table 13 above that you have used. Then write any other types of Emotional Maturity Problems that have resulted in unhealthy, harmful behavior in the space below. Use at least one example of justifying actions based on feelings. If you want, just change the Table 15 statements to fit you.

_____

_____

_____

_____

_____

An important goal of Social Responsibility Therapy is developing emotional maturity (i.e., self-awareness, self-efficacy and self-control) to effectively manage unhealthy, harmful behavior. In order to effectively manage unhealthy, harmful behavior you need to have enough:

1. **self-awareness** to identify thoughts, feelings, motivations and situations that can trigger unhealthy, harmful behavior;
2. **self-efficacy** (confidence) to try learning new ways to deal with emotions, try substituting new positive responses, behaviors and activities for old negative ones and;
3. **self-control** to delay the urge to justify actions based on feelings long enough to consider consequences in order to do the right thing at the right time and keep it up. According to self-control theory, problems with self-control combined with access and opportunity can result in unhealthy, harmful behavior.

In Social Responsibility Therapy, these important attributes build on each other. Self-efficacy/confidence improves with successful management of unhealthy, harmful behavior (i.e., self-control) and self-control improves with self-awareness of what triggers unhealthy, harmful behavior.

"Knowledge is power." The more we know about how we acquired our present behavior patterns, the more confident we can be in understanding ourselves, understanding others, achieving positive life goals and maintaining positive behavior change. Put another way, self-understanding builds the self-confidence needed for self-control. An emotional maturity deficit often begins as a result of the historical, social-emotional, situational and cognitive risk factors that you experienced when you were growing up in the Risk Factor Chain (Figure 13 p. 87, covered in workbook 1) that led to your unhealthy, harmful behavior. Put another way, the Risk Factor Chain that led you to be referred for treatment of unhealthy, harmful behavior often delays the development of self-awareness, self-efficacy/confidence and self-control which sets the occasion for other forms of harmful behavior or problems in other areas of your life. Many repetitions through the Stress-Relapse Cycle (see p. 15- 16 and Yokley, 2011a) makes problems with self-awareness, self-efficacy/confidence and self-control even worse which allows it to grow and spread through an anatomy of factors. Underline any of the Emotional Maturity problems described above that have applied to you in the past and use the space below to give a specific example of what you consider your most serious or most frequent problem.

_____

_____

_____

_____

_____

A. **Review your Awareness and Honesty Exam (Appendix G),** record your Emotional Maturity Deficit ratings in the spaces provided below and add up all of your ratings to get a total. Since your self-awareness may have improved from your use of the Situation Response Analysis log, you may need to update your ratings. Enter your ratings total in the space provided below.

Emotional Maturity Deficit (10 items from Awareness and Honesty Exam, p. 207)

___ 8) Unaware of behavior motivation ___ 20) Viewed things as worse than reality ___ 25) No confidence that things will work out ___ 28) Unable to label emotions when upset ___ 45) Lacking confidence in self ___ 48) Not introspective or insight oriented	___ 56) Preoccupation with situation injustices ___ 60) Preoccupation with consequence injustices ___ 68) External locus of control ___ 86) Lacking confidence in ability to achieve life goals Total = _____

Consult with your therapist or treatment program staff to determine if you are completing the basic form of this exercise or are completing the entire section.

End of basic form- Stop here and skip to part C, "Identifying Self-Awareness, Self-Efficacy and Self-Control Issues" on page 132 if you are completing the basic form. Otherwise, continue on with the section B questions below.

B. Rate the following Emotional Maturity Deficit characteristics.
   Use the numbered ratings on the scales provided below to rate the frequency of your past thoughts or behaviors on the statements listed in this section.

0	1	2	3	4
Never	**Sometimes**	**Half of the time**	**Often**	**Almost Always**

___ 1) After a problem or conflict is over, I have not been sure what I had to do with it.

___ 2) Have had problems feeling confident around others and about my abilities.

___ 3) Have had behavior outbursts resulting in physical action (e.g., throwing things, slamming doors, pushing, shoving, hitting, kicking, spitting, biting).

___ 4) Have had difficulty identifying and labeling my feelings when upset.

___ 5) Had problems feeling confident doing mental tasks (e.g., schoolwork, book learning).

___ 6) Had problems controlling angry or upsetting thoughts.

___ 7) Had difficulty noticing when I felt annoyed or angry.

___ 8) Had problems feeling confident doing physical tasks (e.g., sports, musical instruments).

___ 9) Had problems controlling angry or upsetting feelings.

___ 10) Had difficulty noticing when I felt anxious or fearful.

___ 11) Had problems feeling confident doing social tasks (e.g., making friends, dances, socializing).

___ 12) Had problems controlling my behavior when upset.

___ 13) Had difficulty noticing when I felt sad or depressed.

0	1	2	3	4
Never	Sometimes	Half of the time	Often	Almost Always

____ 14) Haven't really needed anyone's help dealing with my problems and don't believe that things would have gotten worse if others didn't get involved.

____ 15) Have been told that I do not think before I act.

____ 16) Been unsure of my real strengths, positive qualities or what I am good at.

____ 17) Felt out of control so I acted like I had it all together, a person that others could lean on.

____ 18) Have been upset/angry at someone and taken my feelings out on others (or let them leak out on others).

____ 19) Been unsure of my real weaknesses, problems or what I need to work on.

____ 20) Felt helpless, inadequate or insecure.

____ 21) Have apologized for my behavior and told myself or others that I would never do it again but wound up doing it again anyway.

____ 22) Had problems not thinking about why I need to do what I want to do and just doing it without considering how it might affect myself or others.

____ 23) Used making myself look good (e.g., nice clothes, attractive friends) to feel better.

____ 24) Had a strong need to tell others what makes me angry about their behavior and make sure everyone knows my feelings.

____ 25) Blocked my feelings out. For example, found myself sitting in a daze thinking that I am bored when I was probably too shy or withdrawn to talk or get involved.

____ 26) Used substances such as drinking, drugging, smoking or overeating to feel better.

____ 27) Have needed to grow up and act more mature or at least this is what others have said.

____ 28) Once a problem situation was over, I forgot about it and didn't think about whether it was part of a behavior pattern or similar to other mistakes I made in the past.

____ 29) Used activities such as bragging, arguing, fighting, flirting or sex to feel better.

____ 30) Quit something I started because I was upset with my performance or others involved.

____ 31) I haven't thought about my feelings or reasons for why I was saying/doing something.

____ 32) I have thought that there is nothing that I can do to change things in my life.

____ 33) Situations that I have no control over cause feelings that I have no control over.

____ 34) Thought that once I finish my treatment, I can get on with my life and won't have to be looking at my thoughts, feelings and behavior all of the time.

____ 35) Felt that luck or fate determines how things will turn out

____ 36) My feelings are really strong, when I'm mad, I'm really mad, when I'm sad, I'm really sad and when I'm happy I'm really happy and can get out of control.

____ 37) Picked an occupation/career based on what paid well without thinking about what I thought I could do well or would really like.

0	1	2	3	4
Never	Sometimes	Half of the time	Often	Almost Always

____ 38) Felt like I don't have much choice in what will happen to me, what I will become or how my life will turn out.

____ 39) In terms of the future, I never really thought about what I wanted from life and never thought about what I needed to do in order to get what I wanted.

____ 40) I have found myself looking around and seeing that there are a lot of others who have worse problems than me.

____ 41) I have felt socially awkward and lonely, even when around others.

____ 42) Was upset, didn't understand the reasons things were happening to me and asked myself, "Why me"?

____ 43) Have startled easily and reacted negatively without thinking.

____ 44) Had a quick temper, was easily angered by little things and flew off the handle easily.

____ 45) Punched walls and told myself it wasn't as bad as punching a person.

____ 46) Gotten high, went back to smoking, over eating or spent too much money and told myself I'm not hurting anyone but myself.

____ 47) Ran away from home, a problem or relationship and told myself, it's better than fighting.

____ 48) Did something I shouldn't because others were doing it or I wanted to fit in.

____ 49) Did something I shouldn't because it was exciting

____ 50) Did something I shouldn't because of the attention I would get.

Use the space provided below to list and rate any other Emotional Maturity characteristics that have been a problem for you in the past which weren't included above. Get feedback from your treatment group and/or therapist.

_____

_____

_____

_____

C. Identifying Self-Awareness, Self-Efficacy and Self-Control issues.

Use three sets of boxes below to sort your emotional maturity ratings from your Awareness and Honesty Exam (marked with an "A" in front of each statement) and section B ratings (above) into three categories involving issues with self-awareness, self-efficacy and self-control.

Self-Awareness

____ A8) Unaware of behavior motivation ____ A28) Unable to label emotions when upset	____ A48) Not introspective or insight oriented ____ A86) Lacking confidence in ability to achieve life goals

___ 1) Unaware of your part in a conflict	___ 34) Unaware of future treatment utility
___ 4) Difficulty identifying feelings	___ 37) Lacking career foresight
___ 7) Difficulty noticing when angry	___ 39) Lacking goal attainment foresight
___ 10) Difficulty noticing when anxious	___ 40) Looking outside of self
___ 13) Difficulty noticing when depressed	___ 42) Not aware of why things went wrong
___ 16) Unsure of real strengths	___ 43) Startled and reacted negatively
___ 19) Unsure of real weaknesses	___ 44) Quick temper, easily angered
___ 22) Not considering motivation/impact	___ 45) Punched walls
___ 25) Blocking out feelings	___ 46) Relapsed & said "I'm only hurting myself"
___ 28) Not evaluating mistakes	___ 47) Ran from home, a problem or relationship
___ 31) Not realizing how emotions affect speech and behavior	

Self-Efficacy/Confidence

___ A20) Viewed things as worse than reality	___ A45) Lacking confidence in self
___ A25) No confidence things will work out	___ A68) External locus of control

___ 2) Confident problems around others	___ 23) Used looking good to feel better
___ 5) Confident problems with mental tasks	___ 26) Used substances to feel better
___ 8) Confident problems with physical tasks	___ 29) Used activities to feel better
___ 11) Confident problems with social tasks	___ 32) Felt change was impossible
___ 14) Overconfidence in dealing with problems	___ 35) Felt luck/fate determines what happens
___ 17) Felt out of control	___ 38) Felt don't have choices in what happens
___ 20) Felt helpless, inadequate or insecure	___ 41) Socially awkward and lonely

Self-Control

___ A56) Preoccupation with situation Injustices	___ A60) Preoccupation with consequence injustices

___ 3) Physical behavior outbursts	___ 21) Apologized & repeated same problem
___ 6) Problems controlling angry thoughts	___ 24) Strong need to vent feelings
___ 9) Problems controlling angry feelings	___ 27) Told I needed to grow up/act mature
___ 12) Problems controlling behavior when upset	___ 30) Quit something I started
___ 15) Been told I don't think before I act	___ 33) Situations trigger uncontrollable feelings
___ 18) Taken my feelings out on others	___ 36) My feelings can get out of control.

D. Emotional Maturity Deficit Structured Discovery Exercise

On the following five numbered topics, for both the basic and complete form refer to what you underlined and wrote about your most serious or most frequent Social Maturity problems on p. 129 along with your ratings in part C.

1. **Select your top Emotional Maturity Deficit characteristics**.
   Review the statements that you rated in the previous section. Pick out the top three (3) statements that described your particular Emotional Maturity Deficit behavior the most (i.e., that you rated the highest) in each category and circle the numbers of those statements. Use the space provided below to list the top Emotional Maturity Deficit characteristics that you circled in each category. Place your #1 ranked statement in the space provided next to #1 and so on.

> **Note:** If you are completing the basic form and find that it does not cover material that relates to you (i.e., if you do not have at least 3 ratings of "2" or above) go back and complete section B.

Top Three Emotional Maturity Deficit characteristics (complete #1 only for the basic form)

Self-Awareness

1) _____

2) _____

3) _____

> **Hint:** In Section C above, look at Self-Awareness statements A8 and 42. Review the foresight deficit decision examples in Appendix B, 187. If you did workbook 2, look at your Phase 4 example, p. 64.

Self-Efficacy/Confidence

1) _____

2) _____

3) _____

Self-Control

1) _____

2) _____

3) _____

> **Note:** If you did not complete the Candy Bar Exercise on high risk situation access in Appendix D during the last portion (section F) of your Risk Factor Chain work, consult with your therapist or staff about whether to participate in that exercise as part of this Self-Control learning experience.

2. **Record your top Emotional Maturity Deficit characteristic in each category**.
   Record your top descriptive phrase from each category (#1 Self-Awareness, #1 Self-Efficacy and #1 Self-Control statements) in the space provided on your Harmful Behavior Anatomy worksheet (page 161). If you have a tie, circle the one that most applies to you and underline the other one. Put your ties (other highly ranked phrases that you underlined) on the back of your Harmful Behavior Anatomy Worksheet in the space provided along with your other descriptive phrases.

Compute and enter your Emotional Maturity Deficit score.

If you are completing the basic form of this exercise, use the Awareness and Honesty Exam questions that were summarized with descriptive phrases in part A of this section to compute your average rating score by dividing your rating total by the 10 questions you rated. After you have recorded your average rating score in the space provided below and on your Harmful Behavior Anatomy Worksheet at the end of this section, you can move on to the next section.

Total part A ratings on Awareness and Honesty Exam (_____) divided by 10 = _____.

If you are completing the entire exercise, add up all of your part B question ratings. An easy way to do that is to fill in the chart below.

How many questions did you rate as 4? ____ Multiply that by 4 and enter the answer here _____

How many questions did you rate as 3? ____ Multiply that by 3 and enter the answer here _____

How many questions did you rate as 2? ____ Multiply that by 2 and enter the answer here _____

How many questions did you rate as 1? ____ Multiply that by 1 and enter the answer here _____

How many questions did you rate as 0? ____   Add this column, Total part B = _____

(Total should be 50) Total = ____

Compute your average rating score by adding up your part A and part B total scores, then dividing the total by all 60 questions that you rated. Record your average rating score in the space provided below and on your Harmful Behavior Anatomy worksheet (page 161)
.

Total part A (_____) + Total part B = _____ divided by 60 = _____.

3. **Irresponsible Thinking Impact on Emotional Maturity** (See Hint on next page)
   Use the space provided below to give examples of how your Irresponsible Thinking supported problems with Social-Emotional Maturity. Use workspace on page 227 if needed.

Emotional Maturity Problems	Thinking that Supports Emotional Maturity Problems
Self-Awareness Problems (list below)	Thoughts that distract you from what's going on
Self-Efficacy/Confidence Problems (list below)	Thoughts that decrease your confidence
Self-Control Problems (list below)	Thoughts that get in the way of self-control

Hint: Look at your Irresponsible Thinking personal quotes (p. 41). Some common thinking and self-statements that support Emotional Maturity Problems include, "The best way to handle things is just to put them out of your mind", "Once it's done, it's done and there's no sense thinking about it", "It's just a streak of bad luck", "There's nothing I can do about it", "Other people get all the breaks", "If I let it go, they'll do it again", "I have to teach them a lesson". "Nobody messes with me", "Turnabout is fair play"

4. **The Stress-Relapse Cycle Impact on Emotional Maturity**

   As was mentioned in the "Knowledge is power" section (p. 129), going through the Stress-Relapse Cycle typically increases emotional maturity problems with self-awareness, self-efficacy/confidence and self-control.

   Nothing succeeds like success and nothing disappoints like failure- Too many passes through the Stress-Relapse Cycle that ends in falling back into your unhealthy, harmful behavior can develop a serious lack of self-efficacy or confidence in being able to succeed.

   Review the summary of the Stress-Relapse Cycle in this workbook (p. 15- 16) and in Workbook 2, "Why do I keep doing this?" if you have completed it. Then complete the following Stress-Relapse Cycle exercise.

a. Think about and discuss the **Negative Coping** that you used after your unhealthy, harmful behavior and record it in the space provided below. If you completed workbook 2, transfer your Negative Coping comments from Phase 1 to the space below.

   _____

   _____

   _____

b. Think about and discuss the **Cover Up** tactics that you used after your unhealthy, harmful behavior and record it in the space provided below. If you completed workbook 2, transfer your Cover Up comments from Phase 2 to the space below.

   _____

   _____

   _____

c. Think about and discuss the **Stress Buildup** resulting from Negative Coping and Cover Up if your unhealthy, harmful behavior and record it in the space provided below. If you completed workbook 2, transfer your Stress Buildup comments from Phase 3 to the space below.

   _____

   _____

   _____

d. Think about and discuss the **Slips** (lapse) that let to unhealthy, harmful behavior and record it in the space provided below. If you completed workbook 2, transfer your comments on the Slips you made from Phase 4 to the space below.

_____

_____

_____

e. Think about and discuss the **Falls** (relapse) back into unhealthy, harmful behavior that occurred after a Slip and record it in the space provided below. If you completed workbook 2, transfer your comments on taking Falls from Phase 5 to the space below.

_____

_____

_____

f. **Write what you have discovered about yourself through this structured exercise**
Use the space provided below to document how your Stress-Relapse Cycle affected your social-emotional maturity.

Social Maturity (honesty, trust, loyalty, concern and responsibility)

_____

_____

_____

_____

_____

Emotional Maturity (self-awareness, self-efficacy/confidence, self-control)

_____

_____

_____

Hint: Look at the information you listed above in the five Stress-Relapse Cycle phases and questions compare component of social maturity to each *Stress-Relapse Cycle characteristic*. Take a step by step approach to look for a connection, e.g., "How was my honesty, trust, loyalty, concern or responsibility affected by my *Negative Coping, Cover Up* tactics, *Stress Build-Up, Slips (lapse)* and *Falls(relapse)*? Some connections are easy to see like how various forms of Negative Coping feed dishonesty and how Cover Up tactics create distrust. Others require looking closer. Do the same with each component of emotional maturity, e.g., "How was my self-awareness, self-confidence and self-control affected by my *Negative Coping, Cover Up, Stress Build-Up, Slips and Falls*?" Some connections are easy to see like how various forms of Negative Coping can interfere with learning to look at yourself and developing self-awareness and how emotional Stress Build-Up leads to a Slip. Others require looking closer.

5. List the best personal example you can recall of how any of your Emotional Maturity
Deficit characteristics caused a major problem or crisis in your life.

_____

_____

_____

_____

The ART of Calming Down

The ART of Calming down
(Emotional Regulation) is important
in self-control to prevent justifying
actions based on feelings (p. 198).
Learning to follow facts and avoid
acting out feelings is particularly
important in managing the
Emotional Maturity Problems that
support unhealthy, harmful
behavior. The **ART** of Calming
down (Figure 18) involves:
Awareness training on high risk
situations that can trigger unwanted
feelings; Responsibility training on
developing emotional control
confidence (self-efficacy) by
learning the ABC's of calming
down (p. 22- 24) and; Tolerance
training on learning to tolerate
frustration, distress and unwanted feelings by practicing the ABC's of calming down.

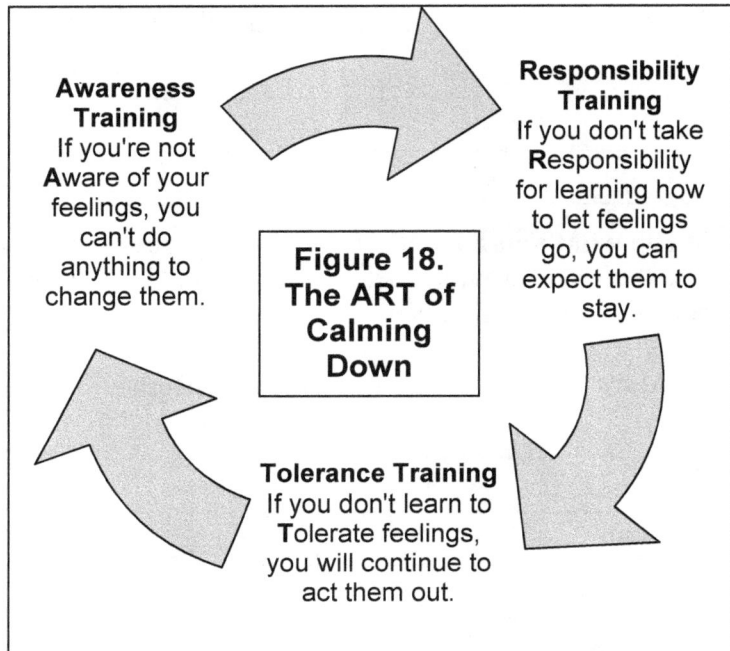

**Awareness
Training**
If you're not
Aware of your
feelings, you
can't do
anything to
change them.

**Responsibility
Training**
If you don't take
Responsibility
for learning how
to let feelings
go, you can
expect them to
stay.

**Figure 18.
The ART of
Calming
Down**

Tolerance Training
If you don't learn to
Tolerate feelings,
you will continue to
act them out.

Awareness training: Developing emotional maturity includes learning the ART of calming
down. If you're not **A**ware of your feelings, you can't do anything to change them. Awareness
training to turn an Emotional Maturity Deficit around involves identifying feelings and using
others feedback to help you identify when you are justifying, magnifying, assuming or falling
into other problems that can trigger following feelings into relapse.

Basic Human Emotions: 101- There are lots of feelings that can set you up for unhealthy,
harmful behavior. Three basic types of unwanted feelings that can result in unhealthy, harmful
behavior are anger, anxiety and depression. These emotions range in severity from mild to severe
and may be begin during the stressful event or may be delayed until much later in time. Anger
can range from a mild frustration to a moderate anger to a severe rage and may be include
regular thoughts about unjust treatment and a desire for revenge. Anxiety can range from mild
social discomfort to a moderate anxiety (fear) to a severe panic attack and may include regular
distressful thoughts about something bad happening. Depression can range from a mild sadness

to a moderate feeling of depression (including feeling helpless) to suicidal despair (including feeling hopeless) and may include regular thoughts about giving up. Three basic ways humans give up when they are overwhelmed with feelings are to: 1) give up on life and start thinking about killing themselves; 2) give up on dealing with feelings, i.e., don't want to kill self but do want to kill feelings so, drink, drug, smoke, eat, spend, have sex to distract self from unwanted feelings and; 3) give up on the situation, i.e., don't want to get rid of self or feelings but definitely want to get rid of the situation (job, relationship, etc.). In summary, you can get angry, anxious or depressed and then justify unhealthy, harmful actions based on those feelings.

In addition to awareness of thoughts and feelings that justify unhealthy, harmful behavior, awareness of Foresight Deficit Decisions (Appendix B, p. 184) is also very important. Review the Foresight Deficit Decision examples in Appendix B and use the space below to write an example of how your problems with self-awareness resulted in making a Foresight Deficit Decision that led to an unhealthy or harmful behavior.

_____

_____

A third important part of Awareness training for emotional maturity development involves learning to value and accept feedback in order to develop emotional control and personal growth. This is particularly difficult because in general, people rarely ask for feedback on their attitude or behavior and "people don't appreciate anything they don't ask for". "You are only limited by your creativity" when dealing with life problems. See Exhibit 3 (p. 177) for ideas and ACTS skills you can use to develop your emotional maturity.

Learning to value feedback- The Mirror Concept (p. 200) helps you value feedback by accepting that "Other people see you better than you see yourself". Think about running out the door late to school or work and forgetting to shave or put on makeup. Since you can't see yourself while talking to others, how would you know unless someone was kind enough to tell you so you could duck into the bathroom and clean up? The goal of the Mirror Concept is to master using other people's feedback as a mirror to see yourself. Initially, this is done by focusing on what is being said, not who is saying it or how it is being said, getting other opinions and accepting feedback consensus, i.e., "If ten people say you're a horse, you're a horse."

Following feelings back into relapse- We all go about our daily lives looking at the world and others but awareness training requires us to look at ourselves. Self-awareness is important because if you're not aware that you are: 1) justify actions based on feelings; 2) blowing things out of proportion (magnifying) and; 3) jumping to conclusions (assuming) without finding out the facts, "following feelings" will continue to lead you back into trouble.

Review what you have learned in Sections A- D of this component about the Emotional Maturity Problems that supports your unhealthy, harmful behavior and answer the question "What kind of Emotional Maturity Problems" support my unhealthy, harmful behavior? Use the space below to list Emotional Maturity Problems beginning with examples of how unwanted feelings led to unhealthy, harmful behavior. Use at least one example of justifying actions based on feelings.

Emotional Maturity Problems (Unwanted feelings)   Unhealthy, Harmful Behavior

_____

_____

_____

Responsibility training: While Awareness training is a necessary first step, if you don't take **R**esponsibility to learn how to let feelings go you can expect them to stay. If you continue the emotional maturity problem of following feelings, your unhealthy, harmful behavior will continue. Review "The ABC's of Calming Down" (p.22- 24). Then use the space below to show how to use the ABC's of Calming down. Pick either letting feelings go or holding on to feelings (whichever fits the situation best for you) to prevent you from acting on the unwanted feelings that you listed in the Awareness training section above. From this point on, develop your emotional maturity by practicing the ABC's of Calming Down, logging your progress on your Situation Response Analysis logs and reviewing it with your therapist or support group.

Action that occurred: _____

_____

Belief problem: _____

_____

Challenging the belief problem: _____

_____

Self-efficacy is the feeling that you can have an effect and make changes which is the opposite of feeling helpless and giving up on change. That being said, start building your self-efficacy by shifting from the helplessness focus on what can't be changed (i.e., the past and other people's behavior) to an empowerment focus on what can be changed (i.e., the present and the client's behavior). Start by doing a nightly self-efficacy review of "three things that went right today and how I made that happen". Write your first self-efficacy review in the space provided below and at the bottom of your SRA log every night afterwards.

_____

_____

_____

Tolerance training: If you don't learn to **T**olerate feelings, you will continue to act them out. Emotional maturity problems also involve over-sensitivity to input and under-sensitivity to output. The perception of what is coming in gets multiplied by two (magnifying) and the perception of what is going out gets divided by two (minimizing). This results in getting your feelings hurt by constructive feedback and snapping back with harsh words. Since the problem starts with magnifying, practice using the Reality Scales to weigh out the real impact of feedback and accept that, "Sticks and stones can break my bones but words can never hurt me" (Northall,1894) is very important. Use the space below to write the last time you overreacted to unwanted feedback and how you could better handle feedback from others in the future using the Reality Scales (See page 24).

_____

_____

_____

Review "Learning to value feedback" in the Awareness Training section above and when you receive feedback from an authority about a mistake, practice going to the opposite extreme of emotional reacting by stating, "Thank you I'll take care of that". Until you are able to accept that this is only proper response to authority you will have to "act as if" you can tolerate unwanted feedback by using the reality scales to help you deal with the frustration and not act your feelings out. When you "act as if" you can tolerate difficult thoughts, feelings or situations, you are practicing being the person you want to be as opposed to the person you were (DeLeon, 2000, p. 81). Tolerating difficult situations isn't easy and "No pain, No gain" is the key point here (DeLeon, 2000, p. 80). If you just act your feelings out and don't go through the pain of dealing with your feelings, you won't gain any self-control.

Use the space below to write the last time you overreacted to unwanted feedback and how you could deal with your feelings by using the ABC's of holding on to feelings to surf the urge to react as the anger wave rises and drops (page 23).[15] Then use the Reality Scales (page 24).

_____

_____

_____

_____

Self-control 101: "You have to go to the opposite extreme to meet the median"
Probably the best example of effective treatments that use high self-control expectations to help with learning to tolerate positive lifestyle change is the Therapeutic Community model. This treatment has a "pendulum concept" tolerance training saying that, "You have to go to the opposite extreme to meet the median". In this "pendulum concept" in order to learn to tolerate positive change, you need to take all of the things that can help with self-control of your unhealthy, harmful behavior (e.g., your irresponsible thinking triggers, your high risk feeling triggers, your high risk people triggers) and swing them like a pendulum from the very low side of self-control before treatment to the opposite extreme very high side during treatment. This is needed so that after treatment when people naturally slip back a little, you don't slip back so far that you fall back into your unhealthy, harmful behavior (Yokley, 2008, p. 137).

Think about the last time you had an emotional overreaction from feelings you got about being told to do something that wasn't your responsibility. From this point on, use those situations to practice going to the opposite extreme by "Earning the right to complain" (Yokley, 2008, p. 166) and "saving your anger for the real injustices". Do the responsibility first, then get back to the person after you earned the right to complain by doing it and tell them you completed it even though it wasn't your responsibility. This allows you to practice self-control and allows them to accept your feedback because you earned the right to complain. Telling yourself that, "What goes around, comes around" helps you get in touch with the fact that everyone needs to develop tolerance for minor injustices and you are not being singled out because the unfairness that comes around to you also goes around to others.

Tolerating change- Answer the question, "What would be the opposite extreme?" of the unhealthy, harmful, Emotional Maturity Problems you listed in the Awareness training section above. Describe the opposite emotionally mature behavior that you need to "Act as if" (p. 12) you already have and practice regularly. Put another way, what would be the right thing at the right time for the right reason? Remember, "If your words are no better than silence, silence is far better than words".

How I reacted before:

_____

_____

New opposite extreme positive responses and activities I need to substitute for old negative ones

_____

_____

E. Make a Positive Plan and Commitment to Change

Review the three Emotional Maturity Deficits that you listed on your Harmful Behavior Anatomy worksheet (page 161). What can you do about it now? How are you going to change these, what are you going to do? (Consult with your therapist or staff and write your plan below)

1) _____

What I can do about it→ _____

What I am going to do about it→ _____

2) _____

What I can do about it→ _____

What I am going to do about it→ _____

3) _____

What I can do about it→ _____

What I am going to do about it→ _____

Get honest about your Emotional Maturity Problems with your therapist or treatment group. Log the date you discussed this issue and who you discussed it with in the space provided below.

Date: _____ Discussed with: _____

"Look before you leap" -- Aesop (620-560 BC)

Name: _____   Date: _____

Definition: Self-defeating habits that involve counterproductive values, behaviors, characteristics, and needs provide firm footing for multiple forms of unhealthy, harmful behavior. Self-Defeating habits support multiple forms of unhealthy, harmful behavior that prevent you from getting what you want in life. Self-defeating habits can also affect many life areas including having a harmful destructive impact on relationships, employment and even personal freedom. Examples include break ups, separation, divorce, getting suspended, expelled, fired or jailed. There are too many self-defeating habits to cover in any one workbook. Just learning to break the self-defeating habit of falling back into your unhealthy, harmful behavior through the Stress Relapse Cycle takes an entire workbook by itself (See Yokley, 2011a). The social maturity problems with honesty, trust, loyalty, concern and responsibility covered in Component 5 can play a part in self-defeating habits that can keep you from getting the relationships and career you want in your life. That being said we will only cover several basic self-defeating characteristics (i.e., ruminating, procrastinating, and giving up) and exaggerated needs (i.e., acceptance, excitement, and attention) that support unhealthy, harmful behavior. Since Self-Defeating Habits can support multiple forms of unhealthy, harmful behavior, once you develop a pattern of self-defeating habits, your harmful behavior can easily spread from one type to another (Figure 19).

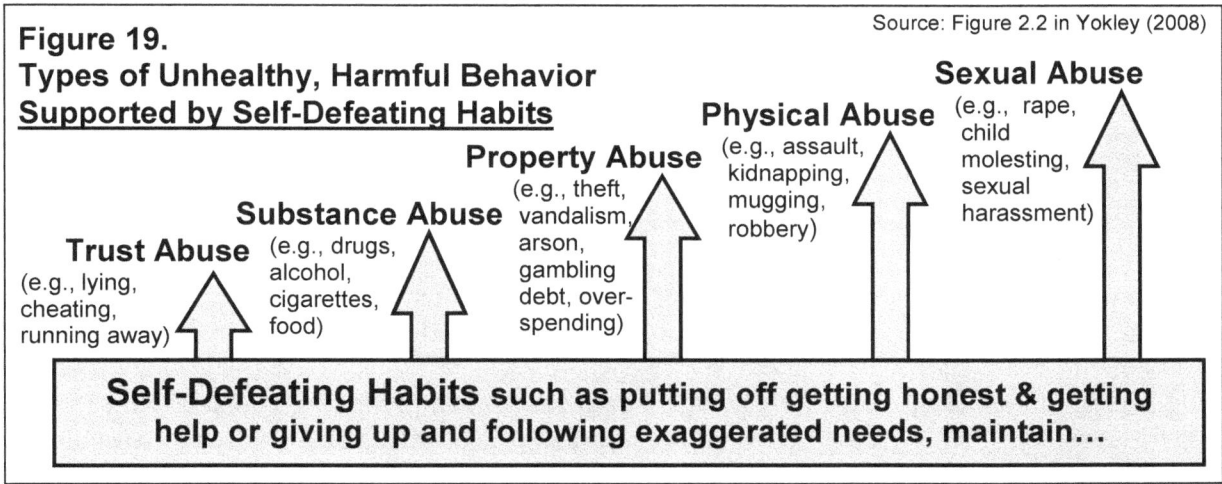

Figure 19.
Types of Unhealthy, Harmful Behavior Supported by Self-Defeating Habits

Source: Figure 2.2 in Yokley (2008)

Sexual Abuse (e.g., rape, child molesting, sexual harassment)

Physical Abuse (e.g., assault, kidnapping, mugging, robbery)

Property Abuse (e.g., theft, vandalism, arson, gambling debt, over-spending)

Substance Abuse (e.g., drugs, alcohol, cigarettes, food)

Trust Abuse (e.g., lying, cheating, running away)

Self-Defeating Habits such as putting off getting honest & getting help or giving up and following exaggerated needs, maintain...

Examples of basic Self-Defeating Habits that support multiple forms of unhealthy, harmful behavior and allow your problems to spread from one type to another are very easy to see. Ruminating is working yourself up by going over and over something in your mind, particularly something that could be unjust, unfair or difficult to handle. Ruminating on perceived or expected injustices is a self-defeating habit that can maintain harmful behavior. For example ruminating on the consequences of getting honest can prevent you from getting help for relationship cheating (trust abuse), drinking (substance abuse), shoplifting (property abuse), domestic violence (physical abuse) or pornography addiction (sexual abuse). In summary, ruminating on the consequences of getting honest results in overestimating the consequences and viewing them as an injustice before any consequences have occurred. This leads to the victim view and a deception to cover up the harmful behavior to avoid expected consequences as opposed to getting honest and getting help. Use the space below to describe a typical situation where you ruminated on something to the point here you got into trouble or relapsed. Since self-defeating habits are patterns, list how often you fall into ruminating (i.e., once in a while, fairly often, very often, all the time).

_____

_____

_____

<u>Procrastinating</u> is putting off something. Typically it's something that is difficult or important and often there is a promise to get it done later. Procrastinating getting help allows you to continue trust, substance, property, physical or sexual abuse until the time you have promised yourself or others that you will get treatment. Sometimes procrastinating involves unhealthy perfectionism by putting things off until the perfect time. Sometimes it involves unhealthy pride and wanting to put off admitting a problem. The problem with procrastinating is that it's just like going to the doctor, the longer you wait the worse the disease gets and the stronger the medicine you have to take to deal with it. Use the space below to describe a typical situation where you have procrastinated dealing with a problem and things got worse. Since self-defeating habits are patterns, list how often you fall into procrastinating (i.e., once in a while, fairly often, very often, all the time).

_____

_____

_____

<u>Giving up</u> on your recovery or your life goals is easily done by compromising yourself to meet exaggerated needs or through the "Slip Give Up Trigger" (p. 104). Compromising yourself (i.e., letting go of what you know is right and doing what you know isn't best) can involve following your needs for attention, acceptance or excitement. Exaggerated needs for attention, acceptance or excitement can involve following others, feelings or urges which can result in giving up and falling back into unhealthy, harmful behavior. For example, compromising yourself to meet needs for acceptance by covering up for others skipping class or work requires lying (trust abuse relapse). Compromising to be accepted by doing too much for others can result in exhaustion or resentment and emotional overeating (diet relapse). If you compromise yourself to be accepted by going with others to an all you can eat buffet or bar, you are likely to fall back into unhealthy eating or drinking (substance abuse relapse). Compromising yourself to meet needs for excitement by gambling, committing a thrill crime (e.g., vandalism, shoplifting) or a sex crime such as frottage (e.g., rubbing against another in a crowd to get sexual excitement) results in property abuse or sexual abuse relapse. Compromising yourself to meet needs for attention by threatening others, calling them out or putting them down in front of peers almost always results

in starting a fight (physical abuse relapse). Use the space below to describe a typical situation where you compromised yourself to be accepted, for attention or excitement and ended up falling back into unhealthy, harmful behavior. Since self-defeating habits are patterns, list how often you fall into compromising yourself (i.e., once in a while, fairly often, very often, all the time). Review the "Slip Give Up Trigger" on page 104. Then comment below on whether you believe you have given up more in the past due to compromising yourself to meet exaggerated needs or the "Slip Give Up Trigger".

_____

_____

_____

Behavior Anatomy Question #10: How could your past experiences have left you with unmet needs or habits that hold you back?

A. Review your Awareness and Honesty Exam (Appendix G), record your Self-Defeating Habit ratings in the spaces provided below and add up all of your ratings to get a total. Since your self-awareness may have improved from your use of the Situation Response Analysis log, you may need to update your ratings. Enter your ratings total in the space provided below.

Self-Defeating Habits (15 items from Awareness and Honesty Exam, p. 207)

___ 5) Giving up	___ 79) If no one says anything it's OK
___ 12) Compromising self to be accepted	___ 95) Rapid relationship involvement
___ 17) Justifying actions based on feelings	___ 98) Normalizing by comparison to the
___ 22) Overly sensitive and critical	more serious
___ 32) Exaggerated need for attention	___100) Fault finding
___ 33) Disorganized	___104) Ruminating
___ 53) Planning problems/Not thinking ahead	___ 131) Can't learn from people I don't like
___ 62) Excusing self but not others	
___ 72) Exaggerated need for excitement	Total = _____

"Do the math" and weigh out your decisions based on facts not feelings

A key self-defeating habit is being too sensitive to rewards and not sensitive enough to consequences. This causes you to follow your feelings (i.e., an exaggerated need for excitement) an avoid looking at the facts (i.e., procrastination- putting off weighing things out). This combination of planning problems and justifying actions based on feelings regularly leads to harmful behavior relapse because you didn't "Do the math" on healthy vs harmful behavior choices. The basic "Do the math" process is simply a more detailed version of thinking things through using the reality scales (p. 24) to weigh out your decisions based on survival, success and severity but doing the math by adding the actual behavior cost to the benefits and drawbacks of your behavior choices. Complete the table below to help you add the actual cost of continuing your unhealthy, harmful behavior. Case #1 and 2 in Appendix H on Decisional Balance provides examples of how to "Do the math" on unhealthy, harmful, self-defeating habits. When the unhealthy, harmful behavior you are dealing with has more physical consequences than the actual costs in dollars, use the three Reality Scales (p. 24) to weigh out your decision as illustrated in Case #3 of Appendix H. When there are serious costs in terms of both cash and consequences (i.e., survival, success and severity) do both (i.e., "Do the math" on cash costs and weigh the pros and cons on the Reality Scales) as illustrated in Case #4 in Appendix H.

"Do the Math" and Reality Scale Decision Sheet

	Benefits/Pros Describe the real benefits in terms of money along with other physical, social or emotional rewards that are received and/or Use the Reality Scales to rate the benefits	Drawbacks/Cons Describe the real drawbacks in terms of money along with other physical, social or emotional benefits that are lost and/or... Use the Reality Scales to rate the drawbacks
Keep Doing the harmful behavior List the behavior here...	3) _____ _____ _____ _____	2) _____ _____ _____ _____
Quit doing the harmful behavior List the behavior and an alternative to doing it here...	1) _____ _____ _____ _____	4) _____ _____ _____ _____

Use the space below to record your reality scale ratings and evaluate the benefits and drawbacks of your unhealthy, harmful behavior based on the Reality Scale ratings. Then write your conclusion about the about cost benefits and drawbacks of your behavior based on the facts you have listed, not the feelings you get.

Reality Scale Ratings

  1) Benefit of quitting- _____   3) Benefit of continuing- _____

+ 2) Drawbacks of keeping it up-_____   + 4) Drawbacks of quitting- _____

  = Need to quit score- _____   = OK to continue score- _____

A Picture is worth 1,000 words: The Fork in the Road

Some people find it easier to weight out the benefits and drawbacks of important decisions if they see it in picture form as a fork in the road with their list of what is likely to happen on both sides of the junction. Try this to see if it's best for you.

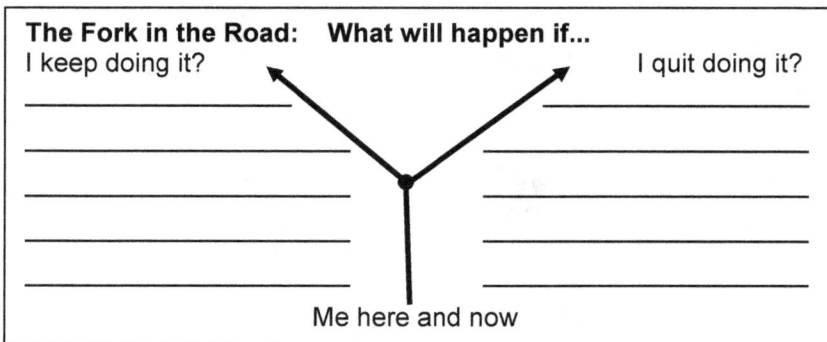

The Fork in the Road: **What will happen if...**

I keep doing it?   I quit doing it?

Me here and now

Self-Defeating Habit Conclusion- When I "Do the math" and weigh out my decisions in the Reality Scales to avoid the self-defeating habit of being too sensitive to rewards and not sensitive enough to consequences, what I learned is...

_____

_____

Consult with your therapist or treatment program staff to determine if you are completing the basic form of this exercise or are completing the entire section.

End of basic form- **Stop here and skip to part C, "Fantasy Addiction as a Self-Defeating Habit" on page 150 if you are completing the basic form. Otherwise, continue on with the section B questions below.**

B. Rate the following Self-Defeating Habits.

Use the numbered ratings on the scales provided below to rate the frequency of your past thoughts or behaviors on the statements listed in this section.

0 Never	1 Sometimes	2 Half of the time	3 Often	4 Almost Always

____ 1) Dropped a relationship or stopped associating with someone based on what was told to me by others and without speaking to that person directly.

____ 2) Quit a job before getting another job.

____ 3) Promised to change when in a lot of trouble and later found myself doing it again.

____ 4) Been able to start at the last minute because I work best under pressure.

____ 5) Have not completed things that I started.

____ 6) Could easily tell when others meant to criticize me even though they would tell me that was not what they meant.

____ 7) Put other things like job, school or relationships as priorities over dealing with my problems or treatment.

____ 8) Avoided thinking about my feelings since that can't help change things anyway.

____ 9) Called myself stupid or other names when I made a mistake.

____ 10) Reacted to others with fear, anger or resentment.

____ 11) Didn't ask a question I had because of feeling nervous or fear of looking dumb.

____ 12) Felt better around others when drinking or a little high on drugs.

____ 13) Would get nervous when things were going too well.

____ 14) Done things to trip myself up when things were going well.

____ 15) Stirred things up for excitement or to break boredom.

____ 16) Wouldn't talk about what was going on with me when I was upset and others asked.

0	1	2	3	4
Never	Sometimes	Half of the time	Often	Almost Always

____ 17 Used pleasure-seeking (e.g., sex, drugs, alcohol, cigarettes, food) to feel better.

____ 18) Used power-seeking (e.g., manipulation, coercion, intimidation or abuse of others) to feel better.

____ 19) Got caught up in thinking about past problems or issues and kept myself upset.

____ 20) Put myself down for making mistakes or compared myself to others and told myself I'm not as good as them.

____ 21) Would go over and over things in my mind and could not seem to let them go without doing something.

____ 22) Haven't really needed to think about consequences because I've always been able to think on my feet and talk my way out of problems.

____ 23) I haven't been able to stand feeling lonely and would do things to avoid it.

____ 24) I would rather quit than take second best.

____ 25) Been a quick thinker and came up with reasons why suggestions won't work.

____ 26) Looked for loop holes or things that haven't been covered in the rules.

____ 27) Had strong needs to be in a relationship with a partner either because I could not stand loneliness or got a natural "high" out of being in a relationship.

____ 28) Started out with lots of motivation at first but let up on self-discipline and let things go after a while.

____ 29) When someone was pointing something out to me, if they had ever done the same thing or had the same problem, I would tell myself there was no sense listening to them because they were no better than me.

____ 30) When someone was pointing something out to me, if they had never done the same thing or never had the same problem, I would tell myself there was no sense listening to them because they couldn't know what I was going through.

____ 31) Being in the middle of conflicts or problems between others has not really bothered me.

____ 32) Thinking of chaotic scenes, violent acts or being a hero has helped me channel feeling nervous into action energy.

____ 33) Thinking of chaotic scenes, violent acts or being a hero has helped me feel confident, a sort of mental build up of energy like pumping one's self up to face a challenge.

____ 34) Haven't paid attention to how I'm feeling until someone would call it to my attention, (e.g., "What's bothering you?").

____ 35) Had strong needs for acceptance and was likely to go along with things that were wrong just to get along or fit in.

____ 36) Felt like "things are OK the way they are so why change?"

____ 37) Told myself I had to like a person in order to learn anything from them.

____ 38) Felt defeated or told myself things like, "I can't make it so why try?"

0	1	2	3	4
Never	Sometimes	Half of the time	Often	Almost Always

____ 39) Been afraid that I will fail if I try to be different, change something about myself or try something new.

____ 40) Felt like others have ruined my life completely and there is little that I can do to make myself feel better except talk about it.

____ 41) Told myself, "Lots of others have done it" either before or after doing something wrong.

____ 42) Told myself, "They told me to do it" either before or after doing something wrong.

____ 43) Told myself, "Lots of others would do it if they had the chance" either before or after doing something wrong.

____ 44) Told myself, "Lots of others would do it if they didn't think anyone would find out", either before or after doing something wrong.

____ 45) Told myself, "Lots of others probably have done it too but no one knows", either before or after doing something wrong.

____ 46) Assumed that others have been telling lies about me to somehow benefit themselves as opposed to really trying to look at the criticism being presented by others.

____ 47) Viewed the negative feelings that are kicked up by life problems as so awful that I can't stand it and must do something.

____ 48) Accused others without first checking the facts.

____ 49) Looked for why recommendations or criticism did not apply to me.

____ 50) Did something I shouldn't because of my feelings.

____ 51) Held on to anger and resentment to the point where I was planning to get even.

____ 52) Others have felt that I need help but I felt my problems had more to do with people getting in the way or holding me back.

____ 53) I couldn't admit a mistake because I didn't want others to criticize me.

____ 54) Told myself that I have to like someone in order to cooperate with or listen to them.

____ 55) Things that were unfair or done wrong to me (i.e., past injustices) have stayed on my mind or kept coming into my thoughts.

____ 56) Hooked up with partners or peers who would encourage, enable or trigger me into doing the wrong thing (e.g., cheat, argue, fight, steal, get high, over eat, smoke).

____ 57) Felt like negative attention was better than no attention at all.

____ 58) Things that I did wrong to others (i.e., past mistakes) have stayed on my mind or kept coming into my thoughts.

____ 59) I have made promises when in trouble that I let go when things started to straighten out.

____ 60) The irritating behavior of certain other people has stayed on my mind or kept coming into my thoughts.

____ 61) Tried too hard to achieve (in school, work, sports, social) like I had something to prove.

____ 62) Didn't try hard enough to achieve (in school, work, sports, social) like I didn't care.

Use the space provided below to list and rate any other Self-Defeating Habits that have been a problem for you in the past which were not included on the statements provided above. Get feedback from your treatment group and/or therapist.

_____

_____

C. Fantasy Addiction as a Self-Defeating Habit

One important Self-defeating habit that can keep you from getting where you want to go is ruminating on fantasies to the point where it takes away from actually trying to achieve positive life goals. It is easy to get caught up in fantasy because fantasy is better than reality. It is easy to generate, takes no work, makes you feel better and always produces the desired effect (turns out the way you want it). As a result, fantasy can be addictive like drugs which are easy to take, make you feel better and always produces the desired effect. Fantasy addiction is particularly damaging when it is focused on the past and other people's behavior because as mentioned earlier the past and other peoples behavior are the only two things you can't change in life. Focusing on what you can't change results in feeling helpless and keeps you from focusing on what you can change (i.e., the present and your behavior). That helpless focus supports relapse in a self-defeating cycle of: 1) rumination on fantasy of past or others; 2) not being aware of high risk situations for self in present (because you are distracted by past fantasy) and; 3) falling back into unhealthy, harmful behavior. List a fantasy (e.g., revenge, hero, violence, romance) that you got too caught up in and tell why.

_____

_____

_____

_____

Record your fantasy question ratings on the Anatomy Components in the space provided below.

Fantasy Problems (6 questions from Harmful Behavior Anatomy Components)

Component 2- Page 48 ___ 1) Fantasy or rumination on past injustice ___ 2) Fantasy or rumination on others behavior Component 2- Page 52 ___ 82) Control & Power anger fantasy ___ 83) Control & Power sex fantasy Component 3- Page 61 ___ 43) Unhealthy Pride fantasy	Component 6- Page 96 ___ 56) Maladaptive Self-Image fantasy Component 7- Page 108 ___ 51) Perfectionism fantasy Component 8- Page 120 ___ 77) Grandiosity fantasy

D. Self-Defeating Habit Structured Discovery Exercise

On the following five numbered topics, if you are completing the basic form refer only to what you wrote about your Self-Defeating Habits on p. 144- 145 along with your ratings in part A. For the complete form include your ratings in parts B and C.

1. **Select your top ten Self-Defeating Habits**.
   Review the statements that you rated in sections A, B and C. Pick out the top ten (10) statements that described your particular Self-Defeating Habit behavior the most (i.e., that you rated the highest in sections A, B and C) and circle the numbers of those statements.

   Examine the top ten Self-Defeating Habit characteristics that you circled and number them in rank order with the #1 statement being the statement that most described your Self-Defeating Habit style, #2 the second most and so on. Use the space provided below to list the top ten Self-Defeating Habit characteristics that you circled. Place your #1 ranked statement in the space provided next to #1 and so on.

Top Ten Self-Defeating Habits (complete first 5 for the basic form)

1) _____
2) _____
3) _____
4) _____
5) _____
6) _____
7) _____
8) _____
9) _____
10) _____

2. **Record at least your top three Self-Defeating Habits** in rank order (highest rated statement first) in the space provided on your Harmful Behavior Anatomy worksheet (page 161). If you have a tie, circle the one that most applies to you and underline the other one. Put your ties (other highly ranked phrases that you underlined) on the back of your Harmful Behavior Anatomy Worksheet in the space provided. Although descriptive phrases (short versions of the questions you have answered) have been provided for you in part A, you will need to make up your own descriptive phrases for part B that will fit on your Harmful Behavior Anatomy worksheet. Don't limit yourself to the top three points if there are important parts that fit in this area. Make sure that you do not leave out any important information about yourself on this topic.

3. **Compute and enter your Self-Defeating Habit score.**
   If you are completing the basic form of this component, use the Awareness and Honesty Exam questions that were summarized with descriptive phrases in part A (p. 145) of this section to compute your average rating score by dividing your rating total by the 15 questions you rated. After you have recorded your average rating score in the space provided below

and on your Harmful Behavior Anatomy worksheet (page 161), you can move on to the next section.

Total part A ratings (p. 145) on Awareness and Honesty Exam (_____) divided by 15 = _____

If you are completing the entire exercise, add up all of your part B question ratings. An easy way to do that is to fill in the chart below.

How many questions did you rate as 4? ____	Multiply that by 4 and enter the answer here ____
How many questions did you rate as 3? ____	Multiply that by 3 and enter the answer here ____
How many questions did you rate as 2? ____	Multiply that by 2 and enter the answer here ____
How many questions did you rate as 1? ____	Multiply that by 1 and enter the answer here ____
How many questions did you rate as 0? ____	Add this column, Total part B = ____
(Total should be 62) Total = ____	

Compute your average rating score by adding up your part A and part B total scores, then dividing the total by all 75 questions that you rated. Record your average rating score in the space provided below and on your Harmful Behavior Anatomy worksheet (page 161).

Total part A (_____) + Total part B = _____ divided by 75 = _____.

4. **Write what you have discovered about yourself through this structured exercise**
   Use the space provided below to document how your Self-Defeating Habits affected your social-emotional maturity. Use the workspace on page 227 if needed.

Social maturity (honesty, trust, loyalty, concern and responsibility)- See Hint on next page.

_____

_____

_____

_____

_____

Emotional maturity (self-awareness, self-efficacy/confidence, self-control)

_____

_____

_____

Hint: If you're having trouble with this, just take the top Self-Defeating Habits that you listed on page 151 and ask yourself questions comparing each Self-Defeating Habit to each component of social maturity looking for a connection. For example, "How did my Self-Defeating Habits affect my (honesty, trust, loyalty, concern, responsibility)?" Do the same with each component of emotional maturity. For example, "How did my Self-Defeating Habits affect my (self-awareness, self-efficacy, self-control)?"

5. **List the best personal example you can recall** of how your Self-Defeating Habits caused a major problem or crisis in your life. Use the workspace on page 227 if needed. Note: An honesty accomplishment award is generally administered for the best example in treatment groups.

_____

_____

_____

_____

Recovery Sabotage Exercise: Putting your Self-Defeating Habits to Work for you

As humans, we often don't know how to plan a perfectly good day, but we all know how to plan a perfectly bad one. In the following exercise, list the unhealthy, harmful behavior you are working on along with the self-defeating habits that hold you back. Then plan a day that is guaranteed to sabotage your recovery. List all of the people, places and things you would need to come in contact with to relapse.

The unhealthy, harmful behavior I am working on is _____

The self-defeating habits that hold me back are _____

_____

The way I could plan a perfectly bad day that would sabotage my recovery and result in relapse back into my unhealthy, harmful behavior is (see "referral problem, p. 4)

_____

_____

_____

_____

Now, put the self-defeating habits you described above on how to plan a perfectly bad day that would result in relapse to work for you. Describe the opposite to plan a perfectly good day that protects your freedom and your recovery. Write the details of what you need to do in order to have a successful recovery day below.

_____

_____

_____

_____

_____

_____

The ART of Social Problem Solving

The ART of Social Problem Solving, is particularly important in managing the Self-Defeating Habits that support unhealthy, harmful behavior. This is because the "habit" part of Self-Defeating Habits results in what Albert Einstein (1879- 1955) called "Insanity: doing the same thing over and over again and expecting different results". Social Problem Solving was designed to break those "insane" Self-Defeating Habits by developing new options for old problems. The **ART** of Social Problem Solving involves getting SET to solve the problem. This requires Awareness training on setting your actual goal (i.e., clarifying- What do I really want?);

Responsibility training on evaluating your progress (How is what I'm doing working for me?) along with your options (What else could I try?); and; Tolerance training on learning to tolerate change, disappointment and barriers to success by taking responsible action by trying one option after another until you find a solution to your problem (Figure 20). Before you go on, review page 25- 27 on how to get SET for solving problems in three steps: 1) Set your goal; 2) Evaluate your progress and options; 3) Take responsible action. "You are only limited by your creativity" when dealing with life problems. See Exhibit 3 (p. 177) for ideas that may help you deal with Self-Defeating Habits.

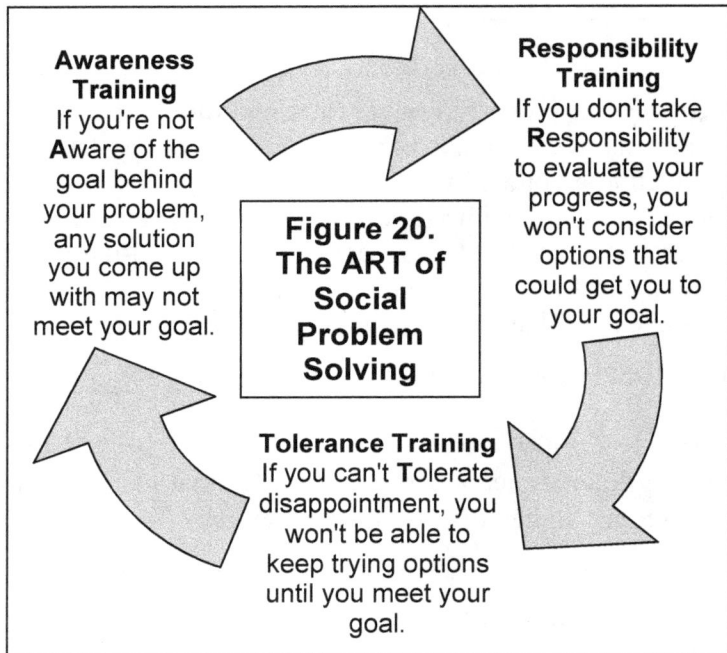

Awareness Training
If you're not **A**ware of the goal behind your problem, any solution you come up with may not meet your goal.

Responsibility Training
If you don't take **R**esponsibility to evaluate your progress, you won't consider options that could get you to your goal.

Figure 20. The ART of Social Problem Solving

Tolerance Training
If you can't **T**olerate disappointment, you won't be able to keep trying options until you meet your goal.

Awareness training: In the ART of Social Problem Solving, if you're not **A**ware of the real goal behind your problem, any solution you come up with may not meet your goal.

Behind every problem there is a goal. Problems are only problems when we are not meeting our goals to get what we want in life. The first step in getting SET to solve the problem is to Set your goal. This requires passing an honesty exam about what you really want. Setting your goal involves getting honest with yourself about your goal. What is my goal? What do I really want? Look at actual problem-solving goals not feelings about the problem. There is a big difference between getting your feelings off and solving the problem.

Practice Example Part 1: <u>Set your Goal</u>- Suppose you have a long track record of family rejection because of your unhealthy, harmful behavior. To make matters worse suppose you would regularly deny it, use cover up tactics to throw them off the track and have angry outbursts to get them off your back (i.e., "winning by intimidation", see p. 194). Imagine that you are now trying to turn things around and haven't done your unhealthy, harmful behavior for a month. You want your family to begin to accept and trust you again but they are still asking the same old questions to check up on you. Because you haven't done it for a month, you are now ruminating (working yourself up) over being unjustly accused when they question you and are having angry outbursts over still not being accepted. Your angry outbursts are making your family think you are still doing wrong, because you used angry outbursts to get them off your back when you were doing your unhealthy, harmful behavior in the past.

Given this situation, you might list your problem as "My family still doesn't trust me even though I've changed" and your goal as "Getting them to believe I've changed, trust and accept me". If you use the "Mirror concept" (i.e., get therapist/group member opinions and use their feedback as a mirror to better see yourself, p. 200), you will become aware that your real problem is, "I have a long track record of unhealthy, harmful behavior including angry outbursts to get my family off my back". Awareness of your real problem allows you to become aware of your real goal, i.e., "Earn their trust and acceptance back by developing a long track record of no unhealthy, harmful behavior and no outbursts when questioned about it".

Problem Example: "~~My family still doesn't trust me even though I've changed.~~" "I have a long track record of unhealthy, harmful behavior including angry outbursts to get my family off my back."

Goal Example: "~~Getting them to believe I've changed, trust and accept me.~~" "Earn their trust and acceptance back by developing a long track record of no unhealthy, harmful behavior and no outbursts when questioned about it."

We can pretty much guarantee that we will stay stuck where we are and never get what we want unless we keep our real problems "up front" (i.e., stay aware of them at all times),[2] become aware of our real goals and deal with the self-defeating habits that block our progress. Use the space below to practice awareness training on a real problem, a real goal and a real self-defeating habit that gets in the way of that goal. Use the "Mirror Concept" by talking this over with your therapist or group and use their feedback to help you better see yourself.

My Problem: _____

_____

My Goal: _____

_____

Review what you have learned in Section A- D of this component about Self-Defeating Habits. Then use the space below to describe the self-defeating habits that get in the way of the goal you described above. Talk this over with your therapist or group and use their feedback to help you.

<u>Self-Defeating Habit(s) that block my goal</u>: _____

_____

_____

Responsibility training: While Awareness training on clarifying the real goal behind your problem is a necessary first step, if you don't take **R**esponsibility to evaluate your progress, you won't consider options that could get you to your goal. After you clarify the real goal behind your problem, you need to take responsibility to evaluate, "What have I been doing, how well has it been working for me and how will things likely turn out if I continue doing the same thing?" This basically means taking responsibility for the self-defeating habits have been getting in the way of your real goal. After that, you will need to take responsibility to come up with other options that could be better solutions to meeting your goal.

Practice Example Part 2: <u>**Evaluate your Progress and Options**</u>- Review the practice example problem and your real goal in part 1 above. Becoming aware of your real goal can help you evaluate the progress you are making towards that goal.

Progress Evaluation Example -
Q: "What have I been doing?
Ans: Ruminating (working yourself up) over being unjustly accused when they question you and are having angry outbursts over still not being accepted.
Q: How well has that been working for me in getting their trust and acceptance back?
Ans: It's not working at all. In fact it's making them think I'm still doing my unhealthy, harmful behavior.
Q: How will things likely turn out if I continue ruminating over not being accepted and having angry outbursts over being questioned?"
Ans: My family will become convicted that I haven't made any positive changes.

Options Evaluation Example - Let's be honest, the first two options you have are....
• "I could just keep getting my feelings off and not solving the problem by ruminating over being unjustly accused when they question me and blowing up over not being accepted."
• "I could always give up by telling myself that I will never be trusted again and they think I'm still doing it anyway so I might as well and go back to my old unhealthy, harmful behavior."
In order to solve the problem, you have to be upset enough to let go of your self-defeating habits and try new options. When coming up with options, "you are only limited by your creativity" but a good place to start would be to review the first three ACTS Healthy Behavior Success Skills (p.20- 25) to see if any of the skills you learned to "avoid trouble, calm down and think it through" might work for you. For example...
• "I could use "the 3 G's", i.e., three-Step Social Responsibility Plan (p. 20) to avoid falling back into another angry outburst when my family questions me."
• "I could use the ABC's of letting my anger go (p. 22) when I start ruminating over how family "should" trust and accept me."
• "I could use the Reality Scales to think my situation through (p. 24) and weigh out how much not being accepted threatens my survival, my success and how severe it really is to me."

Tolerance training: If you can't **T**olerate disappointment, you won't be able to keep trying the different solutions needed to meet your goal. After you become aware of your real goal, evaluate your progress, identify the Self-Defeating Habits that are getting in the way of your goal and come up with several options that are likely to be better solutions to meeting your goal, you need you need to take responsible action. This requires learning to tolerate disappointment by trying one option after another until you find a solution to your problem.

Tolerating disappointment:"Winners never quit and quitters never win"- You have to be able to tolerate disappointment and frustration in order to keep from falling into self-defeating giving up. A good example of self-defeating giving up is described earlier in Component 7 on "Recovery Perfectionism" which involves giving up after one mistake. Tolerating disappointment requires developing tenacity or stick-to-itiveness because changing unhealthy, harmful behavior and achieving life goals are difficult. You may have to accept that progress on both involves two steps up, one back, two up, one back until you finally get there. The bottom line is this, "If at first you don't succeed, try, try again" is the key to making your goals in life and tolerating change means learning to tolerate disappointment.

Practice Example Part 3: <u>Take responsible action</u>- Review practice example part 1 (the real problem and your real goal) and part 2 (your goal progress and options) above . Becoming aware of your real goal can help you evaluate the progress you are making towards that goal.

Since the first three ACTS skills seem to work as options for me, I'm going to use them all to make my goal. Every time I get questioned about my unhealthy, harmful behavior, I'm going to use my three-Step Social Responsibility Plan to avoid falling back into another angry outburst. I will: 1) Get out, excuse myself before they can even read the upset on my face, then; 2) Get honest, that admitting that not being trusted and accepted by family, can't stop my heart or berating (i.e., it's a zero on the survival scale, not dangerous at all), it can't prevent me from achieving what I want in life (i.e., it's a zero on the success scale), it's just disappointing (i.e., about a 5 on the severity scale) so I can handle it without a blow up, then; 3) Get responsible by using the ABC's of letting my anger go. I will remind myself that the <u>Action that occurred</u> (getting questioned about my past unhealthy, harmful behavior); triggered my <u>Belief problem</u>, that my family "should" trust me and accept my word when I tell them I've changed. Using the "should" word on myself magnifies my disappointment and gets me worked up into angry outbursts (see magnifying, p. 200), then; I will <u>Challenge my Belief problem</u> by telling myself "where is the evidence that anyone with a long track record of unhealthy, harmful behavior "should" be trusted after stopping for only a month? This will help me let go of my self-defeating habit of "no concept of track record" (see p. 191) and accept that the only way to earn trust back by after a long track record of unhealthy, harmful behavior is to develop an even longer track record of avoiding that behavior.

Now put it all together by picking a real life problem and using the SET Social Problem Solving skills to solve that problem in the space provided below.

Set your goal: _____

_____

Evaluate your progress _____

_____

and options: _____

_____

_____

_____

Take responsible action: _____

_____

_____

_____

<u>Tolerating change</u>- Describe the opposite healthy, responsible behavior that you need to "Act as if" (p. 12) you already have and practice regularly by answering two questions:
1. "What would be the opposite extreme?" of the self defeating habits listed in the practice example above (i.e., ruminating, winning by intimidation and no concept of track record)
2. "What would be the opposite extreme?" of the "Self-Defeating Habit(s) that block my goal?" that you listed in the Awareness training section above.

_____

_____

_____

Tolerating rejection: Pushing past exaggerated needs for acceptance

Everyone wants to be accepted and no one likes rejection but doing the right thing sometimes involves telling people what they need to hear, not what they want to hear. This means pushing past your need for acceptance and risking rejection by saying or doing the right thing.

It is important to realize that a common reason that we become aware that someone else is making a mistake, slipping and on the way to falling back into unhealthy, harmful behavior is our own experience in making the same mistake ourselves. This may cause us to feel like we shouldn't say anything because we've done it our self (i.e., like a hypocrite). It may also result in rejection because when you tell the person what they need to hear, they may actually discount what you have to say with, "You've done the same thing yourself so don't tell me about it!" Don't make excuses not to speak up when someone is heading for trouble. Do the right thing and if the person says, "You have no right to point out a mistake that you made yourself", tell them that making the same mistake makes you an expert witness on knowing it when you see it.

Be careful not to fall into self-defeating procrastination. The longer you wait to confront the problem, the worse it will get. The longer you put it off, the more time you have to ruminate about the consequences. You already know that the consequences of getting honest with others is risking rejection. Tell yourself, "Nothing to it but to do it" and balance your confrontation with concern so that the person you are getting honest with understands that you are coming from concern and trying to help them avoid problems. The only reason to put off telling someone what they need to hear to avoid relapse or falling into trouble is bounce it off someone you know who is responsible and who will help you balance your confrontation with concern.

Confrontation with Concern

It is important to set unhealthy pride aside in order to be able to receive and give confrontation with concern. Confrontation with concern is a family value concept which dates back to biblical times (i.e., "You are your brother's keeper"). Confrontation with concern is disclosing information about other people's problems when no personal benefit to you will occur or for unselfish reasons which relate only to concern about the individual you are talking about. On the other hand, character assignation and "snitching" involves disclosing information about other people's problems in order to hurt them, get back at them, get yourself out of trouble or some other selfish gain or motive. Confrontation with concern helps you and helps others by increasing behavior awareness. Pushing past your need to be accepted and being your brother's keeper through confrontation with concern helps you maintain both your social maturity. The bottom line here is that if you really care, you will say something and say it so the person can tell there is concern in your confrontation.

One way to do this is with a "Pull Up". Since we view people who do things on purpose differently than those who are not aware of their mistake, a "Pull Up" is based on the assumption that the person making the mistake is not aware of it. A "Pull Up" is a brief constructive feedback designed to pull the other person up to your level of awareness. With pull ups "Less is more" so be brief, be honest and be concerned. A "Pull Up" goes like this, "Excuse me, I need to make you aware that..." (followed by the self-defeating habit or mistake you see). For example...

- "Excuse me, I need to make you aware that if you go to that party, you are setting yourself up for relapse" (compromising self for excitement needs and giving up).
- "Excuse me, I need to make you aware that getting angry over smart remarks and getting even with practical jokes is going too far and someone is going to get hurt" (compromising self for attention and ruminating).
- "Excuse me, I need to make you aware that accepting that movie invitation is putting off studying for finals" (compromising self to be accepted and procrastination).

Hint: Balancing Confrontation with Concern- The SRT "Kite Analogy"
In "the kite analogy," if you yank too hard on the kite string (i.e., provide too much confrontation and not enough concern), it breaks and you lose the kite (i.e., therapeutic relationship). If you give in, go the direction the kite is pulling or run after the kite (i.e., provide too much concern and not enough confrontation, aka "enabling"), the kite crashes. If you stand still and don't pull against it (i.e., fail to provide any more structure than was received in the past), the kite maintains its present level and does not climb higher. If you provide appropriate, positive resistance and consistently pull against the kite (i.e., provide a consistent client needs-based balance of confrontation with concern), it rises to its maximum potential. (Yokley, 2008 p. 152)

E. Make a Positive Plan and Commitment to Change. Review the three Self-Defeating Habits that you listed on your Harmful Behavior Anatomy worksheet (page 161). What can you do about it now? How are you going to change these problems, what are you going to do? (Consult with your therapist or staff and write your plan below)

1) _____

What I can do about it→_____

What I am going to do about it→_____

2) _____

What I can do about it→_____

What I am going to do about it→_____

3) _____

What I can do about it→_____

What I am going to do about it→_____

Update your relapse prevention plan if you have completed workbook 1 or 2. If you haven't completed either workbook, make a relapse prevention plan that works for you (see p. 16) with your treatment staff for the main unhealthy, harmful behavior that brought you to treatment based on what you have learned about what you can do to avoid falling back into it.

Update your promise letter if you have completed workbook 1 or 2. If you haven't completed either workbook, write a promise letter. Start with "Dear (list those you have let down and yourself if you have suffered from the harmful behavior)", and continue with something to the effect of- "I am making a commitment to stop (the unhealthy, harmful behavior) that led to my need for treatment. Be sure to add "I have learned about how I generalized my problem to other areas through The Harmful Behavior Anatomy" and explain what you have learned from this workbook. Add important Harmful Behavior Anatomy information that you are going to use in your relapse prevention plan and commitment to change.

"Two heads are better than one, four eyes are better than two". Discuss your relapse prevention plan and promise letter with your therapist or group. In all of your discussions, use the "Window Concept" (i.e., only shoveling feedback out the window that in not helpful) to help you decide what to apply and the "Mirror Concept" (i.e., learning to use others feedback as a mirror to better see yourself, p. 200) to help you accept and benefit most from what applies. Use this feedback to improve your relapse prevention plan, your letter and your self-awareness.

Get honest about your Self-Defeating Habits with your therapist or treatment group. Log the date you discussed this issue and who you discussed it with in the space provided below.

Date: _____ Discussed with: _____

Congratulations!!! You have now completed your work on the Harmful Behavior Anatomy of factors that allowed your harmful behavior to spread, generalize or transfer to other forms.

The Harmful Behavior Anatomy Worksheet:
How Harmful Behavior was Generalized

Name: _____

Date: _____

The Harmful Behavior Anatomy
(of pathological social-emotional immaturity components that support
<u>multiple forms of unhealthy, harmful behavior</u>)

List all forms of harmful behavior here-

_____

_____

_____

Irresponsible (Score = _____)
Thinking

_____

(Score = _____) **Unhealthy**
Pride

Unhealthy Perfectionism
(Score = _____)

_____

_____

Control
And
Power
Obsession

_____

(Score = _____) **Deception**

H_____

T_____

L_____

C_____

R_____

Grandiosity (Score = _____)

Social
Maturity
Deficit
Score = _____

Emotional
Maturity
Deficit
Score = _____

_____

Self-defeating Habits

Maladaptive Self-image

_____

_____

CAPO
(Score = _____)

_____

_____

(Score = _____)

_____

(Score = _____)

Harmful Behavior Anatomy Worksheet (continued)

Irresponsible Thinking (continued): _____

_____

_____

Control and Power Obsession (continued): _____

_____

_____

Unhealthy Pride (continued): _____

_____

_____

Deception (continued): _____

_____

_____

Social Maturity Deficit (continued): _____

_____

_____

Maladaptive Self Image (continued): _____

_____

_____

Unhealthy Perfectionism (continued): _____

_____

_____

Grandiosity (continued): _____

_____

_____

Emotional Maturity Deficit (continued): _____

_____

_____

Self-Defeating Habits (continued): _____

_____

_____

Understanding Harmful Behavior Summary

"Creativity is the power to connect the seemingly unconnected" -- William Plomer

Look at the ten scores on you Harmful Behavior Anatomy worksheet (page 161) to see your social-emotional maturity strengths and weaknesses.

What is your greatest weakness (i.e., category with the highest score)? _____

What is your greatest strength (i.e., category with the lowest score)? _____

This lets you know where you need to begin work first in your social-emotional growth plan.

Discuss this with your therapist/staff and/or treatment group.

Completing your Harmful Behavior Time Line: Three Case Examples

You are now ready to finish your work on the Harmful Behavior Time Line (Appendix F). When you began various types of unhealthy, harmful behavior (the onset) and how long you continued each type of harmful behavior (the duration) along with the connections between these things are best understood by making and reviewing a harmful behavior time line. If you have a therapist and/or treatment group now is the time to get back to your discussions with them about your harmful behavior history. Just like you did earlier, be socially responsible by initiating a review of everything you did that was harmful first and completing the bottom half of your time line before you move on to discussions about what others have done to you, which is needed to complete the top half of your time line.

> **Hint:** If you have completed workbook 1, start completing the top part of your Harmful Behavior Time Line, start by reviewing your Harmful Behavior Social Diagram (page 42 of workbook 1). Circle the individuals who committed harmful behaviors towards you and record this on your Time Line.

The following three examples were selected to cover the Harmful Behavior Continuum (Table 1) which ranges from unhealthy, harmful behavior that is primarily harmful to self (e.g., food abuse) to behavior that is harmful to self and others (e.g., substance abuse) to behavior that is primarily harmful to others (e.g., sexual abuse). Three different examples are provided at the end of Chapter 2 in Social Responsibility Therapy for Adolescents and Young Adults (Yokley, 2008, p. 125- 131).

Unhealthy Eating (Food Abuse) Referral- The following is a Harmful Behavior Time Line case example of Lucy, a 37-year-old single parent referred for hospital-based outpatient treatment of food abuse behavior and other forms of unhealthy, harmful behavior requiring treatment (e.g., Unhealthy overeating- resulting in morbid obesity, Substance abuse- alcohol, marijuana, cocaine and later heroin along with cigarette smoking, Sexual abuse- Promiscuity, Property abuse- theft and excess spending, Trust abuse- relationship cheating).

Harmful Behavior Time Line- Lucy

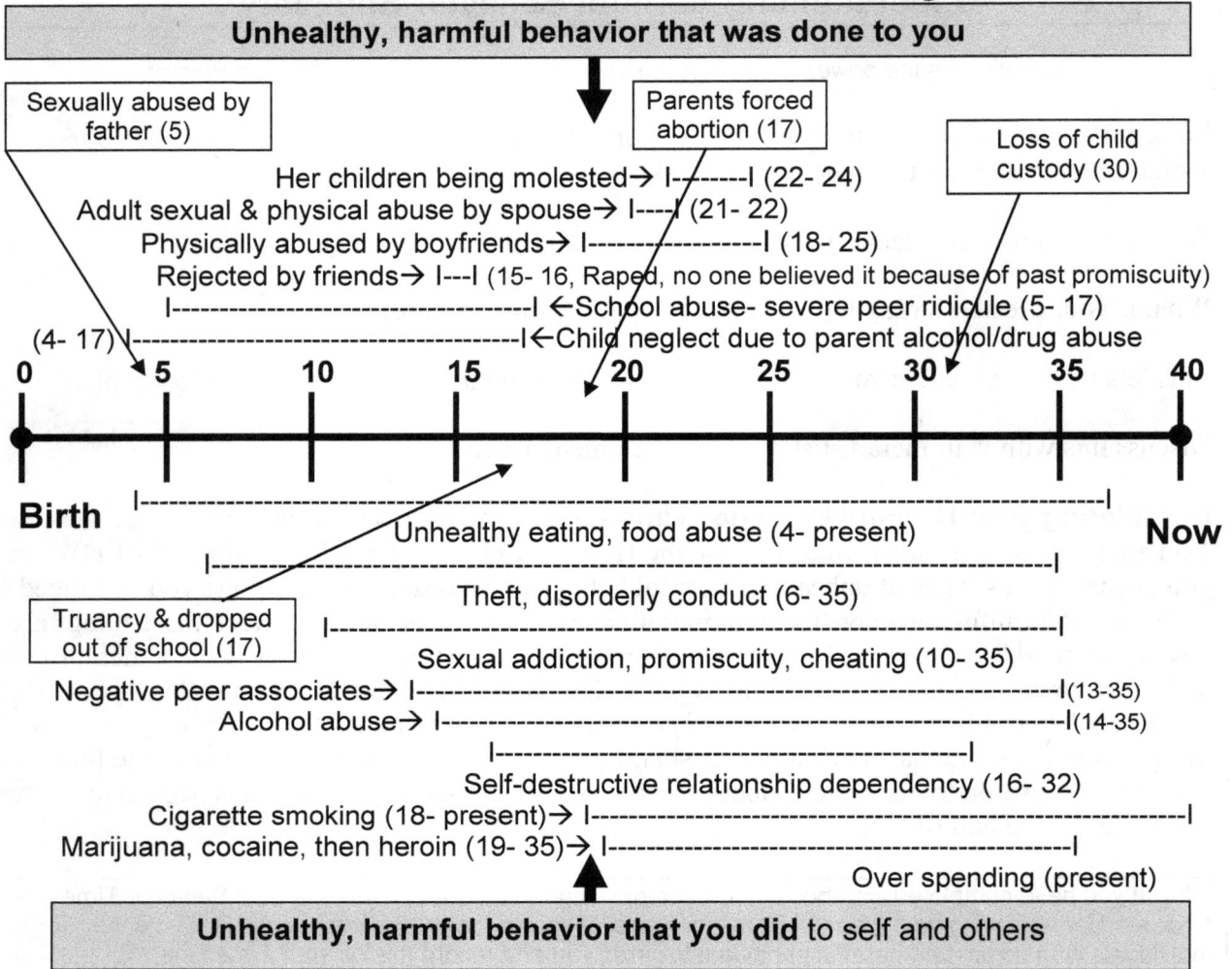

Unhealthy, harmful behavior that was done to you

Sexually abused by father (5)

Parents forced abortion (17)

Loss of child custody (30)

Her children being molested→ I--/-----I (22- 24)
Adult sexual & physical abuse by spouse→ I----/ (21- 22)
Physically abused by boyfriends→ I------/----------I (18- 25)
Rejected by friends→ I---I (15- 16, Raped, no one believed it because of past promiscuity)
I--------------------------------I ←School abuse- severe peer ridicule (5- 17)
(4- 17) I--------------------------------I←Child neglect due to parent alcohol/drug abuse

0   5   10   15   20   25   30   35   40

Birth

I--I
Unhealthy eating, food abuse (4- present)

I---I
Theft, disorderly conduct (6- 35)

Now

Truancy & dropped out of school (17)

I--I
Sexual addiction, promiscuity, cheating (10- 35)

Negative peer associates→ I--I (13-35)
Alcohol abuse→ I--I (14-35)
I--I
Self-destructive relationship dependency (16- 32)
Cigarette smoking (18- present)→ I--I
Marijuana, cocaine, then heroin (19- 35)→ I----------------------------------I
Over spending (present)

Unhealthy, harmful behavior that you did to self and others

Summary: Self-awareness connections made by Lucy from constructing and discussing her time line included awareness of her emotional conversion reaction. This involved, "A problem with feeling helpless by being sexually and physically abused" and converting the unwanted feelings from that abuse into multiple forms of harmful behavior that allowed those feelings to be vented. This process begin with emotional eating to comfort the helplessness experiences from abuse and spread into self-medicating with, cigarettes, alcohol and drugs. In addition, theft (i.e., taking from others without their permission like sex was taken from her) and promiscuity (i.e., "you can't take it from me, I'm giving it away") were used to act those feelings out. Hanging with negative inferiors to and over-spending was used to build self up and feel better. "There was daily neglect where my parents had time for their friends and to party but the kids got put on the back burner. This fed my exaggerated need for attention and willingness to create chaos when I am needing attention".

Substance Abuse (drugs/alcohol) Referral- The following is a Harmful Behavior Time Line case example of Diego, a 19-year-old single male referred for residential (i.e., therapeutic community) treatment of substance abuse and other forms of unhealthy, harmful behavior requiring treatment (e.g., <u>Substance abuse</u>- alcohol, marijuana, opiates (heroin and methadone), drug possession and trafficking charges, <u>Property abuse</u>- vandalism, shoplifting, burglary, <u>Physical abuse</u>- drug-related shooting conviction, assault and battery, menacing, <u>Trust abuse</u>- History of school truancy and home run away, multiple probation violations).

Harmful Behavior Time Line- Diego

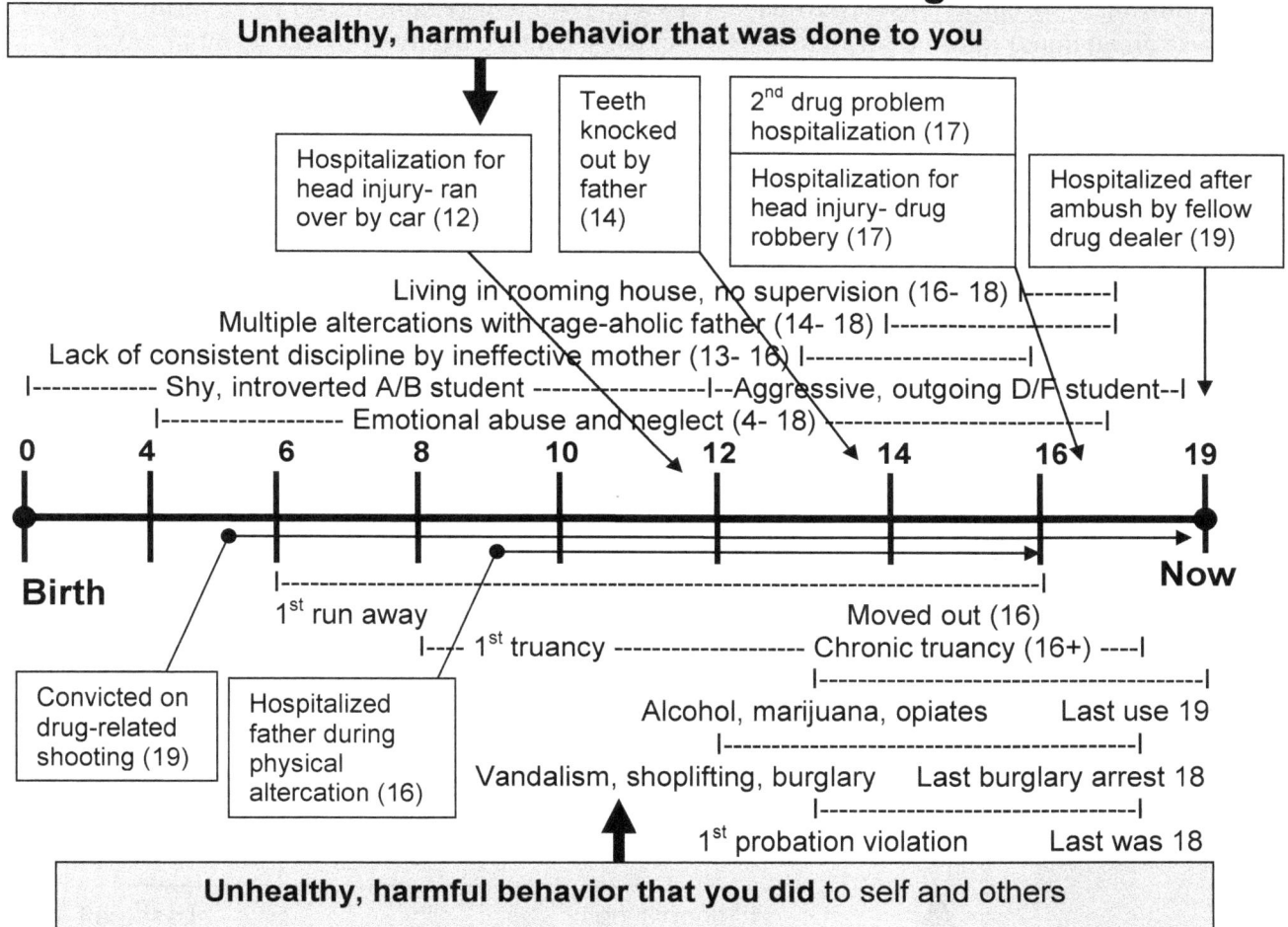

Unhealthy, harmful behavior that was done to you

Hospitalization for head injury- ran over by car (12)

Teeth knocked out by father (14)

2nd drug problem hospitalization (17)

Hospitalization for head injury- drug robbery (17)

Hospitalized after ambush by fellow drug dealer (19)

Living in rooming house, no supervision (16- 18) |--------|
Multiple altercations with rage-aholic father (14- 18) |-----------------|
Lack of consistent discipline by ineffective mother (13- 16) |-----------------|
|------------ Shy, introverted A/B student -----------------|--Aggressive, outgoing D/F student--|
|------------------ Emotional abuse and neglect (4- 18) |-----------------------|

| 0 | 4 | 6 | 8 | 10 | 12 | 14 | 16 | 19 |

Birth

Now

1st run away

Moved out (16)
|--- 1st truancy ------------------- Chronic truancy (16+) ----|

Convicted on drug-related shooting (19)

Hospitalized father during physical altercation (16)

Alcohol, marijuana, opiates   Last use 19
|-----------------------------------|
Vandalism, shoplifting, burglary   Last burglary arrest 18
|-----------------------------|
1st probation violation   Last was 18

Unhealthy, harmful behavior that you did to self and others

Example Summary: Self-awareness connections made by Diego from constructing and discussing his time line included awareness of his emotional conversion reaction. This involved converting unwanted feelings of insecurity from past emotional abuse and neglect into multiple forms of harmful behavior that allowed those feelings to be vented. This process begin with running away from problems and compromising self to be accepted by skipping school, drinking and smoking marijuana with others. Diego's time line allowed him to see his change from shy A/B student to an aggressive D/F student came after his serious head injury. He now remembers that this was when he began making things up and acting like he knew or got things that he didn't. This spread into acting self-confident to cover feeling otherwise and dealing drugs to meet exaggerated needs to be good at something on order to get attention acceptance and excitement. He was able to connect his insecurity, victim view and ruminating on injustices to expecting to be attacked by his frightening rage-aholic father and came to realize by discussing his time line that opiates self-medicated his social insecurity by helping him relax and worry less about being attacked in social situations.

Sexual Abuse Behavior Referral- The following is an Harmful Behavior Time Line case example of Pete, a 16-year-old male referred for residential treatment of sexually abusive behavior and other forms of unhealthy, harmful behavior requiring treatment (e.g., <u>Sexual Abuse</u>- Nine male and female child victims, both relatives and non-relatives between the ages of 5 and 11. <u>Physical abuse</u>- Multiple anger-based peer assaults, <u>Property abuse</u>- petty theft, shoplifting, <u>Substance abuse</u>- Marijuana, tobacco, <u>Trust abuse</u>- Chronic lying, covering up, false abuse allegations) referred for treatment of sexually abusive behavior in a residential group home.

Harmful Behavior Time Line- Pete

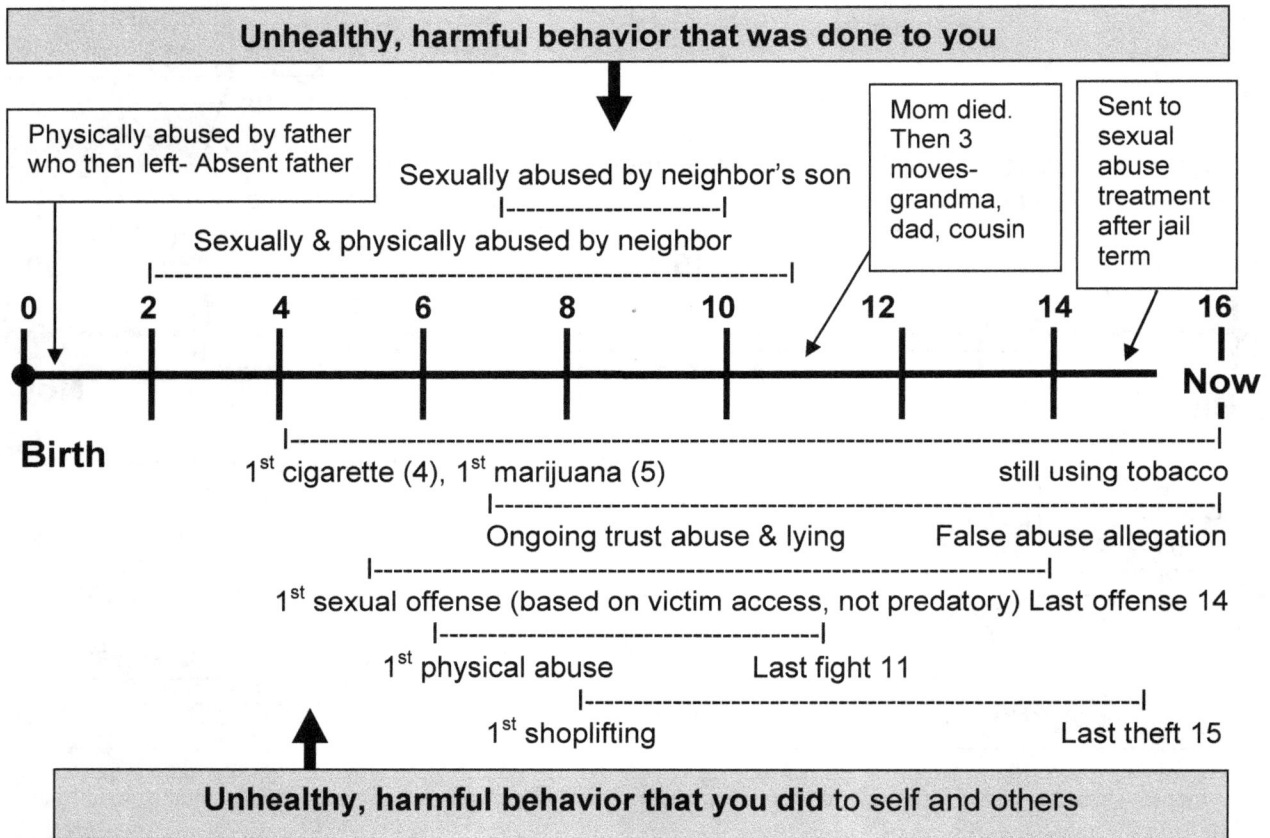

Unhealthy, harmful behavior that was done to you

Physically abused by father who then left- Absent father

Sexually abused by neighbor's son
|----------------------|

Sexually & physically abused by neighbor
|---|

Mom died. Then 3 moves- grandma, dad, cousin

Sent to sexual abuse treatment after jail term

0   2   4   6   8   10   12   14   16

Birth   **Now**

1st cigarette (4), 1st marijuana (5)   still using tobacco
|---|

Ongoing trust abuse & lying   False abuse allegation
|---|

1st sexual offense (based on victim access, not predatory) Last offense 14
|---|

1st physical abuse   Last fight 11
|---|

1st shoplifting   Last theft 15

Unhealthy, harmful behavior that you **did** to self and others

Example Summary: Self-awareness connections made by Pete from constructing and discussing his time line included awareness of his "Vampire Syndrome" behavior repetition compulsion, involving being sexually abused over time and later being sexually abusive to others which also occurred with physical abuse. The difference being that his physical abuse of others stopped when he stopped being physically abused (moved) but his sexual abuse of others continued until he was caught and jailed. The direct connection between becoming trust abusive to cover up his other forms of abuse was also important as was his awareness that his sexual abuse spread to physical abuse and then property abuse showing how abusing power over people had generalized to abusing power over others property (i.e., "I'll do what I want to you and take what I want from you").

Discovering Connections between the Past and the Present

Making Harmful Behavior Time Line Connections

Examine your time line. Look at what you experienced, what was done to you and what you later did. Then write what you have learned about those connections in the space provided below.

_____

_____

_____

_____

_____

_____

_____

_____

_____

Hint: Use the language of responsibility with "I" statements to take ownership of your harmful behavior and don't turn the negative social influence that you were around into blaming others for your behavior. Avoid blaming by identifying who modeled those behaviors by doing them around you, introducing them to you, teaching them to you, or doing them to you while owning responsibility for the choice of whether to adopt or continue behaviors. Put another way, you need to state, "Although I was influenced by my (mother, father, brother, friends, etc.) who (smoked, overate, drank, drugged, assaulted, molested, etc.) around me, got me to try it or did it to me, I knew it was harmful and chose to continue it myself, get others involved or do it to others despite the fact that it was wrong".

Making Social Behavior Diagram Connections

If you have completed workbook 1, review your Harmful Behavior Social Diagram Worksheet (workbook 1, page 42) to complete the table below and help you with your time line. If you haven't completed workbook 1, use the space provided to list the first names of people you know who have been involved in unhealthy, harmful behavior and the type of behavior they were involved in (e.g., overeating, gambling, spending, drugs/alcohol, assault/domestic violence, sexual behavior problems, etc). Do not include this information about the problems of others in your "My Story" presentation (discussed later) which needs to focus on you.

Circle the names of all of the people who committed harmful behaviors around you, to you or showed you how to do it. Next circle the types of harmful behavior that you have done and draw lines connecting the harmful things that were done to you with harmful things that you have done. Did you learn things from others, were you taught, did others behavior rub off on you? Document the connections that you have discovered in the space provided and update your Harmful Behavior Time Line adding new information that you remembered from this exercise.

People	Unhealthy, Harmful Behavior
Friends-	
Family-	
Other-	

Now look at the unhealthy, harmful behaviors that you did on the bottom of your time line and the connections to your hurtful experiences on the top of your time line. Were you using the "Window Concept" (p. 200) at that point in your life? Discuss how hurting yourself is revenging the mistakes of others on yourself and when you hurt others, you hurt yourself through guilt or consequences. Address the question" Why should I hurt me just because other people or other things hurt me?" Record what you learned in the space below.

_____

_____

_____

_____

_____

_____

Life Impact Statement: The Harmful Behavior Anatomy & Time Line

Since humans learn from experience for better or for worse, usually if there's something going wrong in the present it is connected to something that went wrong in the past. Since we are creatures of habit, if we learn something as a survival response or something that worked to get us what we want in the past, we are likely to continue it whether it is still needed or not, even if it is unhealthy or harmful. Use the space below to record connections between each Social Maturity Deficit problem you identified (i.e., problems with honesty, trust, loyalty, concern and responsibility) and the other Harmful Behavior Anatomy factors that you recorded. Ask your therapist or treatment group for a help session on identifying these connections. Use the Life Impact Statement workspace on page 183 if you need more space.

_____

_____

_____

_____

_____

_____

_____

_____

Hint: Consider honesty for example. Dishonesty as a childhood survival technique could be coming out now with connections to Unhealthy Pride and Perfectionism even though it is no longer needed. Here's how you might make that connection. Look at the honesty problems you recorded the Social Maturity Deficit portion of the Harmful Behavior Anatomy (Component 5). Then examine your time line and look for connections to your honesty problem. For example, if your time line includes living in fear of a ragoholic, perfectionist parent who over reacted to your minor mistakes with major punishment, you may have learned to use dishonesty as a survival technique to avoid irrational or extreme consequences. Review your Harmful Behavior Anatomy worksheet. If you also have Unhealthy Pride and Perfection Issues, there may be a connection between the past childhood survival technique of dishonesty to avoid rageoholic parent consequences with present unhealthy pride and need to always look good around peers due to an irrational fear that being less than perfect will bring the same extreme consequences that were received by toxic parents. On the other hand, if you do not have any examples of toxic parenting/abuse, your dishonesty could simple be a Self-defeating Habit repeated because of learning how easy it was and a need to create a Maladaptive Self-Image (cool or tough) or Grandiosity attitude that others are stupid and can't catch you anyway because you have become good at it.

Life Impact Statement connections can also include- Trust issues connected with time line documentation of being hurt in the past and Self-Defeating habit of getting back into unhealthy relationships in the present or fear of commitment rationalized by Perfectionism (finding fault in everyone). Loyalty issues relating to a time line history of abuse or neglect connected to Irresponsible Thinking of "It's every man for himself", "Your either a victim or an offender" or "I'll never let myself be put in a situation where I am helpless again" connected to a defensive Control and Power Obsession (i.e., protecting self by controlling mood with substances or others with manipulations). Concern issues relating to a time line history of neglect, abuse or other forms of not receiving concern and Irresponsible Thinking that "It's OK to treat people the way you are treated", "Turnabout is fair play" can be connected to an offensive Control and Power Obsession (i.e., building self up by putting others down). Responsibility issues relating to a time line which lists a parent history of substance abuse and unemployment is easy to see. What is harder to see is the Grandiosity sense of entitlement to do nothing or Self-defeating habits to hold yourself back that can rub off on you by being in that environment. There are too many examples to list. The number of connections you can make are only limited by your motivation to look into your present behavior and past history.

If this is the only SRT workbook that you have completed, skip this section and go to "Complete the final update of your relapse prevention plan" on page 173.

Putting it all Together

If you have completed SRT workbook 1 and 2, photocopy: 1) The Risk Factor Chain Worksheet and 2) The Stress-Relapse Cycle Worksheet that you completed in each of those workbooks along with 3) The Harmful Behavior Anatomy Worksheet (p. 161) and 4) The Harmful Behavior Time Line (p. 206, instructions p. 34) that you completed in this workbook. Then tape those four sheets together in the manner illustrated in Figure 21 below as the first step in your unhealthy, harmful behavior presentation to others involved in your treatment, support/care circle and life.

Figure 21. Understanding Harmful Behavior: Presentation to Significant Others

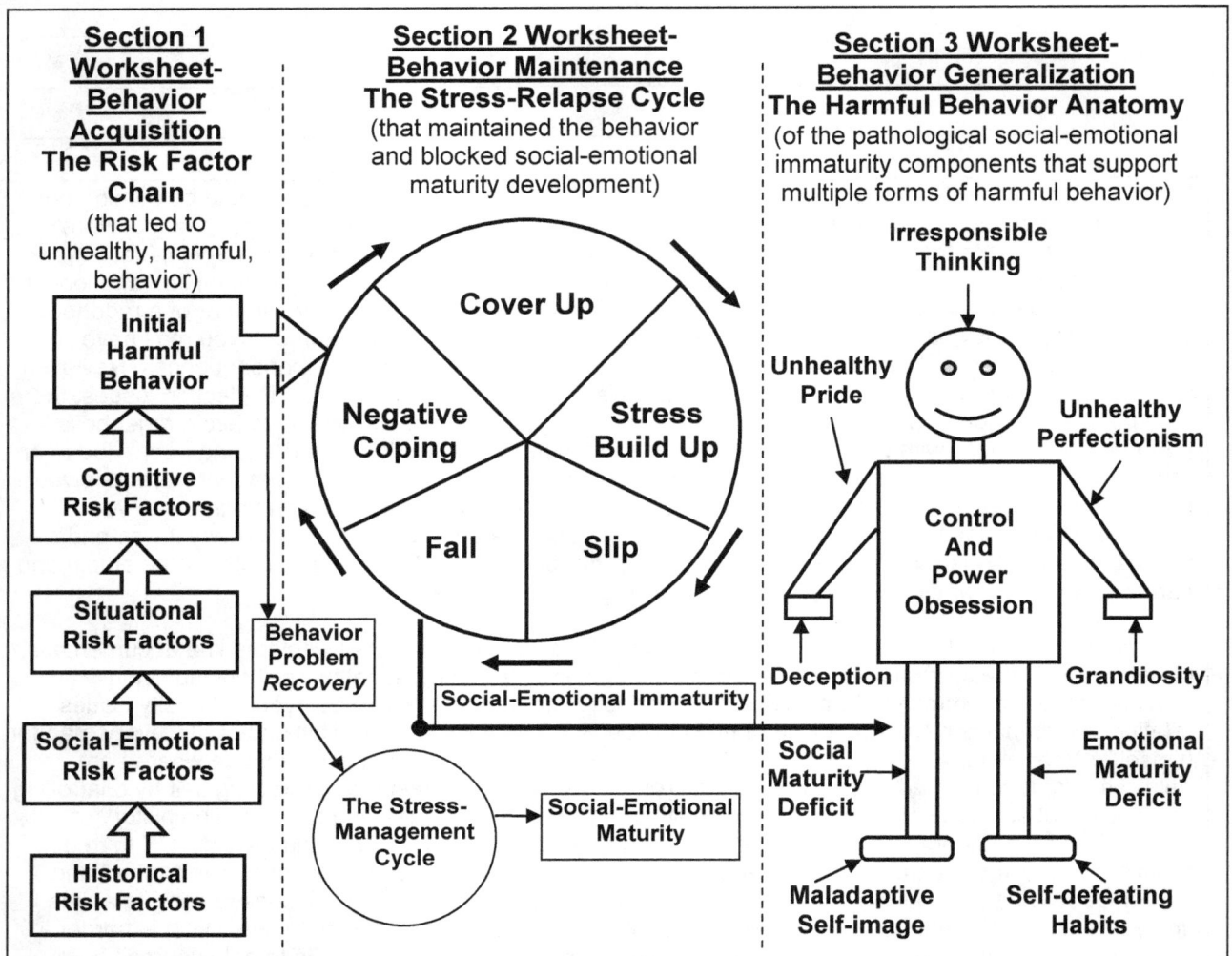

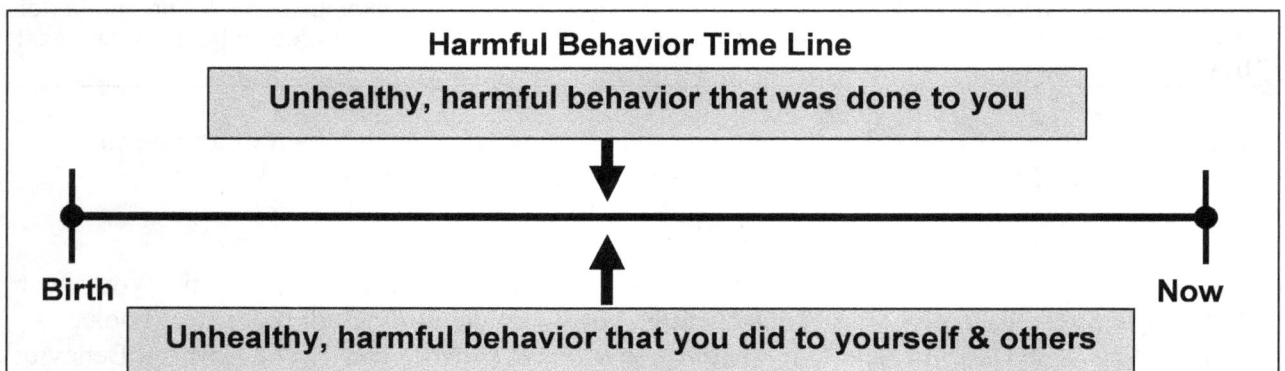

Section 1 Worksheet-Behavior Acquisition
The Risk Factor Chain
(that led to unhealthy, harmful, behavior)

- Initial Harmful Behavior
- Cognitive Risk Factors
- Situational Risk Factors
- Social-Emotional Risk Factors
- Historical Risk Factors

Section 2 Worksheet-Behavior Maintenance
The Stress-Relapse Cycle
(that maintained the behavior and blocked social-emotional maturity development)

- Cover Up
- Stress Build Up
- Slip
- Fall
- Negative Coping

Behavior Problem *Recovery*

Social-Emotional Immaturity

The Stress-Management Cycle → Social-Emotional Maturity

Section 3 Worksheet-Behavior Generalization
The Harmful Behavior Anatomy
(of the pathological social-emotional immaturity components that support multiple forms of harmful behavior)

- Irresponsible Thinking
- Unhealthy Pride
- Unhealthy Perfectionism
- Control And Power Obsession
- Deception
- Grandiosity
- Social Maturity Deficit
- Emotional Maturity Deficit
- Maladaptive Self-image
- Self-defeating Habits

Harmful Behavior Time Line

Unhealthy, harmful behavior that was done to you

Birth — Now

Unhealthy, harmful behavior that you did to yourself & others

The worksheet picture that you constructed outlines how you got your problem, kept it up and spread it to other problem areas in your life in the order listed on your time line. The saying "If you forget where you came from, you're doomed to return there"[12] points out that not only is it important for you to understand how you acquired, maintained and generalized your harmful behavior but to keep what you have learned "up front" and not forget it if you want to avoid falling back into some type of unhealthy, harmful behavior. The Problem Development Triad and Time Line clearly shows where your have been and hopefully will serve to help you avoid returning there. An important first step in keeping your issues up front is sharing them with the significant others in your life.

The Problem Development Triad Presentation- "My Story"

In Social Responsibility Therapy, it is a social responsibility to understand the unhealthy, harmful behavior that has been harmful to yourself and/or others. The phrase "The truth will set you free" only applies if you are able to get it out. The purpose of your Problem Development Triad presentation is to discharge your Social Responsibility to explain the unhealthy, harmful behavior that you have come to understand to those who need to know. Clarifying how you got your harmful behavior in the first place, what maintained it and how it spread out into other areas of your life is an important step in your recovery, in strengthening your relationships and in emotional restitution towards those who were hurt by your unhealthy, harmful behavior and have asked for clarification from you.

"Structured Discovery for solid recovery"- If you have completed all three SRT structured discovery workbooks on understanding your unhealthy, harmful behavior, it is now time for you to put it all together to provide solid support for your recovery. Think back over the types of harmful behavior that you developed. Your workbook assignments on the Risk Factor Chain that led to your unhealthy, harmful behavior, the Stress-Relapse Cycle that maintained it and the Harmful Behavior Anatomy of components that set the occasion for it to spread to other types or areas of your life. These "structured discovery" workbooks were structured to help you discover how you developed the different types of harmful behavior that you reported. It is now time to put this together in a manner that others can understand. It is said that if you want someone to really understand something, get them to teach it to someone else. Putting your presentation together should help you think about how you will explain things to others, which in turn should lead you to a deeper understanding yourself and a more solid recovery. Follow these basic steps.

- Use the four section summary sheets that you completed and taped together (like the illustration in Figure 21 above) to help you write a presentation summary of how you acquired your problem, maintained it and spread it to other areas of your life. If you just have a few people that can sit at a table with you and your treatment staff, make photocopies of your four presentation sections (with identifying information removed) to be collected back after your presentation. If you have more than a few people, use overheads or PowerPoint slides.
- Look at the average rating scores that you recorded on your Harmful Behavior Anatomy worksheet to help you see the areas where you need to do your most work and add this to your promise letter with a commitment to address those issues.
- Review all of the Structured Discovery exercises that you completed and make notes to help you with you explain your understanding of why you did what you did (i.e., the connections that you made from the exercises).
- Do your presentation in the same order that you completed this workbook. Use your harmful

behavior time line to discuss the vampire syndrome (i.e., doing unhealthy, harmful things to others that were done to you or teaching unhealthy, harmful things to others that were taught to you) or conversion reaction (i.e., converting unwanted feelings from problems you experienced into unhealthy, harmful behaviors). Use the "mirror concept" and "window concept"(p. 200) to teach others what you have learned about yourself, to learn more from valuable feedback during your presentation and to avoid over-reacting to difficult feedback. "Knowledge is power" and this self-understanding will help build the self-confidence that you need to maintain self-control. In other words, understanding where you came from and why you are where you are at this point in your life with help maintain your recovery.

Who to invite. Take a close look at The Harmful Behavior Continuum (Table 1) and think about whether your behavior has only affected you or if it has also been harmful to others.

- If your behavior has only affected you, then your only Social Responsibility is to present your understanding of how you got that behavior, what kept it up and how it spread into other areas of your life to your therapist or treatment program staff.
- If you do not have a therapist but are in a Twelve Step Program, it is your Social Responsibility arrange with your sponsor to make your presentation to your recovery group.
- If you do not have a therapist but are completing this workbook as part of a probation requirement to address problem behavior or a human services parenting requirement, arrange with your probation officer or human services caseworker to make your presentation to them and your probation aftercare group or human services parenting group.
- If your behavior was harmful to others and it is fairly low on the severity scale, work with your therapist or program staff to set up a meeting (typically a family session) where you make your presentation.
- In cases where serious harm has come to others as a result of your behavior problem (e.g., physical or sexual abuse), you have a social responsibility to make sure that no further harm comes to them as a result of your actions. This means consulting with your therapist or program staff to determine whether offering this presentation to them could hurt them further. Cooperate with the recommendations of your therapist and do not invite anyone who could be harmed emotionally by what you have to say during your presentation. In general it is not appropriate to invite any victims of serious abuse to your presentation. Respecting their feelings/trauma requires that you complete Emotional Restitution Training (See references-Yokley 2011b) and meet with them along with their therapist and yours in a smaller more private session.

Use the space below to indicate those who need to attend your presentation by checking all that apply. Then make a list the important notes/messages that you want to get across that are not already noted on your worksheets on a separate sheet of paper to use in your presentation.

___Mom (Name: _____)   ___Dad (Name: _____)

___Sisters (Names: _____)   ___Brothers (Names: _____)

___Girlfriend (Name: _____)   ___Boyfriend (Name: _____)

___Wife (Name: _____)   ___Husband (Name: _____)

___Grandmothers (Names: _____)   ___Grandfathers (Names: _____)

___Aunts (Names: _____)   ___Uncles (Names: _____)

___Human services caseworker (Name: _____)

___Probation/Parole officer (Name: _____)

After your presentation- Remember to give copies of your relapse prevention plan and promise letter as part of your commitment to change to the therapists, human services workers and probation/parole authorities who attended along with a signed release of information form. Ask those who attended to be a part of your care circle or support network.

Complete the final update of your relapse prevention plan that works for you (see p. 16) with your therapist or treatment staff based on what you have learned from this workbook about what you can do to avoid falling back into your harmful behavior.. Make sure your relapse prevention plan at least covers the top three unhealthy, harmful behaviors that you listed in your History of unhealthy, harmful behavior (page 4- 6). Be sure to cover the high risk people, places and things that can result in relapse (see p.20). Review types of Irresponsible Thinking, CAPO characteristics, Unhealthy Pride, Deception, Social or Emotional Maturity problems, Maladaptive Self-Image problems, Unhealthy Perfectionism, Grandiosity or Self-defeating habits that could set you up for relapse on the three unhealthy, harmful behaviors that you selected. Be sure to include what you learned from the Harmful Behavior Time Line connections that you were able to make. Copy the final draft of you relapse prevention plan onto the space provided on page 201.

> **Hint:** Take for example, the case of an individual who completed this workbook as part of a referral for food abuse which resulted in becoming severely overweight to the point where it was harmful to their health. Reviewing their Harmful Behavior Time line allowed them to see that overeating started just after they quit smoking. This led to the self-awareness discovery that eating calmed them down the way that smoking used to calm them and helped create a stress relaxation plan after they quit overeating to address their higher risk of returning to smoking.

Update your promise letter. Add anything important that you learned from your final relapse prevention plan or Harmful Time Line to your commitment to change. Copy the final draft of your promise letter onto the space provided on page 220.

"Two heads are better than one, four eyes are better than two". Discuss your relapse prevention plan and promise letter with your therapist and treatment group. In all of your Social Responsibility Therapy discussions, use the "Window Concept" to help you decide what to apply and the "Mirror Concept" to help you accept and benefit most from what applies. Brief definitions of these concepts are on page 200. Use the applicable feedback to improve your relapse prevention plan, your letter and your self-awareness.

Complete your third and final self-evaluation using the form provided in Appendix E. If you are in treatment, discuss your self-evaluation with your therapist or group.

Congratulations! If you have finished the Social Responsibility Therapy Workbooks on "The Risk Factor Chain" that led to your unhealthy, harmful behavior, "The Stress-Relapse Cycle" that maintained it and "The Harmful Behavior Anatomy" of factors that allowed it to generalize or spread to other forms you have a good understanding of the problem development triad and are now ready to explain what you have learned about yourself to others who need to know. If you are in treatment, discuss your how you feel about your accomplishment with your staff.

What's Next: Keeping Your Treatment Path "Up Front"

"No man can know where he is going unless he knows exactly where he has been and exactly how he arrived at his present place"-- Maya Angelou [13]

Recovery from unhealthy, harmful behavior is not at all like recovery from physical disease conditions where treatment typically results in consistent improvement and is discontinued when infections are eradicated or injuries are healed. With unhealthy, harmful behavior recovery in typically two steps up, one back, two up, one back, two up, one back and so on with relapses getting less over time until a track record of healthy, responsible behavior is established and takes over. This occurs because in the words of Dr. Ellis, "We are all fallible human beings" and our Grandiosity sometimes convinces us that our experience or treatment has made us immune to high risk situations that used to trigger unhealthy, harmful behavior. In addition, our Maladaptive Self-Image sometimes gravitates us back to high risk people who exert a negative influence on our recovery. Under these circumstances our Irresponsible Thinking, Self-Defeating Habits and Unhealthy Perfectionism sometimes triggers giving up on self-control kicking in a Social-Emotional Maturity lapse where we succumb to Unhealthy Pride and Deception. In this situation, relapse continues until we win the struggle to get honest with ourselves and others in order to get help, get back on our feet and take the next two steps forward. This leaves us sometimes feeling like we are floundering and getting nowhere, when in fact we are making some progress. Two things must occur to maintain our recovery progress. First, since "No man can know where he is going unless he knows exactly where he has been and exactly how he arrived at his present place" (Maya Angelou) [13] keep your treatment path up front. Stay aware of the Risk Factor Chain that got you there, the Stress-Relapse Cycle that kept you there and the Anatomy of Social-Emotional Maturity Problems that allows you to develop other problem areas. Second, know where you're going by staying focused on your Social Responsibility. Stay focused on maintaining your social maturity (i.e., honesty, trust, loyalty, concern and responsibility) and emotional maturity (i.e., self-awareness, self-efficacy/confidence and self-control). Your social-emotional maturity is your center, your moral compass that will maintain your recovery and guide you to where you need to go.

"Nothing Succeeds Like Success"- In order to continue to build your track record of appropriate social behavior control, don't forget the power of high risk situation access and structure your environment to set you up for success by making self-control as convenient as possible and relapse as inconvenient as possible. Finally, make a commitment to invest yourself in something that will have a lasting positive impact on yourself and others.

"The greatest use of a life is to spend it on something that will outlast it"-- William James (1842- 1910)

Exhibit 1.
Managing Risk Factors for How Harmful Behavior was Acquired:
The Risk Factor Chain (that led to unhealthy, harmful behavior, i.e., biopsychosocial risk factors)
(Summary of risk factor coping skills in Workbook 1- Yokley, 2010a)

Note: A more complete set of "Treatment Notes" with case examples for each one of these categories is provided in "Understanding Harmful Behavior: A Social Responsibility Therapy Perspective." www.srtonline.org.

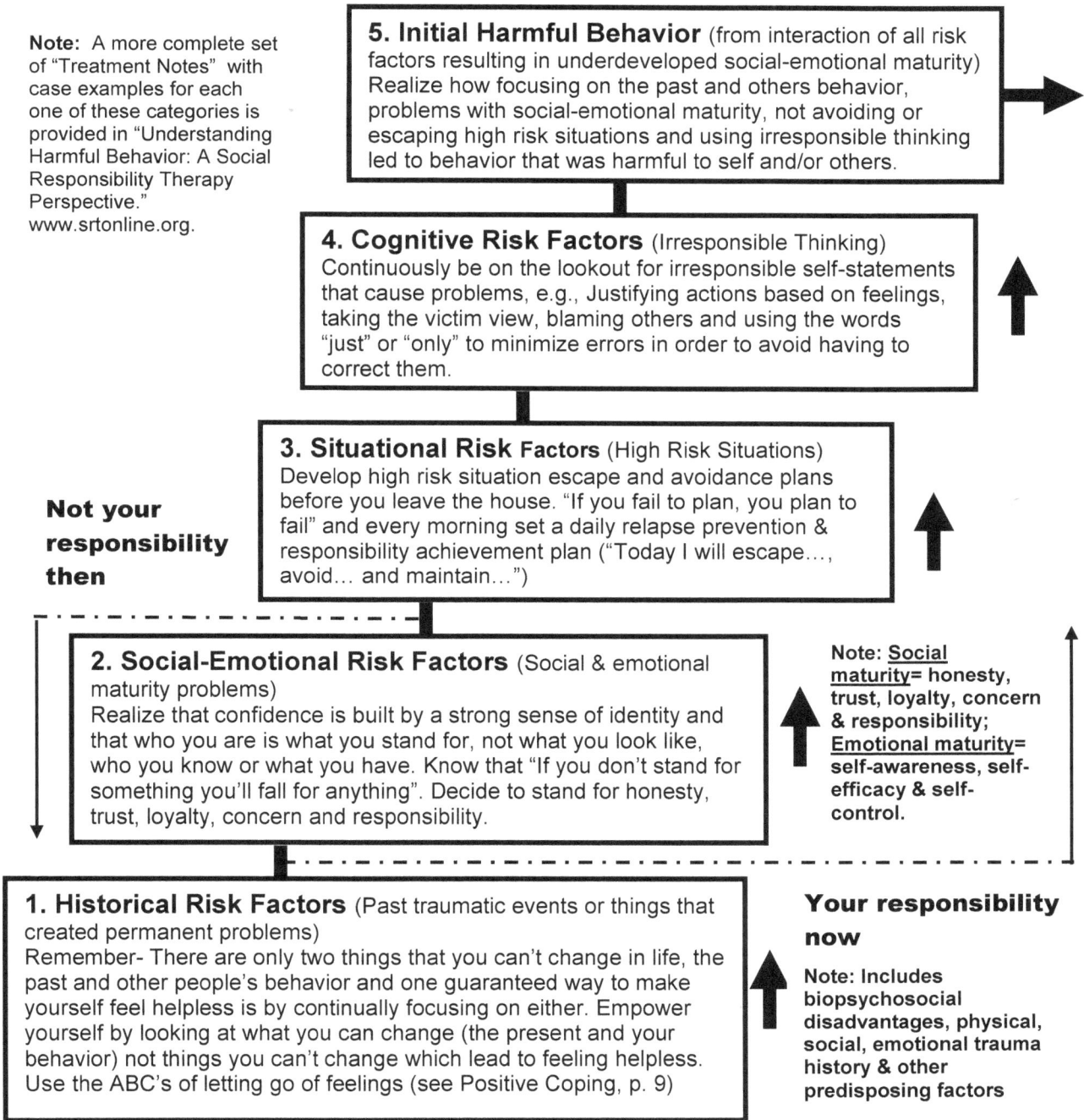

5. Initial Harmful Behavior (from interaction of all risk factors resulting in underdeveloped social-emotional maturity) Realize how focusing on the past and others behavior, problems with social-emotional maturity, not avoiding or escaping high risk situations and using irresponsible thinking led to behavior that was harmful to self and/or others.

4. Cognitive Risk Factors (Irresponsible Thinking) Continuously be on the lookout for irresponsible self-statements that cause problems, e.g., Justifying actions based on feelings, taking the victim view, blaming others and using the words "just" or "only" to minimize errors in order to avoid having to correct them.

3. Situational Risk Factors (High Risk Situations) Develop high risk situation escape and avoidance plans before you leave the house. "If you fail to plan, you plan to fail" and every morning set a daily relapse prevention & responsibility achievement plan ("Today I will escape…, avoid… and maintain…")

Not your responsibility then

2. Social-Emotional Risk Factors (Social & emotional maturity problems) Realize that confidence is built by a strong sense of identity and that who you are is what you stand for, not what you look like, who you know or what you have. Know that "If you don't stand for something you'll fall for anything". Decide to stand for honesty, trust, loyalty, concern and responsibility.

Note: Social maturity= honesty, trust, loyalty, concern & responsibility; Emotional maturity= self-awareness, self-efficacy & self-control.

1. Historical Risk Factors (Past traumatic events or things that created permanent problems) Remember- There are only two things that you can't change in life, the past and other people's behavior and one guaranteed way to make yourself feel helpless is by continually focusing on either. Empower yourself by looking at what you can change (the present and your behavior) not things you can't change which lead to feeling helpless. Use the ABC's of letting go of feelings (see Positive Coping, p. 9)

Your responsibility now

Note: Includes biopsychosocial disadvantages, physical, social, emotional trauma history & other predisposing factors

Exhibit 2.
Recovery Behavior Maintenance: The Stress Management Cycle (that maintains appropriate social behavior control and develops social-emotional maturity)
(Summary of stress management skills from Workbook 2- See Yokley 2011a)

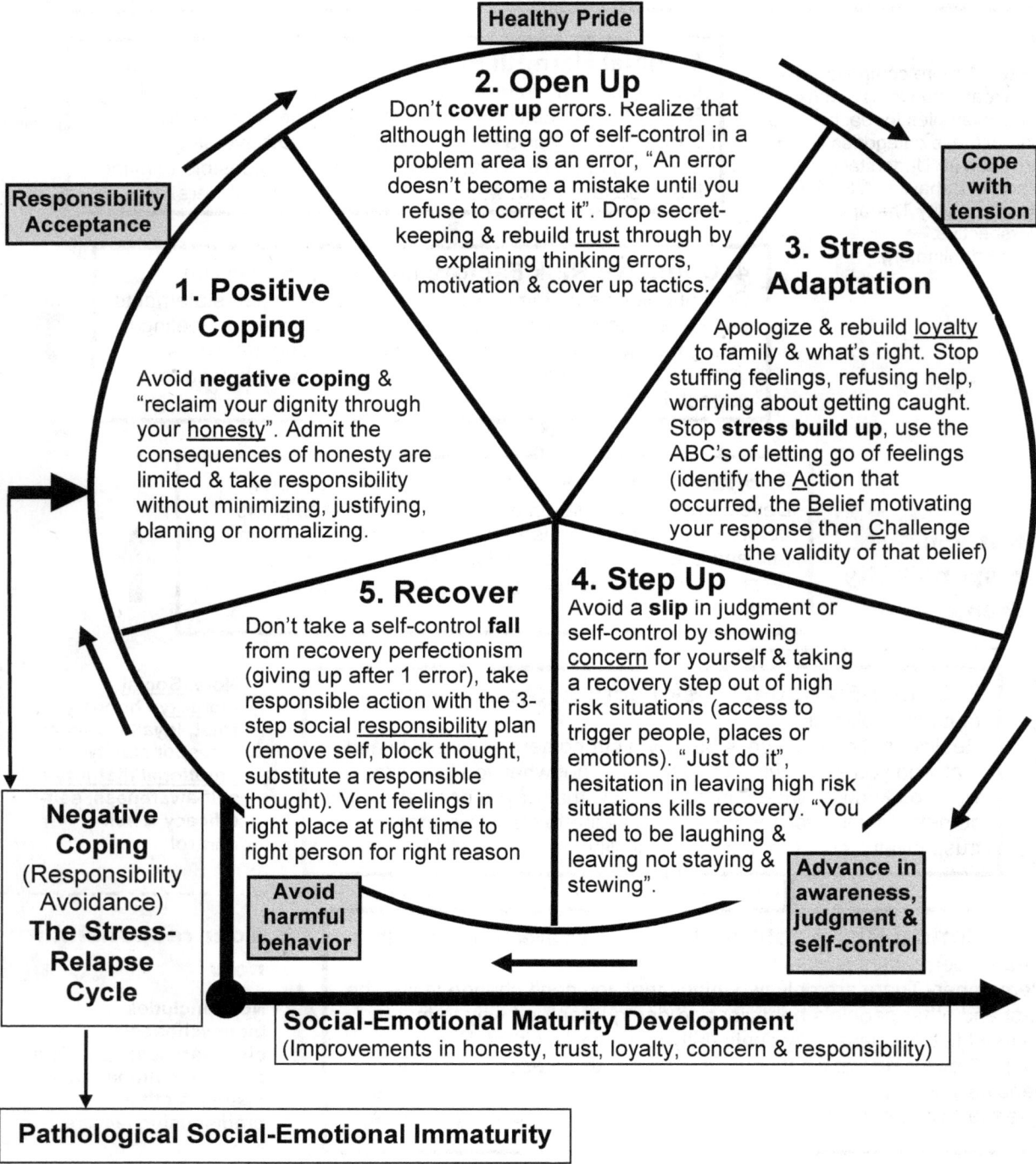

Healthy Pride

2. Open Up
Don't **cover up** errors. Realize that although letting go of self-control in a problem area is an error, "An error doesn't become a mistake until you refuse to correct it". Drop secret-keeping & rebuild trust through by explaining thinking errors, motivation & cover up tactics.

Responsibility Acceptance

Cope with tension

1. Positive Coping

Avoid **negative coping** & "reclaim your dignity through your honesty". Admit the consequences of honesty are limited & take responsibility without minimizing, justifying, blaming or normalizing.

3. Stress Adaptation

Apologize & rebuild loyalty to family & what's right. Stop stuffing feelings, refusing help, worrying about getting caught. Stop **stress build up**, use the ABC's of letting go of feelings (identify the Action that occurred, the Belief motivating your response then Challenge the validity of that belief)

5. Recover
Don't take a self-control **fall** from recovery perfectionism (giving up after 1 error), take responsible action with the 3-step social responsibility plan (remove self, block thought, substitute a responsible thought). Vent feelings in right place at right time to right person for right reason

4. Step Up
Avoid a **slip** in judgment or self-control by showing concern for yourself & taking a recovery step out of high risk situations (access to trigger people, places or emotions). "Just do it", hesitation in leaving high risk situations kills recovery. "You need to be laughing & leaving not staying & stewing".

Avoid harmful behavior

Advance in awareness, judgment & self-control

Negative Coping
(Responsibility Avoidance)
The Stress-Relapse Cycle

Social-Emotional Maturity Development
(Improvements in honesty, trust, loyalty, concern & responsibility)

Pathological Social-Emotional Immaturity

Exhibit 3. Addressing Factors that Support Multiple forms of Harmful Behavior[1]
(Summary of prosocial behavior skills in Workbook 3)

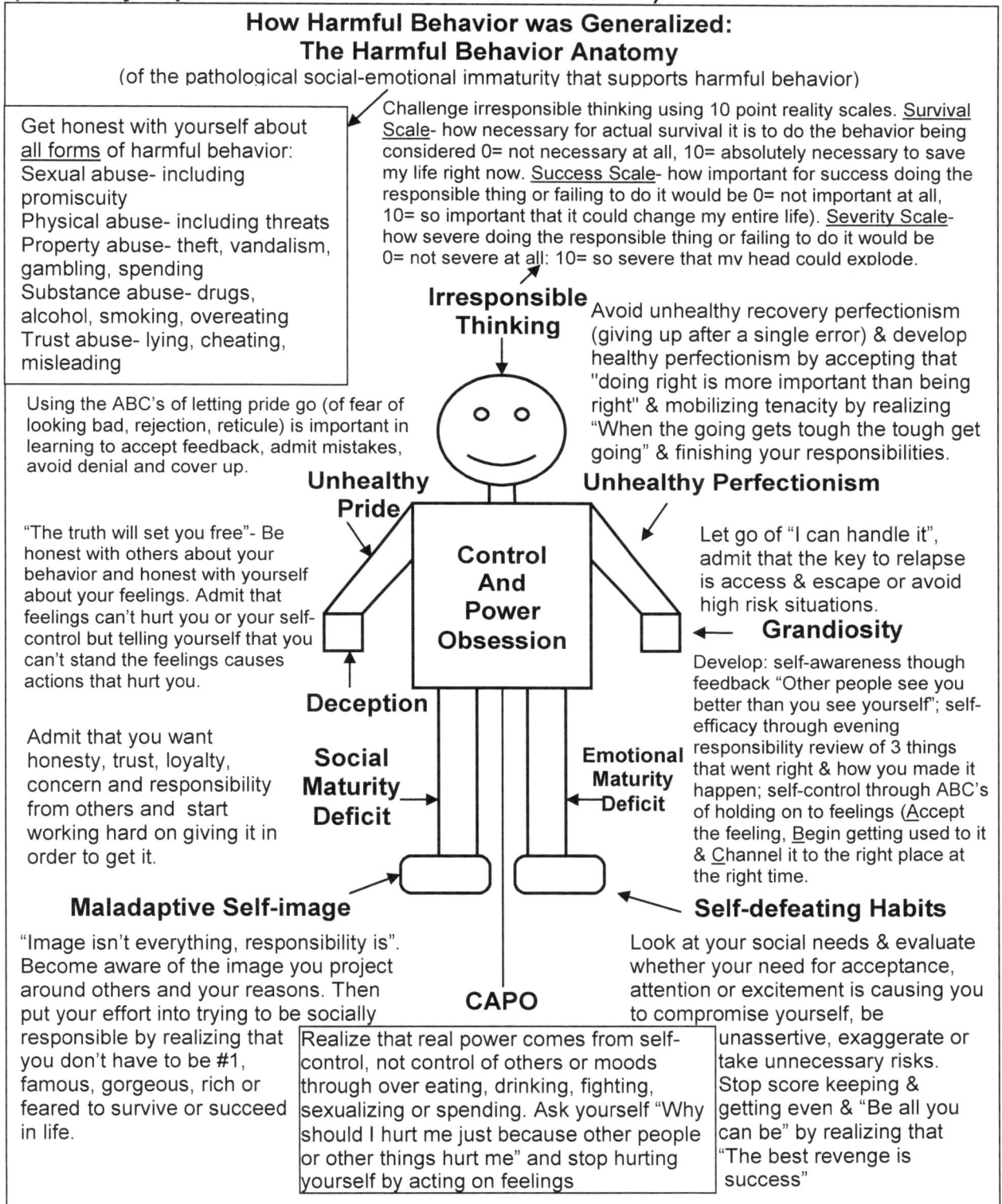

How Harmful Behavior was Generalized:
The Harmful Behavior Anatomy
(of the pathological social-emotional immaturity that supports harmful behavior)

Get honest with yourself about all forms of harmful behavior:
Sexual abuse- including promiscuity
Physical abuse- including threats
Property abuse- theft, vandalism, gambling, spending
Substance abuse- drugs, alcohol, smoking, overeating
Trust abuse- lying, cheating, misleading

Challenge irresponsible thinking using 10 point reality scales. Survival Scale- how necessary for actual survival it is to do the behavior being considered 0= not necessary at all, 10= absolutely necessary to save my life right now. Success Scale- how important for success doing the responsible thing or failing to do it would be 0= not important at all, 10= so important that it could change my entire life). Severity Scale- how severe doing the responsible thing or failing to do it would be 0= not severe at all: 10= so severe that my head could explode.

Irresponsible Thinking

Avoid unhealthy recovery perfectionism (giving up after a single error) & develop healthy perfectionism by accepting that "doing right is more important than being right" & mobilizing tenacity by realizing "When the going gets tough the tough get going" & finishing your responsibilities.

Using the ABC's of letting pride go (of fear of looking bad, rejection, reticule) is important in learning to accept feedback, admit mistakes, avoid denial and cover up.

Unhealthy Pride

Unhealthy Perfectionism

"The truth will set you free"- Be honest with others about your behavior and honest with yourself about your feelings. Admit that feelings can't hurt you or your self-control but telling yourself that you can't stand the feelings causes actions that hurt you.

Control And Power Obsession

Let go of "I can handle it", admit that the key to relapse is access & escape or avoid high risk situations.

Grandiosity

Deception

Develop: self-awareness though feedback "Other people see you better than you see yourself"; self-efficacy through evening responsibility review of 3 things that went right & how you made it happen; self-control through ABC's of holding on to feelings (Accept the feeling, Begin getting used to it & Channel it to the right place at the right time.

Admit that you want honesty, trust, loyalty, concern and responsibility from others and start working hard on giving it in order to get it.

Social Maturity Deficit

Emotional Maturity Deficit

Maladaptive Self-image

Self-defeating Habits

"Image isn't everything, responsibility is". Become aware of the image you project around others and your reasons. Then put your effort into trying to be socially responsible by realizing that you don't have to be #1, famous, gorgeous, rich or feared to survive or succeed in life.

CAPO

Realize that real power comes from self-control, not control of others or moods through over eating, drinking, fighting, sexualizing or spending. Ask yourself "Why should I hurt me just because other people or other things hurt me" and stop hurting yourself by acting on feelings

Look at your social needs & evaluate whether your need for acceptance, attention or excitement is causing you to compromise yourself, be unassertive, exaggerate or take unnecessary risks. Stop score keeping & getting even & "Be all you can be" by realizing that "The best revenge is success"

Appendix A.
Summary Information for Mental Health Professionals
Note: Detailed information is provided in Chapter 9 of the Clinicians Guide (Yokley 2016).

Additional case examples and intervention descriptions for this workbook are provided in "Social Responsibility Therapy for Adolescents & Young Adults: A Multicultural Treatment Manual for Harmful Behavior" (see Yokley, 2008 in references, p. 229). Clinician instructions on using this workbook are also provided (see references, p. 229). Originally developed for client use with therapist input to help those in treatment become more active participants, this workbook provides the high level of structure needed for clients in institutions or residential care where more self-directed workbook structured discovery is necessary. This structured discovery workbook can also provide self-awareness homework assignments for session discussion with outpatient clients in need of structure between sessions and relapse prevention support. The vocabulary bar has been set relatively high for self-help workbooks to encourage cognitive as well as social-emotional growth. This allows therapists to encourage clients whose unhealthy, harmful behavior has interfered with their education to improve their vocabulary by looking up definitions of words that they never learned and sharing them in sessions with therapist prompting. This promotes autonomy, develops self-efficacy and gives the client practice asking for help on less emotionally charged issues.

Using the Unhealthy, Harmful Behavior Anatomy in Time Limited Treatments
Deciding whether to assign the basic vs complete version of this workbook-
This workbook has a "basic form" that can be used with less severe cases in time limited treatment programs or where number of sessions the client can attend is limited. The "basic form" allows the client to skip portions in 8 of the 10 structured discovery learning experience components (i.e., all but Component 1- Irresponsible Thinking and Component 5- Social Maturity Deficit). Clients completing this workbook are instructed to ask their mental health professional whether they should complete the "basic form" or the complete version of each component (see p. iii). Since you can't achieve behavior change without awareness of what you need to change, Awareness Training is central to unhealthy, harmful behavior treatment. Some clients require more Awareness Training than others and the complete version includes more Structured Discovery work on awareness in each component of the Harmful Behavior Anatomy. Although treatment completion time is always a practical factor to consider, other indicators for of the need to assign the complete version of each component include clients:
- who have not completed workbooks 1 and 2;
- in a residential/institutional treatment setting or with more severe behavior;
- who need to increase their awareness of personal symptoms that support harmful behavior.

In addition, to the "basic form", a "focused treatment plan" can be developed by selecting certain components in workbook 3 that fit the individual needs of your client.

Focusing treatment on one component requires three chapter assignments-
It is important to always include assignment of the Introduction to Social Responsibility Therapy & Understanding Harmful Behavior (p. 1) along with Harmful Behavior Anatomy Component 1- Irresponsible Thinking (p. 37). This is needed so that the SRT healthy behavior and relationship success skills along with the irresponsible thinking that interferes with behavior change and achieving personal goals will always be covered. For example, if you want to focus your treatment on your client's problem perfectionism, you would assign the Introduction that covers healthy behavior and relationship success skills and Component 1 on Irresponsible Thinking along with Component 7 on Unhealthy Perfectionism. If you only want to focus your treatment on your client's control and power problem, assign the Introduction, Component 1 and Component 2- Control and Power Obsession and so on.

Recommendations for clients with multiple types of unhealthy, harmful behavior-
If your client has exhibited multiple forms of harmful behavior that is primarily harmful to others (e.g., physical and sexual abuse), they need to complete this entire workbook. If you are using this workbook

for clients with multiple forms of less severe behaviors on the Harmful Behavior Continuum that are not primarily harmful to others (p. 2), a minimum of five components is recommended as follows.

1. **Component 1**- Irresponsible Thinking (Includes the ART of avoiding trouble)
2. **Component 3**- Unhealthy Pride (Includes the ART of thinking it through)
3. **Component 5**- Social Maturity Deficit
4. **Component 9**- Emotional Maturity Deficit (Includes the ART of calming down)
5. **Component 10**- Self-Defeating Habits (Includes the ART of social problem solving)

The "focused treatment plan" listed above is generic and should be modified to meet individual client or program needs. For example...

- Clients whose behavior imposes on others need to have Control and Power problems (Component 2) included as part of their treatment plan;
- Clients with a criminal behavior history or who were not honest about their referral problem need to have Deception (Component 4) included as part of their treatment plan.
- Clients with image problems need to have Maladaptive Self-Image (Component 6) included as part of their treatment plan;
- Clients with denial issues who minimize or cover up problems need to have Unhealthy Perfectionism (Component 7) included as part of their treatment plan and;
- Clients with inflated self-esteem need to have Grandiosity (Component 8) included as part of their treatment plan.

If your client needs some work on all of these issues but treatment time is limited, start with a writing assignment on "What I know about this topic". Then cover the top three key characteristics or concepts to cover and move on to the next section topic. This allows covering more than one section in each treatment session. You can use this time management approach with any of the three workbooks if needed. If you do the Candy Bar exercise in Appendix D, discuss the risk in all cases.

Time limited treatment is not recommended for clients with multiple forms of more severe behaviors on the Harmful Behavior Continuum (p. 2) that are primarily harmful to others (i.e., abuse of power, property and people). Those clients will require completion of all 10 components in the present workbook (i.e., the complete form not the basic form) and all three SRT workbooks in addition to successful completion of their Problem Development Triad presentation.

The Problem Development Triad: Three "Stand Alone" Sections

If you look at Figure 1 on page 8, you will notice three sections in The Problem Development Triad. The first section has five structured discovery learning experience links on understanding of how harmful behavior was acquired. The second has five learning experience phases on how harmful behavior was maintained, The third section covers 10 learning experience components that allow harmful behavior to generalize or be substituted for other problem behavior making a total of 20 structured discovery units to cover in the Problem Development Triad. These three sections are covered in three "stand alone" workbooks that can be integrated into existing treatments individually. If you are seeking to reinforce the portion of your treatment that develops client understanding and insight into how they acquired their condition over time, you can integrate workbook one on, "How did I get this problem?" into your treatment. If you wish to reinforce the relapse prevention portion of your treatment by developing client understanding of how they maintained their problem behavior, you can integrate workbook two on, "Why do I keep doing this?" If your client exhibits multiple forms of unhealthy, harmful behavior or if you wish to address concerns about their harmful behavior generalizing to other problem areas (e.g., behavior migration to another problem during treatment), you can integrate workbook three on, "How did my problem spread?" However, solid recovery support from a thorough understanding of how unhealthy, harmful behavior was acquired, maintained and generalized requires Structured Discovery learning during the completion of all three workbooks along with the successful completion of the Problem Development Triad presentation (See p. 169, "Putting it all together").

Structured Discovery Group Sessions

If you are running a treatment group or program where individuals start treatment at different times, the three workbooks can be completed in any order but require an introduction session before each which has an overview of the Problem Development Triad. As in individual/family therapy a summary of what has been learned is needed at the end of each section along with one presentation session per person in treatment. In group therapy sessions that are time limited (e.g., 1 ½ hours per session for 6- 8 members), it may not be possible to cover all issues for all clients so prioritize by making sure you cover the top three first. This can be done easily by asking each group member to list several section descriptors (i.e., link in workbook 1, phase in workbook 2 or component in workbook 3) that they rated highest and most important to their recovery. Hold one session for each section where the topic of discussion is the characteristics that were rated highest in that section. Reinforce the healthy relationship success skills (p. 17) and teach the healthy behavior success skills (p.19) as indicated. Create "instant identification" by pulling together similarities with a show of hands, e.g., "Who else rated this characteristic as a 2 or above?" discuss those common characteristics (see PRAISE skills outlined below). Then move on to the next person asking for three that haven't been discussed. Usually after several people have talked in a group of 6- 8, the top symptom of that component has been covered for each group member and the group can be moved to processing how that problem affected their life and to generating one positive coping skill to use for each problem characteristic discussed with the homework assignment of using those coping skills on their Situation Response Analysis Logs (Appendix D, p. 202). Note: A simplified version may have to be implemented by the therapist for low functioning groups and examples are available through www.srtonline.org.

SRT PRAISE Participation Motivation and Group Unity Skills

Since unhealthy, harmful behavior is multicultural, the demographic makeup of Social Responsibility Therapy groups is diverse. Given this situation a set of SRT multicultural group unity development "PRAISE" skills was designed for motivational enhancement of client participation in the diverse group setting. These skills are pulled from Yokley (2008) on the page numbers listed in parentheses on these PRAISE cue card (below) and are described further in The Clinician's Guide to SRT (see references). These skills need to be modeled for clients by therapists during all discussions of SRT workbook issues and social-emotional maturity issues to develop multicultural group unity and therapeutic participation. All occasions of clients using these skills in group should be verbally reinforced by therapists.

PRAISE Group Therapy Process Skills (page numbers reference Yokley, 2008)

Helping clients get the most out of their group learning experience requires...

Pulling people in- "Can I borrow that from you? That's a really good point we need to discuss" (Making them a part/Integration), (p. 38)

Responsible reinforcement- "That [took a lot of courage, was impressive, etc] let's give him a hand for his... [honesty, trust, loyalty, concern, responsibility]" (p. 33, 105)

Acknowledgement - "What they are teaching us is..." (p. 38).

Instant identification- "Please raise your hand if you have also..." followed by head count "one, two, three... people here also..." for awareness development (Validation/Recognition), p. 192.

Social mathematics by finding the least common denominator (p. 192) during successive group introductions and when two or more members disclose similar issues- "These two/three have a couple things in common, what are they?/did you notice?" (Cumulative Identification).

Enabling responsibility- "It's not pick on John time, please raise your hand if like John, you have ever been accused of/made the mistake of..." (setting the occasion for honesty & accepting responsibility)

Social Responsibility Therapy Individual/family Sessions

A set of SRT individual therapy problem "REPAIR" collaboration skills was designed for motivational enhancement in individual sessions from two person centered and four SRT participation motivation skills. The "REPAIR" acronym helps SRT therapists remember the following relationship collaboration skills: **R**eflection, **E**ncouraging, **P**ulling the client in, **A**cknowledgement, **I**dentification and **R**esponsible Reinforcement. If you are doing individual/family therapy with a focus on insight into how clients acquired their condition over time, you can complete workbook one in 5- 6 sessions. If you wish to focus individual therapy on relapse prevention of harmful behavior you can complete workbook two in 5- 6 sessions. If your focus is on co-occurring unhealthy, harmful behaviors, you can complete workbook 3 in 10- 12 sessions. Problem Development Triad presentations take between one and two hours per person depending on the extent of the unhealthy, harmful behavior history. Whether implemented individually or in group, all three workbooks can be generally completed in 24- 26 weekly outpatient sessions or an eight week intensive outpatient program with sessions Monday, Wednesday and Friday.

REPAIR Individual Therapy Problem Collaboration Skills

Combined from 2 Person-Centered therapy and 4 PRAISE participation motivation skills

Reflection- "It sounds like you are feeling…", "What I hear you saying is…" (reflecting feelings & message)

Encouraging- "mm-hm," "oh", "yes", "and…", "OK", "go on" and nod acknowledging understanding or repeating a key word (e.g., "upset?") or "Can you talk/say more about that?" [Shows willingness to listen without interrupting, judging or giving advice and tolerate clinical silence].

Pulling the patient in- "Can I borrow that from you? That's a really good point we need to discuss" (Making them a part/Integration), p. 38. [Allows you to interrupt & re-direct without offending patient.]

Acknowledgement - "What you are teaching us is…", "That's an important lesson to remember" [e.g., "having the last word, continues arguments"] (p.38). [Acknowledges important life learning experiences. Allows awareness training with patient ownership- insight development without directive interpretation]

Identification- "I can see/buy/understand that", "Makes sense to me" (Validation/Recognition), p. 192.

Responsible reinforcement- "Thank you for your honesty" or "What you did showed a lot of [trust, loyalty, concern, responsibility]" (p. 33, 105). [Reinforces multicultural prosocial values.]

Repetition

Implement three repetitions in each component to reinforce learning. For example: 1) have client read and complete exercises in a component marking areas that need clarification; 2) review component with client, translating material, clarifying areas as needed and asking key concept questions; 3) have client teach the concepts learned and share personal information/discoveries with appropriate others. This is often done with a component assignment followed by an individual session and a group or family session.

Adjustment for special needs

Reading level can be ahead of math simply because reading is used more in the everyday life of many people. Thus is not uncommon to see clients do well in rating all of the characteristics in a section and transcribing their top three to their worksheet correctly but getting the math wrong and showing low average scores next to severe behavior statements with high statement ratings. If you have individuals like this, handle it by focusing your discussion on the top three rated characteristics in each component which does not require calculating each component average rating score. Special needs in secure residential or correctional settings may require therapists to sign off at the end of each section under the "Discussed with" heading in order to get required completion certificates.

Self-evaluations

Treatment programs addressing harmful behavior often have their participants review their self-evaluations at the end of each Problem Development Triad section in a group treatment setting with their peers and staff. Promotion to the next program phase or requests for increases in program privileges are typically linked to successful progress in social-emotional maturity development (i.e., honesty, trust, loyalty, concern, responsibility, self-awareness, self-efficacy and self-control) which is documented on program behavior incident reports. The same process can be used in family therapy meetings where youth privileges are based on social-emotional maturity progress documented in progress notes.

Client reinforcement
Staff who have used this manual successfully in the past with the highest level of participation have provided client accomplishment awards (e.g., certificates of completion for adults which included tangible reinforcement for youth) after the completion of each workbook. Discussion by clients of their understanding of how their acquired, maintained or generalized their unhealthy, harmful behavior, keeps them in touch with their past which helps them avoid returning there and helps dissipate resentment in mandated treatment cases.

The ART of SRT:
Awareness Training, Responsibility Training & Tolerance Training
During implementation of Social Responsibility Therapy, basic Awareness, Responsibility and Tolerance Training tools are needed to deal with the emotional baggage related to past historical trauma and self-disappointment from acquiring harmful behavior habits.

The ART of Social Responsibility Therapy includes:
- Awareness Training on the antecedents/triggers, consequences/reinforces and social modeling of unhealthy, harmful behavior;
- Responsibility Training on learning the Healthy Relationship and Behavior success Skills (p. 16) needed to manage unhealthy, harmful behavior and;
- Tolerance Training on learning how to tolerate the feedback needed to change, developing the frustration tolerance needed to overcome barriers to goals; tolerate conflict that triggers relapse and tolerate mistakes the trigger relapse through the slip give up trigger (p. 104).

Examples are provided in Components 1, 3, 9 and 10.

Multimethod-Multipath Behavior Therapy
SRT is a multimethod-multipath behavior therapy (see p. 48 in Yokley2008 and Yokley, 2010b). Old habits die hard. Three big categories of barriers to healthy behavior change are: 1) external reinforcement and consequences (e.g., feeling good or better when doing the unhealthy, harmful behavior) that can push us towards it; 2) internal thoughts and feelings (e.g., urges and cravings) that can pull us towards it and; 3) social influence (e.g., friends suggesting it or doing it around us) that can steer us towards it. Since unhealthy harmful behavior

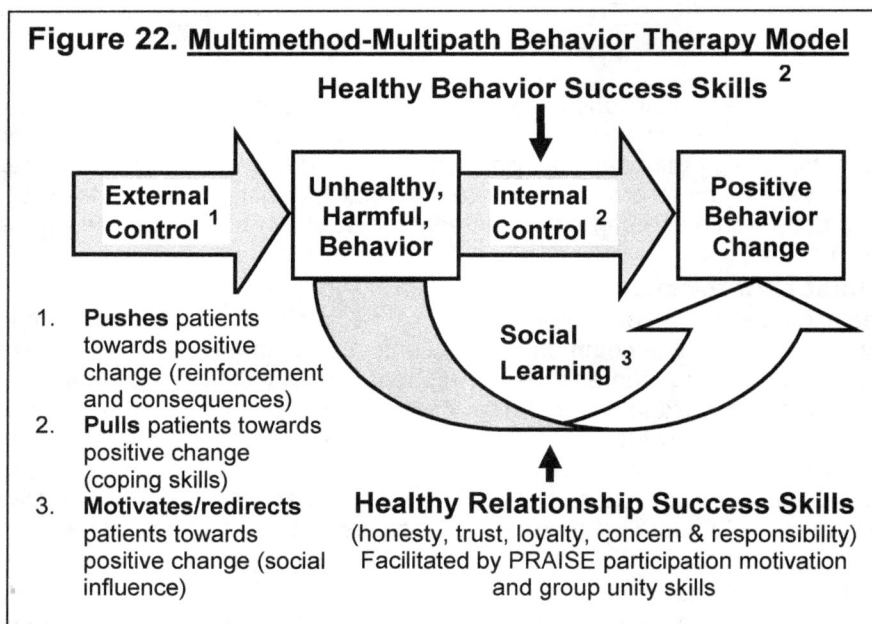

Figure 22. Multimethod-Multipath Behavior Therapy Model

can be self-reinforcing, triggered by thoughts, feelings or social influence, it is often highly resistant to change and requires multiple intervention methods across multiple paths to bring about change. In medicine, this comprehensive three path approach is called the Biopsychosocial Model. Multimethod-Multipath Behavior Therapy (Figure 22) is similar to the medical Biopsychosocial Model in some respects.

Multimethod-Multipath Behavior Therapy:

- **Pushes** individuals with unhealthy behavior toward positive change with external control procedures (i.e., <u>biological</u> positive/negative responses to <u>operant conditioning</u> reinforcement and consequences provided in behavior contracts, token economy programs along with external monitoring of the target behavior thorough urine tests, blood tests, breathalyzers, weigh ins, behavioral observations, AA sign in sheets, medication pill counts, ankle monitors, along with limiting external access to high risk situations for relapse through supervised relapse prevention plans- behavior modification);
- **Pulls** them toward positive change through internal control procedures (i.e., <u>psychological</u> reasoning with <u>cognitive restructuring and coping techniques</u> to manage the target behavior- drilling the SRT healthy behavior success skills to the point where they are automatic reactions to problem situations) and;
- **Motivates/redirects** them towards change with social learning (i.e., <u>social learning and social influence interventions</u> including peer modeling, role modeling and participant modeling by therapists of coping with the problem, support groups, group reviewed SRA logs, PRAISE group participation and motivation skills, social support for healthy relationship success skills in the form of multicultural prosocial values that act as competing factors to unhealthy, harmful behavior, development of positive "care circle" support network, positive peer environments).

Each of these pathways towards positive change involves awareness training, responsibility training and tolerance training methods.

Workspace for Life Impact Statement

_____
_____
_____
_____
_____
_____
_____
_____
_____
_____
_____
_____
_____
_____
_____
_____
_____
_____

Appendix B.
Self-Awareness Problems & Relapse: Foresight Deficit Decisions
(also referred to as Apparently Irrelevant Decisions or Seemingly Unimportant Decisions)
"The road to hell is paved with good intentions" -- John Ray circa 1670

Nowhere is the importance of developing self-awareness and using foresight as clear as in the case of Foresight Deficit Decisions. Foresight Deficit Decisions are decisions made without enough foresight or thinking ahead and awareness of high risk situations. These decisions pave the road to harmful behavior relapse often beginning with good intentions. Relapse from Foresight Deficit Decisions often occurs from Problem priorities or Triage Trouble. Triage is French for "to sort" and refers to emergency room sorting of battle and disaster victims in a system of priorities designed to maximize the number of survivors. Problem priorities involves not keeping the focus on the most important problem first. In terms of harmful behavior relapse prevention, problem priorities involves getting diverted away from "keeping your problem up front". This often relates to good intentions, putting other people or tasks first, forgetting about self and letting priorities slip. This can occur from assuming that good intentions can be substituted for good foresight and planning.

In reality, no matter how good our intentions are, if we don't use positive planning, stick to our recovery priorities (i.e., relapse prevention plan), avoid high risk situations, use Fantasy Fast Forward (p. 187) and the reality scales (p. 24) to think it through and weigh the possible consequences, Murphy's Law will take hold and "whatever can go wrong, will go wrong". Foresight deficit decisions or slips occur in virtually all forms of harmful behavior relapse. The following examples illustrate that the key to controlling harmful behavior is developing enough self-awareness to make relapse prevention decisions and avoid the foresight slips that lead there.

A trust abuse (cheating, overspending) example would be the foresight deficit decision by an individual having partner jealousy problems to stop in a flower shop where an ex-girlfriend worked for two dozen roses to smooth things over (slip #1, diversion away from "keeping your problem up front" by good intentions). The thought that seeing his ex-girlfriend might not be a good idea was immediately replaced by the self-statement, "this would be a good test of our relationship" (slip #2, testing self-control). In the shop, the ex-girlfriend commented about the expensive purchase stating "You must really care" which led to the honest answer that the flowers were to try and patch things up (slip #3, diplomacy lapse). This started a discussion of things that had gone wrong (slip #4, inappropriate self-disclosure) which led to talking about the good times they used to have together which led to being invited over to her place "just for a drink" (slip #5 minimizing). That conversation led to rekindling an old flame which resulted in spending the night and giving the roses to the ex-girlfriend the following morning on the way out the door. Feeling very guilty about cheating, they went online and booked an expensive weekend getaway trip to make it up to their partner which put them back into heavy credit card debt. Thus, the foresight deficit decision to buy roses at a shop where an ex-girlfriend worked in order to smooth over a partner conflict, triggered a chain of events which set the occasion for relapse on cheating and overspending.

A substance abuse (food) example would be the foresight deficit decision by an overweight individual in a diet program to turn down the cash alternative and accept a cruise that they won at the office work incentive program. This occurred as a result of telling themselves, "I know there's a lot of food on those cruises but wouldn't it be great to do something nice for the family?" (slip #1, careless exposure to a high risk situation with good intentions). The first night of the cruise, ballroom dancing was scheduled to follow a gourmet dinner. They ordered healthy food and ate reasonable portions but after dinner the dancing announcement included an invitation to a complete dessert buffet in the adjoining room for those who didn't want to dance. Their partner took their hand and led them into the dessert buffet as opposed to the dance floor as was expected (slip #2, failure to communicate needs and plan ahead). Not wanting to be a burden they went along (slip #3, compromising self to be accepted) telling themselves "I'll just tag along but will leave if it gets too much" (slip #4, testing self-control) which it quickly did and they left to sit down at one of the tables stating "you go ahead, I'm resting up for dancing". Their partner returned to the table with two plates, put one on front of them that was filled with all of their dessert favorites and stated "This is for your hard earned work that brought us here". They told themselves, "Why not, I deserve a reward" and joined in as opposed to speaking up for themselves (slip #5, rationalizing harmful behavior through feelings of entitlement). Thus, the foresight deficit decision to accept a cruise trip as opposed to taking the cash alternative triggered a chain of events which set the occasion for a diet relapse.

A substance abuse (cigarettes) example would be the foresight deficit decision by an individual who just quit smoking to go over and say hello to some friends they see sitting in the smoking section of a restaurant (slip #1, careless exposure to a high risk situation with good intentions). Having not seen them for some time, they accepted an invitation to sit down and visit because they felt a little awkward about eating alone anyway (slip #2, failure to implement a concrete face saving exit strategy and justifying actions based on feelings). After dinner their smoking friends all lit up and the smell filled the air reminding them of that great feeling that they used to get from a cigarette after a good meal (slip #3, dwelling on euphoric recall). They were caught off guard and were in a sort of daydream trance thinking about it when asked, "Want one?" with their favorite brand being dangled right under their nose. They remember thinking "Just one won't hurt" (slip #4, minimizing harmful behavior) as they took the lighter that was being passed to them. Thus, the foresight deficit decision to join some friends in the smoking section of a restaurant to catch up on old times triggered a chain of events which set the occasion for a smoking relapse.

A substance abuse (marijuana) example would be the foresight deficit decision by an individual in their first week of residential substance abuse treatment to call their partner without discussing it with staff to reassure them that everything will work out fine (slip #1, diversion away from "keeping your problem up front" by good intentions). This call triggered feeling emotionally threatened when their partner seemed to be getting along fine without them which led to a fear that the relationship would be lost if they stayed in treatment because their partner might find someone else (slip #2, affect impaired perception). Since the focus of their residential substance abuse treatment was on learning to deal with self and contact with outsiders is initially discouraged, this fear was not disclosed to others (slip #3, unhealthy pride) causing Stress Build-

Up which set the occasion for the belief that "I must go over there to make sure everything is OK or something will go wrong" (slip #4, irresponsible thinking and Control and Power Obsession). This led to calling a friend to pick them up and sneaking out during a community AA meeting (slip #5, deception). When they arrived at their partner's place, a party was going on where everyone was getting high but they do not leave (slip #6, failure to exit a high risk situation) because there are only five other people at the party and they assumed that the party was planned for three couples (slip #7, assuming thinking error). This assumption validated up their fear that they would lose their partner if they stayed in treatment at the same time that someone passed them a joint and they felt the need to smoke marijuana to calm themselves down (slip #8, justifying actions based on feelings). Thus, the foresight deficit decision to call their partner for reassurance triggered a chain of events which set the occasion for a marijuana abuse relapse.

A property abuse (gambling, credit card debt) example would be the foresight deficit decision by an individual in gamblers anonymous to take a weekend convenience store job in addition to their regular office job to pay off their considerable gambling debt and deciding to stay after learning they would be running the store by themselves (slip #1, careless exposure to a high risk situation with good intentions). The fact that lottery ticket sales were a large part of the business wasn't considered a problem because their gambling debt occurred at the horse races (slip #2, rationalizing, tunnel vision). The following weekend, a customer won $1,000 on an instant win scratch off ticket and gave him a $20 tip. He told himself that he wasn't gambling because it wasn't his money (slip #3, self-deception), he put the $20 in the register and scratched off $20 worth of instant win tickets. Telling himself that one more wouldn't hurt (slip #5, pushing back the line), he scratched off another one and when it didn't hit, got mad and told himself, "Why pay for something that isn't worth anything?" (slip #4, justifying actions based on feelings). By the end of his shift he had scratched off $50 worth of instant win tickets and didn't have the cash to pay for them. He had to leave the store unattended to go across the street and use the bank machine putting himself further into credit card debt to avoid being charged with stealing on the job. Thus, the foresight deficit decision to stay in a weekend convenience store job that allowed unsupervised access to lottery tickets in order to pay off a gambling debt, triggered a chain of events which set the occasion for a gambling and credit card debt relapse.

A property abuse (theft) example would be the foresight deficit decision by an individual who was just fined for shoplifting to borrow a nice leather coat for a social occasion from a friend at the last minute (slip #1, not keeping their problem "up front"). Finding the friend absent triggered frustration and borrowing the coat without asking or leaving a note because of being late (slip #2, justifying actions based on feelings). Not waiting to find the person or taking the time to write a note (slip #3, feeding the Problem of Immediate Gratification) set the occasion for telling self, "I might as well keep the coat because I already have it and nobody knows" (slip #4, rationalizing). Thus, the foresight deficit decision to borrow a coat for a social occasion from an absent friend triggered a series of events which set the occasion for a stealing relapse.

A physical abuse (domestic violence) example would be the foresight deficit decision by an individual who was warned by their probation officer to stay away from their ex-partner to drop in and apologize for the way they acted (slip #1, "my way" attitude). Upon arriving at the house they noticed there was a strange car in the driveway which triggered immediate suspicion and jealousy (slip #2, affect impaired perception). Telling themselves, "I have to know", they barged in the house without knocking (slip #3, Control and Power Obsession) only to find their partner hugging someone else. Without thinking, they yelled out "Who are you?" only to hear the same thing back which instantly confirmed their worst fears (slip #4, assuming) and triggered an attack on what later was found to be a cousin in town for a family funeral. Thus, the foresight deficit decision to drop in and apologize to ex-partner for their behavior triggered a series of events which set the occasion for a domestic violence relapse.

A sexual abuse (adult and adolescent) example would be the foresight deficit decision for an adult in sex offender treatment to put off their regular lunch time trip to the dry cleaners at the mall on Friday (when the number of potential victims to stare at is minimal) to take a friend having problems out to lunch (adult slip #1, problem priorities) or for an adolescent in sex offender treatment to accept a babysitting job because they were pressured to do it (adolescent slip #1, problem priorities). The adult became overwhelmed with a sexual urge from being exposed to several attractive potential victims as they walked through the mall on Saturday with their dry cleaning and the adolescent became overwhelmed with a sexual urge after they walked through the door to greet the children on their babysitting job saw their potential victims and heard the parents tell the children, "Now you do everything your babysitter tells you" (slip #2, failure to plan ahead). In both cases, they maintained visual contact which triggered a flood of mental "snap shots" (slip #3, failure to exit a high risk situation) telling themselves they were "just" staring to get a mental picture for masturbation later in private and had no intent to touch the person (slip #4, pushing back the line). The result was that the adult found themselves automatically following someone out into the parking lot and the adolescent found themselves deciding to give one of the children a bath. Thus, the foresight deficit decision of the adult to postpone a regular dry cleaning trip in order to help a friend out or the adolescent to accepting a babysitting job to help an adult out started a chain of events which set the occasion for a sexual abuse relapse.

Fantasy Fast Forward
Foresight Deficit Decisions can be avoided by using "Fantasy Fast Forward". Fantasy Fast Forward involves viewing the situation you are considering (often a favor or something that involves good intentions) like a movie with you as the main character. Run it through your mind and fast forward to think ahead. Play the movie through to the end in your mind, stop at each decision step and ask yourself "In the worst case what could happen if I take this step?" Use a Reality Check (p. 24) to consider the consequences and determine whether to go ahead or tell yourself "I'm not falling into that" and change your course.

Appendix C.
Types of Irresponsible Thinking & Responsible Alternatives

Responsible Self-statement Substitution is identifying and correcting the irresponsible thinking that gets in the way of you getting what you want in life. This basically involves learning to talk to yourself like someone who really cares about you. If you were standing next to your most responsible best friend in the whole world in a high risk situation for relapse, they would encourage you to do the right thing and steer you towards a responsible behavior. Talking to yourself like your own best friend involves asking yourself "what would someone who really cares about me, tell me to do?" Although most of us know our best friends really well, since we can't actually read minds, one easy way to talk to yourself like your own best friend, steer yourself away from irresponsible, harmful, negative behavior and towards a responsible, helpful, positive alternative is to use the Pendulum Concept (p. 14), "go to the opposite extreme" and do the responsible, helpful opposite. Harmful thinking and helpful opposites are listed below.

1. Deception- Examples include… Outright <u>Lying</u> (not being truthful to others) or covering up and avoiding admitting responsibility along with <u>Denial</u> (not being truthful to self), e.g., "It's not my fault", "It just happened", <u>Diversion</u> (changing the subject, disclosing a minor problem to avoid discussion of a major one, shifting the focus to unnecessary facts, details, other problems or people, "They started it") & <u>Division</u> (misleading & splitting people against each other, often into camps that defend or challenge your innocence, "I really didn't do anything wrong"). <u>Vagueness</u>, <u>Dishonesty by omission</u> & <u>Legitimizing</u> (leaving out critical information or misleading with partial information to avoid consequences), A lack of understanding about the difference between dishonesty by omission (withholding information for selfish reasons) and diplomacy (withholding information for unselfish reasons) can also cause problems. <u>Appeasing</u> (telling people what they want to hear), <u>Assenting</u> (agreeing without meaning it and having no intention to comply). Bending the truth to meet needs for attention (e.g., exaggerating a story for entertainment, bragging), acceptance (e.g., gossiping to fit in, giving insincere complements) or excitement (e.g., saying whatever it takes to get someone to have sex) can result in harm to both self and others. Deception which involves basic honesty deficits (not enough) is only one side of the coin. Honesty problems can also involve excesses (too much). Angry over-disclosure of truthful and painful details (brutal honesty) that hurt another's feelings is the most common example. In addition, inappropriate self-disclosure (excessive honesty) for the situation due to social anxiety (nervous talking) can end up hurting you. Disclosing confidential information when asked about someone else (excessive honesty) can result in harm to others. Whether the honesty issues involve a deficit or excess, the results are still harmful to self or others.

Helpful opposite- Get Honest. "Honesty is the best policy" (Miguel de Cervantes, 1547-1616). Admit that the reason honesty is valued so much is the tremendous price attached. Help yourself get honest by realizing that getting honest and taking responsibility is having the courage to face consequences and take pride in your courage to get honest. Use the ABC's of letting feelings go to "Calm down" (see p. 22) so that you don't justify your actions (lying) based on your feelings (fear of consequences). Before you use deception, "Think it through" using the reality scales (p. 24) to weigh out the severity of the consequences to yourself and others. Get honest about your mistakes and the mistakes of others right away to help yourself and others avoid getting in worse trouble later. Tell yourself the truth about the feelings that others could have about your actions and how you feel about the actions of others.

Then avoid stress buildup that can trigger relapse by talking out mistakes and feelings with a therapist or someone who is responsible.

2. Double standards- Examples include… No concept of social exchange where there is an expectation that good deeds are returned & favors are repaid. Everything is one sided. "Do as I say, not as I do". <u>Honesty double standards</u>, not being completely honest and refusing to admit responsibility while telling yourself others "should" level with you. Being more honest with others about their behavior than you are with yourself about yours or being more honest with yourself than you are with others. <u>Trust double standards</u>- Believes they are trustworthy but distrusts others. Has "Trust Entitlement", feels entitled to be trusted (and receive associated privileges based on "innocent until proven guilty" rationalization) despite lack of responsibility but unwilling to trust others. Doesn't understand that trust must be earned by consistent honesty and responsible action. <u>Loyalty double standards</u> involve shifting loyalties and cheating but expecting or demanding loyalty from others. <u>Concern double standards</u>, taking more than you give, being selfish while complaining about, expecting or demanding concern from others. Being a selfish friend or life partner by looking for support and affection without looking for the opportunity to provide it. <u>Responsibility double standards</u>, being irresponsible while complaining about, expecting or demanding responsibility from others. <u>Respect double standards</u>- being disrespectful while complaining about, expecting or demanding respect from others. This can relate to a 2:1 input/output multiplication/division problem occurs when feedback from others is viewed as twice as critical as it was & statements to others are viewed as half as critical as they were. This is because of hypersensitivity to what comes in (magnifying it, multiplying by 2), expecting it to be criticism, aversive or disrespectful in nature (e.g., Viewing "I don't think I agree" as "You turned on me" or "You stupid ass…") & being insensitive to what is let out in terms of criticism, aversive or disrespectful comments (minimizing it, dividing by 2) often due to a role reversal deficit and not putting self in other peoples shoes, e.g., Stating "You back stabbing ass…." or "You dumb ass…" as opposed to "This is important to me so I'd like to know why you don't agree". Viewing disagreement as disrespect and using fear or manipulation to get agreement. In summary, either showing more respect and consideration for yourself than you do for others or showing more respect and consideration for others than you do for yourself. <u>Behavioral double standards</u>- Mistakes you make are considered accidents but mistakes others make are assumed to be on purpose. In parenting, "Do what I say, not what I do".

Helpful opposite- Treat others the way you want to be treated. Use your healthy relationship success skills (p. 18) and practice social exchange by returning favors, compliments, respect and social responsibility (i.e., honesty, trust, loyalty, concern and responsibility). Hold yourself to the same standards that you expect from others. Realize that others are likely to give you the same thing that you give to them. This means being aware of the fact that humans can easily fall into double standards and avoiding double standards in honesty, trust, loyalty, concern and responsibility. Letting go of double standards means having the courage to correct yourself after a mistake in honesty, trust, loyalty, concern or responsibility. Use the reality scales to help you "Think it through" (p. 24) and realize that you can handle correcting yourself after a mistake.

While all double standards are important to work on, trust double standards is particularly important since many people feel that they can be trusted but do not trust others. While trust double standards may relate to years of exposure to television news covering the scandals if those who are not trustworthy, it is still an important issue because "Every kind of peaceful cooperation among men is primarily based on mutual trust and only secondarily on institutions such as courts of justice and police" (Albert Einstein, 1879-1955). Help yourself build trust in others by realizing that there is something in it for you. Realize that you get more privileges as a youth and promotions as an adult "after" you develop trust by being responsible. The key word here is "after". Trust is not a legal right, where you are innocent until proven guilty so don't tell yourself "they should trust me until I prove myself untrustworthy". Since you don't trust others that you don't know well, you can't expect others to trust you without first getting to know you. Just like others have to earn your trust, you have to earn theirs. The point that others are likely to give you the same thing you give them is easy to see with honesty. If you are dishonest with others, they are likely to be dishonest with you. This point can be a little confusing in terms of *building trust* unless you realize that responsibility is involved. If you are responsible with others (i.e., do what you say, when you say for the reason you say), they are likely to trust you and if others are responsible with you, you are likely to trust them. The same thing applies with *learning to trust* which can also be confusing unless you realize that honesty is involved. If you pick honest people to trust and open up with your honest feelings to them, they are likely to view you as an honest person and open up with their honest feelings to you. Picking an honest person to trust is the key here.

3. Irresponsible Loyalty- Examples include… Forming negative ties, developing relationships with irresponsible others. Being loyal to people you can't count on and who get you in trouble by telling you what you want to hear not what you need to hear or asking you to do something wrong. Unhealthy dependency on people who can't be depended on, continuing to give more than you get, overly loyal, remaining in relationships with others who are not dependable or shifting loyalty, problems with attachment and getting close and staying close. Holding Negative contracts, i.e., "I'll cover up your wrong doing if you cover up mine". Defending negative peers. Also includes misplaced loyalty, putting negative peers over positive family or negative family over positive peers. Whether the loyalty issues involve a responsible loyalty deficit (not enough loyalty to the right people or what you know is right) or irresponsible loyalty excess (too much loyalty to the wrong people what you know is wrong), the results are still harmful to self or others.

Helpful opposite- Practice Responsible Loyalty. Be loyal to those who have earned it through their track record of honesty, trustworthiness, concern and responsibility. In relationships, "Think it though" using the reality scales (see p. 24) to help you stand up for what you know is right and who you know is right by: 1) not going along with what is wrong just to get along; 2) not compromising yourself and what you know is right to be accepted by others; 3) not covering up for others wrongdoing (the longer they keep doing wrong, the worse their consequences will be); 4) not picking looks over loyalty in relationships and; 5) not picking negative people over positive ones as friends, "Consider loyalty and faithfulness to be fundamental." (Confucius, c. 551-c. 479 BC).

4. Don't Care Attitude- Examples include… Not caring and not sharing. Includes lack of concern for self by not thinking about consequences before taking action or telling yourself, "I'm only hurting myself". Selfishness- Not thinking about anyone else but yourself. Telling yourself, "Nobody else matters" or "It's every man for himself". Extreme role reversal deficit. Not putting yourself in others shoes or considering the impact of behavior on others. Lacking empathy. Putting others down to build self up. Not sharing with others. Not being socially responsible by being your brother's keeper and sharing your level of awareness i.e., "I shouldn't have to point out problems that others need to change. If I hold myself accountable, that should be enough" A "don't care attitude" about others by those who only care about themselves is only one side of

the coin. Concern problems can also involve excesses with some who have more concern for others than themselves, compromising themselves for others, centering their life around others and thus not really caring enough for self (i.e., "don't care attitude" about self). Whether the concern issues involve a deficit or excess, the results are still harmful to self or others.

Helpful opposite- Show the courage to care, share and try- Take care of yourself and others. Realize that "No act of kindness, no matter how small, is ever wasted" (Aesop, ancient Greek moralist). Let yourself care about what you and do and what is healthy. Help yourself by keeping problems "up front" as a daily priority so that they don't get out of control again. Help others by treating them the way they want to be treated. Push past fears of loss and rejection to let yourself care about others and share your feelings with others who have earned your trust by sharing honest feelings with you. Stop using "who cares" as a face saving excuse not to put effort or energy into getting what you really want. Tell yourself "nothing to it but to do it", push past the fear of failure and try. Add concern to your decision making. Ask yourself, "How will this help/hurt myself or others?" Admit that "If you're not working on the solution, you're part of the problem" and block helplessness by taking responsibility instead of blaming others (i.e., "when you blame other people for your behavior, you give them control over your life"). Use the SET steps to "Solve the Problem" (see p. 25) as opposed to a "don't care attitude" to avoid dealing with the problem.

5. Responsibility Issues- Examples include… <u>No achievement motivation</u>. "I don't need to", "It's not my responsibility", "It's their problem/issue", "I don't want to", puts off doing responsibilities, "I won't because it's not that important", does what they want not what they should. Says they forgot when they ignored it. <u>Not doing their part</u>. Failure to pull own weight. Not <u>"Earning the right to complain"</u> by inconveniencing yourself and finishing a task that was assigned by mistake. <u>Poor work ethic</u>, lazy, "dead beat", borrows and doesn't pay. Feels entitled to top rank pay without starting at the bottom. Includes entitlement dependency attitude, "I don't need to go to school/work" implying that "The world owes me a living". Lack of responsibility motivation involves <u>lack of effort, not finishing what started</u> or finishing but doing half way job. <u>No concept of track record</u> (i.e., telling yourself that you have changed after a few days or weeks when a track record is measured in months and years) is a recovery problem that prevents long term lifestyle change. Puts fun before work is an example of responsibility problem priorities. Also failure to schedule time for responsibilities, and no life achievement goals or motivation to succeed at anything that involves hard work and avoiding responsibilities that are boring or not interesting. Includes "my way" excuses for responsibility refusal, e.g., "I don't have to make it the hard way, I can always… deal drugs, pimp/live off of women, hook/live off of men, go on welfare, depend on my family/friends, gamble or win the lottery". Lack of social responsibility and work effort can be found in the criminal subcultures of societies around the world where realizing that criminal subculture does not represent minority culture determines the unity of these societies. Refusing to accept personal responsibility involving unwillingness to look at ones part in a problem typically involves <u>blaming problems on others or circumstances</u>. Responsibility issues which involve basic responsibility deficits is only one side of the coin with responsibility problems which can also involve excesses by some who take on too much responsibility, do too much for others and blame themselves unnecessarily. Whether the responsibility issues involve a deficit or excess, the results are still harmful to self or others.

Helpful opposite- Accept your responsibilities. "None of us can hope to get anywhere without character, moral courage and the spiritual strength to accept responsibility" (Thomas Watson,

1874-1956). Getting what we want in life requires learning Healthy Behavior Success Skills to **A**void trouble; **C**alm down; **T**hink it through and; **S**olve the problem (see p. 19). These skills help us uphold our responsibilities to maintain self-control, make things right after mistakes (emotional restitution), pull our own weight and learn to accept feedback. Accepting responsibility involves understanding that real men and women have learned to do what they should, when they should for the reason they should. Don't wait for someone to do it for you, try doing it yourself. Take initiative, look for things that need to get done and do them, start your responsibilities without being told and accept reminders. Realize that the only responsible answer when being reminded is, "thank you, I'll take care of that". If you want a break, earn it by finishing what you started or getting to a reasonable quitting point first. Don't get overwhelmed by too much to accomplish. Know that you will get things done if you learn to set and achieve small but realistic goals one at a time. Get honest about being responsible. Admit to yourself that being responsible builds trust which gets you what you want in terms of favors, privileges or promotions. Accept that our number one responsibility is self-control and use "the 3 G's" (i.e., the three-step social responsibility plan, p. 21) to get out of high risk situations and maintain self-control.

6. Blind Ambition- Examples include… Selfishly getting what you want at any cost and not being able to see (being blind to) or consider anything else, including impact on others. "I want what I want when I want it, nothing else matters". In socially irresponsible needs gratification or career achievement, "The ends justify the means" by getting what you want at the expense of others or by putting others at risk for harm. Putting self and career over everything else including family responsibilities, being a selfish "workaholic". Includes flawed definition of achievement and success, using survival as an excuse to exploit others, profit illegally and be a greedy "takeaholic". Putting money over everything. Compromising yourself or your values to get ahead. Being unwilling to accept achievement alternatives that are socially responsible but either require more work or are less rewarding. Blind ambition also includes having "all or nothing thinking" about achievement, ambition or success by adopting an attitude that, "You're either a hero or a zero" or "Second best is the first loser". This thinking focuses you so intensely on ambition that you lose sight of the impact of your behavior (or your absence) on others.

        Helpful opposite- Show Socially Responsible Achievement. Examples include looking at possible consequences to self and others not just what you want no matter what. Realize that "You're #1 but there are other numbers" and while it is important to take care of yourself, you have the social responsibility to avoid harming others. Look for win-win solutions where there is benefit for yourself and others. Admit that since doing the right thing takes more effort, you value it more & feel better about it. Ask yourself who really helped you in your life and take on the social responsibility to help someone else. Use the reality scales (p. 24) to weigh what it takes for your success against the severity of what could happen to others. Let go of your all or nothing thinking about ambition, achievement and success. Include "being a better person" by improving your an honesty, trust, loyalty, concern and social responsibility in your personal success goals.

7. Motivational Blindness- Examples include not being aware of why you do what you do. Lacking awareness- Not being aware of feelings that trigger behavior (e.g., anger, anxiety or depression); thoughts that trigger behavior (e.g., using words like "should" or "must" which trigger reactions) or needs that trigger behavior (e.g., for power, acceptance, attention or excitement). Unable to identify and label types of feelings or types of irresponsible thinking. Found yourself saying "I don't know" when asked why you did what you did. Motivational blindness is often reflected by statements like, "It just happened". Lacking understanding about how you got the problem, what maintained it and how it spread to other problems or parts of your life. <u>Closed minded</u>, only paid attention to what you wanted to hear or people who wouldn't bring up your problems. You never really knew you had problems with awareness, understanding and openness. You have heard others say you were "clueless" or therapists say "They don't even know that they don't even know" about you.

Helpful opposite- Develop your Awareness and Insight. Adopt the "Mirror Concept" (p. 125) that "Other people may see you better than you see yourself" and use other people's feedback as a mirror to see yourself. Slow down your reactions and let yourself feel. Then label those feelings. Look at what triggered them to determine where you are coming from with the action you are considering to decide if you really want to take that action. Learn about the Risk Factor Chain that led up to your unhealthy, harmful behavior, the Stress-Relapse Cycle that maintained it and the Harmful Behavior Anatomy that generalized it to other forms and life areas.

8. "I can't" belief (Opposite of Grandiosity)- Examples include… Two basic types- A. <u>Defeatist attitude</u> involving low self-efficacy (confidence) and insecurity. Doesn't believe in abilities. Has unrealistic negative self-appraisal, may be competent but lacks confidence. Doesn't think they are as capable as they actually are, "I can't do it" or "I won't succeed" belief. Feels inferior to others, helpless. Has fear of failure. Afraid to try new things or extend self socially to new people. Extreme pessimism. Always expecting the worst of self and others. Obsessing on the negative. When evaluating the feedback of others, discounting positive feedback and focusing on the negative feedback. "I can't" and "I quit" attitude. Making things fit the "I can't belief by devaluing accomplishments or discounting achievements. B. <u>Resistance to change</u> involving "Hole punching", telling why solutions won't work without trying them or saying they already did when they heard about it but never really gave it a serious try. Says "I can't" when really means "I won't". Gives excuses for not trying.

Helpful opposite- Build your self-confidence. Get honest about the fact that "I can't" may be true but it is really true if you don't get up the courage to try. Start by looking at why you won't try. For example, some people are afraid to try because they are afraid they will fail so they tell themselves "I can't do it so why even try". Others are afraid to put in 100% because if they do their best and don't make it, they are worried about being thought of as a loser or failure. These are excuses to avoid putting in effort to succeed. Get honest with yourself, lose the excuses and put in the effort. Tell yourself the truth. If you try your hardest and don't make it this just means, you didn't succeed at one thing, not that your whole life is a failure. Stop magnifying (p. 125) and start working on the problems in your life. Realize that "If you are not working on the solution, you are part of the problem" and start using your SET problem solving tools (p. 25) to reach your goals.

9. Grandiosity (Opposite of "I can't" Belief)- Examples include… <u>Extreme optimism</u> and unrealistic positive appraisal of self and abilities Discounting constructive feedback from others. Other people notice my abilities and mess with me because they are jealous "haters". Thinks they are more capable than they are. Feels superior to others, arrogant. Overconfidence in abilities, "I can pull this off", "I won't get caught" or "no one will know". "I don't have to avoid high risk situations, I can handle them". "I don't have to plan ahead to avoid problems because I can talk my way out of anything that happens". Highly unrealistic expectations, impatient and intolerant of "stupidity" and sense of entitlement based on view of self as unique and special, e.g., "If I want it, they will want to give it to me" or "Because I like her, she must like me". Extreme entitlement to special attention, privileges, rule exceptions, as a result of uniqueness (e.g., "This doesn't apply to me") or superiority (e.g., "rules are for fools who need others to tell them what to do"). Highly confident but may lack competence.

Helpful opposite- Be Realistic- about what you want, what you need and what people should do for you. Realize that while everyone wants some recognition, no one needs it to survive and no one is likely to recognize your abilities if you don't demonstrate a consistent track record and bring it to their attention. Telling yourself, "They should" recognize my abilities, what I've done, etc, is assuming that others do not have their own world of worries to address. Grandma had a saying about making others aware of your accomplishments, "You've got to toot your own horn because nobody else will". In life, "First do it, then point to it". Be realistic about what you can and can't do. When it comes to doing things you know you shouldn't, get honest about the fact that "no one will know" is usually not true but "Three can keep a secret if two of them are dead" (Benjamin Franklin) is usually true and don't do it. Use the reality scales (see p. 24) to keep grandiosity in check and keep you in touch with the reality of the possible consequences of your actions to yourself and others. Don't over-estimate your self-control ability. Get honest about the fact that staying in high risk situations is likely to trigger relapse and escape trouble with "the 3 G's" (i.e., your three-step responsibility plan, p. 21). Continue to tell yourself that you can do anything that you put your mind to but accept that just thinking about it will not make it happen.

10. Control Issues- Examples include… "I must be in control" attitude, starting power struggles for fun and to gain control. Plays people against people, rules against rules and concepts against concepts (e.g., being honest vs. being polite to people) to try and get own way. Has attitude of entitlement to do what they want, when they want for the reason they want. Follows Irresponsible Behavior Law, i.e., "What's right is what I want to do and the reason it's right is because I want to do it". Has "Baby My Way" (BMW) fits when they don't get what they want, when they want for the reason they want and reckless BMW driving crashes their relationships. Uses Winning by Intimidation, outbursts to stop others from confronting your behavior, manipulation or any means necessary to get control, continue to do what you want and have things "my way". Self-control motivation deficit and dysfunctional social values, e.g., "It's only wrong if you get caught", "My behavior doesn't bother me so why should I control it?" Physical & verbal bullying, "It's better to be an offender than a victim". "I give ulcers, I don't get them", "I create fear, I don't feel it". "I control other people, they don't control me". Has attitude that power has to do with being in command of (controlling) others not understanding and being in command of (controlling) self & enjoys dominating or manipulating others. Control issues also involve need to control mood or self-medicate by drinking, drugging, eating, spending, sexual indulging or any method that temporarily controls/alleviates unwanted feelings.

Helpful opposite- Work on controlling yourself, not others. Some people who have feelings of helplessness because their lives have been out of control in the past decide to make up for it by controlling others. Others who have been over-controlled (or abused) in the past fall into the "vampire syndrome" and become an over-controlling (or abusive) themselves. Making yourself feel more powerful by over-controlling others results in power struggles or mistreating others and avoids dealing with self. Realize that people who focus too much on being in control could be afraid of feeling helpless often from bad past experiences or repeating what was done to them (the "vampire syndrome"). If any of this applies to you, then conflicts could make you very nervous and too caught up in the extremes of either trying to be in control or trying to avoid conflict. In disagreements or conflicts use the ABC's of letting feelings go to calm down (see page 22) and keep from falling into the extremes of "my way or the highway" or "go along to get along (compromising yourself to be accepted). If past bad memories are triggered by conflicts, remind yourself, "That was then and this is now" and use the reality scales (p. 24) to help you think it through and do the right thing in conflict situations. Decide who you want to run your life, yourself (through decisions you make) or others (who push your emotional buttons and watch you react to feelings they trigger). Get out of those trigger situations, "You need to be laughing and leaving, not staying and stewing". Developing self-control involves using your 3-step social responsibility plan (p. 21) and continually challenging your BMW ("baby my way") thinking, "Why must I always get my way (or always have the last word)?" Weigh out what you are going to say on the reality scales (p. 24) to help you realize that getting "my way" or having the last word is not needed for survival or success and letting it go isn't that severe. Use fantasy fast forward (p. 113) to think ahead by playing the tape in your mind through to the end. Ask yourself, "Is this so important that ten years from now, I will remember not getting my way here?" If the answer is no, let it go. Stop using anger to try and win by intimidation, grow up and admit that anger is a secondary emotion, underneath it you are afraid of not being in control.

11. Image Problems- Examples include… Three basic types- A. <u>Unhealthy pride</u>- Values looking good by being right. Involves unhealthy perfectionism, inability to admit fault, secret keeping and covering up. This is often based on fear of looking bad, stupid, not being accepted or blowing image, by disclosing problems. Reluctant to ask for help, "Keeping up appearances is job #1". B. <u>Criminal pride</u>- Values looking tough/cool. Involves glorifying authority problem tough guy image, viewing kindness as weakness, rules for fools, war story bragging about negative, abusive or criminal behavior and getting over on others, "Being tough is job #1". Criminal pride often involves a fear of being put down and compromising self to fit in, "Being accepted is job #1". C. <u>Superficial values</u>- Valuing what's on the outside (appearance, clothes, jewelry, money) over what's on the inside (honesty, trust, loyalty, concern & responsibility) or who you know over what you know, how you look over how you act. "Looking beautiful/wealthy is job #1". Picking friends based on how that will improve your image or popularity not who is a good person. The superficial values problem of picking looks over loyalty in relationships continues to result in relationship disappointment. All three can involve putting image over integrity, i.e., "Looking good is more important than doing good" and stubborn refusal to back down or change mind.

      Helpful opposite- Be yourself. Examples include not trying to be anyone or anything you're not, just being real about your true thoughts and feelings. Your likes are your likes, your opinion is your opinion and your feelings are your feelings. Unless they are unhealthy or harmful, keep them. Attack unhealthy and criminal pride by being yourself and blowing your image with honesty and humor. Use healthy pride by admitting to self that the reason we value honesty so much is the tremendous cost attached to it. Remind yourself that while "Honesty has its price, the good news is you don't have to pay twice". Realize that being yourself uses less energy which decreases stress build up and improves your life. Don't let unhealthy or criminal pride control your behavior, if you were wrong be strong, back down and apologize.

12. Need Problems- Examples include… Three basic types- A. <u>Exaggerated need for acceptance</u>, "I must be accepted" can result in doing too much for others, going along with things that are wrong to be accepted or not be left out (i.e., "going along to get along" and compromising self to be accepted), worrying about how you will be viewed if you do the right thing, tell the truth or if you try something and fail. B. <u>Exaggerated need for excitement</u>, "I need excitement/must be entertained" or "I can't stand boredom" can result in doing risky, unhealthy or harmful behaviors to break boredom or for excitement/fun, putting what is fun before responsibilities, doing something wrong because it is exciting, instigating to spark a conflict or creating chaos with "Drama Queen" exaggerating and emotional amplification. Sparking conflict excitement- the argument is more important than the issue. C. <u>Exaggerated need for attention</u>, "I must get attention" can result in doing something risky, unhealthy or harmful for attention. "Any attention is better than none" and drawing attention to self overshadows the needs of others to also receive social recognition. Can involve getting for Attention for Support or Sympathy.

Helpful opposite- Get a grip on your needs. Realize that attention, acceptance and excitement are human needs not necessities. Everyone wants some degree of attention, acceptance and excitement in their life but no one needs it to survive, no one is entitled to it as a birth right, no one should entertain you, automatically accept you or devote attention to you without getting to know you first. Don't compromise yourself to be accepted, act out for attention or endanger yourself for excitement. If you want acceptance, accept someone. If you want attention, do something good that deserves it. If you want excitement, try something positive that is new and you have never tried before.

13. Planning Problems- Examples include… Not planning ahead or thinking ahead. Putting things off until the last minute, "Not to make a decision is to make a decision". Like motivational blindness, planning problems can be reflected by statements like, "It just happened". Being disorganized, not writing things down and forgetting to turn work in, being late or missing appointments. Not thinking ahead about the possible consequences of taking an action or failing to do a responsibility. Planning problems also involve a planning skills deficit (i.e., never learning how to put priorities in order with the most important responsibilities first), problem priorities (i.e., putting fun or interesting tasks before more important responsibilities) and pathological priorities (putting harmful but exciting activities first such as drinking, drugging or gambling over more important responsibilities such as homework or child care).

Helpful opposite- Use Positive planning, "Think ahead, plan ahead, get ahead." Examples include playing the mental checkers tape, "If I make this move, they will make that move", "If I do this, the result could be that". Use the reality scales (p. 13) to weigh out the consequences of not planning ahead to get things done. Getting yourself together, means getting organized. Each evening after dinner, whether you have been in school, at work or at home, ask yourself, "What do I need to get ready for tomorrow" and get ready by making a list. Good planners are good performers. Humans perform most poorly when they are caught off guard and good planners are rarely caught off guard. Put another way, "If you fail to plan, you plan to fail". With respect to learning social responsibility, accept that "Accidents happen, behaviors are planned and consequences are earned". Use your three SET steps (p. 25- 27) to make success plans for important life goals.

14. Boundary Problems- Examples include… Five basic types: A. <u>Relationship boundary problems</u>- Not enough boundaries, too accepting, highly trustworthy so overly trusting (assumes others are also), getting too involved too quick, violating personal space, touchy feely. Boundaries too defended, problems trusting and/or untrustworthy, too distant, quick to push away, reject or both (i.e., approach-avoidance in relationships, gets too close, too fast, scares self then pulls too far away too fast). Ownership jealousy- viewing a person as property that you own. Objectifying- viewing others as objects to use to get what you want (e.g., sexual abuse). B. <u>Personal boundary problems</u>- Not respecting personal privacy. Nosey, snooping through others possessions, letters, diary wallet, purse, etc. Trying to be in on everything, eavesdropping or dipping into private conversations, asks inappropriate personal questions. Discloses inappropriate personal information, "Group Leaking", violates group/family therapy confidentiality boundaries (trust abuse). C. Social boundary problems- Viewing elders or superiors as peers and potential partners. Doesn't dress appropriately for age or setting. Acts as if they are a member of a different culture or group. D. Property boundary problems- Property ownership attitude. Theft, borrowing without permission, not returning borrowed property, "What's mine is mine and what's yours is mine" (property abuse), "Give me that!" E. Emotional boundary problems- Doesn't respect other people's feelings by going too far with arguing, teasing horseplay or personal comments. Whether the boundary and trust issues involve a deficit or excess, the results are still harmful to self or others.

Helpful opposite- Show Respect. Treat people like they deserve to be treated. Respect others personal space, personal property, privacy, opinions and feelings. If you want good relationships, take time to get to know the person before getting too involved. If you want to know something personal about someone, ask "Can I ask you a question?" to get them ready. "When in Rome do as the Romans do". This means to respect social boundaries by speaking and acting according to what is appropriate to the setting. For example, if you are at a party and are not Catholic, don't tell jokes about Nuns or Priests. If you want to borrow something from someone and they are not there, don't come back later. Use the reality scales (p. 24) to weigh out how important it is for you to borrow the item in question. If it rates high on the survival or success scales and low on the severity scale (impact on the person you are borrowing from) don't just take it, leave a note and call them as soon as you can. Become aware of your Historical Risk factors in the Risk Factor Chain that led to unhealthy, harmful behavior. Don't transfer your past boundary problems onto present relationships, if you were mistreated, disrespected, devalued or abused put extra effort into respecting others boundaries making sure that others are not treated like servants, property or objects for your personal use.

15. Victim View- Examples include… A preoccupation with injustices, falling into feeling sorry for self and making self miserable in "pity party" ruminating on past issues. Dwelling on past thoughts that reinforce feeling like the victim of things that were not fair. For example, thinking about getting comfort from your mother for the overly harsh discipline of an out of control father that she was too ineffective, depressed or addicted to protect you from or leave. In this regard, the victim view involves rumination (dwelling) on the only two things that can't be changed in life, i.e., the past and other people's behavior. This results in helplessness and a tendency to view self as a victim. The victim view includes attempts to elicit sympathy from others and includes problems accepting personal responsibility, blaming others for your situation, consequences and associated behavior, e.g. "I don't deserve this, it wasn't my fault, they got it started". The victim view can involve the attitude that what happened is either never your fault because someone else got you upset or always your fault because you always mess up. The victim view can also involve being the martyr, trying to get attention for sadness and sympathy. "No one understands" or "You don't understand" or are common victim view responses to those who do understand but just don't agree. Feeling rejected and acting that victim view out was expressed by one young man who said, "It's better to be wanted by the police than not wanted by anyone."

Helpful opposite- Hold yourself Accountable. Let go of your preoccupation with injustices and save your anger for the real injustices. Use the reality scales (p. 24) to help you stop dwelling on the past and other people's behavior. The only two things you can't change in life are the past and other people's behavior. Dwelling on these things makes you feel helpless because you can't change them and feeling helpless keeps your victim view going. Take responsibility for mistakes. Substitute the responsibility tape, (e.g., "What can I do to avoid this in the future?") for the victim rumination tape, (e.g., "This crap ain't right"). Regain control of your life by taking responsibility for your actions. Remind yourself that "It's up to me" to make it in life and "If you blame others for your behavior, you give them control over your life." Stay focused on what you can change (i.e., the present and your behavior), not what you can't change (i.e., the past and other people's behavior). Let go of victim view thinking that, "You don't understand me" and realize that since humans have the same ability to experience feelings it is more likely that they do understand you but simply disagree with your choice in attitude, feelings or behaviors used in your situation. Admit that in the real world, outside of a dysfunctional family, you get consequences as a result of your poor decisions and problem behavior, not because the authorities are taking their bad mood out on you. Put the responsibility for your decisions and behaviors on yourself. Admit that many times you can avoid a problem by avoiding a problem person or a problem place. Accept that , "the best revenge is success" and use your anger from feeling victimized as fuel to succeed by channeling it into getting ahead and making your goals. "If you believe that feeling bad or worrying long enough will change a past or future event, then you are residing on another planet with a different reality system"-- William James (1842- 1910)

16. Justifying Actions

16. **Justifying Actions**- Includes any form of <u>justifying actions based on feelings</u>. For example, excuses and feelings to justify taking action and avoid taking responsibility for self-control such as "I had to hit him, he really ticked me off!" Justifying harmful actions based on unwanted feelings include hurting others based on anger, hurting self based on depression and avoiding or running from problems based on anxiety. Using feelings to justify taking action and excuse the social responsibility of maintaining self-control of behavior that is harmful to others can be summed up in the statement "They deserved it". On the other hand, justifying unhealthy behavior that is harmful to self (e.g., eating, drinking, smoking, drugs, etc) after successfully handling a stressful situation can be triggered by the self-statement, "I deserve it". Justifying actions based on rationalization includes score keeping and getting even. This irresponsible thinking is often based on incorrect assumption that feelings reflect the way things really are (reality). This can also occur in justifying actions based on beliefs (or group membership), e.g., global, political, religious or gang murder/war. <u>Payback Thinking</u>, i.e., "They wronged me so I'm entitled to my revenge". This type of justification can extend into using relationships for payback, e.g., "You care about them, so I'll hurt you by hurting them" or "You care about me, so I'll hurt you by hurting me". Justifying actions also includes entitlement justification, i.e., "Since they accused me wrongly, I'm entitled to do what they accused me of doing".

Helpful opposite- Follow facts not feelings. Remind yourself that although all feelings are valid experiences, they may not reflect facts and find out the facts before taking action. If action has already been taken, don't justify actions with excuses. Find out the facts and get honest with yourself about what you could have done differently. Realize that payback is a socially irresponsible form of working through anger, hurt or loss. Ask yourself, "In the long run, who really suffers if I do something harmful to myself or get caught for doing something harmful to others?" and "Why should I hurt me just because other people or things hurt me?" Use the ABC's of letting feelings go (p. 12) to calm down, then admit that "The best revenge is success" and move on.

17. **Extremism** (Going to Extremes)- Examples include dichotomous (All-or-nothing) thinking. In achievement (school/work/sports) if your performance isn't perfect you're a failure. This is

reflected in statements like, "You're either a hero or a zero", "You're a champ or a chump" or "Second best is the first loser". "Being the best is all that counts so if I can't be the best of the best (e.g., student or athlete), I'll be best of the worst (e.g., druggie or bully)". In relationships, "If they don't accept me, I'm a total reject" or being passive, holding things in until stress builds up and blows up through aggressive words or actions. In negotiation, "My way or the highway" view that you must either win or lose and in discussion, "Either you're with me or you're against me". Extremism can include over involvement (encapsulation) in work or relationships to the extreme where everything else is almost excluded or total lack of involvement and detachment, i.e., "It's all in or it's all over". In personal responsibility, extremism can result in viewing problems as either all their fault (which can trigger anger and blaming others unjustly) or all your fault (which can lead to guilt and blaming self unjustly). In parenting discipline, extremism in can result in being too lenient or too harsh which may relate to shifting back and forth between "Don't care attitude" (p. 116) and "Justifying actions based on feelings" (p. 124). Parenting supervision extremism can result in no supervision at all or no freedom at all.

Helpful opposite- Take a Balanced View. Keep your balance in your life goals, relationships, negotiations and opinions. Be very aware of "all or nothing thinking" and how "Don't care attitude" (p. 116) and "Justifying actions based on feelings" (p. 124) triggers going to extremes. Remind yourself that you don't have to be a hero to get recognition from others, that it is unrealistic to expect everyone to agree with you and don't mistake disagreement on an opinion as rejection of you as a person. Understand that it is impossible to always get your way in life, that everyone deserves to get something out of a relationship and it's important to keep a balance of give and take. Take "all things in moderation", strive for the "happy medium" and look for win-win situations in relationships where there are benefits for all involved.

18. Minimizing (Opposite of Magnifying)- Examples include… Playing down problems (often of self) or consequences (often about not doing the right thing). Minimizing behavior frequency or severity can often be identified by the words "Just" or "Only" (e.g., "I just did it once", "I don't do it that much" or "I only yelled, didn't hit them"). Minimizing problems can occur by excusing actions as something you did when you weren't your usual self, "I was really... upset, angry, drunk, high". Minimizing impact or severity can occur by comparison with more serious problems, "It wasn't as bad as what others have done", for example compared to newspaper articles or TV news on the same topic. Minimizing by normalizing (making it seem normal), examples include, "Lots of people do it" or "Everybody does it so it's no big deal".

Helpful opposite- Call it like it is- Use the "Mirror Concept" to avoid minimizing or blocking out valuable feedback from others. The "Mirror Concept" holds that "other people can see you better than you see yourself" and you need to use their feedback as a mirror to get a better view of yourself to avoid minimizing problems. When a mistake has been called to your attention, don't play it down or blow it off. Look at what you need to do to correct the problem, don't try to correct the person. Use feedback to improve your relapse prevention plan, your promise letter and your self-awareness. Don't block feedback out by pointing out that others have made the same mistake. If they made the same mistake and are calling it to your attention, take it serious. They are not a hypocrite because they have done it themselves, they are an expert witness at seeing it because they have done it themselves. Accept that, "It takes one to know one". Keep the focus on the present and your behavior, not the past and others. Substitute getting defensive with the proper response, "Thank you I'll take care of that" to avoid unnecessary conflict.

19. Magnifying (Opposite of Minimizing)- Examples include… Exaggerating a problem (often of others) or consequences (often about doing the right thing). Blowing things way out of proportion, taking constructive feedback personal. Minor criticism is magnified into "disrespect" that is used to justify retaliation. Overgeneralization to the extreme, often used to justify giving up, acting out or not extending self to others, e.g., "since I broke one rule or made one mistake, I'm failing treatment and might as well quit" (rule violation effect), because one adult mistreated you, all adults will mistreat you. Magnifying "Sorry, I couldn't make it, I had to finish my work" into "I'm not interested in you (or you don't matter)" and then stating "You led me on (or lied to me)" as opposed to "I was looking forward to seeing you (or to a visit) and hope to see you soon". Ruminating on injustices, negative feedback or conflicts to the point where any positive is overshadowed and the negative is magnified into triggering action often by using the word "should" or "must". For example, they "should act the way that I want", they "should not have said that" or "I must drink, drug, smoke, eat, spend, hit, cut or run away to get away from my problems and make myself feel better".

     Helpful opposite- Reel it in- <u>Use the "Window Concept"</u> to avoid magnifying feedback from others to the point where you are upset and at risk for acting feelings out. The "Window Concept" involves looking at everything everyone tells you and deciding what to keep. If it's helpful to yourself or others hold it dear to your heart, if it's not, open the window and shovel it out. One way to see the possible benefit of the feedback is to ask yourself, "What if I actually did what the person is saying?" This can make it easier because, "Go to hell!" will not help you but "Shut up while others are talking" will (i.e., we never learn anything while running our mouths). If there is any doubt about whether to keep and apply the feedback you receive, use group consensus (i.e., "If ten people say you're a horse, you're a horse"). Realize that exaggerating problems and stirring up trouble about the behavior of others sends a signal that: you are trying to take the spotlight off of your mistakes; you are a bored drama addict who needs excitement or; a thin skinned insecure person who is hypersensitive to criticism. Ask yourself if you really want to send any of these signals to others. Remind yourself that fighting over disrespect is an admission that you have nothing more valuable to fight for. Use the Reality Scales (p. 24) to weigh out the real seriousness of injustices, negative feedback or conflicts and don't overreact. Use the Reality Scales to put things in perspective and avoid overreaction by weighing out the real seriousness of injustices, negative feedback or conflicts. When a mistake has been called to your attention, don't blow it out of proportion, realize that honest feedback as a way to learn about yourself and grow.

20. Assuming- Examples include… Jumping to conclusions and making assumptions without facts, proof or other evidence to support the assumption. Also involves not verifying your assumption based on initial information by continuing to gather information. Making judgments about others and decisions about actions to take based on unverified assumptions. Not "looking before you leap". Making negative assumptions that because one thing has gone wrong or one error has been made, all is lost and using that as justification to quit trying or give up.

     Helpful opposite- Verify. Realize that things are not always the way they appear so "when in doubt, check it out." Realize that everybody makes mistakes and don't assume that mistakes were on purpose, i.e., "never mistake incompetence for viciousness". When rumors, opinions or other information presented to you kicks up a desire to take action, don't act. If you are being asked or encouraged to act on unverified information use the proper response, "I need to get back to you about that" and then check it out. If you are made to feel that you must take action right away, be creative and come up with a way to check things out or get other opinions before taking action.

Workspace for Relapse Prevention Plan

Appendix D.   Summary of Situation Response Analysis

The goal of Situation Response Analysis is to increase your self-efficacy (confidence) by learning to analyze your responses to problem situations and by developing your awareness of the Negative Coping that leads to problem responses. Situation Response Analysis is based on the premise that you need to change your internal coping methods (i.e., irresponsible thinking) in order to change your responses to problem situations and break your stress-relapse cycle through positive coping (i.e., responsible, mature, adaptive thinking). In summary, irresponsible thinking maintains irresponsible, emotional and behavioral reactions which in turn tend to be justified by more irresponsible thinking in a continual self-defeating cycle as follows.

- If you always think what you always thought, you will always feel what you always felt.
- If you always feel what you always felt, you will always do what you've always done.
- If you always do what you've always done, you will always think what you've always thought.

Although we all talk to ourselves, that's how we make decisions and solve problems, much of this is automatic and not noticed unless we pay special attention to it. Thus, at first you will probably not be aware of your self-statements (i.e., thinking) that trigger irresponsible, immature or maladaptive reactions to problem situations. Situation Response Analysis is designed to increase your awareness of your thinking during problem situations beginning with helping you review those situations by recording them on a Situation Response Analysis log at the end of each day when you can analyze what needed to be done differently. Consistently analyzing your thinking, associated feelings and reactions to problem situations will help you develop your ability to do "on the spot" substitution of responsible, mature self-statements during actual problem situations. As you begin to develop positive coping through responsible, mature adaptive thinking, you will notice that you are exhibiting less intense emotional reactions and more responsible, mature reactions to problem situations.

Situation	Response		Analysis	
Date and what actually happened in the situation (the facts). People, places, things, sights, sounds or other experiences that triggered irresponsible thinking, unwanted feelings or unhealthy, harmful behavior urges/cravings.	Your response to the situation. What you said to yourself (thoughts), what you were feeling (emotions) and what you did (behavior- What you said & your actions)		Your analysis of your response to the situation. What you said to yourself	
	Cognitive & Emotional Response	**Behavioral Response**	**Positive Coping**	**Negative Coping**
	Your thoughts & feelings- (primary & secondary)	(responsible, or irresponsible reactions)	(responsible, adaptive thinking- See Footnote 1)	(irresponsible, maladaptive thinking- See Footnote 2)

1. This is what you needed to say to yourself after the Situation to avoid the irresponsible, immature, maladaptive Response that causes problems for yourself and/or others. Positive Coping involves self-statement substitution by challenging, disputing and then correcting irresponsible, immature, maladaptive thinking. This type of positive coping leads to assuming responsibility, considering alternative explanations for the Situation and looking at the Situation from the perspective of others. This socially responsible, mature approach to problem situations decreases destructive urges, making appropriate social behavior control easier.
2. This is what you said to yourself after the Situation that led to the irresponsible, immature, maladaptive Response that causes problems for yourself and/or others. Negative Coping through maladaptive thinking includes irresponsible thinking, irrational beliefs, inaccurate attributions and perceptions. Irrational beliefs are unrealistic expectations (e.g., irrational use of "should" or "must"). Inaccurate attribution is responsibility, cause or blame that you attributed or assigned to yourself or others by mistake. Inaccurate perceptions are views, opinions and feelings about yourself or others that are not correct or are assumed but can't be proved for certain.

Be sure to make at least one Situation Response Analysis log entry every day as you will be using what you learned from this log in treatment and all three workbooks.

SRT Appropriate Social Behavior Control Exercise

Developing awareness of high risk situations and irresponsible thinking is the first step towards appropriate social behavior control of urges that can result in harmful behavior. Here are some examples in order of seriousness…

Uncontrolled Urge	Resulting Abusive Behavior
Anxious urge to cover-up mistakes or Grandiosity urge to get over on someone	Trust Abuse (lying, deceiving, misleading, omitting)
Negative mood urge or peer acceptance urge to get high, overeat, smoke	Substance Abuse (drugs, alcohol, tobacco, food)
Envy urge to take or break	Property Abuse (theft, vandalism)
Aggressive urge to get even or get "my way"	Physical Abuse (punch, kick, slap, threaten)
Sexual excitement urge to have sex	Sexual Abuse (rape, child molesting, peer coercion)

Many people in treatment relapse and commit another abusive behavior as a result of entering high risk situations and using irresponsible thinking as opposed to positive coping in those situations. Here are some examples in order of seriousness…

High Risk Situation	Resulting Urge & Irresponsible Thinking
Getting confronted about doing something wrong or making a mistake	Anxious urge to cover-up mistakes or Grandiosity urge to get over on someone, e.g., "I can't stand the consequences so I have to lie"
Being around peers who ask you to get high with them. Smelling weed, cigarettes or food	Negative mood urge or peer acceptance urge to get high, smoke or eat, e.g., "One last time won't hurt"
Hearing someone brag about what they have and feeling inferior or less than them	Envy urge to take or break, e.g., "They can afford t lose it" or "They deserve it for showing off"
Continuing to stick around and listen to someone who is putting you down	Aggressive urge to get even, e.g., "The need to be taught a lesson" or "I'll show you"
Starring at a person that is sexually attractive or at porno, Listening to sex talk or 900 toll calls.	Sexual excitement urge to have sex, e.g., "It's just sex, everybody does it"

Irresponsible Thinking in High Risk Situations: The Candy Bar Exercise

In real estate, the key to good property value is location, location and location. In harmful behavior treatment, the key to relapse is access, access and access (to high risk people, places or things). Since you must learn to identify and eliminate your irresponsible thinking in high risk situations in order to prevent relapse, this exercise is designed to generate some irresponsible thinking for you to address on your Situation Response Analysis log. Bring in your favorite candy bar and have your therapist sign and date it. You will be using your candy bar to represent your high risk situation as a structured exercise to help you discover the thinking that leads a person to relapse when in a high risk situation. Your self-control goal is to turn your candy bar back in next week unopened with no part eaten. You are to carry your candy bar on you at all times in a place where it will not melt. No excuses will be accepted, if you lost it, it will be assumed that you caved into your urge and ate it. Use your Situation, Response, Analysis Log to help you become aware of the high risk situation triggers (thoughts, feelings) that relate to urges along with the positive and negative coping that you use in when in a high risk situation. Discuss your week's worth of logs with your therapist or treatment group. This assignment will be evaluated with equal weight applied to how well you complete your logs and how much of your candy bar you turn in next week. Good luck on learning to become aware of the irresponsible thinking related to urges to eat your favorite candy bar!

Note: If you are in treatment for unhealthy eating, are diabetic, are allergic to candy bar ingredients, have had bariatric surgery which could trigger dumping syndrome or have any condition that could harm you by eating your favorite candy bar, do not begin this exercise without making an informed decision after consulting your therapist about the potential benefits & possible adverse impact of participation. If you are advised to do this exercise with an empty candy bar, empty it during a treatment session, discuss the thoughts/feelings triggered by throwing food away and use that information as your first SRA log entry.

Social Responsibility Therapy   **Situation Response Analysis Log**   Name: _____

Situation	Response	Analysis
Date & Description (What actually happened)	**My Thoughts, Feelings and Behavior**	1. Was my response positive/helpful or negative/harmful? 2. What do I need to do in this situation next time?
	Thoughts-	**Thoughts:** __Positive Coping; __Negative Coping **Feelings:** __Tolerable; __Stressful; __Unbearable **Behavior:** __Healthy/helpful; __Unhealthy/harmful **My positive plan for next time is...**
	Feelings*-	
	Behavior-	
	Thoughts-	**Thoughts:** __Positive Coping; __Negative Coping **Feelings:** __Tolerable; __Stressful; __Unbearable **Behavior:** __Healthy/helpful; __Unhealthy/harmful **My positive plan for next time is...**
	Feelings*-	
	Behavior-	
	Thoughts-	**Thoughts:** __Positive Coping; __Negative Coping **Feelings:** __Tolerable; __Stressful; __Unbearable **Behavior:** __Healthy/helpful; __Unhealthy/harmful **My positive plan for next time is...**
	Feelings*-	
	Behavior-	
	Thoughts-	**Thoughts:** __Positive Coping; __Negative Coping **Feelings:** __Tolerable; __Stressful; __Unbearable **Behavior:** __Healthy/helpful; __Unhealthy/harmful **My positive plan for next time is...**
	Feelings*-	
	Behavior-	

* Rate any cravings/urges to eat, drink, drug, smoke, gamble, fight, get sex (1-10: 1=mild urge, 5=moderate urge, 10=very strong urge)

Appendix E.   Social Responsibility Therapy Self-Evaluation

Do a self-evaluation of your social-emotional maturity progress in each of the areas below.

Name: _____   Date: _____

Honesty (check one and explain): __improved; __problems; __both.

_____

_____

Trust (check one and explain): __improved; __problems; __both.

_____

_____

Loyalty (check one and explain): __improved; __problems; __both.

_____

_____

Concern (check one and explain): __improved; __problems; __both.

_____

_____

Responsibility (check one and explain): __improved; __problems; __both.

_____

_____

Self-Awareness (check one and explain): __improved; __problems; __both.

_____

_____

_____

Self-Efficacy/Confidence (check one and explain): __improved; __problems; __both.

_____

_____

_____

Self-Control (check one and explain): __improved; __problems; __both.

_____

_____

_____

Appendix F.   Harmful Behavior Time Line

Harmful Behavior Time Line Name:

Date:

Harmful behavior that was done to you (e.g., witness to domestic violence, toxic parents, sexually abused, physically abused, neglected, removed from home, bullied, picked on, threatened, intimidated, robbed, manipulated, incarcerated, constantly put down, had to run the house when too young, alcoholic, addicted or absent parents, loss of loved ones, poverty, multiple caretakers or moves)

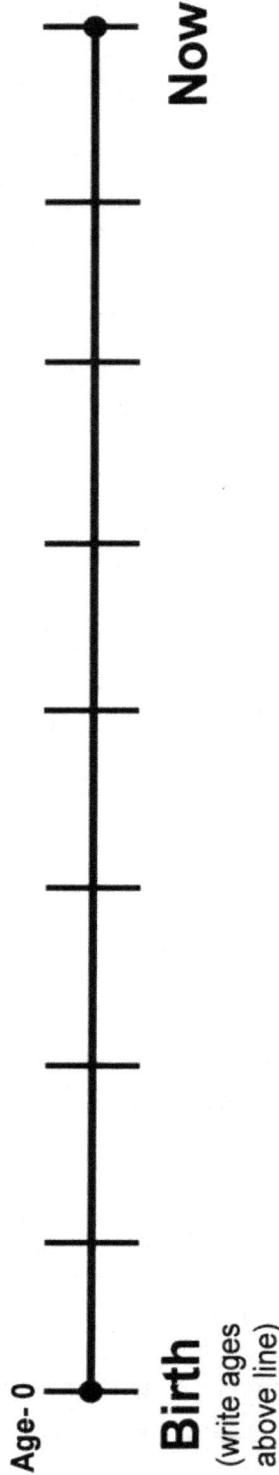

Now

Age- 0

Birth
(write ages
above line)

Harmful behavior that you did to self and/or others (e.g., drugs, alcohol, cigarettes, overeating, over spending, self-harm, quitting school/job, negative relationships, sexual abuse, physical abuse, bullying, gambling, theft, vandalism, arson, cheating, running away)

Appendix G. Awareness and Honesty Examination

"We cannot solve our problems with the same thinking we used when we created them."--Albert Einstein

Name: _____   **Date**: _____

Cognitive Risk Factors involve Irresponsible Thinking that supports and allows irresponsible behavior that is harmful to self or others. Responsible Thinking supports responsible behavior that is helpful to self or others. Irresponsible behavior is associated with being immature and means not acting responsible by doing the right thing at the right time for the right reason. Irresponsible people do what they want, when they want for the reason they want without thinking about whether their actions could be harmful to self or others. Irresponsible thinking that supports and allows unhealthy, harmful behavior includes thinking errors, irrational beliefs, false conclusions, false perceptions and cognitive disinhibitors (thoughts that disinhibit or break down your resistance to unhealthy, harmful behavior). In order to substitute more appropriate, responsible thinking, you need to become aware of the irresponsible thinking that supports and allows harmful behavior. Irresponsible thinking increases the risk of harmful behavior by justifying or minimizing dwelling on harmful behavior thoughts or plans, entering or staying in high risk situations for harmful behavior, or pushing back the line on what you know is wrong and heading for trouble. Not being aware of Irresponsible Thinking puts you at risk for repeating behavior that is harmful to yourself or others.

Awareness and Honesty Examination

Self-awareness and honesty about yourself is very important in your treatment. The following "Awareness and Honesty Examination" is made up of questions designed to see *how aware you are* of the way you think, act and talk to yourself along with *how honest you can be* about your thoughts, feelings and behavior. Everyone makes mistakes and has problems dealing with things that happen to them from time to time. Everyone slips and does things they shouldn't even though they have a feeling that what they are considering may be wrong.

The following Awareness and Honesty Examination covers cognitive risk factors along with social responsibility problems that support harmful behavior and prevent getting the most out of treatment. The items on this exam include ways that people think and act when handling unfortunate events, making mistakes, getting in trouble, conflicts or doing something they shouldn't that could be harmful to self or others.

Taking this exam is the exact opposite of the typical classroom test, job interview or first date where the object is to make yourself look good in order to "score" highly or do well in making a positive impression. In this task, since the object is self-awareness and honesty, "When you're looking bad, you're looking good", that is when you are aware of shortcomings or problem areas and get honest about them (i.e., look bad), you get the highest honesty and awareness score (i.e., look good). Think about each question and mark it if you are aware of it or if you have been made aware of it by others (told that you do it or confronted about it).

When dealing with past situations, please rate how often you have had the following thoughts or behaviors.

Use the numbered ratings on the scale below to rate your answers to the following questions.

0	1	2	3	4
Never	Sometimes	Half of the time	Often	Almost Always

When dealing with past situations, please rate how often you have...

____ 1. Told others what you thought they wanted to hear, not exactly what happened.

____ 2. Not being polite to others while expecting or demanding respect for yourself.

____ 3. Held on to a relationship where you put in more than you got out.

____ 4. Told yourself or others that "you've got to look out for number one" because nobody else will or thought that in life it's "every man for himself".

____ 5. Told yourself "I give up, there's no use in trying".

____ 6. Said "I forgot" or "you forgot to tell me" when reminded about something you knew you were supposed to do.

____ 7. Told yourself that becoming successful is more important than anything else in life.

____ 8. Not been exactly sure why you have done some of the things that you did.

____ 9. Told yourself that you will stay in control and never let anyone hurt you, take advantage of you or get the best of you again.

____ 10. Felt I could do anything if I wasn't held back by others or situations.

____ 11. Felt that people would look down on you if you showed your emotions, admitted you were wrong or admitted a mistake.

____ 12. Went along with things you wouldn't normally do or that you knew were wrong in order to fit in, be accepted, be socially comfortable or avoid being put down.

____ 13. Not written down things that needed to get done and didn't get them turned in or completed.

____ 14. Borrowed things without asking or forgot to return borrowed items.

____ 15. Told yourself that what you did wasn't that bad because you did it on rare occasions, when stressed out or when using drugs/alcohol.

____ 16. Told yourself or others that what happened wasn't your fault because someone else got you upset or you always get blamed whether you did wrong or not.

____ 17. Justified actions based on feelings- For example, told yourself the other person deserved what you said or did because they got you upset or told yourself that you deserved to do something harmful (eating, drinking, smoking, drugs) because you were upset.

____ 18. Thought that if people aren't with you, they're against you.

____ 19. Jumped to conclusions based on how the situation looked at the time.

____ 20. Told yourself or others that a problem others caused or mistake they made was worse than it really was and made a big deal about it.

____ 21. Said "Yes" to someone with no intention of doing what they ask.

0	1	2	3	4
Never	Sometimes	Half of the time	Often	Almost Always

When dealing with past situations, please rate how often you have...

____ 22. Multiplied criticism you received by two (telling yourself it was really harsh) while dividing the criticism you gave in half (telling yourself you weren't that harsh).

____ 23. Put negative peers/friends before family or positive, responsible peers.

____ 24. Been told or thought that you don't care how your actions might affect others.

____ 25. Felt that things always go wrong and will never work out.

____ 26. Not tried your hardest and done things half way or just enough to get by.

____ 27. Put getting ahead, work or making money (including illegally) before family or friends.

____ 28. Not been aware of feeling any certain way (e.g., sad, anxious, angry) when upset over something.

____ 29. Felt very upset when things didn't go the way you wanted them to and told yourself "This is terrible" or "I can't stand this".

____ 30. Been annoyed by people who know less than me trying to tell me what to do.

____ 31. Found yourself worrying about being put down, looking bad, being embarrassed or messing up in front of others.

____ 32. Done something risky or wrong for attention.

____ 33. Been told that you are not organized.

____ 34. Let joking, teasing or horseplay go too far.

____ 35. When considering doing something wrong or explaining what you did to others, found yourself using the words, "just", "only", "a little", "rarely" or "once".

____ 36. Felt that you couldn't help yourself from getting in trouble because you were encouraged or the other person started it.

____ 37. Given others logical explanations that excuse or justify a mistake you made.

____ 38. Felt like "You're either a hero or a zero", that there is nothing in between and anything less than being number one is not good enough.

____ 39. Made decisions without consulting others because the motivations, attitudes or actions of those involved were clear and there was no need to check out the information that was presented.

____ 40. Told yourself or others that a mistake that you made was horrible, made a big deal out of it and turned it into a really upsetting experience.

____ 41. Left out parts of a story or told the part of a mistake, error or problem that wasn't so bad and left out parts that were worse.

____ 42. Told yourself that trust should be given to you without considering that your trust in others is earned by their behavior.

____ 43. Defended negative, irresponsible peers or partners that really didn't deserve my support.

0	1	2	3	4
Never	Sometimes	Half of the time	Often	Almost Always

When dealing with past situations, please rate how often you have...

___ 44. Told yourself that your behavior only hurts you or if you knew it affected others told yourself "it could be worse".

___ 45. Felt a lack of confidence in yourself.

___ 46. Been told that you are unmotivated or lazy about doing anything you don't want to do (including paying back money you borrow).

___ 47. Told yourself or others that you will do anything it takes to get ahead.

___ 48. Found yourself saying "I don't know" to people who asked you why you did what you did and not really caring to think about it.

___ 49. Played people against people to try and get what you wanted.

___ 50. Felt people have been jealous of your unique and special qualities or talents.

___ 51. Felt that people judge you on your looks so looking good is the most important thing.

___ 52. Gone along with others & made fun of someone that you get along with & think are OK.

___ 53. Had problems because of not thinking ahead about the possible consequences of taking an action or failing to do a responsibility.

___ 54. Found yourself listening in on interesting conversations, asking personal questions or looking through others stuff that they left out.

___ 55. Said to yourself or others "It wasn't that wrong", "It didn't do that much harm", "Others have done it also" or "It wasn't as bad as what others have done".

___ 56. Felt that the situation wasn't fair, you weren't given a chance or you didn't deserve what Happened ("This isn't right") after not doing well or making a mistake.

___ 57. Made a mental list of why what you did was OK or why it will be OK for you to do something that you really shouldn't.

___ 58. Felt like if it can't be done perfectly, why do it at all (or if it can't be done just right, it's not worth doing).

___ 59. Thought that because one thing went wrong or one mistake was made, everything is blown and you might as well quit trying.

___ 60. Told yourself or others that a consequence you received was worse than what really occurred.

___ 61. Lied, misled others or covered things up in order to avoid possible consequences.

___ 62. Considered mistakes you made as accidents but were more likely to view mistakes others made as on purpose.

___ 63. Covered for someone who has covered for you or kept negative secrets for and with others to cover up problems or mistakes.

___ 64. Been called selfish by a peer, associate, friend, family member or significant other.

___ 65. Told yourself or others excuses for why you can't do something that you are able to do but just don't want to do.

0	1	2	3	4
Never	Sometimes	Half of the time	Often	Almost Always

When dealing with past situations, please rate how often you have...

___ 66. Told yourself that the problem was with the job, class or person instead of your ability to handle frustration or disappointment.

___ 67. Been told that when it comes to getting what you want, you don't worry about anyone getting hurt but yourself.

___ 68. Thought things just seem to happen to you for no reason that you have no control over.

___ 69. Showed anger towards others (i.e., sarcasm, annoyance, intimidation, threats or aggressive behavior), used coercion, bribery or manipulation in order to try to get what you wanted.

___ 70. Have had total confidence in your ability to talk your way out of problems or situations.

___ 71. Felt that since people view kindness as weakness, being tough is necessary to get respect.

___ 72. Done something risky or wrong for excitement.

___ 73. Told yourself "Live for today, not for tomorrow" and made your plans based on your needs right now without considering the future effects of your decisions.

___ 74. Been jealous in a relationship, possessive or not wanted others to socialize with someone you really like.

___ 75. Told yourself "Others did it with me (or got me into it) and I'm still alive so it's not that bad if I get others involved".

___ 76. Told yourself or others "He/she did it" or "They caused this problem" when you also had something to do with it.

___ 77. Worked yourself up (e.g., "This isn't right") and then followed your feelings into getting even (e.g., "I'll show you").

___ 78. Thought that "If I can't be the best of the best, I'll be the best of the worst".

___ 79. Assumed that if what you said or did was really a problem, someone would bring it to your attention.

___ 80. Exaggerated or blown something that happened to you so far out of proportion that it was absurd or silly.

___ 81. Been vague with others in order to avoid possible problems.

___ 82. Not asked for help because you thought you should be able to do it on your own or that asking for help shows that you are weak.

___ 83. Complained about others responsibility problems before completing your own.

___ 84. Counted on people who couldn't be counted on and been let down or disappointed.

___ 85. Said negative things about others or put them down when they were not present to hear what you were saying.

___ 86. Felt like I would never be able to succeed in my life goals.

0 Never	1 Sometimes	2 Half of the time	3 Often	4 Almost Always

When dealing with past situations, please rate how often you have…

____ 87. Told yourself "It can wait", "I can do this later" or other excuses to put off doing responsibilities.

____ 88. Told yourself that you had to take what you want or use emotions such as anger, tears or guilt trips to get what you want if asking doesn't work.

____ 89. Paid attention to what you liked (i.e., agreeable feedback from others) and ignored what you didn't want to hear (i.e., disagreeable feedback).

____ 90. Argued to try and win control of the situation or just for the fun of the struggle.

____ 91. Have been 100% confident that I could control or handle problems without making any mistakes.

____ 92. Told yourself or others that being afraid is a weakness.

____ 93. Didn't plan ahead and put things off until the last minute.

____ 94. Stirred up an argument or started a conflict to break up the boredom.

____ 95. Got involved quickly in a relationship that didn't work out.

____ 96. Told yourself or others "You don't understand me".

____ 97. Been told that you are not doing your part of work or family responsibilities or felt that you are not pulling your own weight.

____ 98. Compared yourself to others on TV or the newspaper and thought that other people have a lot more problems.

____ 99. Told yourself "What I'm doing is OK because I'm not really hurting anyone but myself".

____ 100. Told yourself that most things are not accidents and what goes wrong is either your fault or their fault.

____ 101. Kept silent in order to avoid having to discuss a problem.

____ 102. Not spoken up about a problem because you didn't want to be viewed as a "snitch" or felt it was none of your business.

____ 103. Thought that you should be given a chance and trusted but haven't really trusted others.

____ 104. Had something that was done wrong to you (or someone you care about) go over and over in your mind, not been able to let it go.

____ 105. Told yourself that your behavior isn't really a harmful problem and if it does effect you "look at the bright side, it could be worse".

____ 106. Found yourself avoiding responsibilities that you find boring or disagreeable.

____ 107. Been told that you don't see things from anyone else's point of view but your own.

____ 108. Got others in trouble or did something to get even because they said or did something to you.

____ 109. Felt that others were better than me in one way or another.

0 Never	1 Sometimes	2 Half of the time	3 Often	4 Almost Always

When dealing with past situations, please rate how often you have...

___ 110. Told yourself "the best way to deal with problems is to put them out of my mind".

___ 111. Been late to or missed important appointments.

___ 112. Realized you got too close too quick in a relationship and pulled back fast to get some space.

___ 113. Found yourself getting angry at others and pointing out their problems/issues after they give you some criticism.

___ 114. Thought that unless there is a good chance of achieving your goal right away, it's not worth trying.

___ 115. Felt that I should get more support, attention and concern from others.

___ 116. Told yourself "Even if my behavior is somewhat harmful, lots of people do it" or "Since I only did with others who have already done it before, it's not that bad".

___ 117. Changed the subject or quickly skipped over to another topic when asked about a problem or mistake.

___ 118. Told yourself or others, "If you care about me you should trust me" or used, "You don't trust me" to get your way.

___ 119. Put someone down because what they did or said was dumb from your point of view.

___ 120. Felt there's no real need to change or listen to those who say they want to help me or lashed out at those trying to help me.

___ 121. Put doing something fun before doing responsibilities or work.

___ 122. Ignored what others said without even giving it consideration because you already knew what you were going to do so why even listen.

___ 123. Told yourself "I couldn't ask because they might have said no".

___ 124. Told yourself or others that you were not afraid when you really were.

___ 125. Told yourself that others should cooperate and go along with you more than they do or been disappointed at others lack of cooperation with you.

___ 126. Considered yourself more mature for your age and looked at older people as equals, friends or possible dating partners (now or at any time in your life).

___ 127. Didn't speak up about a problem or tell others what they should know because I didn't want to get someone in trouble or thought "what they don't know won't hurt them".

___ 128. Found yourself looking for support and affection more than looking for the opportunity to give it to others.

___ 129. Told yourself "Even if my behavior is a problem sometimes, it's a free country so if others don't like it they can hang out with someone else. If they hang around me and something bad happens that effects them, it's their own fault for staying."

___ 130. Complained about aches, pains and a lack of energy to get responsibilities done.

0	1	2	3	4
Never	Sometimes	Half of the time	Often	Almost Always

When dealing with past situations, please rate how often you have...

____ 131. Told yourself that you can't learn from people that you don't like or you shouldn't have to listen to people you don't like.

____ 132. Told yourself or others "Why are they lying?" and assuming that others must be lying because they are not reporting things the way you view them.

____ 133. Brought up the problems of others or put them down to make yourself look better.

____ 134. Told yourself it's better to be an offender than a victim (pick on others as opposed to be picked on, take advantage of others as opposed to be conned).

____ 135. Trusted people that seemed OK but you haven't known for long by telling them personal things about yourself or others and been let down.

____ 136. Brought up something to get people arguing and take the heat off of yourself when being confronted about a problem.

____ 137. Insisted that others let you in on things but kept the information you had to yourself.

____ 138. Told yourself that if you can't get a high paying job, it's better not to work at all.

____ 139. Not bothered to pay any attention at all unless the person got your attention by raising their voice or calling everyone's attention to you.

____ 140. Thought that if people don't agree with me, they are probably trying to put me down in front of others because they don't like me.

____ 141. Been angry at others for not trusting you without asking any questions.

____ 142. Told yourself that if you want to maintain the respect of others, you can't back down even on little points.

____ 143. Shifted to another friend for support after a disagreement to let things "cool off".

____ 144. Admitted to a less serious problem or mistake to get people off of the track when asked about a more serious problem or mistake.

____ 145. Been angry at others for shifting their loyalty to other friends or for cheating when you have done the same.

____ 146. Asked yourself why people bother you about finishing things that they could do themselves if it was really that important.

____ 147. Thought that only someone that has had my kind of problem can understand me and help me.

____ 148. Showing anger about being accused without carefully listening to or thinking about the other persons point of view.

____ 149. Felt that if you admit a mistake to others they will probably use it against you.

____ 150. Pointed out what others who were involved did or that others do it too, in order to take the heat off of yourself.

____ 151. Told yourself that if you are working on a problem area and do something right, people should recognize your accomplishment and treat you like you have changed as opposed to saying "Let's see if you can keep it up".

0 Never	1 Sometimes	2 Half of the time	3 Often	4 Almost Always

When dealing with past situations, please rate how often you have...

____ 152. When someone in authority was talking, found yourself ignoring them.

____ 153. Told yourself or others that people can't be trusted so it is always best to keep things to yourself.

____ 154. Confronted others honesty without first getting honest yourself.

____ 155. Have been told or thought that you have had problems finishing what you started.

____ 156. Felt that if others don't go along or cooperate with you like they should, you will have to do something about it or take things into your own hands and/or told yourself, "It's only wrong if you get caught".

____ 157. Thought that people with the same problems that I have are no better off than me and have no right to act like they can help me.

____ 158. Added unnecessary facts or statements to a story (i.e., purposefully made it too long or got it off track) in order to take the focus off of the main issue and avoid problems.

____ 159. Complained about unfair responsibility assignments before completing them.

____ 160. Told yourself that if others don't keep track of their things, they don't really care about them so there's no need to return those things unless asked.

Please list and other thoughts or things that you say to yourself that have caused past problems. Add feedback from your treatment group, therapist, family or partner about their view.

_____

_____

_____

_____

Look over your ratings. List any patterns or connections that you notice on the items you rated.

_____

_____

_____

Go over your answers to the Awareness and Honesty questions to make sure that you have been completely accurate. Then make a photocopy of these results and turn them into your therapist before continuing any further assignments in this workbook.

I have answered this examination honestly and to the best of my ability without any attempt to make myself look better or worse than my past behavior would indicate.

Signature: _____   **Date Completed**: _____

Awareness and Honesty Exam Scoring Instructions

Review your "Awareness and Honesty Examination" questions and record your 0- 4 rating for each question in the blank space provided before each question number in the "Exam Questions" column on the scoring sheet. Add up all exam questions in each of the 20 Irresponsible Thinking categories listed. Divide the total of all question ratings in each category by the total number of questions in each category. For example to calculate the exam score in category one (Deception), if the first 4 questions were rated as "Often" (i.e., 3's) and the remaining questions were rated as "Almost Always" (i.e., 4's), the Exam Total would be $(3 + 3 + 3 + 3) + (4 + 4 + 4 + 4 + 4 + 4 + 4) = 40/12 = 3.33$, rounded off to 3.3 which should be recorded as the complete exam score in the space provided. If any of your Complete Exam Total scores were less than 1.0 or more than 4.0, check your math.

Awareness and Honesty Examination Scoring Sheet

Exam Category	Exam Questions	Category Scores
1. Deception	___ 1, ___ 21, ___ 41, ___ 61, ___81, ___101, ___117, ___136, ___144, ___150, ___158	Category Total ____/11 = ____
2. Double Standards	___ 2, ___ 22, ___ 42, ___ 62, ___83, ___103, ___118, ___128, ___ 137, ___ 145, ___ 154	Category Total ____/11 = ____
3. Irresponsible Loyalty	___ 3, ___ 23, ___ 43, ___ 63, ___ 84, ___127	Category Total ____/6 = ____
4. Don't Care Attitude	___ 4, ___ 24, ___ 44, ___ 64, ___ 85, ___ 105, ___ 119, ___ 129	Category Total ____/8 = ____
5. Responsibility Issues	___ 6, ___ 26, ___ 46, ___ 66, ___ 87, ___ 97, ___106, ___121, ___ 130, ___ 138, ___ 146, ___ 151, ___ 155, ___ 159	Category Total ____/14 = ____
6. Blind Ambition	___ 7, ___ 27, ___ 47, ___ 67, ___ 88	Category Total ____/5 = ____
7. Motivational Blindness	___ 8, ___ 28, ___ 48, ___ 68, ___89, ___107, ___122, ___131, ___ 139, ___ 147, ___ 152	Category Total ____/11 = ____
8. "I can't" belief	___ 5, ___ 25, ___ 45, ___ 65, ___ 86, ___ 109, ___ 120	Category Total ____/ 7 = ____

Exam Category	Exam Questions	Category Scores
9. Grandiosity	___ 10, ___ 30, ___ 50, ___ 70, ___ 91, ___ 115, ___ 125, ___ 132, ___ 140	Category Total ____/9 = ____
10. Control Issues	___ 9, ___ 29, ___ 49, ___ 69, ___ 90, ___ 108, ___ 123, ___ 133, ___ 141, ___ 148, ___ 153, ___ 156, ___ 160	Category Total ____/13 = ____
11. Image Problems	___ 11, ___ 31, ___ 51, ___ 71, ___ 82, ___ 92, ___ 102, ___ 110, ___ 124, ___ 134, ___ 142, ___ 149, ___ 157	Category Total ____/13 = ____
12. Need Problems	___ 12, ___ 32, ___ 52, ___ 72, ___ 94	Category Total ____/5 = ____
13. Planning Problems	___ 13, ___ 33, ___ 53, ___ 73, ___ 93, ___ 111	Category Total ____/6 = ____
14. Boundary Problems	___ 14, ___ 34, ___ 54, ___ 74, ___ 95, ___ 112, ___ 126, ___ 135, ___ 143	Category Total ____/9 = ____
15. Victim View	___ 16, ___ 36, ___ 56, ___ 76, ___ 96	Category Total ____/5 = ____
16. Justifying Actions	___ 17, ___ 37, ___ 57, ___ 77, ___ 99, ___ 113	Category Total ____/6 = ____
17. Extremism	___ 18, ___ 38, ___ 58, ___ 78, ___ 100, ___ 114	Category Total ____/6 = ____
18. Minimizing	___ 15, ___ 35, ___ 55, ___ 75, ___ 98, ___ 116	Category Total ____/6 = ____
19. Magnifying	___ 20, ___ 40, ___ 60, ___ 80, ___ 104	Category Total ____/5 = ____
20. Assuming	___ 19, ___ 39, ___ 59, ___ 79	Category Total ____/4 = ____
Total Scores	**Exam Score** Add all complete exam category totals & record the result here ____ Divide this total by 160 & record the Exam Score here ____	

Look at each your answers in each category, the closer your answer is to…
- **zero** the more likely it is that you **never** exhibit this type of thinking or characteristics
- **one** the more likely it is that you **sometimes** exhibit this type of thinking or characteristics
- **two** the more likely you exhibit this type of thinking or characteristics **half of the time**
- **three** the more likely you exhibit this type of thinking or characteristics **often**
- **four** the more likely you exhibit this type of thinking or characteristics **almost always**

If you scored below average on this Awareness and Honesty exercise, i.e., have no category ratings at 2.0 (average) or above, and you are completing this exercise because you have been referred for a problem that is harmful to yourself or others refer to "Low score trouble shooting" (below) and consult with your therapist or treatment staff.

Low Score Trouble Shooting: "When you're looking bad, you're looking good"

As was mentioned at the beginning of this exercise, unlike the typical job interview or first date where the object is to "score" highly on making a positive impression, the object of the Awareness and Honesty Exam is to determine how aware you are of shortcomings or problem areas and how honest you are able to be about them. Thus, an overall low score on this exercise which makes you look good in terms of minimal problems, makes you look bad in terms of awareness or honesty and may block the development of an optimal treatment plan for you.

What's normal? The answer depends on whether you are working on changing behaviors that are primarily harmful to self or others. In general, normal ratings for those who have behavioral excesses, go overboard and do something too much are not 0's (Never) or 1's (Sometimes). When dealing with behaviors that are primarily harmful to self, the behavior is likely to be occurring "half the time" (2) or more if it has interfered with your life or required a treatment referral. This is not the case with any behavior that can cause serious harm to self if not changed and this is also not the case when dealing with behaviors that are primarily harmful to others. In cases of danger to self or harm to others "once is enough" to warrant a treatment referral and ratings of 1 (sometimes) on those behaviors reflect a need to seek treatment.

"To thine own self be true" is a 12 Step Recovery Program saying that emphasizes the importance of getting honest with yourself as a first step towards dealing with problems. If you scored below average on this Awareness and Honesty exercise, i.e., have no category ratings at 2.0 (average) or above, and you are completing this exercise because you have been referred for a harmful behavior, a number of factors could have contributed to this low score including…
- You may have simply been reading the questions too rapidly and should go back through them again taking your time to think about each one to see if that increases any of your rating scores.
- You may have simply been reading the questions too literally and should go back through them again to see if your problem rating the question hinges on one or two words. If that is the case, cross those one or two words out and change them to so that you are able to answer in a manner that discloses the problem characteristics that are unique to you and your treatment referral. After making changes to tailor the questions to you, re-rate and re-score

the exam to see if you were able to obtain a higher score.

- You may have an Unhealthy Pride image problem that is blocking you from getting honest with others even though you are able to use the mirror concept in treatment (p. 200), have gained insight from questionnaires and the feedback of others and are aware of the thinking and characteristics that resulted in your referral for treatment. This could require group session treatment work to desensitize you to the social anxiety associated with getting honest and open about problems kept secret that need to be let go of in order to free you up to be a more self-confident person.
- You may have a Motivational Blindness that is blocking you from using the mirror concept in treatment where you are able to use questionnaires and the feedback of others to look at yourself, gain insight and self-confidence (i.e., develop inner strength through awareness of thinking weaknesses). This could require individual session treatment work to develop your self-awareness to the point where you can identify important thinking problems and characteristics that contributed to your referral for treatment.
- You may have missed information that relates to you. This may be a result of "all or nothing" thinking when rating questions and dropping a rating do to one word that does not apply. Go back and cross out the words that do not apply, write in words that make the statement apply to you but do not change the basic meaning of the statement and then rate it again.

Please consult with your therapist or treatment staff if you have low Awareness and Honesty exam scores, i.e., have no category ratings at 2.0 (average) or above.

Now label your Complete Exam rating scores by using the "Exam Frequency Labels" table below to find the frequency label associated with each Complete Exam score. For example, if your Complete Exam score for category 1, Deception was 3.3, that score would fall in the "Often" range in the table below and you would enter the label "Often" in the margin next to Exam Category 1, "Deception" on page 216. Do this for each of the 20 Irresponsible Thinking Categories. Record scores that fall on the borderline as follows. If your Category 20, Assuming ratings were 3 19, 3 39, 3 59, 1 79, your Complete Exam score would be 10/4= 2.5, you would enter "Between Half of the time and Often" next to the Exam Category 20, "Assuming" on page 217.

Exam Frequency Labels

Complete Exam Score	Frequency Label
0.0 to 0.5	Never
0.6 to 1.5	Sometimes
1.6 to 2.5	Half of the time
2.6 to 3.5	Often
3.6 to 4.0	Almost Always

Irresponsible Thinking Structured Discovery Exercise #2
Identify and record the most frequent the types of past irresponsible thinking that you listed on your Awareness and Honesty Exam. The complete Awareness and Honesty Exam can be expected to show higher scores because there are more Irresponsible Thinking questions to rank. In order to deal with this additional information, you will be looking at your top 5 types of Irresponsible Thinking as opposed to the top three that you previously identified. These top 5 may include some or all of "at lease the top 3" that you previously identified (in Appendix C or the Risk Factor Chain in workbook 1) but not necessarily since your use of your Situation Response Analysis Log may have made you aware of other Irresponsible Thinking that is used

more frequently. Use the space provided to write a brief summary of what you discovered from this structured exercise about the Irresponsible Thinking that supported your harmful behavior using the following steps…

a. Review your Category Scores (216- 217) and circle your top five Exam Scores.

b. List each of your top five types of Irresponsible Thinking categories, the Scores and Frequency Labels (i.e., never, sometimes, half the time, often, almost always) in the spaces provided below.

1. Irresponsible Thinking= _____ Score = _____ Frequency=_____

2. Irresponsible Thinking= _____ Score = _____ Frequency=_____

3. Irresponsible Thinking= _____ Score = _____ Frequency=_____

4. Irresponsible Thinking= _____ Score = _____ Frequency=_____

5. Irresponsible Thinking= _____ Score = _____ Frequency=_____

c. Compute the average of your top three types of Irresponsible Thinking. Then use Table 4 above to get the Frequency Label and record this information in the spaces provided below.

Irresponsible Thinking Type #1 score _____ + #2 score _____ + #3 score _____ / 3 = _____

Frequency Label: On average, I used Irresponsible Thinking (check one)...
__never, __sometimes, __half the time, __often, __almost always

---

Workspace for Promise Letter

_____

_____

_____

_____

_____

_____

_____

_____

_____

_____

_____

_____

Appendix H.
Decisional Balance:
How to "Do the math" and use the "Reality Scales"- Four Case Examples

---

Case #1: Kelsey- Doing the math on unhealthy eating

Kelsey was a 29-year-old professional female enrolled in a weight management program as a result of obesity from emotional comfort eating since childhood when she was molested. Her later involvement in a long term unhealthy relationship provided further emotional turmoil that fueled continued comfort eating. She volunteered for double shifts to avoid being at home with her partner and when she was home would spend her time on the computer so she wouldn't have to deal with him. She initially stated that her late work hours left no time to prepare food causing her to drive through fast food restaurants order all of the high calorie comfort food extras with her burger and eat in her car on the way home every night. Later she disclosed this was part of her eating in secret to prevent people from seeing her unhealthy eating. She feels discriminated against at work because of weight- related comments that she has overheard. Making up for feeling looked down on by doing too much for others adds further emotional stress and comfort eating. She is currently 5 feet tall, weights 200lbs and every weeknight after work engages in fast food drive through comfort eating getting a large regular coke instead of unsweetened tea, saying yes to supersizing her fries and adding a hot fudge sundae or baked apple pie to her regular two order of 2 Big Macs. She justifies comfort eating based on unwanted feelings which are commonplace in her life. She hurts herself with drive-through fast food comfort eating after other people hurt her. She tells herself it's OK because she walks an hour after work on weeknights which actually relates more to the need to avoid her partner and vent her feelings on the cell phone to her other overweight work friend than trying to manage her weight.

1) Benefits of Quitting (fast food comfort eating). Healthy grocery eating, saves $1,023/year on food. Healthy grocery eating contributes to weight loss which can result in: a) less weight-related fatigue and pain; b) less frequent physician visits and medical bills for weight-related physical illness; c) more energy and better sleep; d) less weight comments and higher self-esteem. Monetary cost of fast food comfort eating- 2 Big Macs, large fries, large regular soda = $7.19. Monetary cost of grocery shopping and preparing a healthy meal: 2 turkey burgers w whole grain buns, 3 oz baked fries, 32 oz unsweetened tea = $3.27 Monetary cost of comfort eating: Additional $3.92/meal. Driving through every weeknight = $1,023 more each year. Calorie cost of fast food comfort eating- 2 Big Macs, large fries, large regular soda - 2450cal Calorie cost of grocery shopping and preparing a healthy meal: 2 turkey burgers w whole grain buns, 3 oz baked fries, 32 oz unsweetened tea = 1000cal. Calorie cost each meal =additional 1450 calories each weeknight, 378,450 in a year resulting in a 108 lb weight gain (at 3500cal/lb) with no exercise, 91 lb gain even with her regular 1 hour walk every evening after work (260 nights burning a total of 59,280cal). Medical cost of weight-related physical illness (i.e., type 2 diabetes, sleep apnea, high cholesterol, high blood pressure, back pain) = $340/year. $20 co-pay for monthly physician visits = $240/year, $5 prescription co-pay on five generic medications, 3 month refills = $100/year for prescription medications. Exercise cost of fast food comfort eating- In order to burn off the additional 1450 calories from drive through comfort food eating on the way home every weeknight, Kelsey would have to jog two hours, swim laps for two and a quarter hours, bicycle 4 hours or walk over 6 hours.

Calories burned in 1-hour Activity if you weigh 200 pounds			
Jogging, 5 mph	728cal	Bicycling, < 10 mph, leisure	364cal
Swimming, laps	637cal	Walking, 2 mph	228cal

2) Drawbacks of continuing (fast food comfort eating). Expected loss of $1,363/year. Expected gain of additional 91 lbs over the next year requiring further clothing expenses, resulting in more weight comments and less self-esteem. Fast food is twice as expensive as grocery store shopping and preparing a healthy meal ($1,023 more each year). Fast food has twice as many calories as grocery shopping and preparing a healthy meal (2450cal vs 1000cal). More calories more weight, worse weight-related physical illness symptoms and $340/year in medical costs to treat those symptoms, more weight related fatigue, pain and sleep disturbance,
3) Benefits of continuing (fast food comfort eating). Fast food is faster than grocery shopping and preparing a healthy meal. You get emotional comfort from eating comfort foods. It satisfies cravings. You don't have to socialize with partner if you drive through and eat in car.
4) Drawbacks of quitting (fast food comfort eating). Takes more time to grocery shop and prepare meals. Takes planning. Takes energy to cook after work. Feel deprived from not satisfying craving.

Kelsey's "Do the Math" Decision Sheet Ratings

	Benefits/Pros Reality Scale Benefit Ratings	Drawbacks/Cons Reality Scale Drawback Ratings
Keep Doing Fast food comfort eating	3) How important for my life success is it for me to keep fast food comfort eating dealing? <u>Success scale</u> rating is? (0- 10) <u>0</u>→ Not important for success at all.	2) How severe could the consequences be if I keep fast food comfort eating? <u>Severity scale</u> rating is? (0- 10). <u>10</u>→ -91lb expected weight gain, low self-esteem, Lose $1,363/year.
Quit Fast food comfort eating	1) How necessary for my survival is it for me to quit fast food comfort eating? <u>Survival scale</u> rating is? (0- 10). <u>8</u>→ Weight loss, healthier.	4) How severe will the consequences be if I quit fast food comfort eating? <u>Severity scale</u> rating is? (0- 10). <u>7</u>→ Takes time and energy to shop & prepare meals.

Kelsey's Reality Scale Summary

```
 1)  8 (Benefit of quitting)              3) 0 (Benefit of continuing)
+ 2) 10 (Drawbacks of keeping it up)     + 4) 7 (Drawbacks of quitting)
 = 18  Need to quit score                 = 7  OK to continue score
```

Self-Defeating Habit Conclusion- The combination of being too sensitive to rewards and not sensitive enough to consequences as a result of not doing the math on fast food eating and justifying actions based on feelings resulted in the following. Although Kelsey understood the concept of "Why should I hurt me (by comfort eating) just because other people or other things (such as past abuse of present weight comments) hurt me" she rationalized continuing her drive through fast food comfort eating because she walks for an hour after work every weeknight which she believed "should" burn her comfort food off. She never did the math on her fast food drive through comfort eating. As a result she now takes medications for weight-related problems including type 2 diabetes, sleep apnea, high cholesterol, high blood pressure, back pain. She is spending $1,363/year on her fast food comfort eating habit and associated medical bills. Despite her energy to "walk and talk" her feelings out after work, she states her weight-related fatigue robs her of the energy she needs to prepare healthy meals which keeps her driving through for fast food in a self-defeating cycle. Even with continued weeknight walking, she stands to gain an additional 91lbs over the next year if she continues to follow her feelings and not the facts.

Case #2: Jesse- Doing the math on drug dealing

Jesse was a 18-year-old, male, referred for residential drug treatment as a condition of his parole by the State Department of Youth Services on drug-related convictions which basically resulted from not being able to do math. He states developed a fast money addiction from dealing crack cocaine due to his belief that dealing was easier than any job that might interest him, paid more met his needs for attention, excitement, acceptance and gave him feelings of power and being looked up to as successful. "When you're selling it, you get money hungry and addicted not only to the drug but to the power. I loved the power and people looking up to me." When ask if there were any legal jobs that might interest him, Jesse stated police officer. When asked to compare dealing with the jobs he selected, this is what Jesse discovered.

1) Benefits of Quitting (dealing and getting a police officer job). **Income estimate-** Police officer 1 and 2 earn $16.38 and $19.38 per hour (Hours- 5 days, 8 hours/day. 40 hour work week). Paid sick leave, vacation & health benefits. No job risk of losing freedom by going to jail. Both during work and after, female dating partners are available. Regular scheduled pay raises.
2) Drawbacks of continuing (dealing). Risk of being robbed, shot. Risk of going to jail goes up with number of customers (More customers, higher chance of someone getting caught and turning you in). Legal fees and fines. Risk of physical, sexual assault in jail. No female dating partners in jail. No pay raises, health insurance, vacation, sick leave.
3) Benefits of continuing (dealing). **Income estimate-** Dealing estimate by sales volume: Monthly total = $1,200 or $300.00/week (cash and barter goods) without expenses. Selling 7 grams crack/week for $750- $450 product price = $300/week profit the first week of each month. Weeks 2- 4 after first of month customer checks were spent resulted in less actual cash crack sales. Jesse's creative solution to this cash flow problem was robbery to purchase crack and exchange crack for needed materials (stolen by customers) which he would have purchased for cash from direct crack sales during the first week of the month. Dealing hours: Work week- Work until 4am, sleep until 1pm, work day = 15 hours, work week = 105 hours. Time off- Past year of dealing, spent half in jail so 50% of available work time was unpaid. Quality of life- Cruising in his rented Cadillac with friends was fun but tense. He had to carry gun was assaulted, pistol whipped, robbed and unable to seek medical care as that would involve the police. Hourly dealing pay: $300.00 per week/105 work hours per week = $2.86/hour. When you subtract 50% from salary due to jail, hourly dealing pay was $1.43/hour.
4) Drawbacks of quitting (dealing). Don't get to set own work hours, can't use illegal drugs.

Jesse's "Do the Math" Decision Sheet Ratings

	Benefits/Pros Reality Scale Benefit Ratings	Drawbacks/Cons Reality Scale Drawback Ratings
Keep Dealing Drugs	3) How important for my life success is it for me to keep dealing? Success scale rating is? (0- 10) 0→ $1.43/hour is not success in life.	2) How severe could the consequences be if I keep dealing? Severity scale rating is? (0- 10). 10→ Long term prison risk.
Quit Drug Dealing & get a legal job	1) How necessary for my survival is it for me to quit dealing? Survival scale rating is? (0- 10). 10→ High risk of getting robbed again.	4) How severe will the consequences be if I quit dealing? Severity scale rating is? (0- 10). 5→ Don't get to set own work hours.

Jesse's Reality Scale Summary

1) 10 (Benefit of quitting)   3) 0 (Benefit of continuing)
+ 2) 10 (Drawbacks of keeping it up)   + 4) 5 (Drawbacks of quitting)
= 20 Need to quit score   = 5 OK to continue score

Self-Defeating Habit Conclusion- The combination of being too sensitive to rewards and not sensitive enough to consequences as a result of not doing the math on dealing and justifying actions based on feelings resulted in the following. Jesse is broke and will go back to jail if he doesn't complete his residential drug treatment. He knew there was risk but the money in his pocket and cruising in a nice car made him feel successful. He justified his actions of continued dealing based on his needs for attention, excitement, acceptance and gave him feelings of power and being looked up to as successful, not the facts. He never did the math on dealing and now feels angry about being played and going to jail for following his feelings and not the facts.

Case #3: Dave- Using the Reality Scales on smoking decisions

Dave was a 17 year-old youth male with multiple forms of harmful behavior referred for polysubstance dependence in a residential drug treatment center largely supported by antismoking funds with strict no smoking rules. After a recent smoking relapse, he was placed on a last chance contract before treatment termination and knew that his parole would be violated if his treatment was terminated. He was open about ½ pack/day habit and smoking regularly with another resident. At first he stated that he didn't know why he relapsed. After accepting that without knowing why he did it, he would likely repeat it, Dave came up with several important contributing factors and weighed out his decisional balance sheet as follows.

Dave's Reality Scale Decision Sheet Ratings

	Benefits/Pros Reality Scale Benefit Ratings	Drawbacks/Cons Reality Scale Drawback Ratings
Keep Smoking	3) How important for my life success is it for me to keep smoking? Success scale rating is? (0- 10) 0→ "I don't need it for success in life."	2) How severe could the consequences be if I keep smoking? Severity scale rating is? (0- 10). 10→ "I will get a parole violation and lose my freedom. It costs me $45/month."
Quit Smoking	1) How necessary for my survival is it for me to quit smoking? Survival scale rating is? (0- 10). 10→ "I need to quit to avoid lung cancer and survive. My social life will survive if I stop my smoking with friends before school."	4) How severe will the consequences be if I quit smoking? Severity scale rating is? (0- 10). 3→ "Not that severe, doing without calming myself by smoking in order to get off parole isn't that bad."

Dave's Reality Scale Summary

1) 10 (Benefit of quitting)   3) 0 (Benefit of continuing)
+ 2) 10 (Drawbacks of keeping it up)   + 4) 3 (Drawbacks of quitting)
= 20 Need to quit score   = 3 OK to continue score

Self-Defeating Habit Conclusion- After reviewing his reality scale scores, Dave came to the conclusion that, "I'm fining myself to kill myself". He realized that he has been too sensitive to rewards, not sensitive enough to consequences and quitting outweighs continuing to smoke. He believes that if he had completed his decision sheet earlier, he probably wouldn't have jeopardized his freedom by smoking. In discussing his decision sheet, he became aware of a number of contributing factors to his smoking including: thinking about it at movies the night before (seeing people smoke) but not doing it then as he was with staff; ruminating on wanting to smoke the next day and telling himself he would at first available chance; being asked by if he wanted to smoke at school (peer pressure) and; being angry at a teacher.

Case #4: Buck- Doing the math and using the Reality Scales on sexual abuse

Buck was a 19-year-old, male, on parole from the state penitentiary for sexual abuse that he referred to as "party sex". He was beaten by his alcoholic father and molested by one of his mothers multiple boyfriends that she had after his father went to prison. As a result of his childhood abuse, Buck viewed people as either victims or offenders and decided it was better to hurt than be hurt. As a result of being physically beaten and sexually forced into homosexual acts, he had both the need to prove himself a man and the ability to minimize his predatory sexual behavior as "party sex" because he didn't use force like was done to him. According to Buck, he would regularly go to parties at 2- 4am after everyone was so drunk and high that they were passed out. He would then select the passed out girls of his choice, carry them into the room where all the coats were on the bed and rape their unconscious bodies. He maintained that he wasn't doing anything really wrong for several reasons including, "they probably already had sex with whoever they came to the party with", "I'm not hurting anyone because I don't force them" and "what you don't know don't hurt you". He blamed the victim, "these party girls must not care about who does what to them or they wouldn't get so high they pass out". He justified his actions of sexual abuse based on his feelings of fear that he was gay and reported feeling like a "real man" after his "party sex".

Buck's "Do the Math" and Reality Scale Decision Sheet Ratings

	Benefits/Pros Reality Scale Benefit Ratings	Drawbacks/Cons Reality Scale Drawback Ratings
Keep Doing the harmful behavior List the behavior here... **Sexual abuse**	Feeling like a "real man" after sexually abusing "party girls". **3)** How important for my life success is it for me to keep sexually abusing? <u>Success scale</u> rating is? (0- 10) <u>0</u>→ "It will actually prevent me from succeeding in life."	Harm to victim. Loss of freedom/Prison, $5,000 legal fees and fines. Parole with permanent sex offender registration and labeling. Pay docked with fee to victim's assistance fund. Exposure to physical, sexual assault in jail. No female dating partners in jail. Pay $30/session out of pocket for weekly sex offender therapy. **2)** How severe could the consequences be if I keep sexually abusing? <u>Severity scale</u> rating is? (0- 10). <u>10</u>→ "It does severe emotional damage to my victims and results in getting me victimized."
Quit doing the harmful behavior List an alternative to the behavior here... **Peer dating**	Peer dating faces fear of being gay without sexually abusing others and jeopardizing freedom. Not having further "party sex" protects freedom, prevents parole violation and allows progression in sex offender treatment with emotional restitution training needed for re-integration back into existing family. **1)** How necessary for my survival is it for me to quit sexually abusing? <u>Survival scale</u> rating is? (0- 10). <u>10</u>→ Received death threats from two victim family members.	Not having "party sex" means continuing to harbor fear of being gay. Peer dating risks possible rejection by potential female dating partners, particularly when sex offender status is disclosed. **4)** How severe will the consequences be if I quit sexually abusing? <u>Severity scale</u> rating is? (0- 10). <u>5</u>→ "Somewhat, I feel gay without party sex and am shy around girls my age".

Bucks Reality Scale Summary

1) <u>10</u> (Benefit of quitting)   3) <u>0</u> (Benefit of continuing)
+ 2) <u>10</u> (Drawbacks of keeping it up)   + 4) <u>5</u> (Drawbacks of quitting)
= <u>20</u> Need to quit score   = <u>5</u> OK to continue score

Self-Defeating Habit Conclusion- The combination of being too sensitive to rewards (i.e., meeting his own needs) and not sensitive enough to consequences (i.e., the needs/rights of others), not doing the math (in terms of consequences to self and others) and justifying his actions based on his feelings resulted in the following. Buck ended up on parole as a registered sex offender and holds $5,000 in legal fee debt. While in prison, he received death threat letters from two families of his victims. In addition, he was sexually molested in the prison chow hall bathroom by another inmate who ripped an empty a coke can in half and threatened to slit Bucks throat with the jagged edge if he didn't comply. After reviewing his reality scale scores and discussing his decision sheet in treatment, Buck came to the conclusion that the cost of making himself feel more like a man at the expense of others through non-consenting sexual abuse was far higher than the cost of risking rejection by potential female dating partners. Although Buck has progressing well in his sex-offender therapy, has reached a point where he is willing to let go of the need to build himself up at the expense of others and has the desire to enter into a healthy, consenting peer relationship, his sex offender registration threatens to end any relationship that he is able to initiate. He never did the math on his non-consenting "party sex" and suffered personal re-victimization as a result of victimizing others.

Decisional Balance: Three ways for "Thinking it Through" on Big Decisions

Start Easy, begin by learning to use the "Fork in the road" decision map as described below...

1. Fork in the road (easiest- only 2 things to think about). Make a list under each. Talk to partners, parents and peers to gather as much information for each ending as you can. Diego (p. 165) received a "fork in the road" sign as a reminder to get back on track during treatment.

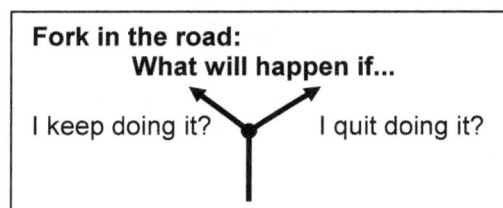

> **Fork in the road:**
> **What will happen if...**
> I keep doing it?   I quit doing it?

2. Reality Scale Review (more difficult- 3 things to think about)

	Reality Scale 0 = not at all necessary or important/no impact; 10= absolutely necessary or important/very severe impact		
Decision Check one: __doing; __saying; __trying; __not doing, __not saying, __not trying	**Survival Scale** How necessary for my survival is it for me to...	**Success Scale** How important for my success is it for me to...	**Severity Scale** How severe could the consequences be if I...
List the behavior being considered ...	Survival scale rating is (0- 10)	Success scale rating is (0- 10)	Severity scale rating is (0- 10)

What is the most responsible decision to make? _____

3. Reality Scale Decision Sheet (most difficult- 4 things to think about)

	Benefits/Pros Use the Reality Scales to rate the benefits	**Drawbacks/Cons** Use the Reality Scales to rate the drawbacks
Keep doing it	3) How important for my life success is it for me to keep doing it? Success scale rating is? (0- 10)	2) How severe could the consequences be if I keep doing it? Severity scale rating is? (0-10).
Quit doing it	1) How necessary for my survival is it for me to quit doing it? Survival scale rating is? (0- 10).	4) How severe will the consequences be if I quit doing it? Severity scale rating is? (0- 10).

  1) ___ (Benefit of quitting)   3) ___ (Benefit of continuing)
+ 2) ___ (Drawbacks of keeping it up)   + 4) ___ (Drawbacks of quitting)
  = ___ Need to quit score   = ___ OK to continue score

Which has the higher score, "Need to quit" or "OK to continue"? _____

The Harmful Behavior Anatomy Workspace (Label your work)

"The highest reward for a man's toil is not what he gets for it, but what he becomes by it"
John Ruskin (1819- 1900)

_____
_____
_____
_____
_____
_____
_____
_____
_____
_____
_____
_____
_____
_____
_____
_____
_____
_____
_____
_____
_____
_____
_____
_____
_____
_____
_____
_____
_____
_____

The Harmful Behavior Anatomy Workspace (continued)

_____
_____
_____
_____
_____
_____
_____
_____
_____
_____
_____
_____
_____
_____
_____
_____
_____
_____
_____
_____
_____
_____

Footnotes

1. Adapted by Research Engineer Russell Yokley for practical problems from 1968 San Francisco speech by Eldridge Cleaver (1935- present, American Black Leader, Writer), "What we're saying today is that you're either part of the solution or you're part of the problem".
2. You have to "keep your problem up front" as a Second Genesis therapeutic community recovery maxim (founded in 1970 by Harvard Psychiatrist Sidney Shankman and evaluated by Nemes, Wish and Messina, 1999).
3. "Act as if" by behaving like the positive person you want to be than the negative person you have been is a key therapeutic community training method for positive change towards " right living" (Chapter 5, DeLeon, 2000) dating back to the early therapeutic community development period in the

United States (1958- 1971). "If you want a quality, act as if you already had it"-- William James (1842-1910).

4. Practicing going to the opposite extreme of negative attitudes and irresponsible behaviors by modeling positive attitudes and responsible behaviors is a key therapeutic community training method for positive change towards " right living" (Chapter 5, DeLeon, 2000) dating back to the early therapeutic community development period in the United States (1958- 1971). "You have to go to the opposite extreme [in treatment through the primary values of right living] to meet the median [after treatment]" is a time honored therapeutic community recovery maxim from Second Genesis founded in 1970 by Harvard Psychiatrist Sidney Shankman and evaluated by Nemes, Wish, Messina, (1999).

5. A Singapore graduate student saying that reflects both Henry David Thoreau, "In the long run men hit only what they aim at. Therefore, though they should fail immediately, they had better aim at something high" (1817- 1862) and W. Clement Stone (1902- 2002), "Aim for the moon. If you miss, you may hit a star".

6. The healthy behavior success skills utilized were drawn from the following four research-supported intervention areas: Relapse Prevention; Emotional Regulation; Decisional Balance and; Social Problem Solving.

7. Rational Emotive Behavior Therapy (REBT) was developed by Dr. Albert Ellis. See Ellis & Bernard (2006) for further description of the REBT approach with children and Ellis & Velten (1992) for further description of REBT with adults exhibiting harmful, addictive behavior.

8. Adapted from "Knowledge is of two kinds. We know a subject ourselves, or we know where we can find information upon it." - Samuel Johnson (1709- 1784).

9. "Right living" is a therapeutic community healthy positive lifestyle goal described in Chapter 5 of DeLeon, 2000 dating back to the early therapeutic community development period in the United States (1958- 1971).

10. "My jailhouse image of a man is killing me" was an important self-image learning experience taught by Phoenix House and Second Genesis (see footnote 4) Therapeutic Community Director Edward Flowers to help young men let go of their socially callous criminal pride and "get back to the basics" of socially mature honesty, concern and responsibility.

11. Adapted from "Courage is doing what you're afraid to do. There can be no courage unless you're scared" -Eddie Rickenbacker, US WWI aviator & businessman (1890 - 1973).

12. Adaptation of "Those who cannot remember the past are condemned to repeat it" (George Santayana) for the Therapeutic Community setting by Harvard Psychiatrist Sidney Shankman.

13. Maya Angelou- born Marguerite Ann Johnson on April 4, 1928 is international recognized for her autobiographical series, most notably "I Know Why the Caged Bird Sings" (1969), has been awarded over 30 honorary degrees and was nominated for a Pulitzer Prize for her 1971 volume of poetry.

14. A detailed description of 18 maladaptive schemas and the practice of schema therapy is provided in Young, Klosko & Weishaar (2003).

15. "Urge-surfing," is a mindfulness-based relapse prevention technique often included as a component in substance abuse treatment. For a detained description, see Bowen, Chawla & Marlatt (2011).

References

Bowen, S., Chawla, N. & Marlatt, G. (2011). *Mindfulness-Based Relapse prevention for Addictive Behaviors: A Clinician's Guide.* New York: Guilford Press.

Clancy, J. (1996). *Anger and addiction: Breaking the relapse cycle: A teaching guide for professionals.* Madison, CT, US, Psychosocial Press.

Clancy, J. (1997). *Anger and relapse: Breaking the cycle.* Madison, CT, US, Psychosocial Press.

DeLeon , G. (2000). *The Therapeutic Community; Theory, Model and Method.* New York, Springer.

Dutton, D. G. (2007). *The abusive personality: Violence and control in intimate relationships (2nd ed.).* New York, NY, US, Guilford Press.

Ellis, A., & Bernard, M. E. (Eds.). (2006). *Rational emotive behavioral approaches to childhood disorders: Theory, practice and research.* New York, NY: Springer Science & Business Media Inc.

Ellis, A., & Velten, E. (1992). *When AA doesn't work for you: Rational steps to quitting alcohol.* Fort Lee, New Jersey: Barricade Books, Inc.

Kahn, T. (1996). Pathways: A guided workbook for youth beginning treatment. Brandon VT: Safer Society

Law, B. (2005) Probing the depression-rumination cycle: Why chewing on problems just makes them harder to swallow. *Monitor on Psychology*, (36), 38- 39.

Nolen-Hoeksema, S. & Davis, C. (1999). "Thanks for Sharing That" Ruminators and Their Social Support Networks, *Journal of Personality and Social Psychology*, 77(4), 801-814

Nower, L. & Blaszczynski, A. (2006). Impulsivity and pathological gambling: A descriptive model. *International Gambling Studies*, Vol 6(1), Jun 2006, 61-75.

Passmore, J. (2011). Motivational interviewing: A model for coaching psychology practice. *The Coaching Psychologist, 7*(1), 36-40.

Schulherr, S. (1998). The binge-diet cycle: Shedding new light, finding new exits. Eating Disorders: The Journal of Treatment & Prevention. 6(3), 267-271.

Schulherr, S. (2005). Exiting the Binge-Diet Cycle. In Shapiro, Robin (Ed), *EMDR solutions: Pathways to healing.* (pp. 241-262). New York, NY, US: W W Norton & Co.

Yokley, J. (2011a). *Why do I keep doing this? Social Responsibility Therapy: Understanding Harmful Behavior Workbook 2.* N. Myrtle Beach, SC: Social Solutions Press. ISBN: 978-0-9832449-1-2.

Yokley, J. (2011b). Emotional Restitution Training in Social Responsibility Therapy for Sex Offender Referrals. In B. Schwartz (Ed.), Handbook of Sex Offender Treatment (Chapter 56). Kingston, NJ: Civic Research Institute. ISBN: 978-1-887554-03-9.

Yokley, J. (2010a). How did I get this problem? Social Responsibility Therapy: Understanding Harmful Behavior Workbook 1. N. Myrtle Beach, SC: Social Solutions Press. ISBN: 978-0-9832449-0-5.

Yokley, J. (2010b). Social Responsibility Therapy for Harmful, Abusive Behavior, *Journal of Contemporary Psychotherapy,* 40(2), p. 105- 113.

Yokley, J. (2008). *Social Responsibility Therapy for Adolescents and Young Adults: A Multicultural Treatment Manual for Harmful Behavior*, New York, NY, US: Routledge/Taylor and Francis Group. ISBN: 978-0-7890-3121-1.

Yokley, J. (2016). *The Clinician's Guide to Social Responsibility Therapy: Practical Applications, Theory and Research Support.* N. Myrtle Beach, SC: Social Solutions Press. ISBN: 978-0-9832449-4-3.

Yokley, J. & Dudich, J. (in press). *Social Responsibility Therapy for Preteen Children: A Multicultural Treatment Manual for Harmful Behavior.* Bloomington, Indiana: Trafford Publishing.

Young, J. E., Klosko, J. S., & Weishaar, M. E. (2003). Schema therapy: A practitioner's guide. New York: Guilford Press.

Workspace for Envelope Exercise

Social Responsibility Therapy for Adolescents and Young Adults
A Multicultural Treatment Manual for Harmful Behavior
James M. Yokley, Ph.D.

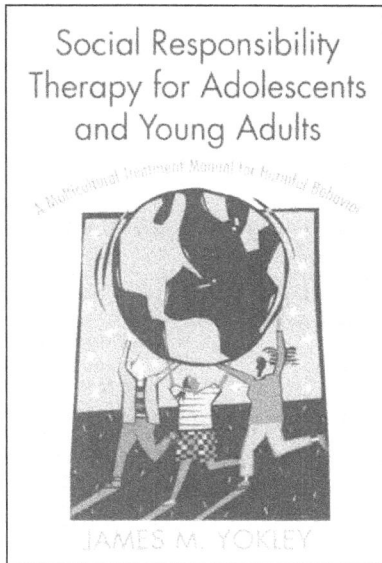

Social Responsibility Therapy for Adolescents and Young Adults: A Multicultural Treatment Manual for Harmful Behavior provides a comprehensive explanation of Social Responsibility Therapy, its advantages, and the intervention evidence-base for multiple forms of harmful behavior. This text discusses in detail the multicultural intervention approach, its rationale, and content. Implementation methods and treatment protocol are explored. The book includes illustrated case studies, tables, figures, and references to additional available readings.

Topics discussed in Social Responsibility Therapy for Adolescents and Young Adults: A Multicultural Treatment Manual for Harmful Behavior include:
- evidence-based procedures used in Structured Discovery learning experiences to target harmful behavior
- helping clients discover how they acquired, maintained, and generalized a broad range of harmful behavior
- addressing target behavior problems, negative social influence problems, and the dose-response problem
- five areas of human functioning that are critical to the wellbeing of self and others which can only be addressed through psychotherapy and forensic parenting
- developing prosocial behavior alternatives which contribute to both relapse prevention and personal development and much more!

Social Responsibility Therapy for Adolescents and Young Adults: A Multicultural Treatment Manual for Harmful Behavior is an essential resource for social workers, counselors, psychologists, and psychiatrists whose caseloads include a multicultural population of young people who exhibit multiple forms of unhealthy, harmful behavior.

Table of Contents
Chapter 1. Social Responsibility Therapy Overview, Intervention Evidence Base and Multicultural Approach. **Chapter 2.** Client Awareness Training: The Problem Development Triad. **Chapter 3.** Social Responsibility Therapy Implementation Methods and Treatment Protocol. **Chapter 4.** Research Support for Social Responsibility Therapy Methods & Procedures. Notes. References.

About the Author
James M. Yokley, Ph.D., is a Clinical Psychologist on the medical staff in the Department of Psychiatry at MetroHealth Medical Center in Cleveland, Ohio, as well as an Assistant Professor at Case Western Reserve University School of Medicine and Department of Psychology. He has expertise in cognitive-behavior therapy with multiple forms of unhealthy, harmful behavior, has authored over 50 research publications, book chapters, and professional presentations, and is a regular conference speaker on this topic.

Paperback: 978-0-7890-3121-1. $49.95 • May 2008, 357pp

Order online through
www.socialsolutionspress.com

Social Responsibility Therapy for Adolescents and Young Adults
A Multicultural Treatment Manual for Harmful Behavior
James M. Yokley, Ph.D.

"A valuable contribution to the field, confronting important issues at the psychological and societal levels. Provides a comprehensive framework for managing some of the most challenging clinical problems. Provides useful guidelines for promoting prosocial values and behaviors in delinquent youth. The treatment strategies balance the notions of therapeutic structure with client discovery. Many interesting and provocative quotations are laced throughout the text. A valuable addition to any library."
  —James C. Overholser, PhD, ABPP, professor of psychology,
  director of clinical training, Case Western Reserve University

Social Responsibility Therapy for Adolescents and Young Adults: A Multicultural Treatment Manual for Harmful Behavior is a crucial treatment manual for mental health professionals whose caseloads include a multicultural population of adolescents and young adults who exhibit multiple forms of harmful behavior. This unique therapy enhances relapse prevention in harmful behavior treatment by addressing the target behavior problem, negative social influence problem, dose-response problem, and the behavior migration problem. It also acknowledges that harmful behavior is multicultural, and it addresses the key criticisms of multicultural therapy through a theory-driven treatment approach that utilizes methods and procedures from existing evidence-based treatments with known multicultural applications.

This text provides a comprehensive explanation of Social Responsibility Therapy, its advantages, and the intervention evidence-base for multiple forms of harmful behavior. It discusses in detail the multicultural intervention approach, its rationale, and content; describes the implementation methods and treatment protocol; and includes illustrated case studies, tables, figures, and references to additional readings. This book is an essential resource for mental health professionals from all disciplines, including social workers, counselors, psychologists, and psychiatrists who are involved in the treatment of multiple forms of harmful behavior.

James M. Yokley, PhD, is a clinical psychologist in the Department of Psychiatry at MetroHealth Medical Center in Cleveland, Ohio, and is an assistant professor at Case Western University School of Medicine and Department of Psychology.

Routledge
Taylor & Francis Group

www.routledgementalhealth.com

Printed in the U.S.A.
Cover design: Elise Weinger Halprin

ISBN: 978-0-7890-3121-1
90000

9 780789 031211

an **informa** business

The Social Responsibility Therapy:
Understanding Harmful Behavior Workbook Series

The Social Responsibility Therapy workbook series on Understanding Harmful Behavior was designed to help individuals with unhealthy, harmful behavior understand how they got that problem, what kept it going and how it spread to other areas through "The Problem Development Triad".

Workbook 1- "How did I get this problem?" focuses on understanding how unhealthy, harmful behavior was acquired through "The Risk Factor Chain". ISBN: 978-0-9832449-0-5.

Workbook 2- "Why do I keep doing this?" focuses on understanding how unhealthy, harmful behavior problems were maintained by "The Stress-Relapse Cycle". ISBN: 978-0-9832449-1-2.

Workbook 3- "How did my problem spread?" focuses on understanding how unhealthy, harmful behavior problems were generalized to other areas using "The Harmful Behavior Anatomy". ISBN: 978-0-9832449-2-9.

For workbook questions or further support, contact dave@socialsolutionspress.com

The Clinician's Guide to Social Responsibility Therapy:
Practical Applications, Theory and Research Support

The Clinician's Guide to Social Responsibility Therapy: Practical Applications, Theory and Research Support (ISBN-978-0-9832449-4-3) supplements the Social Responsibility Therapy Treatment Manual for Adolescents & Young Adults (Yokley, 2008) by providing: Practical clinical applications, case examples and exercises illustrating the treatment model; A positive lifestyle change description integrating theory, research support and practical examples; Clinician support for using the three Social Responsibility Therapy workbooks on understanding and managing unhealthy, harmful behavior described above.

Further description and order information is available at
www.socialsolutionspress.com

For volume or non-profit organization discounts, e-mail order information (Name, zip code and number of workbooks, organization and population served) to...
info@socialsolutionspress.com

Note:

Social Responsibility Therapy is a
Social Solutions Healthy Behavior Lifestyle Project

www.srtonline.org   www.socialsolutionspress.com   www.forensicare.org

www.ingramcontent.com/pod-product-compliance
Lightning Source LLC
Chambersburg PA
CBHW081414270326
41931CB00015B/3271